# THE GOLDEN MOMENT

## THE NOVELS OF F. SCOTT FITZGERALD

# THE GOLDEN MOMENT

## THE NOVELS OF

# F. SCOTT FITZGERALD

## Milton R. Stern

UNIVERSITY OF ILLINOIS PRESS

*Urbana, Chicago, London*

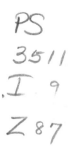
Permission from Charles Scribner's Sons to reprint material from the following works of F. Scott Fitzgerald is gratefully acknowledged: *The Beautiful and Damned* (Copyright 1922 Charles Scribner's Sons; renewal copyright 1950 Frances Scott Fitzgerald Lanahan); *The Great Gatsby* (Copyright 1925 Charles Scribner's Sons; renewal copyright 1953 Frances Scott Fitzgerald Lanahan); *Tender Is the Night* (Copyright 1933, 1934 Charles Scribner's Sons; renewal copyright 1961, 1962 Frances Scott Fitzgerald Lanahan); *This Side of Paradise* (Copyright 1920 Charles Scribner's Sons; renewal copyright 1948 Zelda Fitzgerald); and *The Letters of F. Scott Fitzgerald* edited by Andrew Turnbull (Copyright 1963 Frances Scott Fitzgerald).

Permission to reprint from the following is also gratefully acknowledged: Percy Marks, *The Plastic Age* (Copyright 1924 The Century Co.); Edwin Arlington Robinson, "Cassandra," *Collected Poems* (Copyright 1916 Edwin Arlington Robinson; renewal copyright 1944 Ruth Nivison); F. Scott Fitzgerald, "Lamp in a Window" (Copyright 1935, 1963 The New Yorker Magazine, Inc.; the variant version quoted here is that of Fitzgerald's manuscript in his papers in the Princeton University Library).

*This one, with abiding love, is for*
HARRIET, KATHY *and* PAUL

# CONTENTS

Acknowledgments are a happy matter. I am pleased to thank the American Council of Learned Societies for a grant given long ago, which, also long ago, must have been written off as a dead loss—for various reasons it took longer to complete this book than I had thought it would. Always I acknowledge Russell B. Nye, who first opened American literature to me; Leonard F. Dean, whose amused and friendly understanding of "all that American Studies stuff" is wise and challenging; Sherman Paul, who constantly remains a source of energy, ideas, and purpose. Most of all, for this book I wish to acknowledge Frank Hodgins of the University of Illinois and Irving Pitman Cummings of the University of Connecticut for the kind of debt that can never be repaid in acknowledgments but only in kind: the careful, sympathetic, encouraging, time-consuming and selfless readings with which true friends help friends who are struggling with manuscripts. They were both totally and constructively helpful. Finally I want to say thanks, publicly, to my wife, for all the long hours uncomplainingly spent in the dull chore of proofreading.

# Gentle Reader

THIS IS an old-fashioned and personal book. When I say, however, that in this book I try to show how Fitzgerald attempted to work out the meanings of his life in his novels, I am not indulging in the old fashion of using Literature as Life. My aim is not the surface facts of biography. When I see Fitzgerald's fiction as a continuing exercise of the autobiographical impulse, I am not using his fiction to illuminate his life so much as I am trying to use his life to illuminate his fiction and, I hope, the "identity crisis" of our American time. But to do one is to do the other inevitably; and to whatever extent this book is biographical, it is the biography of an imagination. Actually, I do not try to furnish or even recapitulate a biography. Mizener and Turnbull and "the Fitzgerald revival" have made Fitzgerald's life familiar to everyone—a national property—and I take that for granted throughout this book.

Arthur Mizener, of course, consolidated the Fitzgerald revival with *The Far Side of Paradise*. In that revival there have been countless periodical pieces that examined bits of Fitzgerald. The full-length treatments, other than the essentially biographical, were either specialized studies of Fitzgerald's development, like

Kuehl's examination of Fitzgerald's literary apprenticeship, or studies of a milieu, like Goldhurst's. If they were critical studies like Lehan's or Miller's or Perosa's, I found that though they were informative and suggestive, they seemed to miss the point (my point, that is), and that if they were biographical-critical, like Piper's, they were divided in intention (my intention, that is) and, therefore, in insight. They are all good books, useful and intelligent; but, like Miller's study, they were concerned with matters other than what I thought was the center of Fitzgerald's imagination: the uses of history, the American identity, the moral reconstruction of the American past. But Mizener and Turnbull in biography, and Turnbull in the edition of the letters (though I have some arguments with the edition), provided constantly new starting points for critical exploration. When I began this book, some of what I wanted to say had already been said in bits and pieces in several good introductions and articles and, here and there, in the book-length studies. When I was halfway through with the last chapter of this book, I read Sklar's *F. Scott Fitzgerald: The Last Laocoon*, and felt that finally Fitzgerald criticism was coming to the important center of what I felt within my own self had been the Fitzgerald self. But what still remained to be written, it seemed to me, was an extended study that would go beyond all the fragmentary good things that have been said about Fitzgerald and organize a statement that would parallel Sklar's by talking about the national rather than the literary development of Fitzgerald's talent.

What I still had to do, I felt, was to complete a book not for Fitzgerald experts, to whom I will have little new to offer except for the organization of a total perspective (which will, I hope, offer strongly wrought interpretation), but for interested readers who, knowing the Fitzgerald facts, would want a unified view of the meaning of those facts. Therefore, this book is a study that attempts to illuminate the fiction by trying to see it through Fitzgerald's personality, a study that tries to bring together from one central perspective the portions of Fitzgerald's yearning imagination that were manifested in the novels, the writings best known to the reading public. To try to discuss everything Fitzgerald wrote in terms of my central thesis would be tediously repetitive. So I limited myself to the novels, despite the many brilliant short pieces that Fitzgerald wrote. (Even after all the years of the "revival," he is only now beginning to come into his own as a writer of short stories. Yet, I think, he will continue to be remembered primarily for his novels.) I have omitted *The Last Tycoon* because, as brilliantly promising as it is, it is completely unfinished. Anyone familiar with Fitzgerald's practices of revision is aware of how putative every statement about *The Last Tycoon* must be. To point out the germinal material within the fragment would only reiterate what I hope I've demonstrated in the other novels, which *can* be talked about as completed instances of whatever thesis.

As I became more and more aware of what Fitzgerald's novels intend to do, I thought of calling this book *The Americanness of Scott Fitzgerald*, or *Fitzgerald and the Uses of History*, or *The Autobiografiction of F. Scott Fitzgerald*. When I became convinced of the significance of Fitzgerald's uses of his "composite characters," and the central vision of his betrayed, golden, imagined world became clear to me, I found that I could not decide between the first two titles, and I settled for something simpler than the third; but I mention them because they help to suggest what this book is about. The biographies concentrate on Fitzgerald's life and come obliquely at his art thereby. I wanted to do just the opposite, to write the complementary explanatory analysis that would fit the biographies, so that after reading Mizener or Turnbull and the complementary explanation, the reader would say, "There. Now I know what Fitzgerald is about." I hope this is that book.

# THE GOLDEN MOMENT
## THE NOVELS OF F. SCOTT FITZGERALD

*The compensation of a very early success is a conviction that life is a romantic matter. In the best sense one stays young. When the primary objects of love and money could be taken for granted and a shaky eminence had lost its fascination, I had fair years to waste, years that I can't honestly regret, in seeking the eternal Carnival by the Sea. Once in the middle twenties I was driving along the High Corniche Road through the twilight with the whole French Riviera twinkling on the sea below. As far ahead as I could see was Monte Carlo. . . . It was not Monte Carlo I was looking at. It was back into the mind of the young man with cardboard soles who had walked the streets of New York. I was him again—for an instant I had the good fortune to share his dreams, I who had no more dreams of my own. And there are still times when I creep up on him, surprise him on an autumn morning in New York or a spring night in Carolina when it is so quiet that you can hear a dog barking in the next county. But never again as during that all too short period when he and I were one person, when the fulfilled future and the wistful past were mingled in a single gorgeous moment—when life was literally a dream.*

October, 1937. "Early Success," in *The Crack-Up.*

# CHAPTER I

# THIS SIDE OF PARADISE

## *A Brummagem God*

"I FEEL I have an enormous power in me now, more than I've ever had in a way, but it works so fitfully and with so many bogeys because I've *talked so much* and not lived enough within myself to develop the necessary self-reliance. Also, I don't know anyone who has used up so much personal experience as I have at 27." Writing this to Maxwell Perkins, Fitzgerald was commenting about *The Great Gatsby*, his new book, which, he said, would be the product of "the sustained imagination of a sincere yet radiant world."[1] He was really commenting about his entire life as a writer. Almost no other American writer used so much of himself, his life, his friends and family as did Scott Fitzgerald, and no one could have been more aware than he of the self-consuming process that turned out, as final products, a ruined and courageous life, a used-up heart, and the short stories and novels.

There is really little point in making lists of sources and analogues, balancing columns of Life against columns of Art. Fitzgerald didn't write *romans à clef*. He used bits and pieces of what

[1] April 1924, in *The Letters of F. Scott Fitzgerald*, ed. Andrew Turnbull (New York, 1963), p. 163; hereafter referred to as *Letters*.

*3*

people presented to him as selves, and he turned them into composite beings who usually shifted and changed into himself with
each story, each new idea.[2]

He had a running argument with Ernest Hemingway about it.
Hemingway insisted that the composite character—the character
made up of bits of many real people—would ruin the fiction; Fitzgerald insisted that it was superior to the character borrowed integral and whole. Each man was right, but for himself alone, of
course, and the argument was foolish—as though the one could
use for his eyestrain the treatment prescribed to the other for a
wrenched shoulder. There is a certain historical interest in equat-
ing, for instance, Harvey Stone or Robert Cohn of *The Sun Also
Rises* with Harold Stearns and Harold Loeb: done well or badly,
for truth or lie, they are "complete" characters, and they provide
the necessary distortions of one writer's view of "the way it was,"
to use Loeb's phrase, in an enormously exciting literary period.
But there is at best a very limited value in knowing that in *This
Side of Paradise* Ginevra King was the model for both Rosalind
and Isabel throughout *The Romantic Egotist* version of the book,
and that she was only Isabel in the final version, where Zelda
Sayre became Rosalind. Certainly a list of equations is possible:
Monsignor Darcy (Dr. Dudley in the earliest version) is Monsignor
Sigourney Webster Fay; Thornton Hancock is Henry Adams;
Thomas Parke D'Invilliers is John Peale Bishop; Burne Holiday

---

[2] As an imaginative extension of himself, everything Fitzgerald wrote was autobiographical in one way or another. Most of his critics and commentators have
pointed out fully and correctly the extent to which his experience was his fiction. See
particularly Arthur Mizener's classic work in Fitzgerald scholarship, *The Far Side of
Paradise* (New York, 1949) and Kenneth Eble's *F. Scott Fitzgerald* (New York, 1963),
which is, in effect, a condensed study of the autobiographical elements in Fitzgerald's
writing. In addition, the biography, *Scott Fitzgerald* (New York, 1962), and *The
Letters of F. Scott Fitzgerald* (New York, 1963), both by Andrew Turnbull, indicate
for any interested reader the many parallels—and shifts and reworkings of the parallels—between Fitzgerald's life and fiction. These works, together with the innumerable periodical pieces on the subject, liberate me and all other commentators on
Fitzgerald's writing from the necessity of demonstrating the facts of the parallels
and leave us free to *use* the fact.

is, partly, Henry Strater, the student leader of the anti-club movement when Fitzgerald was at Princeton; the title of the real Triangle Club's "Ha-Ha Hortense!" was "Fie! Fie! Fi-Fi!"; but, finally, it is of no more moment to know that than to know that Amory Blaine was Francis Scott Key Fitzgerald. Fitzgerald was not interested in taking off a character as much as he was in defining a type. He used parts of himself and those he knew for parts of the composite characters he created; the borrowing was eclectic, not representational. What Fitzgerald wished to present was a social character, a national type that fascinated and repelled him, in which he felt his identity as an American, and in which he saw the history of America as it was written meaningfully for him: in the attitudes and characteristics of the businessmen and debutantes and tycoons and college boys whose actions made for him a composite portrait of American values and morality.[3]

There are three basic characters in Fitzgerald's fiction. There are the characters that Fitzgerald took from himself: first, the innocent; and second, the moral commentator. The innocent has high hopes. He is completely a romantic. He believes in the Ameri-

---

[3] When I was almost finished writing this book, Robert Sklar published *F. Scott Fitzgerald: The Last Laocoon* (New York, 1967). I was delighted to discover that my own conclusions about Fitzgerald were corroborated by Mr. Sklar's book, especially because Mr. Sklar examines Fitzgerald's fiction from a very different beginning point than my own. He finds that the types Fitzgerald wrote about are descendents of the romantic genteel hero, epitomized in Tom Sawyer and popularized in the boy-heroes of Booth Tarkington. By exerting his will and his imagination, the romantic genteel hero outrages and amuses his elders, winning by unconventional means the conventional goals of girl, money, and a respected place in the community. Examining the short stories as well as the novels, Mr. Sklar argues that Fitzgerald's "type" gradually moves away from the genteel hero to a man with un- and even anti-conventional values, but that the genteel hero always continued to represent for Fitzgerald a memory of an older America with handsome manners. As my own book indicates, I think that Fitzgerald's "type" never really abandons the older America, but I agree with Mr. Sklar that beneath the chic and mode of Fitzgerald's characters and materials there is a nostalgic conservatism in Fitzgerald's assessment of his culture. I do not use the genteel hero as a basis for my discussion of what I call Fitzgerald's "composite characters," for my point of departure is concerned more with the autobiographical impulse in Fitzgerald's writing than with literary influences, but without question Mr. Sklar has introduced a valuable and very significant consideration into the world of Fitzgerald criticism.

can Dream: through his dedication or talent or shrewdness or
charm he will either remake the world or will discover a success
in which the flood of money gained will wash him onto an enchanted shore of brilliance and gaiety and endless invulnerable
youth in which the inhabitants really are "different from you and
me," as he said in "The Rich Boy." The moral commentator is
the Fitzgerald who knows better, who is aware of the historical,
actual America *as well as* of the America that is a metaphor for
the dream of the New World, the Golden West, the Paradise regained of happy youth and immortality. He is the person through
whose intelligence the events are filtered, the Nick Carraway of
*Gatsby;* he is the person who enjoys a real, self-destructive imaginative superiority to others, the Monroe Stahr of *The Last Tycoon.* Like Dick Diver of *Tender Is the Night,* he is the one whose
recognitions record the true, the inner, the imaginative history
of America, and, when all is said and done, the distinction between
the two characters is of only minor usefulness: the faces of the
innocent and the moral commentator both blur and merge, as
they do in Dick Diver, as do saintliness and ravaging experience
in the photographs of Fitzgerald himself.

The third basic composite character is the Golden Girl, and as
Fitzgerald knew, recognizing the feminine in himself, she too was
as much a part of his own self as she was a composite of other
people. She presents to the innocent the epitome, he thinks, of
what he seeks. She is the romantic prospector's West, the America
of the imagination. The moral commentator knows that the promise represented by the golden girl is an appearance that both
clothes and is the result of the arrogant carelessness and overwhelming selfish irresponsibility born of precocious good looks,
physical health, pampered youth, and wealth. For Fitzgerald, as
for his iconoclastic generation, these are national characteristics,
the glittering, tawdry power and incomparable beauty of the
U.S.A., the young golden girl of the nations. The betrayal of the

seeking innocent by his own naiveté and by the golden girl to whom he dedicates his entire identity is a national history observed by the moral commentator. An ethical participant rather than judgmental voyeur, even in many of the short stories the moral commentator lurks in the "objective" narrator of action presented in the third person. It is the story that Fitzgerald tells over and over again; and in the compulsive insistence with which he makes the story symbolically and inevitably American, Fitzgerald's fiction becomes a story of the extent to which the actual America is a whore to the prototypical, romantic, Columbus of the imagination, how she leads him on, and, in betraying his expectations, destroys his Adamic, redemptive identity.

After his affair with Ginevra King, the overwhelming golden girl of his youth, Fitzgerald identified poor Zelda with the attainment of all his dreams of success. The popularity of her, the desirability of her, the sheer charm of her occupied him with a total possession. To win fame and fortune was to win Zelda. To win Zelda was to win the dream of the world and the world of the dream. Even at the moment that he wrote Maxwell Perkins the news of his finished novel, *The Education of a Personage* (the rewritten version of *The Romantic Egotist* and itself rewritten and published finally as his first book, *This Side of Paradise*), he was impatient that a delay in success would be the loss of his own golden girl. Please, if you publish me, hurry, he said. The question he really wanted to ask was not, "Will the book be published?" but, "If I send you the book by August 20th and you decide you could risk its publication (I am blatantly confident that you will) would it be brought out in October, say, or just what would decide its date of publication?"[4] And a little later, the appeal more desperate, he writes again: "Terms, etc., I leave to you but one thing I can't relinquish without a struggle. Would it be utterly impossible for you to publish the book Xmas—or,

4 July 26, 1919, *Letters*, p. 137.

say, by February? I have so many things dependent on its success—
including of course a girl—not that I expect it to make me a fortune [and how excitedly he hoped for it to make both fortune and
fame] but it will have a psychological effect on me and all my
surroundings and besides open up new fields. I'm in that stage
where every month counts frantically and seems a cudgel in a
fight for happiness against time. Will you let me know more
exactly how that difference in time of publication influences the
sale and what you mean by 'early spring?' "[5] For a moment it did
look as though all would be lost, and life seemed to be a schedule
of despair. "I feel I ought to tell you something," he wrote in the
summer of 1919 to a confidante to whom he had spoken about
Zelda, "because you're the only person in the world that knows.
. . . I've done my best and I've failed—it's a great tragedy to me
and I feel I have very little left to live for because until everything
is as it should be I'll have that sense of vacancy that only this can
give. I wish you'd tear up this letter and I know you'll never say
what I told you in an hour of depression. Unless some day she
will marry me I will never marry."[6] Just a little more than a year
later, when the whole tone of his life had changed and had come
closer to the tone of the dream, he reported to Shane Leslie that
"I am married and living rustically in Connecticut—working on
a second novel. I married the Rosalind of . . . [*This Side of Paradise*], the southern girl I was so attached to, after a grand recon-
ciliation."[7] To his mother he had been able to report in the winter
of 1919 that "My novel is autobiographical in point of view but
I've borrowed incidents from all my friends' experiences."[8]

The "nervousness" of that famous courtship of Zelda and the
values involved in it are what were "autobiographically" important to Fitzgerald in his composite re-creation of character and

[5] September 18, 1919, *ibid.*, p. 139.
[6] June 24, 1919, *ibid.*, pp. 455–56.
[7] August 6, 1920, *ibid.*, p. 376.
[8] *Letters*, p. 455.

experience. Those values were stated explicitly in *This Side of Paradise* and were to be restated in more complex terms in Jay Gatsby's courtship of Daisy Fay. In life, as in "autobiography," he always saw the Gatsbylike elements of his "just personal" history as material for a moral commentator. The extent to which he saw the waste of enthusiasm and dedication, the blight of the expectations of innocence, is not an aspect of his early vision only. It is clear in the admonitory letter he wrote his daughter just ten months before his death:

I'm sorry about the tone of the telegram I sent you this morning, but it represents a most terrific worry. You are doing exactly what I did at Princeton. I wore myself out on a musical comedy there for which I wrote book and lyrics, organized and mostly directed while the president played football. Result: I slipped way back in my work, got T.B., lost a year in college—and, irony of ironies, because of scholastic slip I wasn't allowed to take the presidency of the Triangle.

From your letter I guess that you are doing exactly the same thing and it just makes my stomach fall out to think of it. Amateur work is fun but the price of it is just simply tremendous. In the end you get "thank you" and that's all. You give three performances which everybody promptly forgets and somebody has a breakdown—that somebody being the enthusiast.

*Please, please, please* delegate every bit of the work you can and keep your scholastic head above water. To see a mistake repeated twice in two generations would be just too much to bear.[9]

But it was a lifelong "mistake." The extent to which Princeton provided the emotional material for Amory Blaine is not greater, finally, than the extent to which Fitzgerald's youthful midwestern yearning provided the composite characteristics of what Franz Gregorovius in *Tender Is the Night* was to call the "very American" Dick Diver qualities of the innocently hopeful enthusiast.

Fitzgerald never hid his composite debts for his composite materials—one of the facts of his life which has allowed the legend

9 April 12, 1940, *ibid.*, pp. 69–70.

sometimes to get in the way of the writings, even retrospectively. Indeed, for example, writing to Shane Leslie, he acknowledges his debt to one of Leslie's letters (describing the funeral of Monsignor Fay) for part of his description of the funeral of Monsignor Darcy; he also acknowledges his use of Monsignor Fay's letters and poem as the letters and poem of Monsignor Darcy.[10] Writing to John Peale Bishop he insists upon the extent to which the composite borrowing must be complete. If the borrowing is someone else's style, someone else's ideas, the borrowing is mere plagiarism. If the borrowing is material, *experience*, provided by others, but cast in the light that only your own eye can cast, then there is the beginning of art. He advised Bishop:

First, conscientiously you must try to cut all traces of other people out of yourself. . . . Frank Norris, speaking of Kipling, said, "the little colonial, to whose pipe we must all dance"—but by that general admission of the tremendous power of certain stylists he announced that he, for one, would fight shy of any effect that he might gain by using their rhythms to cradle his ideas or to fill gaps with reminiscent echolalia. Several times I saw patterns in . . . [your manuscript] which derived background and drama from Faulkner, or cadences from Hemingway, and each time you might have produced something much stronger by having more of a conscience, by fighting against that tendency, cutting out the passage no matter how satisfactory it may have been in itself, and building up the structure with something that *is* yourself. In any case, that has been my experience, and I pass it on to you for what it's worth.[11]

A letter to Frances Turnbull, the sister of Fitzgerald's biographer and editor of the letters, is so clear on this point that it is worth quoting in full.

I've read . . . [your] story carefully and, Frances, I'm afraid the price for doing professional work is a good deal higher than you are prepared to pay at present. You've got to sell your heart, your strongest

10 *Letters*, pp. 376, 378.
11 January 30, 1935, *ibid.*, p. 365.

reactions, not the little minor things that only touch you lightly, the little experiences that you might tell at dinner. This is especially true when you *begin* to write, when you have not yet developed the tricks of interesting people on paper, when you have none of the techniques which it takes time to learn. When, in short, you have *only* your emotions to sell.

This is the experience of all writers. It was necessary for Dickens to put into *Oliver Twist* the child's passionate resentment at being abused and starved that haunted his whole childhood. Ernest Hemingway's first stories, *In Our Time*, went right down to the bottom of all that he had ever felt and known. In *This Side of Paradise* I wrote about a love affair that was still bleeding as fresh as the skin wound on a haemophile.

The amateur, seeing how the professional, having learned all that he'll ever learn about writing, can take a trivial thing such as the most superficial reactions of three uncharacterized girls and make it witty and charming—the amateur thinks he or she can do the same. But the amateur can only realize his ability to transfer his emotions to another person by some desperate and radical expedient as tearing your first tragic love story out of your heart and putting it on pages for people to see.

That, anyhow, is the price of admission. Whether you are prepared to pay it, or whether it coincides or conflicts with your attitude on what is "nice" is something for you to decide. But literature, even light literature, will accept nothing less from the neophyte. It is one of those professions that wants the "works." You wouldn't be interested in the soldier who was only a *little* brave.

In the light of this, it doesn't seem worth while to analyze why this story isn't salable but I am too fond of you to kid you about it, as one tends to do at my age. If you ever decide to tell *your* stories, no one would be more interested than

Your old friend<br>F. Scott Fitzgerald

P.S. I might say that the writing is smooth and agreeable and some of the pages very apt and charming. You have talent—which is the equivalent of a soldier having the right physical qualifications for entering West Point.[12]

[12] November 9, 1938, *ibid.*, pp. 577–78.

Perhaps the most telling comment about the depth and intensity of Fitzgerald's composite use of his experience and of people
appears in this comment to an author-friend, James Boyd:

I have just emerged not totally unscathed, I'm afraid, from a short
violent love affair which will account for the somewhat sentimental
cadence of this letter and for the lack of ink in the vicinity. It's no one
I ever mentioned to you but it was in the bag when I came to Southern Pines [a resort] and I had done much better to let it alone because
this was scarcely a time in my life for one more emotion. [This was
written in the depths of Fitzgerald's agonizing bad years, in the mid-
nineteen thirties.] Still it's done now and tied up in cellophane and—
maybe someday I'll get a chapter out of it. God, what a hell of a profession to be a writer. One is one simply because one can't help it.[13]

The basic "borrowing" for Fitzgerald remained those experiences and complexes of memory that provided the emotional
frame of reference for his basic characters—that sharp, lifting, joyous hopefulness not for money itself but for what money would
bring. He always had what he described as the smoldering hatred of
the peasant for the rich, and therefore he was a snob. He smoldered
as well with a yearning to put an end once and for all to his social
luftmensch-ship, and the firm point of land—founded firmly on a
fairy's wing—he steered for was the mythical East Egg of Gatsby's
adolescent dreams.

For one thing, the family had pretensions to aristocracy. On his
mother's side, his Grandfather McQuillan had left a personal
estate of over a quarter of a million dollars and a business that
grossed a yearly income figured in the millions.[14] On his father's
side the family "was descended from Maryland families that had
figured prominently in the colonial legislatures and on the gover-
nor's councils."[15] His great, great, great granduncle was Francis
Scott Key, after whom he was named. Yet, especially after his

13 August 1935, *ibid.*, pp. 528–29.
14 See Andrew Turnbull, *Scott Fitzgerald*, p. 3 and Chapters I, II, and III, *passim*.
15 *Ibid.*, p. 5.

father, Edward Fitzgerald, lost his job as a salesman for Procter and Gamble, the family enjoyed only a shabby gentility. For Scott the visible sign of decline was the growing distance between his home and the Summit Avenue hilltop mansion of J. J. Hill, the railroad magnate and pinnacle of St. Paul society. But at the same time, the family never slid into real economic obscurity, below the level at which they could be free both of memory and pretension. Fitzgerald grew up in a social and psychological condition for which he himself supplied the metaphor: "In a house below the average/ Of a street above the average/ In a room below the roof/ With a lot above the ears."[16] The conceited and sensitive boy's interior reality, where the meanings of the outward signs lived, was insecurity born of a sense of the importance of all the money the family no longer had, of a lost paradise that was to have been not only regained but vouchsafed.

But the sense of having been cheated by the adolescent dream's golden promise of wealth and social popularity was coupled at the same time with an excited sense of the expectations of the fulfillment of its memory. As his past was in his future, so, like Gatsby's, his future was in the past of his imaginative youthfulness. After all, more was due to the child of such familial possibilities than the actualities of penurious history afforded. Ahead lay the glamorous world of fulfillment, an America where one belonged with all the "right" people. Ahead it lay, and to the east, where the great life swirling in the white and shining towers of the *real* cities offered more than even J. J. Hill could represent.

As a grown man, Fitzgerald articulated his consciousness of the dross that the dream turned out to hold. But even as a youngster, moving from town to town and street to street, vain of his appearance, enslaved by his concern with popularity, conscious of a rightful place among princes, imaginative and theatrical in his enjoyments and visions, shallow, nostalgic, precocious, snobbish,

[16] September 22, 1919, *Letters*, p. 456.

excitable, elated, and scared, he already knew that the excitements of expectation were defined by the certainties of what had been lost. Hope and nostalgia are peculiarly American bedfellows —the restoration of the loss is what the future promises to give; the national insistence on the future tense as an ideological norm is not so much an act of possession as a constant and desperate hope of repossession. If the Amory Blaine of young Fitzgerald closes *This Side of Paradise* with a radiant and morning world awaiting him, he does so with a consciousness that his future is free only so long as it is dispossessed of the past. The Gatsby of an older Fitzgerald devotes five years to a future which will remake a past composed of losses. Dick Diver, later yet, learns that the night so tender with nightingale song is the real darkness of the fact that the present, constantly becoming the past, is never the fulfillment of the future world dreamed of from the magic casements of youth. The reality to which he had dedicated his youth and passion and past betrayed him with his own dreams and expectations: "the fancy cannot cheat so well as she is famed to do, deceiving elf!"

As Wright Morris has said, the territory ahead lies behind us;[17] the dream filled and burst before the frontiers did. As Fitzgerald dramatized it, Gatsby's dream future lay behind him, somewhere in the obscure fields of the Republic that rolled on under the night. So for the young Fitzgerald—he died so young that perhaps "the Fitzgerald of early success" is more accurate—for him the postures of the future, of achievement, were poses made breathlessly evanescent by hope and brilliant by snobbish desperation and social dis-ease. How that youthful triumph overwhelmed Scott and Zelda both! What enviable madness it must have been

[17] W. Morris, *The Territory Ahead* (New York, 1963). Although the Fitzgerald chapter in *The Territory Ahead* is but one brief essay in the welter of Fitzgerald scholarship, it is—especially in the context of the book's contents—one of the most suggestive, illuminating, and rewarding of all the works written about Fitzgerald and deserves much greater recognition than it receives.

to pipe with wild (and deliciously, uneasily, incredulous) pleasure the attainment of the dream at last, to say to oneself, "*This* is it. It! Now, right *now!*" How the miraculous quality of that wedding between self and dream, "when the fulfilled future and the wistful past were mingled in a single gorgeous moment," must have been further proof, as it was for Gatsby, that the world was firmly founded on a fairy's wing. And if that wing bore a trademark, surely it must have said, "Made in America."

To coalesce the poles of past and future into an achieved electric unity of a golden and endless present, however, one had to escape the middle-class placelessness that was the actuality of Fitzgerald's experience. The New Eden and limbo, after all, are hardly the same neighborhood. It is not insignificant that the problem to which Fitzgerald addressed himself in his first book is the crisis of identity that exists for "The American" suspended in time and class.[18] For one thing, by way of example, Amory's contact—and throughout *This Side of Paradise* Amory is very much a fictional expression of Fitzgerald's autobiographical im-

---

[18] Although James E. Miller, *F. Scott Fitzgerald: His Art and His Technique* (New York, 1964), pp. 1–44, convincingly and quite properly places the Fitzgerald of *This Side of Paradise* among the "saturationists" and Wells-ites in the Henry James–H. G. Wells controversy, he rides his central thesis too strongly over the book when he implies (p. 25 *in context*) that it has no single thematic organizing center, none of the Jamesian "aboutness" that Percy Lubbock was demanding at the turn of the decade. He characterizes the novel with Edmund Wilson's phrase, "a gesture of indefinite revolt." Without doubt Miller is correct to accuse the novel of diffusion and diffuseness of recollection and inclusions for their own sakes. But there is something more at stake than architectural efficiency. A novel can fail in selection, yet still make clear its intentions even though it fails to frame (create) that intention fully or successfully. (This is not to touch at all the central question of criteria or Mr. Miller's implicit assumption that James was unquestionably correct, as though all novels are or should be the same kinds of art with the same kinds of purposes.) It is permissible, after all, for the critic to picture the blueprint in the collapsed wreck. What I wish to pursue in this chapter is what I think is unquestionably the book's "aboutness," the clear intention of reproducing a young American's romantic imagination in contact—for illusion or disillusion—with the objects and values that make it glow. *That*, I think, is the intended theme of this adolescent and self-dramatizing novel, and is no less the central spine of this, Fitzgerald's first book, than of the last. Indeed, that is the book's useful and premonitory significance for any study of Fitzgerald's themes.

pulse—with "the lower orders" is always attended by disgust or buffoonery. What Amory tried to cultivate as a Princeton manner shows through in *his creator's* consistent attitude toward menials in the book. The trip to Asbury Park is typical. Assuming a condescending attitude toward those who wait on them, the young men will have their college-boy pranks, and on manner alone they successfully carry off their inability to pay their bills. That's nothing to pay special attention to. They're just schoolkids building up class reunion memories. But the *tone* of the episode has something to say:

"What's the bill?"
Someone scanned it.
"Eight twenty-five."
"Rotten overcharge. We'll give them two dollars and one for the waiter. Kerry, collect the small change."
The waiter approached, and Kerry gravely handed him a dollar, tossed two dollars on the check, and turned away. They sauntered leisurely toward the door, pursued in a moment by the suspicious Ganymede.
"Some mistake, sir."
Kerry took the bill and examined it critically.
"No mistake!" he said, shaking his head gravely, and, tearing it into four pieces, he handed the scraps to the waiter, who was so dumbfounded that he stood motionless and expressionless while they walked out.
"Won't he send after us?"
"No," said Kerry; "for a minute he'll think we're the proprietor's sons or something; then he'll look at the check again and call the manager, and in the meantime—"[19]

Fitzgerald participates a little too joyfully with the boys. It is he, not one of the characters, who calls the waiter a "suspicious Ganymede." He leers at the waiter over the reader's shoulder,

[19] *This Side of Paradise* (New York, 1960), pp. 75–76. All further references to the novel are to this text, and page numbers throughout this chapter will be indicated by parentheses.

nudging the reader: "Some young lords, eh? That's me, second from the right." Or again when the gay dogs ridiculingly consort with a poor, ugly, half-wit girl at dinner, their undergraduate humor is far less admirable in the reader's eyes than in Fitzgerald's intentions:

"She prefers her native dishes," said Alec gravely to the waiter, "but any coarse food will do."
All through supper he addressed her in the most respectful language, while Kerry made idiotic love to her on the one side, and she giggled and grinned (p. 77).

Granted that what is happening is part of what Amory and the reader are to come to repudiate rather than admire, still in its undergraduate humor the episode nags us a bit too insistently to admire. What is pathetic is not so much the half-wit girl as Fitzgerald's obvious desire, in Amory's pitying condescension, to let us know that he was part of such groups of snappily slumming gay rascals. (One fact often overlooked by commentators on the novel is that Fitzgerald was very aware of a personal audience, on which he counted for sales, when he wrote the book. He knew that many smiling and admiring collegiate and socialite readers would see Scott Fitzgerald quite specifically in Amory Blaine.) What is pathetic is the inescapability of the problem of identity exposed in the implicit snobbishness. If one has a smoldering hatred for those above, he hates them at least in part for the self-image their ascendancy forces on him as one below. He hates them for defining the distance between where he is and where he wants to be. It is a definition of the distance between the tenses as well as the classes. It is a definition of the distance between The Democracy as metaphor, in which we were all liberated young demigods, or will be, and the democracy as actuality, in which our point-present identities are too often quite mortally something else. It is the distance between the Summit Avenue of the expectations and "a house below the average." We want to be with the gay dogs and young demigods, not with the waiters and half-wits. No one wishes to lose the delusions of American ideology (every man in God's Country is a King), and one so robbed hates the robber because one so robbed is made to hate himself where and for what he disappointingly is. (In his own lifetime, as he makes clear in letters and in the imagery of *The Great Gatsby*, even before the superhighway transformation that followed World War II, Fitzgerald recognized the significance of America as a nation on wheels, the physical mobility becoming both sign and guarantor of a yearning, seeking social mobility—and, ironically at the same time, a proof of placelessness and namelessness. The expectations and assumptions in the "cure" compound the disease being fled.) As for those below the seeker—what are they but examples of what he must avoid, the identity to be feared as the point furthest from where he wants to be and what, in the decline from what was, he is so fearfully close to. "We're the damned middle class!" Amory exclaims in the impatience born of fear of all below and desire for all above. With one's own identity at stake in a society where identity is both social and fluid, the self is grouped with those above by condescending scorn of those below.

The paradox is that in America, which prides itself on democracy, the very democratic fluidity of that society, where all ideologies bespeak expectation and success, breeds middle-class snobbishness: one's desired passage to identity in the future is to be up, certainly, not down. Writing to Helen Hayes about why European girls make excellent governesses and American girls never do, Fitzgerald proved himself acutely aware of the snobbishness of one's place ironically inherent in the egalitarian mobility of American expectations and self-identification.

I think it is impossible to get a first rate American governess who will not make home a hell. That's reason number one for procuring a French, English, or German number who will have a precise knowledge of her so-called "place." The position of a governess, which is halfway between an employee and a servant, is difficult for anyone to keep up with dignity—that is, to be a sort of an ideal friend to the child and yet maintain an unobtrusive position in regard to mama and papa. It is utterly un-American, and I have never seen one of our countrywomen who was really successful at it. They don't succeed in passing on any standards, save those of the last shoddy series of movies. On the contrary, from a European upper servant, a child learns many short cuts, ways to dispose of those ordinary problems that irk us in youth. The business of politeness is usually deftly handled without any nonsense— and what a saving! The self-consciousness, if any, is eradicated smoothly and easily; the nerves are somehow cushioned by a protective pillow of good form, something which would be annoying to a formed adult but for a child is a big saving of wear and tear. . . . The pace of American life simply will not permit a first-rate woman to take up such a profession.[20]

He pointed out, like James and Hawthorne before him, that in America, the ease, though not the readiness, of "vertical" social intercourse is prevented by a loss of the presentness of the past, an absence of the small amenities which buffer social contact in mutually understood prepared identities and rituals on which the European can depend.

But for the overwhelming personal differences made by his talent and intelligence, Fitzgerald himself could so readily have been *An American Tragedy*'s Clyde Griffiths. Despite the differences between Dreiser and Fitzgerald in identification with literary schools of the moment (and Fitzgerald admired the realism of Norris and Dreiser as the "real" literature), Fitzgerald's thematic community with Dreiser is clearly seen in their similar views of class distinction defined by social mobility and defining the importance of money.[21] It is clearly seen in their admiration for

[20] September 16, 1937, *Letters*, pp. 554–55.

[21] Fitzgerald thought of Norris and Dreiser as courageous artists whose societies rejected them because of their experimental realism. He thought of their realism as a mark of strong and serious—as opposed to popular and successful—fiction. His admiration of them was an admiration for their attitudes, especially for their concern with failure in American life, which to him meant seriousness. Writing to

some of the assumptions of naturalistic literature and their agreement about the psychic and moral emptiness of class distinctions
and mobilities in the dehumanized and purely social, selfish
personality that commercial success defines and which is all that
the innocent climber finds when he arrives, seeking his new humanity. The community between Fitzgerald and Dreiser is seen
perhaps most disturbingly in the significance of Fitzgerald's constant and casual snobbery in his references to delivery boys,
shopgirls, Jews, Negroes—references in the very works that repudiate the values which give the references their frame of implicit
attitudes. The tension between democratic earthiness and snobbish racism never completely left Fitzgerald, as it never really
left Dreiser or most of the writers who seriously tried to dramatize
their distrust of and desire for American wealth. On the one hand
a participant in his particular localities of the American scene and
on the other hand a moral commentator on them, Fitzgerald could
at once identify himself with the rich and identify himself as a
Marxist; could take whacks at Jews and caution his daughter that
"whacks at Jews" are "a moron's game"; could recognize that a
lot of himself was a spoiled playboy and could yet be the most self-
disciplined worker; could riot in an atmosphere of irresponsible
hedonism and yet insist, from the depths of his belief, on the necessity for being good, in the most old-fashioned sense of the word.

---

Maxwell Perkins in February 1920, a month before *This Side of Paradise* was released for public sale, he said,

> I was afraid all along because of . . . the agitation against Dreiser. . . . What
> in hell is the use of trying to write decent fiction if a bunch of old women
> refuse to let anyone hear the truth?
>     I've fallen lately under the influence of an author who's quite changed my
> point of view. He's a chestnut to you, no doubt, but I've just discovered him—
> Frank Norris. I think *McTeague* and *Vandover* are both excellent. . . . There
> are things in *Paradise* that might have been written by Norris—those drunken
> scenes, for instance—in fact all the realism. I wish I'd stuck to it throughout
> (*Letters*, pp. 143–44).

Though later in life he would refer to "poor old Dreiser," Fitzgerald never lost a
basic respect for him as an honest and serious artist.

For Fitzgerald's readers, the importance of the tensions between the aspects of the world that went into his composite characters is that they could result in first-class fiction. The sophomoric
attitudinizing of *This Side of Paradise* results not only in crack-
ups but also in the high and dramatic irony of *The Great Gatsby*
and *Tender Is the Night*. Perhaps Adam and Vespucci and Cabeza
de Vaca, certainly Norris, Veblen, Twain, and Dreiser could have
told Fitzgerald what he already knew: the quality of those tensions is peculiarly American. Like Twain and Dreiser he knew
the attractions of the world of money and the nausea in the realization of its actualities. With a few callow pretensions and a few
changes in background, Tom Sawyer becomes Amory Blaine,
just as, with a few talents, Clyde Griffiths becomes Jay Gatsby.
Twain's destruction, like Fitzgerald's, like Jay Gatsby's, was "just
personal," but it was archetypally personal for all of us. What
can one say about our Hawthornes and Twains and Hemingways
and Fitzgeralds, intensifications of our national selves, self-consciously (there's the horror!) destroyed by their very success?
What can one say but what Owl Eyes said of Gatsby: the poor
son of a bitch. Dreiser's books, like Twain's, are filled with the
effect of money on human personality in a vastly luxurious, fluid,
snobbish, pretentious, and democratic, commercial society.[22] If
the sparkle of the gay life is based on the vulgarity and artificial
distinctions within that society, then the hero is indeed nowhere.
What he is offered by his culture as identification is not salvation
or redemption, but *two* Fords in his future. If Sinclair Lewis was
the reporter of emotional sterility and spiritual poverty within
American commercial life, after F. Scott Fitzgerald the imaginative identification of its opulence with the Adamic American hero
was not again a serious literary possibility and the hero was to go

[22] So pervasive was the idea of wealth in the psychology of both men that in their
public as well as their private writings, their works are shot through with rhetorical
figures of subject-material as capital and of emotional resources as banked wealth.

into the underground resistance. In the world of fictional models and influences, the popularity of F. Scott Fitzgerald, like the modish bourgeoisie-baiting of his literary generation, announced the death of Horatio Alger in American fiction. Norris and Dreiser and the muckrakers were engaged in the social and historical identification of the American, particularly at a moment of the great influx of immigrants from eastern and southern Europe; Scott Fitzgerald addressed himself to the modern-dress mythic consequences of that reidentification while still identifying, Catholic though he had been, with WASP supereminence.

As for Fitzgerald himself in the tension of placelessness, he tells us in his novels about "others" what he told John O'Hara about himself:

I am half black Irish and half old American stock with the usual exaggerated ancestral pretensions. The black Irish half of the family had the money and looked down upon the Maryland side of the family who had, and really had, that certain series of reticences and obligations that go under the poor old shattered word "breeding" (modern form "inhibitions"). So being born in that atmosphere of crack, wisecrack and countercrack I developed a two-cylinder inferiority complex. So if I were elected King of Scotland tomorrow after graduating from Eton, Magdalene to Guards, with an embryonic history which tied me to the Plantagenets, I would still be a parvenue. I spent my youth in alternately crawling in front of the kitchen maids and insulting the great.

I suppose this is just a confession of being a Gael though I have known many Irish who have not been afflicted by this intense social self-consciousness. If you are interested in colleges, a typical gesture on my part would have been, for being at Princeton and belonging to one of its snootiest clubs, I would be capable of going to Podunk on a visit and being absolutely booed and overawed by its social system, not from timidity, but simply because of an inner necessity of starting my life and my self-justification over again at scratch in whatever new environment I may be thrown.[23]

23 July 18, 1933, *Letters*, p. 503.

Although the bit of Fitzgerald-O'Hara correspondence reflects peculiarly Irish overtones in the autobiographical utterances of Yeats, Shaw, Joyce, O'Casey, O'Neill, still the Irish uncertainty about a dependable social self is intensified by the American fluidity of the Irish American. In the fictive extension of his social self, the inner necessity to continually start self-justification all over again exists because Fitzgerald is aware that we never know at what dark moment our souls and our history will catch up with our national assumption that being The Kid, the New-Man, the Stranger, the Adam, is an unadulterated blessing, the best of all possible identities in the most promising of all worlds. The need to begin anew in each new place and time and circumstance is especially true if The Kid belongs to the drifting middle class, for like his rebellious literary contemporaries, Fitzgerald felt that to belong to the middle class is to belong to a nowhere of transit in time and status, and therefore in identity. Tom Buchanan finally destroys Gatsby when he calls him "Mr. Nobody from Nowhere." It is not only an oversimplification, but it is foolish and wrong to say, as has often been said, that America ruined Scott Fitzgerald. It is quite something else, however, to recognize that as the victim of his own circumstances he was in many ways an acutely representative American and that the agony that went into his "autobiographical" fiction gives Americans, for better or for worse, that most composite of all his characters, themselves.

II

In the 1920's *This Side of Paradise* occupied a midpoint between two other popular books in the *Bildungsroman* literature of the Young Man Finding Himself During His College Years. It was influenced by Compton Mackenzie's *Sinister Street* as, in turn, it provided an example for a book of much smaller stature, Percy Marks's *The Plastic Age*. The context provided by contemporary

samples of the genre is instructive, for the differences between *This
Side of Paradise* and the other two books indicate what is unique
about Fitzgerald's imagination.

*Sinister Street*, at least for American readers, is a very British,
and by now a very dated, book. It is the kind of novel that, as one
reviewer put it, is "the best sort of history." As history it is peculiarly British because it is a detailed and evocative profile of
upper-class English life at the turn of the century; it makes the
stereotype of the tweedy, pipey, educated young English esquire
breathe audibly. Beneath the stereotypical verisimilitudes, the
book offered its times some vital heat that must have had at least
a double flame. One fire must have warmed the historical and
sociological particulars of the book, for a young American reader
like Scott Fitzgerald found therein not only a rhetoric but a society that he scanned with wistful and emulative admiration. Another fire must have warmed the general matter of the book, for
young readers, regardless of nation or class, found in its hero,
Michael Fane, a living example of their own need to find a place
in the world, if not in the sun. In our own time, my metaphor is
inaccurate, for *Sinister Street* has cooled considerably; it is a thin
bed of pleasantly glowing embers rather than a burst of flame.
But there is no doubt that in its day it did fire the imagination
of the young Scott Fitzgerald. "While it astonished me that so few
critics mentioned the influence of *Sinister Street* on *This Side of
Paradise*," he said, "I feel sure that it was much more in intention
than in literal fact. It occurred to me to write an American version
of the history of that sort of young man—in which, no doubt, I
was hindered by lack of perspective as well as by congenital
shortcomings.

"But I was also hindered by a series of resemblances between
my life and that of Michael Fane which, had I been a more conscientious man, might have precluded my ever attempting an

autobiographical novel."[24] The lack of perspective, like the congenital shortcomings, was a consequence of the American condition of Fitzgerald's vision and experience. He could not see with a British eye, no matter how much he might have wanted to see himself in his dream doppelganger, Charles Michael Saxby Fame, the unacknowledged bastard of a powerful British lord.[25]

In the "Britishness" of *Sinister Street*, the young Fitzgerald found something that the "Americanness" of his hungry expectations and insecurities could feast upon. The class point of view, natural and organic to the world Mackenzie portrays, was seized by Fitzgerald's imagination as a storehouse of poses and attitudes that were to be associated with success and with belonging rather than with that indeterminate arriviste world of middle-class decline and quick new wealth that marked his own sense of identity. Mackenzie's hero can indulge in a tedious speculation about "good eggery" and "bad eggery" without appearing foolish, though he is boring. His speculation is merely a catalogue of the facts of social behavior historically belonging to defined groups within English society. Michael Fane, as young-man-finding-himself, might not know where he belongs in the universe, but he knows where he belongs in the world. The act of speculation turns out to be merely an act of reference, of evoking understood conventions. But Fitzgerald's hero, Amory Blaine, has to define the "good egg," or more accurately the *successful* egg by creating him out of the social actualities that aren't supposed to exist. (In 1920 Fitzgerald was no more free from the American artist's need to make the world anew each morning than was Fenimore Cooper, with his new American, one hundred years earlier.)

The successful egg—the "slicker"—is a concealed reality. Signif-

24 February 26, 1921, *ibid.*, pp. 468–69.
25 For a discussion of the influences on technique exercised by *Sinister Street* upon *This Side of Paradise*, see Miller, pp. 16–26.

icantly, his qualities are not an inheritance from an established past and present, but are signs of a deliberate calculus at success in the future. The "big man," as opposed to the "slicker," is merely the dupe of the moment. He is constantly in demand as a friend in need. The big man is a nice guy, but the slicker is a successful one.

The slicker was good-looking or *clean*-looking; he had brains, social brains, that is, and he used all means on the broad path of honesty to get ahead, be popular, admired, and never in trouble. He dressed well, was particularly neat in appearance, and derived his name from the fact that his hair was inevitably worn short, soaked in water or tonic, parted in the middle, and slicked back as the current of fashion dictated. . . . The slicker seemed distributed through school, always a little wiser and shrewder than his contemporaries, managing some team or other, and keeping his cleverness carefully concealed. . . .

| The Slicker | The Big Man |
|---|---|
| 1. Clever sense of social values. | 1. Inclined to stupidity and unconscious of social values. |
| 2. Dresses well. Pretends that dress is superficial—but knows that it isn't. | 2. Thinks dress is superficial, and is inclined to be careless about it. |
| 3. Goes into such activities as he can shine in. | 3. Goes out for everything from a sense of duty. |
| 4. Gets to college and is, in a worldly way, successful. | 4. Gets to college and has a problematical future. Feels lost without his circle, and always says that school days were happiest, after all. Goes back to school and makes speeches about what St. Regis boys are doing. |
| 5. Hair slicked. | 5. Hair not slicked. |

(pp. 34, 35, 36)

For Michael Fane, the hazing of a poor and unattractive scholarship student can be abjured from a sense of noblesse oblige which can be exercised without embarrassment or pretension. Fane's life simply does not reveal the same conditions to which Amory is subject. Fane is not prone to fears of class and position and social identity; if he has to find himself internally, he does not have to define himself externally. For the American, the two needs seem very much to be one. Michael Fane and Amory Blaine are both lonely as they begin college, but they are subject to loneliness in significantly different ways.[26] Fane's problem disappears easily, although he begins his career at Oxford in circumstances that seem similar to Amory's at Princeton.

The list of freshmen, pinned up on the board in the Lodge, was a discouraging document to those isolated members of public schools other than Eton, Winchester, Harrow or Charterhouse. These four seemed to have produced all but six or seven of the freshmen. Eton alone was responsible for half the list. What chance, thought Michael, could he stand against such an impenetrable phalanx of conversation as was bound to ensue from such a preponderance?[27]

But beneath the uneasiness that comes to any stranger among strangers, there is an easy community of gentlemen who do not have to prove themselves as belongers. They merely have to feel each other out until they have announced to each other the mutuality of identity that transcends the tribal pride attaching to the words "Etonian," "Harrovian," "Jacobean," "Carthusian," and "Wykehamist":

". . . Are you a Harrovian?"
Michael shook his head. . . .
"My name's Lonsdale. I think we're on the same staircase—so's Mackintosh. It's a pity he's a Harrovian, but I promised my mother I'd look him up. . . . I don't mind telling you that the Etonians up here are a pretty poor lot. . . . I say, are you really from St. James's?"

[26] The surface similarity of the names is merely a similarity in sound. Fitzgerald wrote to critic Frances Newman, "It seems to me you have marred a justified criticism [the dependence of *This Side of Paradise* on *Sinister Street*] by such pettinesses as comparing the names 'Blaine' and 'Fane'. . . ." February 26, 1921, *Letters*, p. 469.
[27] Compton Mackenzie, *Sinister Street* (Harmondsworth, Middlesex, 1960), p. 384.

Michael replied coldly that he was.

"I say, come and have coffee with me after hall. One or two O.E.'s [Old Etonians] are coming in, but you won't mind?"

. . . Now at any rate there was a perceptible relaxation of tension. Still the conversation was only general in so much as that whenever anybody spoke, the rest of the table listened.

. . . "How these Wykehamists love one another," laughed an Etonian.

This implied criticism welded the four Winchester men present in defiance of all England. . . .

. . . [But] the unwieldly bulk of sixteen freshmen was beginning to break up into bridge fours. Friendships were already in visible elaboration. The first evening had wonderfully brought them together. Something deeper than the superficial amity of chance juxtaposition at the same table was now begetting tentative confidences that would ultimately ripen into intimacies. Etonians were discovering that all Harrovians were not the dark-blue bedecked ruffians of Lords nor aggressive boors of Etonian tradition. Harrovians were beginning to suspect that some Etonians might exist less flaccid, less deliberately lackadaisical, less odiously serene than the majority of those they had so far only encountered in summer holidays. Carthusians found that athletic prowess was going to count pleasantly in their favor. Even the Wykehamists extended a cordiality that was not positively chilling, and though they never lost an opportunity to criticize implicitly all other schools, and though their manners were so perfect that they abashed all but the more debonair Etonians, still it was evident they were sincerely trying to acknowledge a little merit, a little good-fellowship among these strange new contemporaries. . . .[28]

Michael Fane is not alone. He is a jolly good gentleman among jolly good gentlemen.

But the American—particularly the American who, like Fitzgerald, is acutely class conscious, and who has strong class pretensions but no clearly defined class identity—cannot play the British game without generating a great deal of confusion. Being a stranger among strangers does not, for "damned middle class"

28 *Ibid.*, pp. 384–91.

Amory, lead to a discovery of class oneness with others, but rather to an egalitarian resentment of class distinctions. The sting of actual social exclusion calls for the ideological balm of that rebellious social democracy which is supposed to be American.

"Amory had decided definitely on Princeton, even though he would be the only boy entering that year from St. Regis' . . ." (p. 36). Arriving at Princeton, he

alone from St. Regis', watched the crowds form and widen and form again; St. Paul's, Hill, Pomfret, eating at certain tacitly reserved tables in Commons, dressing in their own corners of the gymnasium, and drawing unconsciously about them a barrier of the slightly less important but socially ambitious to protect them from the friendly, rather puzzled high school element. From the moment he realized this Amory resented social barriers as artificial distinctions made by the strong to bolster up their weak retainers and keep out the almost strong (p. 43).

The Princetonian does not enjoy the casual certainties of the Oxonian. Although the English gentlemen compete among themselves, the competition is intellectual and athletic. Finally, it is not social. At the basic level of identity, the professional amateurism and apparently easy serenities—the true gentleman's life as a process of quiet understatement—of the English campus are nonexistent on the American. Lacking the historical reality beneath appearances, "belonging" on the American campus is a lonely business of hectic social competition in which very process one not only proves oneself, but thereby *finds* oneself. It is only surfaces and appearances and outward signs that one has with which to identify. For the American students, "from the day when, wild-eyed and exhausted, the jerseyed freshmen sat in the gymnasium and elected someone from Hill School class president, a Lawrenceville celebrity vice-president, a hockey star from St. Paul's secretary, up until the end of the sophomore year it never ceased, that breathless social system, that worship, seldom named, never really admitted, of the bogey 'Big Man.' " From the very first, the democratic fluidity of the American's existence is fever as well as opportunity, a lack of a past—or at least any understanding of its necessity and meaning—as well as an emphasis on the future. It relegates the present to lost moments and turns faces into hasty masks. It is the paradox, at once creatively strenuous and destructive, of anonymous individuality. It is the paradox in which the British gentleman, representing a conventional and aristocratic way of life, has the security that allows the eccentricity, individuality, idiosyncrasy, which, because he cannot afford to appear out of place, are denied to the parvenu American—who is supposed to represent an individualistic democracy. The democrat cannot afford *not* to be a snob.

Democratic impulses remain on the level of ideology, but nowhere in Amory's world, in his journey toward identity, do they rest upon solid reality in the way that class security does for Michael Fane. Amory's resentment of social barriers is stated by Fitzgerald, the momentary American democrat, and stated, at that, in a sour-grapes recollection of social insecurity. Amory's anger at caste is merely a conscious and temporary gesture on the part of Fitzgerald. But the writer in Fitzgerald, recalling and dramatizing the social impulses of his experience and his personality, creates an Amory whose longings and actions do not substantiate the ideologies of democracy. Amory's adolescent self-conscious and self-important postures are the imaginative actuality, regardless of Fitzgerald's telling us that "Amory resented social barriers as artificial distinctions." For, "By afternoon [of his first day at Princeton] Amory realized that now the newest arrivals were taking him for an upper classman, and he tried conscientiously to look both pleasantly blasé and casually critical, which was as near as he could analyze the prevalent facial expression" (p. 38). Of course, like any freshman, Michael Fane also wishes to be taken for an old inhabitant. But beneath Fitzgerald's deliberate consciousness of Amory's awareness of appearances is the constant of the competitive need to discover channels that will *create* the belonging which the Englishman only need learn to clothe fashionably, because he already has it. For Michael, finding himself at Oxford means finding a means of defining and expressing an established identity: it is a matter of vocation. For Amory, finding himself at Princeton means creating an entity: it is a matter of advantages, finding which *is* one's American vocation. *This Side of Paradise* repeatedly concerns the reader with the identities that overlay "the fundamental Amory," and the overlays are all the phoney and tinsel stances from which the poseur expects to derive an advantage.

Amory found that writing for the *Nassau Literary Magazine* would get him nothing, but that being on the board of the *Daily Princetonian* would get any one a good deal. His vague desire to do immortal acting with the English Dramatic Association faded out when he found that the most ingenious brains and talents were concentrated upon the Triangle Club, a musical comedy organization that every year took a great Christmas trip. In the meanwhile, feeling strangely alone and restless in Commons, with new desires and ambitions stirring in his mind, he let the first term go by between an envy of the embryo successes and a puzzled fretting with Kerry as to why they were not accepted immediately among the elite of the class.

". . . We're the damned middle class, that's what!" he complained to Kerry one day as he lay stretched out on the sofa, consuming a family of Fatimas with contemplative precision.

"Well, why not? We came to Princeton so we could feel that way toward the small colleges—have it on 'em, more self-confidence, dress better, cut a swathe—"

"Oh, it isn't that I mind the glittering caste system," admitted Amory. "I like having a bunch of hot cats on top, but gosh, Kerry, I've got to be one of them" (p. 45).

Because there *is* a top, vaguely represented by Princeton in the first place (that's why "we come to Princeton"). And at the top there is an "elite of the class." That knowledge, within the ambiguities of American democracy, exacerbates the itch to belong. More bitingly does the itch burn precisely because of the tantalizing possibilities that arise from the absence of any clear certainty of the limits of one's caste. Yet, seeing the belongers, one is surrounded by proofs that caste exists. One is plunged into a world slightly Kafkaesque in its mystery. The belief is in democratic equality. The fact is social inequality. The belief makes the components of the fact hard to define. One must define "the top" at the same time he strives for it. But how define it, unless one is there to see it? The seeing is in the striving, the definition is in the climbing, and all the climber has, finally, is an uneasy sense that everybody is somewhere except himself. (At the early height of his own "gaudy spree," Fitzgerald could not bear to be left out, and revelled in the stage-center position that he and Zelda occupied as king and queen of the jazz age, at the same time that he recognized the destructive spuriousness of what he delighted in.

> There'd be an orchestra
> Bingo! Bango!
> Playing for us
> To dance the tango
> And people would clap
> When we arose
> At her sweet face
> And my new clothes.[29]

In later years, in essays like "Echoes of the Jazz Age" [1931] and "My Lost City" [1932], he would declare a repudiation of that spree mingled with nostalgia for it, crying out not for the return of a place or a time as such, but for the return of a condition of being: "Come back, come back, O glittering and white!")

Those at the top have in common a language of belonging. They share the people, places, experiences, and attitudes that

29 F. Scott Fitzgerald, *The Crack-Up*, ed. Edmund Wilson (New York, 1956), p. 159.

the climber must pretend to have in order to be accepted there. The absurd-pathetic talk of "old sport" Gatsby and his fabricated experiences and acquaintances, for instance, are shattered, to his dismay, that hot afternoon at the Plaza, when Tom, Nick, and Daisy begin to reminisce about friends in the Yale and Chicago society world that Gatsby could only pretend to, but had never entered. The necessity for pretense is the climber's constant reminder that he doesn't belong to a world which, in its inner relationships, seems closed to him and yet which seems to be the most attractive of all possible worlds. So even choosing a dwelling place is a crucial matter of identity in the social statement made by the choice. In Michael Fane's world, one's college is either chosen by whim (a childhood picture of a college tower), or by the custom of one's people. When one goes into "digs," one chooses a location and a decor according to personal tastes. But for Amory, one's "digs"—the Princeton eating clubs—are matters of public image and therefore of identity itself:

Amory was far from contented. He missed the place he had won at St. Regis', the being known and admired, yet Princeton stimulated him, and there were many things ahead calculated to arouse the Machiavelli latent in him, could he but insert a wedge. The upper-class clubs, concerning which he had pumped a reluctant graduate during the previous summer, excited his curiosity: Ivy, detached and breathlessly aristocratic; Cottage, an impressive mélange of brilliant adventurers and well-dressed philanderers: Tiger Inn, broad-shouldered and athletic, vitalized by an honest elaboration of prep-school standards; Cap and Gown, anti-alcoholic, faintly religious and politically powerful; flambuoyant Colonial; literary Quadrangle; and the dozen others, varying in age and position (p. 44).

But it's a never-ending round, for making the proper club, the proper activity, the proper identity, must appear to be effortless, the natural and just consequence of one's place at the top—that very place to which the climber pretends in order to make the proper club, the proper activity, the proper identity. One must conform to be allowed to belong, one must belong to be allowed to conform:

Anything which brought an under classman into too glaring a light was labelled with the damning brand of "running it out." The movies thrived on caustic comments, but the men who made them were generally running it out; talking of clubs was running it out; standing for anything very strongly, as, for instance, drinking parties or teetotalling, was running it out; in short, being personally conspicuous was not tolerated, and the influential man was the non-committal man, until at club elections in sophomore year every one should be sewed up in some bag for the rest of his college career (pp. 44–45).

There is a double involution here: the insistent amateurism of Fane's British world is a consequence of the solid recognition of one's being: a gentleman does not take advantage of his superiority by insisting on it—the amateurism is phoney only insofar as the gentleman works hard indeed for his grades, for the expertise that allows him to wear the mantle of amateurism. Socially he doesn't run it out because of his sense of noblesse oblige. Amory, the American, is likely to let his studies go in order to achieve the social status in which he can pretend that he belongs so securely to the elite that he too need not insist upon it. He must sweat like hell in order to be able to pretend that he never perspires. The insistence upon not running it out is a much more ingeniously empty and desperate matter for the Princetonian than for the Oxonian. The latter can disregard the status of high or central position because he so surely has it. The former must pretend to disregard the status of high or central position because that is the pretense of the man he pretends to be. " 'But just now, Amory,' " says Kerry in response to Amory's desire to live at the top, " 'you're only a sweaty bourgeois.'

"Amory lay for a long moment without speaking.

" 'I won't be—long,' he said finally. 'But I hate to get anywhere by working for it. I'll show the marks, don't you know' " (pp. 45–46).

At the sight of one "hot cat on top," Amory "sighed eagerly. There at the head of the white platoon marched Allenby, the football captain, slim and defiant, as if aware that this year the hopes of the college rested on him, that his hundred-and-sixty pounds were expected to dodge to victory through the heavy blue and crimson lines." Craning his neck suddenly at the street, Amory sees other worthies go by as he is called to the window by Kerry, his roommate: " 'There's Langueduc, if you want to see what he looks like—and Humbird just behind.'

"Amory rose dynamically and sought the windows.

" 'Oh,' he said scrutinizing these worthies, 'Humbird looks like a knockout, but this Langueduc—he's the rugged type, isn't he? I distrust that sort. All diamonds look big in the rough' " (p. 45).

Again the significance lies in the extent to which the American is in an earlier stage of development than the European. Michael Fane went through his puppy-love crushes of hero worship at the proper time—when he was a little boy at Randell House, the first school he attended. Too young yet to have any real sense of himself, he was engaged in the universal and feral conflict that results from the self-declarative necessity of each ego to proclaim its existence. Michael learned the protective coloration of majority behavior. He sought out heroes and worshipped them. He developed tribal fealties and loyalties. Consequently, by the time he entered public school at St. James's he was more established as a social being, and, when war broke out, was even secure enough to rebel against the mindless patriotism of the majority. By the time he entered Oxford, he belonged to a caste, a set and defined, if unspoken, world of self-identifications. Learning Oxfordisms was a matter of propriety, not of being.

As the Englishman grows up faster, the American, years be-

hind him, remains younger, the constant adolescent. The fundamental young Fitzgerald, creating out of himself the fundamental
Amory, gives us the American college man who is still learning
what was provided for the English little boy back in Randell
House. Particularly does the disparity between his poses and his
certitudes make him a little schoolboy in contrast. He is foolish,
and it is the foolishness of adolescence that marks Fitzgerald and
his materials. And therein, paradoxically, is his strength.

Consider Fitzgerald's personality: more self-conscious than
most, hungrier than most, more self-declarative than most, he
had the narcissistic, solipsistic, strong, and terribly aware personality of the artist. If, to begin with, the itch to belong is irri-
tated in America by the conflict between ideology and actuality,
by the formlessness of social identity, how much more is it intensified for the personality which feels its own existence very acutely.
How much sharper is the urge for the personality which must find
itself because it makes such a clamor to be found and yet which
must define itself according to every nameable American mythic
optimism, which must belong according to the democratic expectations of American mythic egalitarianism, which must fulfill
itself according to the American mythic sense of the absolutely
liberated new-man—all this among the hot cats at the top according to American burgeois actualities!

Indeed, the poses in which the silly and adolescent Fitzgerald
arranged his silly and adolescent Amory are silly and adolescent.
But by what inner necessity is the pose impelled and what a cultural revelation the adolescent pretension makes! This is not to
say that because *This Side of Paradise* is excellent material for
the historian or sociologist it is a good book. It is not a good book.
It *is* a silly and adolescent book with many lovely and promising
passages. But it is a very significant book for an understanding of
the nature of American literary materials and cultural attitudes
toward American experience; it is a highly important book for

an understanding of the writings of Fitzgerald. As Fitzgerald grew, became the artist primarily and the American boy only retrospectively and wanly and, finally, tragically, he enlarged his composite materials into a metaphor for our national experience, making out of the history of America the betrayal of adolescent innocence in dimensions of art that attain universalities well beyond anything achieved by Compton Mackenzie. When Amory grows up, ruined by his growth, into the protagonists that follow him in other books, his stature is significantly greater than that of the Englishman who preceded him.

The young Edmund Wilson, writing to the young Scott Fitzgerald shortly after the publication of *This Side of Paradise*, hit exactly upon Fitzgerald's adolescent posing as the force behind Amory's posing. And of course Wilson was right, as he almost always is when he turns his critical intelligence loose upon a book. But how wrong he was, at the same time. (As Fitzgerald put it five years later, and speaking about quite another letter, "We enjoyed your letter enormously, colossally, stupendously. It was epochal, acrocryptical, categorical . . . . But you are wrong . . . . You are always wrong—but always with the most correct possible reasons.")[30] Wilson's early (Nov. 21, 1919) personal reaction to *This Side of Paradise* is worth quoting in full.

Dear Fitz:

I have just read your novel with more delight than I can well tell you. It ought to be a classic in a class with *The Young Visitors;* Amory Blaine should rank with Mr. Salteena. It sounds like an exquisite burlesque of Compton Mackenzie with a pastiche of Wells thrown in at the end. I wish you hadn't chosen such bad masters as Mackenzie and the later Wells: your hero is an unreal imitation of Michael Fane who was himself unreal and who was last seen in the role of the veriest card-board best-seller hero being nursed back to life in the Balkans. Almost the only things of value to be learned from the

[30] October 7, 1924, *Letters*, p. 340.

Michael Fane books are pretty writing and clever dialogue and with both of these you have done very well. The descriptions in places are very nicely done and so is some of the college dialogue, which really catches the Princeton tone, though your hero as an intellectual is a fake of the first water and I read his views on art, politics, religion and society with more riotous mirth than I should care to have you know. You handicap your story, for one thing, by making your hero go to the war and then completely leaving the war out. If you thought you couldn't deal with his military experiences you shouldn't have had him go abroad at all. You make him do a lot of other things that the real Amory never did, such as getting on the *Prince* and playing on the football team, and thereby you produce an incredible monster, half romantic hero and half F. Scott Fitzgerald. This, of course, may be more evident to me than it would be to some reader who didn't know you, but I really think you should cultivate detachment and not allow yourself to drift into a state of mind where, as in the latter part of this book, you make Amory the hero of dramatic encounters with all the naive and romantic gusto of a small boy imagining himself as a brave hunter of Indians. The love affairs seem to me to be the soundest part of the book as fiction; the ones with Isabelle and Rosalind are the realest. I was, of course, infinitely entertained by the Princeton part; but you put in some very dubious things,—the party at Asbury Park, for example, where they beat their way through the restaurants. If you tell me that you have seen this happen, I point to the incident in which the Burne brothers, who are presumably not supposed to be cads, are made to play an outrageous and impossible practical joke on the girl who comes down for the game. I was almost very much shocked when poor old John Bishop's hair stands straight on end at beholding the devil.

I don't want to bludgeon you too brutally, however, for I think that some of the poems and descriptions are really exceedingly good. It would all be better if you would tighten up your artistic conscience and pay a little more attention to form. Il faut faire quelque chose de vraiment beau, vous savez!—something 'which the world will not willingly let die.' I feel called upon to give you this advice because I believe you might become a very popular trashy novelist without much difficulty.

The only first-rate novel recently produced in this *genre* is James

Joyce's book [*A Portrait of the Artist as a Young Man*] and that is one of the best things in English because of its rigorous form and selection and its polished style and because the protagonist is presented with complete detachment, with the ugly sides of his life as accurately depicted as the inspired and beautiful ones. But what about the ugly and mean features of Amory's life! You make some feeble attempts to account for them in the beginning, but on the whole your hero is a kind of young god moving among demi-gods; the Amory I hear about in the book is not the Amory I knew at Princeton nor at all like any genuine human being I ever saw. Well, I concede that it is much better to imagine even a more or less brummagem god and strike off from him a few authentic gleams of poetry and romance than to put together a perfectly convincing and mediocre man who never conveys to the reader a single thrill of the wonder of life, like Beresford's Joseph Stahl and a lot of other current heroes, but I do think the most telling poetry and romance may be achieved by keeping close to life and not making Scott Fitzgerald a sort of super-Michael Fane. Cultivate a universal irony and do read something other than contemporary British novelists: this history of a young man stuff has been run into the ground and has always seemed to me a bum art-form, anyway,—at least when, as in Beresford's or Mackenzie's case, it consists of dumping all one's youthful impressions in the reader's lap, with a profound air of importance. You do the same thing: you tell the reader all sorts of stuff which has no bearing on your story and no other interest,—that detail about how Amory's uncle gave him a cap, etc.

I really like the book, though; I enjoyed it enormously, and I shouldn't wonder if a good many other people would enjoy it, too. You have a knack of writing readably which is a great asset. Your style, by the way, has become much sounder than it used to be.—Well, I hope to see you here soon. Thanks for the novel.[31]

Wilson does here what a score of critics did later. He takes Fitzgerald to task for including all kinds of autobiographical details, and then berates him for not being accurately autobiographical enough. In the sneer at the book's pretentiousness, Wilson

[31] The papers of F. Scott Fitzgerald, Princeton University Library.

doesn't see with his intellect what Fitzgerald already could see
with his instincts: a brummagem god is the kind most visible to
the adolescent who, like Jimmy Gatz, has only the "vast, vulgar
and meretricious beauty" of his culture with which to form his
platonic conception of himself. If Wilson has the better mind,
he also has the cooler soul. He never itched, at least not as Fitzgerald did. His personality was not a feverish child of middle-
class vulgar expectation coupled with the wide-eyed vanity of
the artist. Both elements are equally important in Fitzgerald's
personality.[32] It's too simple to say that America is cheap, America
is vulgar, America is a land of will-o'-the-wisps. The dramatic
sense of what lies beneath or behind such a simple statement is
to be had most personally in the alembic of the imagination *most
susceptible* to the tinsel and glitter of America, as Wilson, in the
armor of his more strongly critical and disenchanted (probably
never-enchanted) intelligence, was not. The susceptibility is all.
Not ripeness, but adolescence, which is the certainty of golden
ripeness to come, Gatsby's "heightened sensitivity to the promises
of life." The vision is not of the solid life after the successful
climb, but is the puerile daydream of attaining the peak, the
moment, suspended out of sequence, in which the crowd is always roaring its love and approval—that's what Fitzgerald could
understand about the young and vainly daydreaming Amory:
". . . before he fell asleep he would dream one of his favorite
waking dreams, the one about becoming a great halfback, or the
one about the Japanese invasion, when he was rewarded by being

---

[32] "Indeed," says Turnbull, "Wilson and Fitzgerald were so different that it is
surprising they got along as well as they did. . . . Wilson's strength lay in logical
analysis, in his ability to reason a problem through to plausible conclusions. He was
a master of the literary case or argument, marshaling his evidence with the cogency
of a legal brief and pushing his point across in persuasive, common-sense prose. Fitzgerald's mind and sensibility ran counter—towards the imaginative, the evocative,
the inconsistent, the magical, even the mystical. He was a natural poet as Wilson
was a natural critic. . . . Compared to Fitzgerald, he saw life a little coldly on the one
hand and on the other a little indirectly through the veil of what he had read" (pp.
313–14).

made the youngest general in the world. It was always the becoming he dreamed of, never the being. This, too, was quite characteristic of Amory" (pp. 17–18).

The susceptibility to the vision of the self as hot cat (and why
not! this is America, isn't it?) with which, as Wright Morris put
it, "Fitzgerald dropped to the deep, dead-end center of the American mind . . . deeper than Hemingway and Twain, deeper than
the Mississippi and the Big Two-Hearted River, down to that
sunken island that once mythically flowered for Dutch sailor's
eyes," made and destroyed him.[33] It let Fitzgerald into the secret
dream-corners of the great American adolescent soul, and let him
down from the fulfillment that success is supposed to bring in
the adolescent dream. Let him in and let him down. The adolescent romantic who becomes the disillusioned man of experience can look back most tellingly upon the romantic adolescent, can have the double view, can identify so lovingly and
longingly with the very meretriciousness he repudiates.[34]

Later in his career, Edmund Wilson peered into the pages of
*Life* magazine and said that not only does it represent a land he
does not wish to live in, but that it's an unreal land, a world he
doesn't recognize. Had Fitzgerald lived, he would have agreed
with the condemnation, but he would have recognized every fea-
ture in the terrain. It is exactly because he was "the damned middle class" in his aspirations as well as in his pocketbook and
address that Fitzgerald, in his transcendent imagination, dramatically captured the fevers and pretensions of his age as Wilson did
only intellectually. Exactly because, as Wilson said so truly, he
easily "might become a very popular trashy novelist," Fitzgerald

[33] *The Territory Ahead*, p. 158.
[34] In his introduction to the one-volume edition of *The Great Gatsby, Tender Is
the Night*, and *The Last Tycoon* (New York, 1953), Malcolm Cowley recreates Fitzgerald's "romance of money," brilliantly recapturing and presenting Fitzgerald's
doubleness. All statements about Fitzgerald's double self as "spoiled priest" and
as one of the hot cats on top—and there are many in the corpus of Fitzgerald scholarship—owe a debt of homage to this seminal essay.

knew the adolescent tawdriness of imagination at work on American experience, debasing the zillion-carat big rock candy mountain to the rhinestone as big as the Ritz. Wilson's trouble, reading Fitzgerald, was that he couldn't ever be at home in the five-and-ten of the emotions and the intellect. When one is concerned with true diamonds only, sometimes the very exquisiteness of his jeweller's eye prevents him from recognizing the significance and beauty of the brummagem article, gods and gems alike. The favorite game of Fitzgerald's detractors—announcing his adolescence in tones of implicit condescension—is about played out. It's necessary to recognize that his materials, the adolescence together with the realization of its rhinestone significance, was the source of his fire and of his true diamond art, as it was, for him, the source both of American energy and the five-and-dime shabbiness of that energy's moral product. The trick is to consider Fitzgerald's *uses* of adolescence and to evaluate those. After all, if Michael Fane was last seen in the Balkans in another cardboard pose, Amory Blaine Fitzgerald was later seen in the composite magnificence of *The Great Gatsby* and *Tender Is the Night*.

### I I I

As I have indicated, I do not intend that cultural significance should be confused with critical justification. To the extent that Wilson was undeniably right—Amory's adolescent posing was the sign of Fitzgerald's adolescent pretentiousness—the book is filled with touches that make one wince, laugh, or sneer at the author.[35] For instance, patterning Beatrice Blaine after Mrs. Fane

---

[35] After all, what could be expected of a young man who struck such objectionable poses as those revealed in this portion of a letter (from Fort Leavenworth, Kansas, January 10, 1918) to Edmund Wilson: "This insolent war has carried off Stuart Walcott in France, as you may know, and really is beginning to irritate me—but the maudlin sentiment of most people is still the spear in my side" (*Letters*, p. 323). This, at the moment of composition of one of the drafts of *This Side of Paradise*. Seven years later, having finished *The Great Gatsby*, he could write (with his usual

and the mother of a friend, the young Fitzgerald thought he was creating a beautiful, sad, disengaged, eccentric and aristocratic woman by telling us that in "her less important moments she returned to America, met Stephen Blaine and married him—this almost entirely because she was a little bit weary, a little bit sad. Her only child was carried through a tiresome season and brought into the world on a spring day in ninety-six" (p. 4). It couldn't have taken *too* much to tire Beatrice: when Amory returned to Beatrice from Minneapolis, "He could not reconcile himself to her beauty, that was mother to his own, the exquisite neck and shoulders, the grace of a fortunate woman of *thirty*" (p. 20). The italics are mine, but the accent on youth is Fitzgerald's: Amory, at that point, is fifteen.

Yet cross himself as he does with his affectations, even this early in his artistic consciousness Fitzgerald's dramatic self-awareness tells him that they are affectations. Always he tries to compensate for what he can't help. A few passages after we are told about Beatrice's "less important moments," we have this: "From his fourth to his tenth year . . . [Amory] *did* the country with his mother in her father's private car, from Coronado, where his mother became so bored that she had a nervous breakdown in a fashionable hotel, down to Mexico City, where she took a mild, almost epidemic consumption. This trouble pleased her, and later she made use of it as an intrinsic part of her atmosphere—especially after several astounding bracers" (p. 4). Yet, although Amory is aware of the phony in his elders, Fitzgerald was not consistently self-aware of fakery when it came to youth. There is no satiric redemption, for

uneasy spelling) to Gertrude Stein, "It honestly makes me shiver to know that such a writer as you attributes such a significance to my factitious, meritricious (metricious?) *This Side of Paradise*. It puts me in a false position, I feel" (June 1925, *Letters*, pp. 484–85). And during the years of horror he could write to Maxwell Perkins that he is informed "that *This Side of Paradise* is now out of print. I am not surprised after eighteen years (looking it over, I think it is now one of the funniest books since *Dorian Gray* in its utter spuriousness—and then, here and there, I find a page that is very real and living) . . ." (April 23, 1938, *Letters*, p. 277).

instance, for the pretentiousness that comes with such representative moments as the one in which Isabelle, who is to be Amory's first grand love, is told by her cousin that Amory

"knows you're—you're considered beautiful and all that"—[her cousin] paused—"and I guess he knows you've been kissed."

At this Isabelle's little fist had clinched suddenly under the fur robe. She was accustomed to be thus followed by her desperate past, and it never failed to rouse in her the same feeling of resentment; yet—in a strange town it was an advantageous reputation. She was a "Speed," was she? Well—let them find out.

Twenty three, skidoo. Isabelle is sixteen years old, and that grimly fist-clinched determination to show 'em what for can only arouse again the hooting hilarity with which Wilson, and later Fitzgerald himself, read the novel.[36] Authorial youth in *This Side of Paradise*, however, is too stationary and clear a target to require much aim.

Our sights are better fixed, in this book, on Fitzgerald's intentions. One of the points he wishes to make was one that he would reiterate throughout his life. Three years before his death he wrote to his daughter:

Where on earth did you get the preconception that I think of you as a scarlet woman? Hell, you're romantic, but that's not in your disfavor. It's all right to like affection, but not when you drive, in the immortal words of Mitzi Green. I simply don't want you in danger and I don't want you to do anything inappropriate to your age. For premature adventure one pays an atrocious price. As I told you once, every boy I know who drank at eighteen or nineteen is now safe in his grave. The girls who were what we called "speeds" (in our stone-age slang) at sixteen were reduced to anything they could get at the marrying time. It's in the logic of life that no young person ever "gets

36 For a while an admirer of Frank and Charles Norris, Fitzgerald later wished that he had stuck closer to the kind of realism that they represented to him. The Isabelle passage cited here certainly must have come to be for him one of the passages of unrealistic silliness. See footnote 21, above.

away with anything." They fool their parents but not their contemporaries.[37]

And a year later he wrote on the same subject, quoting to Scottie
what he had already written to Harold Ober:

Those debutante parties in New York are the rendezvous of a gang
of professional idlers, parasites, pansies, failures, the silliest type of
sophomores, young customers' men from Wall Street and hangers-on
—the very riff-raff of social New York who would exploit a child like
Scottie with flattery and squeeze her out until she is a limp colorless
rag. In one more year she can cope with them. In three more years it
will be behind her. This year she is still puppy enough to be dazzled.
She will be infinitely better off here with me than mixed up with that
sort of people. I'd rather have an angry little girl on my hands for a
few months than a broken neurotic for the rest of my life.[38]

The sense of waste attendant upon precocious sexual easiness
becomes one of Fitzgerald's preachments from the devil scenes
in *This Side of Paradise* to his insistence, almost exactly a year
before his death, that ". . . following the footsteps of Cole Porter
and Rodgers and Hart . . . might be . . . excellent. . . . Sometimes I
wish I had gone along with that gang, but I guess I am too much
a moralist at heart and really want to preach at people in some
acceptable form rather than to entertain them."[39] Fitzgerald's
letter to Scottie and his dismissal of Porter, Rodgers, and Hart as
"that gang," at first seem bleak remnants of the dismal lace-
curtain Irish respectability in his background. But in the depths
of his life they were not. They were signs of his growing awareness
of the personal and social necessity for what he called "goodness,"
and which he defined most fully as altruistic responsibility in
*Tender Is the Night.* Even as early as *This Side of Paradise,* a
worthy target for the critic is the moralizing self-distrust within

[37] July 5, 1937, *Letters,* pp. 15–16.
[38] To Scottie, November 18, 1938, *ibid.,* p. 43.
[39] To Scottie, November 4, 1939, *ibid.,* p. 63.

the silly melodrama and phoniness that Fitzgerald created around
his early hero-self.

For one thing, Fitzgerald wants you to believe that Amory thinks
that his true superiority does not lie in the adolescent visions and
appearances of self (the young man who can master the "speed,"
the football hero, the heroic commander of the armed forces, the
hero of the "quest novel"), but in the internal world of his superior mind. Again, it is important to remember that while he wrote
the novel, Fitzgerald self-consciously saw his readers seeing him as
Amory. It would be important to him that Amory be a desirably
ideal self, just as, in conflict with that self, it was important to Fitzgerald's growing artistic conscience that he try to be honest about
what he "preached at people in some acceptable form." In short,
the confusions in the book reveal matters of greater significance
for an evaluation of Fitzgerald as an American artist than the
simple and obvious fact that he was very young and vain and ambitious when he wrote it.

So, Fitzgerald tries to rig Amory up as a potential artist-hero.
When Amory loses Isabelle, the compensatory sense of superiority
is clear to him: "He took a sombre satisfaction in thinking that
perhaps all along she had been nothing except what he had read
into her; that this was her high point, that no one else would make
her think. Yet that was what she had objected to in him; and
Amory was suddenly tired of thinking, thinking!" (p. 94). Up to
this moment Amory has not yet once evidenced any thinking, let
alone any "thinking, thinking!" The passage is embarrassing because Fitzgerald was so caught up in his interior self-image of the
young hero with dramatic, young-debutante troubles, that in his
mind all kinds of evocations cluster around the action, but never
actualize on paper for the reader. But, when Amory is presented
as a "mind," when the all-engrossing image of the golden girl does
not obscure the action, Fitzgerald is able to see more clearly what
his hero looks like on paper, and, more aware, becomes slightly

uncomfortable. The following is typical of an "intellectual" evening in which the current literary situation is being sized up:

> "Fifty thousand dollars a year," [Tom] D'Invilliers would cry. "My God! Look at them, look at them—Edna Ferber, Gouverneur Morris, Fanny Hurst, Mary Roberts Rinehart—not producing among 'em one story or novel that will last ten years. This man Cobb—I don't think he's either clever or amusing—and what's more, I don't think very many people do, except the editors. He's just groggy with advertising. And—oh Harold Bell Wright oh Zane Grey—"
>
> "They try."
>
> "No, they don't even try. Some of them *can* write, but they won't sit down and do one honest novel. Most of them *can't* write, I'll admit. I believe Ruppert Hughes tries to give a real, comprehensive picture of American life, but his style and perspective are barbarous. Ernest Poole and Dorothy Canfield try but they're hindered by their absolute lack of any sense of humor; but at least they crowd their work instead of spreading it thin. Every author ought to write every book as if he were going to be beheaded the day he finished it . . . there's a few of 'em that seem to have some cultural background, some intelligence, and a good deal of literary felicity but they just simply won't write honestly; they'd all claim there was no public for good stuff. Then why the devil is it that Wells, Conrad, Galsworthy, Shaw, Bennett, and the rest depend on America for over half their sales?"
>
> "How does little Tommy like the poets?" (p. 217).

The giveaway is "How does little Tommy like the poets?" What has been boring at that moment becomes embarrassing because it becomes so patently forced and "clever." Fitzgerald has enough young pride in his catalogue of writers to let it stand—indeed, he brazens it out for another page through Tom's verse rejecting contemporary American poets. So the "little Tommy" is not condescension. It does not really come from Amory, who has no opposition to or condescension toward Tom's pronouncements. If anything, Amory takes "intellectual" positions, a critic among critics—he takes the stuff seriously. The satiric tone of "little Tommy" comes from Fitzgerald, who is trying to do two things at once. He's trying to show how smart and slangy is the inside talk we literary guys make in our rooms, and he is at the same time uneasily aware that perhaps the reader will not take the "criticism" as seriously as young Fitzgerald would really like him to. The comment implicit in the tone is a shabby attempt to forestall objections by voicing them before anyone else can. If the reader is gulled, then Amory's talk is inside smart talk. If he's not, Fitzgerald can nod and wink with the reader—a bit uncomfortably.[40] The young Fitzgerald, on the make in every way, wanted so much to impress the world—to win Zelda, to become the hero in the adolescent dream, to flash and scintillate and sparkle, to impress readers with the jazzy brilliance of his novel. Just as onlookers, in the dreamworld of *This Side of Paradise,* turning to look at Amory in the theater, are compelled to say, "What a *remarkable* looking boy," so readers will say in the dreamworld of F. Scott Fitzgerald, "What a *remarkable* book!" which will really be the gratification of the young Fitzgerald's adolescent vanity and the fulfillment of his enormous adolescent expectation: "What a *remarkable* young writer!" But he's uncomfortable. He's afraid of snickers in the audience. Even at the very beginning of his career he is already dimly aware that he will be tricked by, damaged by the tinsel he admires. Characteristically, at the moment he is "insulting the great," he is "grovelling before the kitchen maids."

He was aware of the possibility of ridicule because of that "spoiled priest" in him that he called his puritanism. He knew that the good man must work, for the night cometh. He knew that there was an enormous difference between the world of appearances and the world of work. It was his own self-announced puri-

[40] I am not even certain that Fitzgerald was fully conscious of his intention. I cannot document my conclusion. So much depends on tone. The combination of tone, intention, biography—a general sense of what Fitzgerald was like—makes me certain of what Fitzgerald was doing, if not certain of Fitzgerald's consciousness of it.

tanism (unfortunately, few contemporary readers really took it seriously) that saved him in his vanity from settling for appearances alone. Unlike Mackenzie and Michael Fane, Fitzgerald and Amory did not take their uneasiness from devout Catholicism. If anything, the creation of Monsignor Thayer Darcy suggests that for Fitzgerald, Catholicism belonged to the gorgeous adolescent dreamworld of rich appearances. In Monsignor Darcy the splendor of Catholicism is worldly rather than spiritual. To be sure, Monsignor's advice and his influence on Amory are supposed to be moral, spiritual. And he is always urging Amory to rest on the rock of the Church. Nevertheless, the Monsignor we come away from the book with is an urbane and glittering representative of a resplendent power whose world is more cosmopolitan than theological, whose rich color heightens aphorism rather than pietism, whose machinery is graciousness rather than grace. Monsignor Darcy is a man with whom young Amory can be at home precisely because he does not insist upon any puritanic confusion of virtue and acceptable public behavior. Yet, significantly, the one area in which Monsignor Darcy is effective in Amory's life is neither the world of the Church nor the world of social brilliance, but that personal world of the man at home in both. The secret of that personal world is a very "puritan" secret. It is work.[41]

In the distinction that Monsignor Darcy makes between personality and personage lies a major key to the book as well as to

[41] Five years after he had finished *This Side of Paradise*, Fitzgerald was so far from feeling himself a Catholic that he could write breezily to Ernest Boyd about his stay in Rome: "We're tired of black skirts and dirty teeth and the parades of Pope [Siphilis] the Sixth . . ." (February 1, 1925, *Letters*, p. 478). In *This Side of Paradise* Fitzgerald has this to say about Amory: "He was not even a Catholic, yet that was the only ghost of a code that he had, the gaudy, ritualistic, paradoxical Catholicism whose prophet was Chesterton, whose clacqueurs were such reformed rakes of literature as Huysmans and Bourget, whose American sponsor was Ralph Adams Cram, with his adulation of thirteenth-century cathedrals—a Catholicism which Amory found convenient and ready-made, without priest or sacraments or sacrifice" (p. 125). On page 172 of his Ledger, Fitzgerald noted that 1917 was his "Last year as a Catholic." Quoted in Eble, *F. Scott Fitzgerald*, p. 160, n.15.

the character of Fitzgerald. It is, partly, the distinction between
Fitzgerald's social puritanism—a puritan prissiness of manners
that he both shocked and represented and that he thought of as
what is "nice"—and his moral puritanism, that deep sense of
ethics, responsibility, and work that is supposed to be the real,
underlying meaning of social manners, and that he thought of as
what is "good." In his fashionable rejection of what is "nice," he
joined the contemporaries whose purpose was to épater le bourgeois. In his dedication to what is "good," he retained allegiance
to the old American Protestant ethic, which by his day had become
a matter of scorn in its connection with the middle class that had
hypocritically commercialized it.

"A personality is what you thought you were," explained Monsignor
to Amory. "Personality is a physical matter almost entirely; it lowers
the people it acts on—I've seen it vanish in a long sickness. But while
a personality is active it overrides 'the next thing.' Now a personage,
on the other hand, gathers. He is never thought of apart from what
he's done. He's a bar on which a thousand things have been hung—
glittering things sometimes, as ours are, but he uses those things with
a cold mentality back of them."

He works. The glittering ornaments of his being are his achievements, and both identity and function are inseparable from the
achievements:

"And several of my most glittering possessions had fallen off when
I needed them." Amory continued the simile eagerly.
"Yes, that's it. . . . The thing to do now is to collect some new ones,
and the farther you look ahead in the collecting the better. But remember, do the next thing."
". . . I was beginning to think I was growing eccentric till I came up
here. It was a pose, I guess."
"Don't worry about that; for you not posing may be the biggest pose
of all. Pose —"

"Yes?"

"But do the next thing" (p. 104).[42]

The Amory-Fitzgerald who was the romantic egotist only and puritan not at all, could see only the brilliant visions of personality, could only pose. But as Fitzgerald had to work hard—to actually write the book about his adolescent self-image, in which one magically becomes someone without the tedious interim of accomplishment—so Amory too has to learn to become a personage and do the next thing.

Entranced by the idea of Princeton as Michael Fane was entranced by the idea of Oxford, the romantic egotist lies in the wet Princeton grass, contentedly dreaming of his place in the bright Princeton sun. " 'Damn it all,' he whispered aloud, wetting his hands in the damp and running them through his hair. 'Next year I work!' Yet he knew that where now the spirit of spires and towers made him dreamily acquiescent, it would then overawe him. Where now he realized only his own inconsequence, effort would make him aware of his own impotency and insufficiency" (p. 54). The fear of snickers, the fear of showing the marks, the fear of falling in public, keep him from doing the next thing. It is the fear known to the personality rather than to the personage, and that fear, together with the counteracting moral puritanism and the imaginative ambition, is "the fundamental Amory."

[42] Cribbing from his yet unpublished novel, Fitzgerald used some material which sheds dim light upon the distinction. Writing to Sally Pope Taylor, daughter of the model for the "Cousin Clara" of the novel (Mrs. Richard Pope Taylor), he said:

> I did enjoy your letter, Sally, and I believe you're going to be quite a personage. A personage and a personality are quite different—I wonder if you can figure the difference. Your mother, Peter the Hermit, Joan of Arc, Cousin Tom, Mark Antony and Bonnie Prince Charlie were personalities. You and Cardinal Newman and Julius Caesar and Elizabeth Barrett Browning and myself and Mme. de Staël were personages. Does the distinction begin to glimmer on you? Personality may vanish at a sickness; a personage is hurt more by a worldly setback (June 19, 1918, *Letters*, p. 453).

Perhaps in his patronizing eagerness to show off the kind of "wisdom" he so proudly thought he was putting into *This Side of Paradise*, Fitzgerald was unaware of how murky his "distinction" was in this letter.

If his reactions to his environment could be tabulated, the chart would
have appeared like this, beginning with his earliest years:

 1. The fundamental Amory

 2. Amory plus Beatrice.

 3. Amory plus Beatrice plus Minneapolis.

Then St. Regis' had pulled him to pieces and started him over again:

 4. Amory plus St. Regis'.

 5. Amory plus St. Regis' plus Princeton.

That had been his nearest approach to success through conformity.
The fundamental Amory, idle, imaginative, rebellious, had been
nearly snowed under. He had conformed, he had succeeded, but as
his imagination was neither satisfied nor grasped by his own success,
he had listlessly, half-accidentally chucked the whole thing and become again:

 6. The fundamental Amory (pp. 98–99).

The search for a really personal identity, which is the emergence
from personality to personage—the fleshing out of "the fundamental Amory" in the contacts between his imagination and his
experience—is the central wire of the book on which all the characteristic Fitzgerald materials are hung. The discovery of self
lies in two major sets of materials: Dick Humbird and the devil,
who provide the epitome of personality, and the romances with
Isabelle, Rosalind, and Eleanor, who provide all that is needed
to complete the adolescent dreamworld of the Successful American Personality. Both sets of materials are a discussion of evil—
the moral center of the book—which the fundamental Amory
must understand before he can repudiate them and achieve an
identity as a personage.

It is the commitment to the discovery of moral meanings beneath manners that makes *This Side of Paradise* a serious, if ju-
venile, book. In comparison to the surfaces of *Sinister Street*, the
surface world of manners and mannerisms in *This Side of Paradise*
is clumsily handled and puerile. Yet in comparison to the world

of "evil" in *The Plastic Age*, a popular "college book" that was hailed as a successful example of the genre, *This Side of Paradise* offers a glimpse into the nature of the difference between the serious and the merely popular novel. Percy Marks's novel, influenced by *This Side of Paradise*, uses all the materials advanced by Fitzgerald. The novel is a long bull session about college, flaming youth, and post-Victorian mores. But in his sparser imagination, Marks could only see the materials, not their meanings. If *This Side of Paradise* is foolish, largely dated, and promissory, *The Plastic Age* is merely foolish and completely dated. "Evil" in Marks's book is nothing more than the shallowest of unexamined clichés: says one of the college boys, Carl, to his roommate, Hugh, who is the hero of the book, his voice sharp with scorn:

"You see, I'm a bad egg [compare with Michael Fane!]. I drink and gamble and pet. I haven't gone the limit yet—on account of my old lady—but I will."

Hugh was relieved. He had wondered more than once during the past week "just how far Carl had gone." . . .

"I've never gone the limit either," he confessed shyly.

Carl threw his head back and laughed . . . "You're just kinda pure; that's all. I'm not pure at all; I'm just a little afraid—and I keep thinkin' of my old lady. I've started to several times, but I've always thought of her and quit."[43]

When Carl finally does succumb completely to sex, he regards himself as Hugh regards him: a ruined man who can never again take his place in decent society. In a wonderful and unintended (by Marks) oedipal guilt, Carl flinches before the picture of his mother. "He began to undress rapidly. The eyes of the 'old lady' in the picture seemed to follow him around the room. The thought of her haunted him. Desperately, he switched out the light.

43 Percy Marks, *The Plastic Age* (New York, 1924), p. 53.

Once in bed, he rolled over on his stomach and buried his face in the pillow. 'God!' he whispered. 'God!' "[44]

Marks enters equally shallow channels of exploration in his discussion of drink:

As the evening wore on . . . [Hugh] danced with a good many girls who had whiskey breaths. One girl clung to him as they danced and whispered, "Hold me up, kid; I'm ginned." He had to rush a third, a dainty blond child, to the porch railing. She wasn't a pretty sight as she vomited into the garden; nor did Hugh find her gasped comment, "The seas are rough to-night," amusing. Another girl went sound asleep in a chair and had to be carried up-stairs and put to bed.

A number of the [fraternity] brothers were hilarious; a few had drunk too much and were sick; one had a "crying jag." There were men there, however, who were not drinking at all, and they were making gallant efforts to keep the sober girls away from the less sober girls and the inebriated brothers.

Hugh was not drinking. The idea of drinking at a dance was offensive to him; he thought it insulting to the girls. The fact that some of the girls were drinking horrified him. He didn't mind their smoking—well, not very much; but drinking? That was going altogether too far."[45]

Humanity, sympathy, virtue exist on the same thin surface. They are defined in this moment following defeat in the Big Game:

When the hymn was over, the Sanford men quietly left the grand stand, quietly formed a long line in groups of fours, quietly marched to the college flagpole in the center of the campus. A Sanford banner was flying from the pole, a blue banner with an orange S. Wayne Gifford loosened the ropes. Down fluttered the banner, and the boys reverently took off their hats. Gifford caught the banner before it touched the ground and gathered it into his arms. The song-leader stepped beside him. He lifted his hand, sang a note, and then the boys

44 *Ibid.*, p. 152.
45 *Ibid.*, p. 213.

sang with him, huskily, sadly, some of them with tears streaming
down their cheeks:

> Sanford, Sanford, mother of men,
> Love us, guard us, hold us true.
> Let thy arms enfold us;
> Let thy truth uphold us.
> Queen of colleges, mother of men—
> Alma mater, Sanford—hail!
> Alma mater—Hail!—Hail!

Slowly the circle broke into small groups that straggled wearily
across the campus. Hugh, with two or three others, was walking behind two young professors—one of them, Alling, the other, Jones of
the economics department. Hugh was almost literally broken-hearted;
the defeat lay on him like an awful sorrow that never could be lifted.
Every inch of him ached, but his despair was greater than his physical
pain. The sharp, clear voice of Jones broke into his half-deadened
consciousness.

"I can't understand all this emotional excitement," said Jones
crisply. "A football game is a football game, not a national calamity.
I enjoy the game myself, but why weep over it? I don't think I ever
saw anything more absurd than those boys singing with tears running
into their mouths."

Shocked, the boys looked at each other. They started to make angry
remarks but paused as Alling spoke.

"Of course, what you say, Jones, is quite right," he remarked calmly, "quite right. But, do you know, I pity you."

"Alling's a good guy," Hugh told Carl later; "he's human."[46]

What makes *The Plastic Age* funny is not so much the fact that
it is dated as the way in which it is dated. What should be universal is merely a matter of official high-school mores, publicly
acceptable attitudes, clichés of the time and place. As the uni-
versals take on different clothing and all that's left is the clothing,
the discarded surfaces lie in the past, a pile of junk. We look at
that pile of old clothes and laugh at how silly we would appear

46 *Ibid.*, p. 92.

wearing that trash—how silly, therefore, anyone must have appeared in it. There is nothing in the derisive laughter that responds to evocations of times past, for there is nothing evoked that gives us the sense of anything lost. Junk, unlike souvenirs of history after all, is not treasured but thrown away. In Fitzgerald's books, we are nostalgically aware of the evanescence of the youthful sense of high promise. In Marks's book, we are hilariously aware of the evanescence of mores.

In its frailty, Marks's book demonstrates once more that Fitzgerald's strength lay not in the materials themselves, with which he has been too completely identified—Fitzgerald is not recognized as a serious writer merely because of our interest in the 1920's—but that it lay precisely in what *The Plastic Age* didn't do and what *Sinister Street* couldn't do for peculiarly American materials: provide a mediation between momentary manners and national experience, between social identities and moral identities, between school experiences and lasting meanings, between souvenirs and junk. It is in the universalizing attempt to dramatize the moral significance of personality and personage that the adolescence of *This Side of Paradise*, unlike the adolescence of *The Plastic Age*, does evoke a nostalgic sense of a particular time and place as well as a sense of evil understandable today, giving it a value beyond that of the forgotten fifth-rate literary curios among which *The Plastic Age* mercifully remains.

## I V

If "evil" is merely a matter of silly surfaces in *The Plastic Age*, it is quite something else in *This Side of Paradise*. For Fitzgerald, its essence lies in the spurious beauty of American wealth.

Amory's identification with the "very rich," so "different from you and me," is not an identification with money. Not for itself, anyway.[47] The Utopian fulfillment of the adolescent American dream is, finally, a liberation from conditions and circumstances. The state of always becoming, at the moment of triumph, is really release from the condition of time itself, for whether it is the Emersonian transcendent moment or the capture of the green light at the end of Daisy's dock, it is the American belief in the possibility of indefinitely extending the golden moment, of Eden unforfeited. The representatives of the gilded world of the hot cats on top are gilded youths. To be forever young, forever golden, is the fundamental quality of the Utopian personality in the ever-New World, which by its very nature makes anticipation and nostalgia the dominant national emotions. Where does our youth exist if not in optimistic anticipation of tomorrow, of the new year, the new model, the word NEW on the label? Where does our youth exist if not nostalgically in our past? For the vain and adolescent itching dreamer, not to belong to the gilded world is

47 "The rich were dull and they drank too much, or they played too much back-gammon," wrote Hemingway in the original version of "The Snows of Kilimanjaro." "They were dull and they were repetitious. He remembered poor Scott Fitzgerald and his romantic awe of them and how he had started a story once that began, 'The very rich are different from you and me,' and how someone had said to Scott, Yes, they have more money. He thought they were a special glamorous race and when he found they weren't it wrecked him just as much as any other thing that wrecked him." In the famous exchange between Fitzgerald and Hemingway, triggered by "The Snows" before Hemingway changed the name from "Scott" to "Julian," and by Hemingway's brutal reaction to the article titled "The Crack-Up," Fitzgerald intended the pathetic and apparently indefensible postscript in the deepest possible way:

Dear Ernest:
    Please lay off me in print. If I choose to write *de profundis* sometimes it doesn't mean I want friends praying aloud over my corpse. No doubt you meant it kindly but it cost me a night's sleep. And when you incorporate it (the story) in a book would you mind cutting my name?
    It's a fine story—one of your best—even though the "Poor Scott Fitzgerald, etc." rather spoiled it for me.
                                        Ever your friend,
                                        Scott

Riches have *never* fascinated me, unless combined with the greatest charm or distinction (August 1936, *Letters*, p. 311).

to be locked out of the golden world; is to be denied immortality; is, therefore, to be locked out of a state of being that transcends mortal actuality and experience. And to be locked out of paradise is to be constantly reminded of how far less than Utopian one's actual, sweaty, middle-class condition is.

So Amory singles out Dick Humbird as an epitome of his own desires and fancies. So Fitzgerald makes the character of the personality-idol a matter of moral instruction as well as social report. When Amory and his Princeton friends descend, lordly and all but penniless, on Deal Beach and carry their day among the peasants—cheating waiters and ridiculing half-wit girls—Amory's central reaction to their behavior is to try to classify the manner, the sense of differentness from you and me, that makes it possible. His concern at this point is personality, not morality. Amory

wondered how much each one contributed to the party, for there was somewhat of a spiritual tax levied. Alec and Kerry were the life of it, but not quite the center. Somehow the quiet Humbird, and Sloane, with his impatient superciliousness, were the center (p. 77).

Whatever judgment of Humbird Amory can make is negated by his admiration for him.

Dick Humbird had, ever since freshman year, seemed to Amory a perfect type of aristocrat. He was slender but well-built—black curly hair, straight features, and rather a dark skin. Everything he said sounded intangibly appropriate. He possessed infinite courage, an averagely good mind, and a sense of humor with a clear charm and *noblesse oblige* that varied it from righteousness. He could dissipate without going to pieces, and even his most bohemian adventures never seemed "running it out." People dressed like him, tried to talk as he did. Amory decided that he probably held the world back, but he wouldn't have changed him (p. 77).

Like the people on the pavement in Robinson's "Richard Cory," Amory thought that Humbird was everything to make him wish that he were in his place. It is inevitable that Fitzgerald's des-

perate middle-class snobbishness should emerge again in association with this paragon, this calm King of Personality: "He differed
from the healthy type that was essentially middle class—he never
seemed to perspire. Some people couldn't be familiar with a chauffeur without having it returned; Humbird could have lunched at
Sherry's with a colored man, yet people would have somehow
known that it was all right" (p. 77). *There's* the man to be. There's
the one who occupies the world Fitzgerald peered at so greedily
when he read about Michael Fane. He's all complete, caste in-
violably wrapped around him so that everyone knows his place.
Imperturbably he's the center in the envied actuality of the American dream that is *not* the democratic earthiness of ideology associated with Whitman or Lincoln. How enviable! One can
actually even come into direct contact with those locked out—
yes even with "colored men" and shopgirls—and never have one's
identity threatened. The only thing that Amory would not be
able to accept about Humbird would be a taint of sweat, any real
connection with the earth. For to connect Humbird with "next
things" or with any marks that show would threaten the image that
insures the existence of the gilded identity Amory hungers for.

[Humbird] was not a snob, though he knew only half his class. His
friends ranged from the highest to the lowest, but it was impossible to
"cultivate" him. Servants worshiped him and treated him like a god.
He seemed the eternal example of what the upper class tries to be.
   "He's like those pictures in the *Illustrated London News* of the
English officers who have been killed," Amory had said to Alec.
   "Well," Alec had answered, "if you want to know the shocking
truth, his father was a grocery clerk [shades of Edward Fitzgerald
and Grandfather McQuillan!] who made a fortune in Tacoma real
estate and came to New York ten years ago."
   *Amory had felt a curious sinking sensation* (p. 78; the righteous
italics are mine).

The appearances in America are tricky, where generations are
speeded up in a world which, nostalgically anticipating its

imagined golden past in the future, is divorced from the past and pretends that time is conquered. In *The Great Gatsby*, Fitzgerald will mature and complete his statement about the American relationship of time to identity, but in this first book, "fast movie" time is only glimpsed in the introduction of Amory's idols. The idols can be forgiven anything but the same pretense that characterizes their worshippers—or what is left that's safe to worship? What is left that offers the identity hungered for so terribly? There is no real involution of identity in Fitzgerald's giving Humbird a background reminiscent (though inverted) of his own. The book, after all, is a confession, Fitzgerald's disguised act of public penance, the artist's coming to terms with his American materials of adolescence. But for puritan-artist-Fitzgerald-the-personage, Humbird is what Amory-Fitzgerald-the-personality *would have chosen to be*. Fitzgerald is looking back at himself (young yet, and looking back in the harsh nearness of an immediate past), even this early in his life. Aware of what looking back means, he knows more than Amory does, for he knows what's coming. Among other things he knows even this early that the brummagem god is not the imagined self of the romantic egotist's adolescent dream, but the Humbird upon whom it is patterned. He knows that the gilded world is not the golden world. Nor does he wait until Tom and Daisy Buchanan to unmask his illusions publicly. In name Humbird is both humbug and hummingbird, which flits and flits in gay color, but does not amass the solidity of "next things."

For, having identified Humbird with the personality beyond earth and time, he proceeds to show that earth and time are what every man sweatily belongs to. The beguiling appearances of Dick Humbird are, therefore, a fatal misrepresentation; they are the evil nightmare underside of the dream, for they provide a *false* mold in which the creative energies of the heightened sensitivities to the promises of life are contained. Personality, in short, becomes evil. Fitzgerald begins Amory's education into evil by reducing Humbird to the actualities of the time, earth, and mortality that his appearances had seemed to deny. Killed in an automobile accident, Humbird is something other than what he seemed:

The doctor had arrived, and Amory went over to the couch, where some one handed him a sheet to put over the body. With a sudden hardness, he raised one of the hands and let it fall back inertly. The brow was cold but the face not expressionless. He looked at the shoe-laces—Dick had tied them that morning. *He* had tied them—and now he was this heavy white mass. *All that remained of the charm and personality of the Dick Humbird he had known—oh, it was all so horrible and unaristocratic and close to earth.* All tragedy has that strain of the grotesque and squalid—so useless, futile . . . the way animals die . . ." (pp. 86–87, italics mine).

To allow the artist to emerge, Fitzgerald had to subordinate his personality to his personage. He had to kill Humbird. One sign of the tension involved in the struggle is the terror and heartbreak with which Amory witnesses Humbird's death. More frighteningly certain a sign that it's hard to keep Humbird in his grave is the appearance of the devil.[48]

48 Readers have had a hard time with the appearance of the devil in the novel. The general reaction has been either to chalk it off to Fitzgerald's early desire to include in this book everything he had written, whether it fit or not, or else to see it as a remnant of Fitzgerald's Catholic sensibility or of his Irish "mysticism." Actually, when the episode is seen in its proper function as an attempt to dramatize rather than merely sermonize the theme of evil in the novel, it is perfectly explicable. My objection to the episode is that the mode is wrong. The serious quality with which the supernatural is presented asks the reader to accept the supernatural as part of the literal events. Some readers have tried to explain the section as Amory's hallucination, but there is nothing to prepare the reader for the supposition that Amory literally hallucinates, nor does such an explanation—the novel is nowhere psychiatric in intent or direction—go anywhere. Nor does Fitzgerald make it clear enough that Amory is confronted by a hallucination of his own moral, if not psychic, sensibilities. Indeed, the fact that Tom D'Invilliers also senses the presence of the devil does externalize the supernatural into the literal narrative events, where it does not belong, for nothing in event, attitude, or tone of the book prepares the reader any-where to accept the supernatural as part of the objective world the novel occupies. There is no question that the incident is a dramatization of that area where Fitz-

Amory goes out with Sloane (significantly, the other personality who, with Humbird, was at "the center") on yet another party. It is not the petting and drinking themselves that attract the devil. Fitzgerald was too self-consciously representative of the *welt-schmertz* of "flaming youth" and of the break from the Victorianism of the Popular Daughter's bewildered parents to be completely a social puritan. No, the evil is not so much in the manners as in the character that they disclose. What partyboys and partygirls and partymanners came to represent early and lastingly for Fitzgerald was the fascinating, attractive, and life-destroying ascendency of personality, whose essential trait is irresponsibility. What Fitzgerald comes to associate with Humbird is a way of life that denies earth, and, inorganic and freakish, devours the personage, the worker. It is as though Fitzgerald were saying that his American materials were the very evil that threaten to damn the artist, who can, in turn, exorcise those materials only by using them in repudiation, outgrow them in participation—knowing them only by living them. So Humbird is hard to kill.

The devil comes after Amory at the height of his party with Sloane, and Amory flees through the same El Greco landscape that Nick Carraway dreams at the end of *Gatsby*—a landscape on which is enacted a dream that is the very epitome of irresponsibility. In Amory's flight the landscape is the home of the Humbird-people: people as transitory, flitting, flighty, and impersonal as the name implies. It is a city street where repeated anonymity is the sign of a world of partypeople. The houses are the apartments where the young Princetonians have their digs, where the Popular Daughters are called for. They are the "glittering and white" city filled with clever and sophisticated people who never

gerald sees the social and moral concerns of the novel coming together, but he made a critical error in not presenting a dramatization that would at once be symbolic and also in keeping with the realistic mode of the rest of the book. See footnote 51, below.

show the marks. But that sweatless cleverness turns out to be a horror, for just as in Carraway's dream, the city of personality is the home of facelessness, of that ultimate evil of depersonalization where, his transcendent Utopian identity a lie, and devoid of his earthly identity as a human personage, a man is ready for his subterranean hell-identity as the anonymous hero of the adolescent dream now become nightmare: ". . . piling intimately into a taxicab, they drove out over the hundreds and drew up at a tall, white-stone apartment house. . . . Never would [Amory] forget the street. . . . It was a broad street, lined on both sides with just such tall white-stone buildings, dotted with dark windows; they stretched along as far as the eye could see, flooded with a bright moonlight that gave them a calcium pallor. He imagined each one to have an elevator and a colored hall-boy and a key-rack; each one to be eight stories high and full of three and four room suites" (pp. 111–12), such as the party-suite he has just left. Pursued by the devil, Amory fled down this street, and down

the long street came the moon, and Amory turned his back on it and walked. Ten, fifteen steps away sounded the footsteps [of the devil]. They were like a slow dripping, with just the slightest insistence in their fall. Amory's shadow lay, perhaps, ten feet ahead of him, and soft shoes was presumably that far behind. With the instinct of a child Amory edged in under the blue darkness of the white buildings, cleaving the moonlight for haggard seconds, once bursting into a slow run with clumsy stumblings. . . .

If he met anyone good ["*good*," now, not "right" or "nice" or "clever"] —were there any good people left in the world or did they all live in white apartment-houses now? Was everyone followed in the moonlight? But if he met some one good who'd know what he meant and hear this damned scuffle . . . then the scuffling grew suddenly nearer, and a black cloud settled over the moon. . . . Suddenly he realized that the footsteps were not behind, had never been behind, they were ahead and he was not eluding but following . . . following" (pp. 114–15),

as he had been following Sloane and Humbird and every bright
hero who seemed to deck out his dream and promise satisfaction
to his hunger. The following of the demon of personality is fittingly landscaped: what exists within Amory is endlessly and iden-
tically repeated within the faceless buildings that stare down at
him. The poison is exactly the food he wanted; the sophistication,
the false adolescent cleverness, the imitation, the glibness, the
belonging to the "center." He had almost surrendered completely
to the world of Humbird and the falseness of the dream—only
a bit of himself as human, as personage, as real and earthly man
remains: "Only far inside his soul a little fire leaped and cried
that something was pulling him down, trying to get him inside a
door and slam it behind him. After that door was slammed there
would be only footfalls and white buildings in the moonlight,
and perhaps he would be one of the footfalls" (p. 115). Perhaps
he would then be the perfect and emulated gilded zombie, the
haunting Humbird-devil deracinating the innocents who would,
in turn, believe in him. But there remained "somehow this fire . . .
that was as near as he could name it afterward. He remembered
calling aloud:

" 'I want someone stupid. Oh, send someone stupid!' This to
the black fence opposite him, in whose shadows the footsteps
shuffled . . . shuffled. He supposed 'stupid' and 'good' had become
somehow intermingled through previous association" (pp. 115–
16). And then, this much clear to him about his clever, glittering
world, he saw the face in the earthless dream turned to torment,
he saw the face of what he had been following, the face of personality, the face of evil: "Then something clanged like a low
gong struck at a distance, and before his eyes a face flashed over
the two feet, a face pale and distorted with a sort of infinite evil
that twisted it like flame in the wind; *but he knew, for the half
instant that the gong tanged and hummed, that it was the face of*

*Dick Humbird"* (p. 116). The italics, significantly, are Fitzgerald's own.

To leave no doubts about his ultimate allegiance, Fitzgerald creates a personage-idol as a complementary opposite to Humbird. Unfortunately the character of the good angel, Burne Holiday, is buried beneath the clutter and claptrap of young Fitzgerald's attempts to sound like an intellectual (the conversations between Burne and Amory must have been high on the list of things that made Edmund Wilson laugh), but his outlines remain clear even beneath all the debris.

As Burne perched on a table and launched into argument with Tom, [Amory] looked at this revolutionary more carefully than he ever had before. [Burne is a revolutionary in the most fitting way: he leads a movement to abolish the eating clubs, which are the essence of class, caste, aristocracy, wealth, and all the clever, sophisticated appearances represented by and aligned with Humbird.] Broad-browed and strong-chinned, with a fineness in the honest gray eyes that were like Kerry's, Burne was a man who gave an immediate impression of bigness and security—stubborn, that was evident, but his stubbornness wore no stolidity, and when he had talked for five minutes Amory knew that this keen enthusiasm had in it *no quality of dilettantism.*

The intense power Amory felt later in Burne Holiday *differed from the admiration he had had for Humbird.* This time it began as purely a mental interest. With other men whom he had thought as primarily *first-class, he had been attracted by their personalities, and in Burne he missed that immediate magnetism to which he usually swore allegiance.* But that night Amory was struck by Burne's intense earnestness, a quality he was accustomed to associate *only with the dread stupidity,* and by the great enthusiasm that struck dead chords in his heart. Burne stood vaguely for a land Amory hoped he was drifting toward—and it was almost time that land was in sight (pp. 122–23, italics mine).

Typically, Burne does not worry about belonging. He does not care about his clothes. No one tries to emulate him. He follows his own passions and beliefs regardless of whether he appears to be running it out. A nonconformist in social thought, politics, and economics, his goal is not a place in the center of the hot cats on top, but is (very vaguely defined by the young Fitzgerald) "social service."[49] In his nonpersonality is his identity as a human person and a personage: "the logic of Burne's objections to the social system dovetailed so completely with everything they [Amory and Tom] had thought, that they questioned rather than argued, and envied the sanity that enabled this man to stand out so against all traditions" (p. 125). "Goodness" is not necessarily stupidity, Amory discovers, although the sham sophistications of status *are* necessarily evil. "Being Burne," Amory realizes one day, "was suddenly so much realler than being clever" (p. 125). The man ridiculed by the Humbirds is a man of "next things," who does work, regardless of social appearances, for an end he considers a social good. As the weeks passed in Burne's campaign against the eating clubs, and as the clubs, in increasing pique and frustration, levelled ridicule at him, Burne continued to remain firm and unbroken, indifferent to prestige or establishmentarian status.

Yet, Fitzgerald's American materials don't give him the redemptive New-Man for his history of American values any more than they did to Melville (whose Ishmael could not reform the lee shore with the story of Ahab) or Twain (whose Huck had to light out for the territory ahead of the rest of all those who had filled up the known America) or James (who couldn't follow the

---

[49] Talking about Fitzgerald's use of *Sinister Street*, *The Research Magnificent* (H. G. Wells), and *None Other Gods* (Robert Hugh Benson) as quest books—Fitzgerald characterized *This Side of Paradise* as a quest book—James E. Miller appropriately identifies the quest book's search for social ideals with an attempt to saturate the novel with glimpses of "the way it really is." (See Miller, *F. Scott Fitzgerald: His Art and His Technique*, p. 18.) However, it is almost beside the point here to dismiss the quest book models simply as examples of "saturation novels," as influences in technique. The James-Wells controversy is not as illuminating of *This Side of Paradise* as is seeing that the very idea of the quest is an inextricable part of the moral center of the book, the exploration of evil in the choice of values open to the romantic innocent's search for his imagined identity.

redeemed Newman back to San Francisco) or Dreiser (whose Carrie will never realize the happiness she dreams). Burne drifts out of the story and disappears, whereas it is the Humbirds, in their various metamorphoses, who return.

The face of Humbird reappears, in various avatars, in the female faces of the Popular Daughter, the American Pet, the Golden Girl, who, like Humbird, is at once the center of adoration, beauty, adulation, youth, emulation—and destruction. Daisy, Rosemary, Nicole, have their birth in Isabelle, Rosalind, and Eleanor. They, in turn, have their birth in Fitzgerald's hungry anticipations of the glittering white cities, anticipations and expectations that he imaginatively read into the actualities of Ginevra King and Zelda Sayre. It is tasteless to do more than mention the parallels. Even a cursory reading of Fitzgerald's letters and of Mizener's and Turnbull's biographies in the context of Fitzgerald's novels indicate how deeply and how much, though in complex transmutations, Zelda and Ginevra exist in the golden girls. The point is hardly that Zelda was evil-and-destructive-as-well-as-beautiful-and-a-source-of-inspiration, or that we are to create out of Ginevra King the source of the "belle," the "flirt," or the "baby vamp." The point is that Fitzgerald wanted these girls very, very much, just as he wanted the crazy ecstasy of the dream-success he had when *This Side of Paradise* was published. The point is what they represented intensely in his imagination. It is their transformations and life in his art rather than their actualities and life in his history that should matter to us now that all the phantoms are exorcised and there is only a thin sadness evoked by the ghostly rumble among the drums.

Although there are complex and real differences between, say, a Rosemary, a Nicole, and a Daisy Fay, the constant function of the golden girl in Fitzgerald's novels and stories is basically simple. It is to represent at once the object of our collective American longing, the dream, and the revelation of the vast, vulgar, shallow, adolescent emptiness and meretriciousness of that dream in its attainment. The wooing of the golden girl is the following of a grail, with all the accompanying ritual and liturgy, and it is the absorption of the follower into his ideal. The winning is a destructive triumph, a handful of dust. It all seems so simple to the quester with the innocent eye. All he need do is win America, that West, wherever it is, that had so long ceased to be a western geographical location and had become, by Fitzgerald's time, the glittering and white eastern city. In the city, the ideal land is the personality fulfillment and status of that golden room in the topmost floor of the highest alabaster building. In that room is the golden girl, the king's daughter, the eastern princess of the golden west.

It is not simply winning a sexual victory that the liberated flaming youth sought against all the mores of his parents. Fitzgerald's fiction really has surprisingly little to do with the bedroom. No, winning the golden girl is winning—oh, at last!—face, place, name, and being. That being is the constantly extended golden moment of arriving of the dream-hero in the young Amory's fantasies. To be a god, freed finally and forever from the necessities of the next thing because he has remade time to his own desires, is what drives Amory to the window to catch a glimpse of Dick Humbird as inexorably as it drives Jay Gatsby with the certainty that he can "turn back the clock," on his long journey to the blue lawn in West Egg.

The golden girls—either at first or at last—destroy personal relationships in personality relationships. Their indulgence in their self-needs prevents them from lastingly giving their selves to the lover in the total, absurd, wonderful, and pathetic way in which the lover self-sacrificially devotes himself to the girl. For the personality has no lasting, inner self to give. Even Nicole Diver, *when restored to her self* out of pain and deprivation, is restored to the self-preserving hardness that gives her, once again,

THIS SIDE OF PARADISE

the "white crook's eyes" of the rapacious Chicago Warren family. And the "tweet ickle durls," who have never known pain or deprivation of any sort, are the merest apparitions, at once empty and yet more experienced and selfish than the innocent, seeking lover. In his vanity, filled with innocent belief and a transcendental hope, the seeker furnishes the energy on which the beauty, wealth, and health of the golden girl feed. In a vampire symbiosis, she destroys his vitality with the very qualities that lure him in the first place. The candle destroys the moth, and its flame is fattened in the burning. So, for Fitzgerald, America to the American. The idea of her, the beauty of her unleash his energies; the actuality of her destroys him.

It is illuminating for readers of Fitzgerald to keep in mind at all points Fitzgerald's increasingly historical use of the golden girl. There is nothing adventitious about his female characters: the scenes in which they carry their burden of moral meaning are not merely convenient settings but a constant "scene" which, in a Jamesian sense, is the story itself. The "scene" is always one of social and economic supremacy, and the details that present it—a dance, a fabulous house or room, an exciting party—become a set background against which the golden girl betrays the seeker, so that the immorality of her act refers back to and includes those details, reverberating back and forth between her and the form of her life. She becomes the setting, her *things;* they become her; she becomes completely an external creature. In Fitzgerald's increasingly historical imagination, there is every reason why (beyond the fact of Zelda) the dream should be embodied now in the white bitch goddess and why the problem of personality and personage should be a problem for America in a larger context than that of the 1920's. As he indicates in but one of many examples, the history of Dan Cody in *The Great Gatsby,* Fitzgerald sees that American history since the robber barons has simply become a visible manifestation of what had always been an underlying truth about the dream of the Golden West. The visibility increases when the literal facts embodying America's social history and values—the setting, the scene, the things—have shifted from the pioneer dream and the image of the western land to the materialistic society world of urban, moneyed existence. The Emersonian self-reliant hero is transformed into the self-reliance of the marketplace and the typal figure for national emulation and identification is no longer the earthy, sweaty Crockett or Bunyan, male or female, in Whitmanesque stance, but Miss America, male or female, in the advertisements of *Vogue* or of *Esquire*, for which Fitzgerald wrote so often. The Isabelles and Rosalinds and Eleanors, like Gloria of *The Beautiful and Damned* and Daisy of *The Great Gatsby* and Nicole of *Tender Is the Night*, become in their settings the national jewels, the dreams whose very natures become summations of Fitzgerald's historical sense of the degeneration of national vision, and the consequent failure and shallowness of American moral identity.

In this connection one can understand Fitzgerald's reverence of Edith Wharton and her own fictional materials at the same time that he respected and admired writers like Dreiser and Norris. As Professor Francis Hodgins has suggested:

In terms of technique, Dreiser and Norris were (at their best) naturalistic social novelists, and Fitzgerald's own talent was something quite different. In this respect a closer analogy is Edith Wharton, who moves toward the kind of symbolic social novel that Fitzgerald writes. *The House of Mirth* deals with a long list of Fitzgerald's subjects: the relationship of beauty and wealth, the human flower (Lily) who is both poisoned and poisonous, the displacement of values from internals to externals, the corruption of American expectation when it shifts from social meaning to "society." Gatsby is upside down in Seldon, who refuses the dream and opts for a safe and private sterility. Lily is the late Gloria and something of Daisy. And so on.

There is every difference of meaning between this novel and Fitzgerald's first two, but the difference has a fundamental source: the imaginative meaning of history is profoundly different in the two writers. Wharton's sense of history is far denser in *form*. Those glittering palaces, how they came to be and what goes on there, these things are far more specific—and far more realized—in her novel than in Fitzgerald's first two novels. Intricacy of physical scene fits intricacy of social relationship, from dinner party to boudoir. But the *substance* of history is simplistic. Money has changed hands and thereby changed class relationships and human values. From being the support of a (presumed) graciousness, it has become the support of ostentation. But the historical fact is simply that. To "think old" is to be stupid and priggish, to mourn nothing more than the social customs of one's own past. Those who "think new" have nowhere to go except into more of what they have (none of Fitzgerald's "next things"), or into Seldon's total unconnectedness and irresponsibility. It is interesting that Wharton at once encourages nostalgia and a sense of the future, a longing for the past and a hope of deliverance, and that both are vague and essentially meaningless. They are meaningless because there is no substance in her "historical" perspective, no firm and coherent core in it. History is, in effect, only the recoil of social class and custom; it can be all shown (brilliantly) in a single street of houses. In a far more limited and literal way than Fitzgerald, she might have said this was "all" her material.

Fitzgerald is just the opposite kind of symbolic social historian. There is little denseness of form in his history; his eye is for the evocative detail, his sense is for the aura or the atmosphere of things. But the *substance* of his imaginative history is firm and coherent. Autobiography is not simply "all" his material but the appropriate contemporary expression of ancient possibilities and desires. In that sense his symbols are anything but arbitrary.

He is less of a chronicler than Wharton and more of a historian. In *This Side of Paradise* and *The Beautiful and Damned*, Fitzgerald is seen in the process of learning how to bring together the form and the substance of his sense of American history, how to bring together the vision and the details in which it resides for him. His little golden girls become the focus of the necessary coalescence. When he learns them thoroughly through his first two novels and his early short stories, he has perfected the setting for his American drama and he is then free to perfect the questing and believing innocent who would gain them and change the world. The fever and the betrayal of the old, old American dream of transcendent existence becomes dramatized in the relationship between the golden girl and her questing lover. When he perfects that relationship in *The Great Gatsby* and *Tender Is the Night*, Fitzgerald takes his place with America's serious writers, from Cooper on, who, like Hawthorne and Twain and James, find that they can discover and articulate their own identities in the careers of their "just personal" yet national, fictional heroes.

(Is it any wonder that so many of our feeling commentators—F. O. Matthiessen, Richard Chase, D. H. Lawrence, Wright Morris, Sherman Paul, R. W. B. Lewis—found again and again that our serious writing is quest literature, from *Walden* and *Moby-Dick* to Gatsby with his green light and Dick Diver with his never-written revolutionary reclassification of psychiatric knowledge? Any wonder that whether it is the hopeful expectation of Thoreau or the despair of Melville, the goal itself—as it exists *in the imagination* of the believer—is never *actually* reached by book's end? Still an undiscovered bourne by the time Fitzgerald writes his books, in all our books the ideal America, the metaphor, evades its Columbuses, the seekers of total expectation. Everyone's first love and never anyone's first and unspoiled beloved, in our serious literature she is whore to the prototypical American's adolescent hungers, succubus to his energies.)

In *This Side of Paradise*, what we have is preparation for Fitzgerald's later and more fully realized statements about the golden girl. Later, the girls and boys will have some meaningful adversity to cope with; in *This Side of Paradise*, still playing among the kids, we can see what will be father and mother to the later and more complex characters. Our first introduction to the golden

girl is a generic description of our national Big Date: "The Popular Daughter becomes engaged every six months between sixteen
and twenty-two, when she arranges a match with young Hambell,
of Cambell and Hambell, who fatuously considers himself her
first love, and between engagements the P. D. (she is selected by
the cut-in system at dances, which favors the survival of the fit-
test) has other sentimental last kisses in the moonlight, or
the firelight, or the outer darkness" (p. 58). No more than in the
episode of the devil is Fitzgerald's condemnation merely the
product of the Old Lady from Dubuque. He distrusts the personality's lack of human depth and the consequent unlikeliness
of a lasting and meaningful relationship. The man who really
wants to belong *to the* moment doesn't want to belong just *for
a* moment. But the moment is all Amory gets from the P. D.

The "belle" had become the "flirt," the "flirt" had become the "baby
vamp." The "belle" had five or six callers every afternoon. If the P. D.,
by some strange accident, has two, it is made pretty uncomfortable for
the one who hasn't a date with her. The "belle" was surrounded by a
dozen men in the intermissions between dances. Try to find the P. D.
between dances, just *try* to find her.

The same girl . . . deep in an atmosphere of jungle music and the
questioning of moral codes. Amory found it rather fascinating to feel
that any popular girl he met before eight he might quite possibly kiss
before twelve.

"Why on earth are we here?" he asked the girl with the green combs
one night as they sat in some one's limousine, outside the Country
Club in Louisville.

"I don't know. I'm just full of the devil."[50]

[50] The devil indeed! I have no idea whether Vladimir Nabokov read *This Side of
Paradise* before the revision and completion of *Lolita,* but how well he, the visitor,
understood the strangeness of the Fitzgerald-natives. There are interestingly curious
parallels. The incredible—to the point of being hilariously funny—emphasis on
youth so typical of Fitzgerald is part of the adolescence that fascinated both writers.
Humbert-Humbert loved Lolita, as Amory loved the Humbird people, because, when
all was said and done, Lolita was the most beautiful thing he had ever seen. Humbird
is the devil as, inverted, Humbert-Humbert is the funny, criminal, pathetic, believing, loving seeker enslaved by what destroys him: he is the enchanted hunter

. . .

"Let's be frank—we'll never see each other again. I wanted to come
out here with you because I thought you were the best-looking girl in
sight. You really don't care whether you ever see me again, do you?"

"No—but is this your line for every girl? What have I done to deserve it?"

"And you don't feel tired dancing or want a cigarette or any of the
things you said? You just wanted to be—"

"Oh, let's go in," she interrupted, "if you want to *analyze*. Let's not
*talk* about it" (pp. 59–60).

Granted that the girl has every right to consider Amory an
idiot, what Fitzgerald wishes to convey is a sense of his hero as
a man who does wish to analyze precisely because he wants the
honesty of a relationship that will offer more than moments.
Amory's "line" is the spoken desire not so much for the giving of
the lips to lead to the giving of the body as for the desire that in
any case the giving should be a giving of the self. It should mean
something. Amory's line is Fitzgerald's badly delivered but meaningful moral puritanism, the recoil from the age with which he
boasted his identification. He tries to recognize the difference
between honest freedom and promiscuity. If there is no self to
give, if there is only personality, what can be given except moments? The free giving of all moments to all takers, Fitzgerald
concludes, is indeed the core of promiscuity as it is not of love or
honesty.

Immediately after the introduction of the typical P. D., Fitzgerald personifies her by bringing Isabelle on stage. And, of

---

as Lolita, the golden girl whom Nabokov identifies with American values and mores,
is the hunted enchanter. Fitzgerald kills Humbird as Humbert-Humbert kills his inverted alter-ego, Quilty the guilty. And yet, all the time, just as Amory seeks to be
Humbird, he shares Humbird's destructive identity in exactly the way that Humbert-
Humbert and Quilty are the same. There's little profit, finally, in this kind of aside.
It becomes too preciously involved and igenious. But I think it useful to point out
this particular possibility of parallelism because I find it significant that not only
do so many of our serious native writers agree in their various assessments of our
wealthy, youth-centered culture, but that a cosmopolitan—and hardly adolescent!—
newcomer with keen eye and quick wit, freshly observing our journey in midstride,
corroborates the judgment.

course, Isabelle's existence *is* her appearance. She is the teen-age queen of moments and surfaces.

She had never been so curious about her appearance, she had never been so satisfied with it. She had been sixteen years old for six months . . . . Isabelle had been for some time capable of very strong, if very transient emotions. . . . All impressions and, in fact, all ideas were extremely kaleidoscopic to Isabelle. She had that curious mixture of the social and the artistic temperaments found often in two classes, society women and actresses. Her education or, rather, her sophistication, had been absorbed from the boys who had dangled on her favor; her tact was instinctive, and her capacity for love affairs was limited only by the number of the susceptible within telephone distance. Flirt smiled from her large black-brown eyes and shone through her intense physical magnetism (pp. 60–61, 63).

This little "absorber," though capable of limitless love affairs, is not capable of love. Too young, too shallow, too chameleonlike, all of her qualities make her the child of a blithe, pampered, and unaware irresponsible selfishness.

Almost the same terms could describe Amory. He can match Isabelle's vanity, narcissism, and solipsism. He knows, as completely as Isabelle, that he is playing a game. In the world of moments and surfaces, he seems not to be innocent and wears a mask as much as she:

Isabelle and Amory were distinctly not innocent, nor were they particularly brazen. Moreover, amateur standing had very little value in the game they were playing, a game that presumably would be her principal study for years to come. She had begun as he had, with good looks and an excitable temperament, and the rest was the result of accessible popular novels and dressing room conversation culled from a slightly older set. Isabelle had walked with an artificial gait at nine and a half, and when her eyes, wide and starry, proclaimed the ingenue most, Amory was proportionately less deceived. He waited for the mask to drop off, but at the same time he did not question her right to wear it. She, on her part, was not impressed by his studied air of blasé sophistication (p. 66).

Amory's arrival into the coveted world is appropriately measured by the shallow values of his vanity and of surfaces:

He had arrived, abreast of the best in his generation at Princeton. He was in love and his love was returned. Turning on all the lights, he looked at himself in the mirror, trying to find in his own face the qualities that made him see more clearly than the great crowd of people, that made him decide firmly, and able to influence and follow his own will. There was little in his life now that he would have changed. . . . Silently he admired himself. How conveniently well he looked, and how well a dinner coat became him (pp. 88–89).

But there is a crucial difference. Amory waits for Isabelle's mask to drop. Isabelle, however, exists for the masks of the game "that would probably be her principal study for years to come." Amory is aware of himself beneath the mask as Isabelle is only aware of herself as an appearance absorbed from the hints and admiration of others. His ebullience is the product of that moment in youth when the appearances do serve to feed the internal hungers, when the romantic egotism, the narcissistic sense of self, and the surfaces coalesce on the same plane for a magic moment: "As he put in his studs he realized that he was enjoying life as he would probably never enjoy it again." The past is the other side of each present instant—the transiency of youth breeds its own nostalgic sense of loss at the peak of its own joy. "Everything was hallowed by the haze of his own youth. . . . 'Isabelle!' he cried, half involuntarily, and held out his arms. As in the story-books, she ran into them, and on that half-minute, as their lips first touched, rested the high point of vanity, the crest of his young egotism" (pp. 88–89).

Aware always that the enchanted moment is as impermanently evanescent and lovely as a bubble, Fitzgerald breathes on everything he uses the sigh of nevermore. For instance, even at the very beginning of this, his first and youngest book, in presenting the Beatrice for whom he has both contempt and an amused fondness, he produces a sense of "in those days" as of some desirable life irretrievably lost: "All in all Beatrice O'Hara absorbed the sort of education that will be quite impossible ever again; a tutelage measured by the number of things and people one could be contemptuous of and charming about; a culture rich in all arts and traditions, barren of all ideas, in the last of those days when the great gardener clipped the inferior roses to produce one perfect bud" (p. 4). When Fitzgerald identifies the nostalgia born of the transitory magic of youth too strongly with his own adolescent fantasies (when he *is* Amory), he is ridiculous—he creates the sixteen-year-old "speeds" and the "jaded old women" of nineteen. When the artist, the personage, controls the sense of transience—as in the "old time table" passages in *Gatsby*, he is unmatchable in his mastery of nostalgia, the sense of the irrevocable deadness of what was once so very much alive.

In *This Side of Paradise*, Fitzgerald's tropistic movement toward nostalgia is indicated by the repeated existence of "ghosts" of all sorts, when-shall-we-ever-see-their-like-again kinds of ghosts of departed friends and departing contemporaries, so that "ghosts" become a sign of dispersion: the cohesive mutuality of youthful experience is breaking up and the world will ever after wear more somber colors.[51] The sense of ghosts is constantly created by the kind of romantic language for which Fitzgerald had an instinctive affinity, phrases of evocation, such as in Amory's "Summer Storm" poem to Eleanor: "Faint winds, and a song fading and leaves

---

[51] Then the night came that was to be the last [at Princeton]. Tom and Amory, bound in the morning for different training-camps, paced the shadowy walks as usual and seemed still to see around them the faces of the men they knew.

"The grass is full of ghosts tonight."

"The whole campus is alive with them" (p. 153).

However, the use of ghosts throughout the novel does not prepare for the devil episode. Either the "ghosts" are clearly a metaphor, or, as in the "appearance" of Monsignor's ghost at the window of the hotel room, they are not so much objective and external facts apparent to others as they are signs of Amory's developing conscience and consciousness out of the amalgam of his past and present experiences.

falling,/ Faint winds, and far away a fading laughter. . . ." The glory of the story-book instant is not compatible with next things. As if by instinct, Fitzgerald *ends* the moments of story-book song and laughter precisely at *"the crest* of young egotism."

The next chapter begins one fraction of an instant after "that half-minute, as their lips first touched," and the moment of coalescence is finished. Certainly the actual incident is trivial enough: Amory's stud, during the kiss, bruises Isabelle's skin. The next chapter opens not on a note of continued coalescence but with "Ouch, let me go!"

" 'What's the matter?'

" 'Your shirt stud—it hurt me—look!' She was looking down at her neck, where a little blue spot about the size of a pea marred its pallor." Isabelle finds the marred appearance unforgivable. Her pout leads to an argument which in turn leads to the dissolution of the relationship. For Amory the kiss was important for its meaning as the fulfillment of all previous anticipation. For Isabelle, no such thing. Furious that her appearance is marred in even so infinitesimal a way, she pouts, weeps, and finally flounces off in unforgiving indignation in the face of Amory's attempt to jolly her out of her anger.

It won't do, really, to wave away the incident with the recognition of the surface that Fitzgerald is successful in creating— these are kids and Isabelle, especially, is only a spoiled little girl. The nature of the spoiled child here is protypical of the older golden girls to come. It's the marring of the appearances that leads to Isabelle's open resentment of Amory's desire for "something deeper," for the pledges within the kiss (Daisy is to tell Jay Gatsby, "You ask too much"). " 'You're a nervous strain'—this emphatically—" says P. D. Isabelle to Amory. " 'And when you analyze every little emotion and instinct I just don't have 'em' " (p. 93).

The moment is exactly as fragile as Isabelle's staying—or transit

—power. She will flit, humbirding, from moment to moment, like the Daisy she will grow into, the Daisy Buchanan who always watches for the longest day of the year and then misses it. Amory, like Gatsby on the other hand, has devoted not the moment but the year to her, subordinating all else to his puppy-love. Isabelle is bitter because she "shows the marks" of the moment; Amory closes the chapter with, "Damn her! She's spoiled my year." The dream can't bear actualization because the actuality itself has no insides to withstand the pressure of the lover's hug. Thematically and instinctively the nostalgia is inevitable because the loss is. Seventeen years later, Fitzgerald could still remember that "in *This Side of Paradise* (in a crude way) and in *Gatsby* I selected the stuff to fit a given mood or 'hauntedness' or whatever you might call it. . . ."[52] "Whatever you might call it" is inevitable when the anticlimactic voice from within the grail, by the very act of speaking, can only relegate the moment of communion itself to the past:

"Ouch! let me go!"


Older, Rosalind is not so simple a quantity as Isabelle. Also the irresponsible and spoiled little beauty, "she wants what she wants when she wants it," but her "fresh enthusiasm, her will to grow and learn, her endless faith in the inexhaustibility of romance, her courage and fundamental honesty—these things are not spoiled." Yet that courage and that faith in romance, which she shares with the innocent quester, will both be defeated by her pampered centrality as an "absorber" in the golden world. She too is created for moments rather than a lifetime of next things. "She is quite unprincipled; her philosophy is *carpe diem*

[52] July 1937, *Letters*, p. 551.

for herself and *laissez faire* for others" (pp. 170–71). Again the essential difference: as the personage in Amory finally begins to overshadow the personality, the personality in Rosalind over-shadows the personage.

From the very beginning, her honesty and courage are mixed with what Amory and Rosalind detest. "Women she detested. They represented qualities that she felt and despised in herself—incipient meanness, conceit, cowardice, and petty dishonesty" (p. 171). Her courage, like her total being, is courage for the stunning impact of the golden moment, not the kind that lasts through next things. During a swimming party she can bravely and beautifully perform a breathtaking high-dive from the top of a rickety shack because she had heard that Annette Kellerman had done the same. She even reproves her boyfriend, whom she forced to imitate the act—reluctantly and precariously—because he stooped over when he dived. " 'It didn't make it any easier,' she said, 'it just took all the courage out of it' " (p. 189). Amory, of course, is delighted when he hears about it. Yet only five weeks later she does not have the lasting courage equal to the mundane prospects offered by Amory's penniless love.

Indeed, "Monsignor Darcy would have been quite up a tree whether to call her a personality or a personage. She was perhaps the delicious, inexpressible, once-in-a-century blend" (p. 172). But the blend is compounded of instability and will not last beyond the high moments. Her own honesty affords her prescience which, like the climactic second with Isabelle, foresees a future that relegates the moment of attainment to the past at the very instant it comes into being:

AMORY: (*Softly—the battle lost*) I love you.
ROSALIND: I love you—now.
    (*They kiss*)
AMORY: Oh, God, what have I done?
ROSALIND: Nothing. Oh, don't talk. Kiss me again.

AMORY: I don't know why or how, but I love you—from the moment
I saw you.
ROSALIND: Me too—I—I—oh, tonight's tonight.
   (*Her brother strolls in, starts, and then in a loud voice says*: "Oh,
   excuse me," *and goes.*)
ROSALIND: (*Her lips scarcely stirring*)
   Don't let me go—I don't care who knows what I do.
AMORY: Say it!
ROSALIND: I love you—now. (*They part.*)
   Oh—I am very youthful, thank God—and rather beautiful, thank
   God—and happy, thank God—(*She pauses and then, in an odd burst
   of prophecy adds*) Poor Amory! (p. 185).

It's a "battle" because in the personality's fascinating attraction
for the quester, one must capitulate to the other. It's "lost" because once more Amory is betrayed by love into staking his hopes
and identity upon a P. D., the nature of whose self he knows
generically. With what's left of her internal honesty—her personage—she proclaims her desire to belong to the world of moments,
when love is just for tonight, which is . . . just tonight. Despite
all the real agony that renouncing Amory (who, without money,
represents to her a future of next things only) costs them both,
Rosalind *does* renounce him. And it is clear that all her honesty,
her personage, is used honestly to make a whore's, the personality's, choice. She sacrifices a very real love in order to marry the
money (represented by Dawson Ryder) which is the quintessential
element in the maintenance of the youth-and-beauty world of
golden moments. Like E. A. Robinson's Cassandra, the young
Fitzgerald guesses that the seemingly ever-young Americans pay
for all they have with all they are. For Rosalind, finally, the expensive hairdo can't be sacrificed, for the appearances *are* her
being.

AMORY: (*Quickly*) Rosalind, let's get married—next week.
ROSALIND: We can't.
AMORY: Why not?

ROSALIND: Oh, we can't. I'd be your squaw—in some horrible place.

AMORY: We'll have two hundred and seventy-five dollars a month all told.

ROSALIND: Darling, I don't even do my own hair, usually . . .

AMORY: Rosalind, you *can't* be thinking of marrying someone else. Tell me! You leave me in the dark. I can help you fight it out if you'll only tell me . . .

ROSALIND: Oh—it *is* Dawson Ryder. He's so reliable, I almost feel that he'd be a—a background.

AMORY: You don't love him.

ROSALIND: I know, but I respect him, and he's a good man and a strong one . . .

AMORY: All the years never to see you, never to kiss you, just a gate shut and barred—you don't dare be my wife.

ROSALIND: No—no—I'm taking the hardest course, the strongest course. Marrying you would be a failure and I never fail . . .

AMORY: We've got to take our chance for happiness. . . .

ROSALIND: I can't, Amory. I can't be shut away from the trees and flowers, cooped up in a little flat, waiting for you. You'd hate me in a narrow atmosphere. I'd make you hate me.

(*Again she is blinded by sudden uncontrolled tears.*)

AMORY: Rosalind—

ROSALIND: Oh, darling, go—don't make it harder! I can't stand it—

AMORY: (*His face drawn, his voice strained*)

Do you know what you're saying? Do you mean forever?

(*There is a difference somehow in the quality of their suffering.*) . . .

ROSALIND: (*A hard note in her voice*)

You're being a baby now . . .

AMORY: Are you going to marry Dawson Ryder?

ROSALIND: Oh, don't ask me. You know I'm old in some ways—in others—well, I'm just a little girl. I like sunshine and pretty things and cheerfulness—and I dread responsibility. I don't want to think about pots and kitchens and brooms. I want to worry whether my legs will get slick and brown when I swim in the summer.

And after Amory leaves, Rosalind stands "*misty-eyed* . . . . *And deep under the aching sadness that will pass in time, Rosalind feels that she has lost something, she knows not what, she knows not why"* (pp. 193–97).

But once he gets through the maudlin prose which is sentimentally disproportionate to the actual pettiness of the romance, the reader knows what Rosalind has lost. No longer is there the confusion Monsignor Darcy would have had in categorizing her. Whether this is Fitzgerald taking a long, dream-secret, lateral glance at his frenetic courtship of Zelda (with all its uncomfortable parallels), or whether he is unconsciously taking a forward look from Dawson, Rosalind, and Amory to Tom, Daisy, and Gatsby, his imaginative and historical realities are both filled with a peasant's smoldering knowledge (to know and love her is to hate her) of the American bourgeois lady. Is it silly, at this point, to insist on what so few of Fitzgerald's contemporary readers, listening to Fitzgerald's admiration of the golden girls, have noted? He hated them. Oh yes, he loved them, wanted them, admired them, surely, but along with his sympathetic fondness, understanding, and awe there is a driving resentment of everything they are in his vision. He hated the hard, petty, rapacious selfishness that protects their chrome-bright, pampered, and fashionable desirability, their appearances that reduce men to lost battles. The unsympathetic Baby Warren, who with her ascendent self-engrossed whorish virginity "had broken the moral back of a race and made a nursery out of a continent," is the logical successor to the sympathetic Rosalind, who gives up the possibility of internal wealth for the actuality of external riches, and indeed, as we shall see, the disappearance of both manhood and womanhood will form one of the centers of *Tender Is the Night*.

The loser goes off on the prescribed three-week bat. But what of the "winner"? He, stolid nothing, fit mate for The Girl, is "a—a background," against which the surfaces can scintillate enticingly. He is the perennial good provider and idiot male who bumbles his way through the folklore of our atrocious popular "family situation" programs. Dawson Ryder, prefigure of the Tom Buchanan All-American Male, "a good man and a strong one," is absorbed by the golden impossibility he wanted. He wants beefily what the quester wants with all the heightened sensitivities of the imagination. Reduced and unimaginative, he's had not only a castration, but a prefrontal lobotomy as well, and has never learned that gilding is gelding. In his fatuous solidity, he doesn't even know that what makes him and the quester over whom he triumphs ruined brothers beneath the skin is that winner takes nothing because there, beneath the surface, is nothing. The virile "tom" buys a "daisy" whose white dresses are an indication not of chastity but of the virginity of an emptiness that never had any real human juices to lose—"the absence of all desire," Nick Carraway calls it. He finds his manhood—fittingly—only in the nostalgic memory of a football game disappeared forever into a past that had promised the entire future, or in the vulgar senti-mentality and tastelessness of a whore, Myrtle, who is a panting chunk of meat filled with the animal juices he never found in his daisy. The oooh of acquiescence at the petting party is one with "Oh, darling, go—." As Nick Carraway was to realize when he stared, that last night, out at Long Island Sound, the golden dream fades into insubstantiality the moment it is touched, and its pan-dering daisy of a whisper, that smooth and delectable voice of inconstancy and insubstantiality, is only a honeyed and throatier version of that bright little petulance that squeaked, when still a teenager in the first book, "Ouch! let me go!"

When Eleanor is presented, we are given this card of introduc-tion: "Eleanor was, say, the last time that evil crept close to Amory under the mask of beauty . . . ." In the contemporary con-text of "flaming youth," there is really nothing so very evil about her. Rather she is the representative of all the modishly insurrectionist attitudes of her contemporaries, a rather (unintentionally) ludicrous Byron-ette whose romantic egotism feels (oh, so painfully, oh, oh) the *weltschmertz* of liberation in a world pointlessly governed and repressed by anybody's Queen Victoria. With all of the young Fitzgerald's tiresomely dramatic sophomorisms, she is transformed into the complete cliché representative of the lost generation. She Walks in the Rain; is Alone and Beautiful; is Mysterious and Impulsive; doesn't Honor the Flag; doesn't Revere Mother. As Amory walks in the cornfields chanting "Ulalume" to himself, she lies alone on a haystack under the lightning "deliver[ing] Verlaine in an extemporaneous tune." She is supposed to have not only an independent spirit but an original mind and a courageous honesty that is the instrument of her fierce and disenchanted disposition. Given her sympathetic (for her anti-establishmentarian audience) romantic egotism, her "evil" is not only in keeping with her contempt for mere innocence, but, for what it is, is not really so very evil:

She had lived in France with a restless mother whom Amory imagined to have been very like his own, on whose death she had come to America, to live in Maryland. She had gone to Baltimore first to stay with a bachelor uncle, and there she insisted on being a débutante at the age of seventeen. She had a wild winter and arrived in the country in March, having quarreled frantically with all her Baltimore relatives, and shocked them into fiery protest. A rather fast crowd had come out, who drank cocktails in limousines and were promiscuously condescending and patronizing toward older people, and Eleanor with an esprit that hinted strongly of the boulevards, led many innocents still redolent of St. Timothy's and Farmington, into paths of Bohemian naughtiness (p. 232).

But beneath all of his familiar foolishness about the desperate wildness of a seventeen-year-old "fast crowd," Fitzgerald is after something not so easily laughed away. The "devilishness" of Eleanor does not exist in the surfaces any more than evil existed in the surfaces of the drinking party that brought devilishness to an open confrontation of Amory. The confusion of the appearances and their meanings is the young Fitzgerald's confusion. He had not yet completely grasped what he was working toward: a distinction between his heritage of social puritanism (what is "nice") and his attempt to articulate his moral puritanism (what is "good"). Again, the evil exists in what generates the surfaces. Beneath is the emptiness created by an irresponsible and posturing abandonment of all moral values. As Humbird offered only a manner and a surface and so led to death and the devil, so Eleanor is now to Amory what Amory had once been to Monsignor Darcy. Now it is Amory who argues for the existence of a necessity for some morality by which human beings treat human beings humanely. We cannot take very seriously his unwillingness to abandon belief in a supernatural God—an insistence which, in the context of all his previous career, only succeeds in making him appear a bit of a prig—but we must take seriously Fitzgerald's intentions underlying Amory's sudden religiosity. In the past, when Amory was told that "Monsignor Darcy still thinks you're his reincarnation, that your faith will eventually clarify," he replied, "Perhaps . . . I'm rather pagan at present. It's just that religion doesn't seem to have the slightest bearing on life at my age." And Eleanor makes his "paganism" swell and soar. Obviously what Fitzgerald had in mind was to identify a growing belief in God on Amory's part with a belief in the necessity for moral standards, which would be a mark of the personage and which would appear old-fashioned or irrelevant to the selfish shallowness of the personality. It's Fitzgerald's way of saying to the reader, See? Amory's becoming a personage. Unfortunately, there is no more preparation for Amory's sudden pietism than there was for the appearance of the devil, and the device doesn't transform the intention into a successful actuality. Furthermore, as a representative of the zeitgeist, Amory already has been identified *positively* with contemporary disenchantment and rebellious, romantic paganism. His disappointment in the academic deadness of his classes, his sense of his professors as fools and of the older generation as smug and immobile hypocrites who will not admit to the actual wartime disintegration of the world they had made for the young, are matters that his creator, Lieutenant Fitzgerald of the Lost Generation Battalion, was self-dramatizingly and self-consciously serious about when he created Amory as the public self-image that he could picture his contemporaries examining. No, the business about the existence of God is neither a theological nor philosophical argument between Eleanor and Amory. "Oh," argues Eleanor, "you're just an old hypocrite, too. Thousands of scowling priests keeping the degenerate Italians and illiterate Irish repentant with gabble-gabble about the sixth and ninth commandments. It's just all cloaks, sentiment and spiritual rouge and panaceas. I'll tell you there *is* no God, not even a definite abstract goodness; so it's all got to be worked out for the individual by the individual here in high white foreheads like mine, and you're too much the prig to admit it" (p. 239). Fitzgerald, the romantic rebel, does indeed tellingly give the best lines to Eleanor, against his intentions. In the argument she's right about Amory. With "his materialism, always a thin cloak . . . torn to shreds by Eleanor's blasphemy," he can only offer coldly righteous platitudes in return: "Like most intellectuals who don't find faith convenient . . . you'll yell loudly for a priest on your deathbed." They are platitudes that Amory, sharing the paganism of his contemporaries, hasn't earned. The whole argument is a study in Fitzgerald's confusion. He has an obvious temperamental affinity, as a spokesman of "flaming youth," with Eleanor, and yet he is forced by his equally strong need to discover moral standards, his need to show that Amory is becoming a personage, to give the victory to Amory. On the level of piety, it is a fruitless game to

try to assign labels of right and wrong, so much is Fitzgerald both
Eleanor and Amory. In fact, that, finally, is what leads to a recognition of Eleanor's identity.

First of all, Fitzgerald makes Eleanor into another personality.
Like Rosalind, her nerve does not last. After the Ingersoll pose
("If there's a God let him strike me—strike me!"), she attempts to
dive on horseback over a cliff to prove her contempt for life, God,
traditional belief. But at the last minute fear forces her from the
horse, which plunges alone to its death. What leads to death, as
with Humbird, what leads to loss, as with Rosalind, is the irresponsible tyranny of the moment. As Rosalind had courage for
the grandstand play, but lost her nerve at the final instant before
commitment to love and next things, so Eleanor is not equal to
a more than momentary commitment to her despair. The point
is not that Eleanor should have jumped over the cliff. The point
is that there is something just as stagey about her despair and
dark urges as there was about Amory the personality.

Her essential identity, as personality, is to serve as mirror for
Amory. She is the dramatized externalization of Amory as personality, allowing for a dramatized externalization of the struggle
between Amory the personality and Amory the personage. She
is completely the doppelganger. Amory's family fortunes have
disappeared and he is orphaned. He visits with Maryland relatives. Eleanor is orphaned and goes to live with Maryland relatives. Eleanor is beautiful, Amory is handsome. Both are romantic egotists. Like Amory's, the most striking features of her
appearance are "eyes that glittered green as emeralds." Like the
"fundamental Amory" she too is aware of "my black old inside
self, the real one, with the fundamental honesty that keeps me
from being absolutely wicked by making me realize my own sins"
(p. 237). Their minds are the same, like their spirits: "As long as
they knew each other Eleanor and Amory could be 'on a subject'
and stop talking with the definite thought of it in their heads, yet

ten minutes later speak aloud and find that their minds had followed the same channels and led them each to a parallel idea, an idea that others would have found absolutely unconnected with the first." Their tastes are the same. "They seemed nearer, not only mentally, but physically, when they read, than when she was in his arms, and this was often, for they fell half into love almost from the first." Like Amory, Eleanor considers herself an intellectual, and, on the brink of destruction (as Amory was when the devil almost claimed him), she pauses on the brink of the cliff and wishes for stupidity. Finally, meeting Eleanor is not a self-conscious step into an untried, make-believe relationship, but a return to himself: "He had never met a girl like this before . . . . He didn't at all feel like a character in a play, the appropriate feeling in an unconventional situation—instead, he had a sense of coming home." In every respect, Eleanor is Amory, only more so. If the Isabelles accuse Amory of being too much a thinker, and the Rosalinds accuse him of being too romantic, Eleanor says to him, "You're stupider than I am . . . I'm too bright for most men, and yet I have to descend to their level and let them patronize my intellect. . . . I'm not sentimental—I'm as romantic as you are."

The distillation of Amory that is Eleanor becomes explicitly clear. The exponent of momentary impulse ("I've got a crazy streak") and the sophisticated appearances that Amory almost followed to the devil (I like *clever* men and *good-looking* men"), Eleanor herself announces her identity: "No one cares more for personality than I do." And when Amory sees the fundamental Eleanor, his "love waned slowly with the moon. . . . For a minute they stood there, hating each other with a bitter sadness. *But as Amory had loved himself in Eleanor, so now what he hated was only a mirror.* Their poses were strewn about the pale dawn like broken glass" (p. 240, italics mine).

The love affair with Eleanor is indeed an externalized re-

capitulation of Amory's entire internal history. He had in fact
fallen in love with all the adolescent vanities of personality,
narcissistically within himself and yearningly with the Humbirds
outside himself. And as Eleanor mirrors his personality-vanity,
she mirrors his identification with romantic moments, fleeting
beauty, and the apparent triumph over time in the extension of
the moment over any necessity for the next thing. The speculation Amory wrote for Eleanor is an explicit statement of the
vanity of the moment in love with the vanity of the moment:

When Vanity kissed Vanity, a hundred happy Junes ago, he pon-
dered o'er her breathlessly, and, that all men might ever know, he
rhymed her eyes with life and death:
"Through Time I'll save my love!" he said . . . yet Beauty vanished
with his breath, and, with her lovers, she was dead . . .
—Ever his wit and not her eyes, ever his art and not her hair:
"Who'd learn a trick in rhyme, be wise and pause before his sonnet
there" . . . So all my words, however true, might sing you to a thou-
sandth June, and no one ever *know* that you were Beauty for an
afternoon.[53]

The beauty that is created in the artist's vision of it finds its
materials in beauty like Eleanor's. "Pagan" is the word that

[53] Fitzgerald used up a lot of old poems in *This Side of Paradise*, obviously unwilling to let them go without a public christening. "I wish [Thomas Wolfe] could
have seen the disgust in Edmund Wilson's face when I once tried to interpolate part
of a rhymed sonnet in the middle of a novel [*This Side of Paradise*] disguised as
prose," he wrote to Maxwell Perkins (April 17, 1935, *Letters*, p. 262). The "Vanity
kissed Vanity" is but one of many such sections in *This Side of Paradise*. Fitzgerald
sent a copy of the original (a speculation about Shakespeare's Dark Lady) to Edmund
Wilson as early as September 26, 1917, three years before the novel was published
(*Letters*, p. 318):

> When Vanity kissed Vanity
>    A hundred happy Junes ago
> He pondered o'er her breathlessly,
>    And that all time might ever know
> He rhymed her over life and death,
>    "For once, for all, for love," he said . . .
> Her beauty's scattered with his breath
>    And with her lovers she was dead.

Fitzgerald associated with that kind of beauty, and Eleanor's real inside self always gives way to the pagan, impulsive self. "Pagan," like "personality," "egotist," and "clever," becomes the term that names the evil of the irresponsible gilded world of appearances, shorn as it is of all moral commitments and therefore free for the exercise of any impulse. The freedom of moments is the freedom that makes and breaks identities and relationships in the same breath. When Amory meets Eleanor in the instantaneous light of the momentary lightning, "his paganism soared." The lighting is perfect for the landscape and the conversation of the pagan love.

"I never fall in love in August or September," [Amory] proffered.

"When then?"

"Christmas or Easter. I'm a liturgist."

"Easter!" [Eleanor] turned up her nose. "Huh! Spring in corsets!"

"Easter *would* bore spring, wouldn't she? Easter has her hair braided, wears a tailored suit."

> Bind on thy sandals, oh, thou most fleet.
> Over the splendor and speed of thy feet—

quoted Eleanor softy, and then added: "I suppose Hallowe'en is a better day for autumn than Thanksgiving."

"Much better—and Christmas Eve does very well for winter, but summer . . ."

"Summer has no day," she said. "We can't possibly have a summer love. So many people have tried that the name's proverbial. Summer . . . has no day."

"Fourth of July," Amory suggested facetiously.

Don't be funny," she said, raking him with her eyes.

> Ever his wit and not her eyes,
>     Ever his art and not her hair.
> "Who'd learn a trick in rhyme be wise
>     And pause before his sonnet there."
> So all my words however true
>     Might sing you to a thousandth June
> And no one ever *know* that you
>     Were beauty for an afternoon.

"Well, what could fulfill the promise of spring?"

She thought a moment.

"Oh, I suppose heaven would, if there was one," she said finally, "a sort of pagan heaven—you ought to be a materialist . . ." (pp. 230–31).

Only a pagan heaven could fulfill the pagan moment by being its eternal extension. The light of social puritanism—of philistine, bourgeois, Fourth of July America—is no light for Eleanor. But the attractive surface paganism of lovely lights is the mask for that underlying paganism in which no moral values, no responsibility, no sense of earthbound necessity for next things are attached to actions, and human beings become mere appendages of personality's instantaneous will. What Isabelle, Rosalind, and Eleanor represent in cumulative intensity as they come nearer and nearer to being the distillation of personality within Amory himself is what Nick Carraway, in the moral puritanism of his "provincial squeamishness," condemns as the murder that is a consequence of the golden, irresponsible Buchanan world of impulse: "They were careless people, Tom and Daisy—they smashed up things and creatures and then retreated back into their money or their vast carelessness, or whatever it was that kept them together, and let other people clean up the mess they had made."

Amory finds Eleanor, lightning-lit, in the dark. In the dark the devil comes. In the dark the pagan rules. Eleanor is a creature of the dark who boasts about having no fear of the dark and who consciously insists upon materialistic consciencelessness (". . . I know I'm a materialist. . . . Conscience—kill it like me! Eleanor Savage, materiologist. . . ."). Savage, pagan, devil, personality, emptiness, beauty, irresponsibility, the golden girl is the ultimate ghost of the Humbird-self inhabiting the dark night of the soul— and the most attractive denizen of the national social landscape.

There is one golden girl who, at first, doesn't seem to fit the
pattern. The others were pagans to Fitzgerald's moral puritanism,
but Clara is an angel, as almost every image describing her insists. "Amory wasn't good enough for Clara, Clara of the ripply
golden hair, but then no man was." The only thing she seems to
have in common with the golden girl is that (yet once more) "she
had had a harried life from sixteen on." Her life has been bent
in a direction opposite to deviltry. The others have been educated on "the boulevards" of wicked cities or in naughty Europe.
Clara was brought up in a convent. Clara "was very devout,
always had been, and God knows what heights she attained and
what strength she drew down to herself when she knelt and bent
her golden hair into the stained-glass light" (p. 144). The others
are all little "devils." "Oh, Clara," says Amory, seeing her as an
angel, "what a devil you could have been if the Lord had just
bent your soul a little the other way." The poem Amory writes
to her is not from Vanity to Vanity, but is a worshipful poem to
"St. Cecelia." And, as the others are creatures of moments, Clara
is a competent inhabitant of the world of next things: "When
Amory found her in Philadelphia he thought her steely blue
eyes held only happiness; a latent strength, a realism, was brought
to its fullest development by the facts that she was compelled to
face. She was alone in the world, with two small children, little
money . . . . She could do the most prosy things . . ." (pp. 138, 139).
In total contrast to Eleanor, she says, "You know me well enough
to know that I'd never marry a clever man," and at one point
Amory, his voice trembling, says to her, "I think . . . that if I lost
faith in you I'd lose faith in God" (pp. 144, 145).

If Clara is supposed to be a moral platform, a stable point from
which the others can be measured, she is a significant failure as a

character. Fitzgerald can do nothing with this kind of composite, for to create her he had not so much to borrow bits and pieces from various models (mostly his cousin "Ceci," Mrs. Richard Taylor) as to create her out of whole cloth and pattern her into the actualities of his experience. It is significant, for instance, that Fitzgerald is unable to make his creature of perfection realized, his lady of light, really inhabit the earth. Her babies are accidents, immaculate conceptions. It is inevitable that her husband is dead, the marriage bed occupied only by herself. Eleanor insists that love is ninety-nine per cent sex, and all the golden girl P. D.'s are always in and out of love. But Clara? "I have never been in love," she says, and Amory "realized slowly how much she had told him . . . never in love . . . . She seemed suddenly a daughter of light alone. His entity dropped out of her plane and he longed only to touch her dress with almost the realization that Joseph must have had of Mary's eternal significance" (p. 145). Further, she insists that she will never marry again.

The golden girl in Fitzgerald's golden American land is either a fleshless ideal or a bitch. The bitches, with the moral shallowness beneath their ideal appearances, are very much a reality for the world of his fiction. The ideal, when not an appearance but "real" clear through, has no concretion and is very unreal in that world. What the seeker attains of the dream can exist only in what "St. Cecelia" points out is his greatest strength, his imagination. In a world where unreality is real and perfection is not, only in the imagination does there exist that transubstantiation of the inescapable American world of unfulfilled promises and lying appearances into (unattainable) angels. The reality to be transmuted into meaning, the meretricious beauty to be transmuted into artistic beauty, is the corrupted filth of Humbird's corrupting gorgeousness. Muses Amory, thinking of America's national sport, "Isabelle, Clara, Rosalind, Eleanor, were all-American. Eleanor would pitch, probably southpaw. Rosalind was outfield, wonderful hitter. Clara first base, maybe. Wonder what Humbird's body looked like now" (p. 259).

V

If the real nature of evil is everything subsumed under the All-American Personality, Amory is aware that "probably more than any concrete vice or failing [he] despised his own personality" (p. 261). The basis on which the possibilities of personage are built is the fundamental honesty of the fundamental self about its own qualities. The personality-delights of corruption are all involved in the process of losing one's innocence. And having fought himself free of the devil once, Amory does not want "to commit moral suicide," which would be committed by "becoming really insincere—calling myself 'not such a bad fellow,' thinking I regretted my lost youth when I only envy the delights of losing it. Youth is like having a big plate of candy. Sentimentalists think they want to be in the pure, simple state they were in before they ate the candy. They don't. They just want the fun of eating it all over again. The matron doesn't want to repeat her girlhood—she wants to repeat her honeymoon. I don't want to repeat my innocence. I want the pleasure of losing it again" (p. 258). Amory, via the young Fitzgerald, is becoming aware that the moral commentator is the being who makes the innocent meaningful. To be merely innocent is to be unaware of one's state, which is to be unaware of the meaning of one's state. Only in the loss of the state of innocence is its meaning discerned, is the seeker then awakened within the self by the recognition of the future that the innocence had promised. But the young Fitzgerald is as yet unable to separate out his themes completely. He knows where he wants to go, and foreshadows all the major themes and materials of his later books, but he has not yet controlled his powers enough to be really in full control of his materials. As the introduction of paganism makes evident, Fitzgerald's allegiances, like his personality and his desires, are divided. On the one hand he recognizes the justice of his age's general experimental rebelliousness, which in large part he champions. On the other hand, repudiating its shallow excesses, he identifies with the moral stability of an older, lost time: his radicalism and his conservatism get in each other's way. Consequently, he confuses his social puritanism (the shock of the innocent) with his moral puritanism (the understanding of the moral commentator) just as he occasionally confuses the real immorality of personality with the "evil" behavior of the flaming youth with which he can not help but identify. In the book's attempted exploration of evil and responsibility, there are some instances in which it is impossible *not* to identify evil as drinking, as partying, as petting, much as we find it in *The Plastic Age*. Enamored as he is of his materials, Fitzgerald cannot leave out any good items, whether or not they apply, and, knowing that his job *is* to subject his materials to moral judgment, sometimes gets all mixed up between mores and morality.

On the one hand, he can be very clear about the difference between, say, whoring and really being evil. For instance, Amory saves Alec Connage's name one night in an Atlantic City hotel by gallantly and untruthfully telling the house detective that he, not Alec, is the one who brought a girl to the room. As he makes the decision, "Amory realized that there were other things in the room besides people . . . over and around the figure crouched on the bed there hung an aura, gossamer as a moonbeam, tainted as stale, weak wine, yet a horror, diffusively brooding already over the three of them . . . and over by the window among the stirring curtains stood something else, featureless and indistinguishable, yet strangely familiar . . ." (p. 247). The stale weak taint is what is left of his perception of Humbird the night the devil came.

"Once he had been miraculously able to scent evil as a horse detects a broken bridge at night, but the man with the queer feet in Phoebe's room [the devil] had diminished to the aura over Jill [the girl in the hotel room]" (p. 262).

The thing in the window watching it all is the ghost of Monsignor Darcy. "On a dazed Sunday night, a telegram told him of Monsignor Darcy's death in Philadelphia five days before. He knew then what it was that he had perceived among the curtains of the room in Atlantic City" (p. 253). As Amory makes a choice between the preservation of his own public appearance and an altruistic act, appearing to be identified with sin (Amory is the one who's booked with Jill) is nothing compared to the reality of his unselfishness. Fittingly, the ghost of Monsignor watches the beginning of the change from personality to personage.

Yet, on the other hand, Amory's diminishing sense of evil is a mixed thing. If his sense of evil is his growing understanding that being identified with naughtiness is not necessarily a sign of evil and that the official keepers of public conscience can be wrong, it is also his growing awareness of the loss of innocence, the emergence into the gilded world of personality, which makes him sometimes unable to dissociate the activities of naughtiness from evil. After all, Clara, the one "good" girl who is not evil, is also the one who is not naughty. Also, Fitzgerald says bluntly, "The problem of evil had solidified for Amory into the problem of sex. He was beginning to identify evil with the strong phallic worship in Brooke and the early Wells" (p. 280). There is in Fitzgerald, after all, a genteel commitment to the establishment at least as strong as his dissenting impulses.

Yet, for all his confusion, the *major* direction of Fitzgerald's mind is clear. He himself bemoans the Lost Generation's confusion in which evils and virtues remain undefined. It is with a sense of loss, after all, that Fitzgerald says of Amory that the strong sense of evil had diminished to the faint aura over Jill, that Amory's "instinct perceived the fetidness of poverty, but no longer ferreted out the deeper evils in pride and sensuality" (p. 262). The weakened perception sees cleanliness in wealth, which staves off poverty. "Poverty may have been beautiful once but it's rotten now. It's the ugliest thing in the world," thinks Amory. "It's essentially cleaner to be corrupt and rich than it is to be innocent and poor" (p. 256), and we are off and running on the same circle all over again. All that remains attractive is the corrupt and corrupting fascination of the golden world, and Fitzgerald's basic theme never changes in all his books. He himself observed that every author only has one basic story to tell and he tells it again and again.

The reason to which Amory assigns his own and his generation's confusion is one of the elements that helped make the book popular among his contemporaries: " 'Victorians, Victorians, who never learned to weep/ Who sowed the bitter harvest that your children go to reap,' scribbled Amory in his note-book" (p. 151). "There were no more wise men; there were no more heroes. Burne Holiday was sunk from sight as though he had never lived [like Clara he cannot be a *real* part of the world that Fitzgerald explores]; Monsignor was dead. Amory had grown up to a thousand books, a thousand lies; he had listened eagerly to people who pretended to know, who knew nothing. The mystical reveries of saints that had once filled him with awe in the still hours of the night now vaguely repelled him" (p. 262). Neither school nor church offers answers anymore. Even Monsignor had moments when his faith was shaken, "Monsignor upon whom a cardinal rested." Even he "had moments of strange and horrible insecurity —inexplicable in a religion that explained even disbelief in terms of its own faith: if you doubted the devil it was the devil that made you doubt him. Amory had seen Monsignor go to the houses of stolid philistines, read popular novels furiously, saturate himself in routine, to escape from that horror" (p. 264). What is left is cynical dislike of platitudes and the old pieties. What is left is disillusion, which the generation melodramatically caught up; and Fitzgerald provided what his own temperament and contemporaries greedily snapped at: "Life was a damned muddle . . . a football game with every one off-side and the referee got rid of—everyone claiming that the referee would have been on his side." (p. 265).[54]

In the disillusioned world in which the old gods are dead, the frame of reference that provided for fair and foul died with the Referee. This knowledge made the age, for Fitzgerald, something more than mere indulgence in the license attendant upon the abrogation of the rules. He knew that in a search for positive values to replace the ones no one could believe or find any longer, that "man in his hunger for faith will feed his mind with the nearest and most convenient food" (p. 263). The most attractive food had to be carefully examined, and he examined what his contemporaries gorged on in place of the old moralities: the adolescent dream epitomized by the liberated P. D. and by the Dawson Ryder wealth that defeated the ugliness of poverty. (I cannot overemphasize the suggestion that Fitzgerald's quarrel was not with the real, cultural, and spiritual experimentation and sense of newness in his post–World War I world, but, like Hemingway's quarrel, it was with the easy licentiousness of the serious experimentation's cheap imitators. Until, *as an artist,* he could sort out the brummagem from the real—until *Gatsby,* that is—his

[54] *This Side of Paradise* "rather damns much of Princeton," Fitzgerald wrote to Edmund Wilson. "But it's nothing to what it thinks of men and human nature in general. I can most nearly describe it by calling it a prose, modernistic *Childe Harold* and really if Scribner's takes it I know I'll wake some morning and find that the debutantes have made me famous over night. I really believe that no one else could have written so searchingly the story of the youth of our generation" (January 10, 1918, *Letters,* p. 323).

moral orientation as the moralist within the writer remains divided and confused.) Amory's summation of the golden girl nourishment is Fitzgerald's summation of his materials:

Women—of whom he had expected so much; whose beauty he had hoped to transmute into modes of art; whose unfathomable instincts, marvelously incoherent and inarticulate, he had thought to perpetuate in terms of experience—had become merely consecrations to their own posterity. Isabelle, Clara, Rosalind, Eleanor, were all removed by their very beauty, around which men had swarmed, from the possibility of contributing anything but a sick heart and a page of puzzled words to write (p. 263).

Fitzgerald found the licentious self-indulgence of his disillusioned generation of P. D.'s and lounge lizards just as dishonest in its flashy moral emptiness as the Victorian repressions that had preceded it. Or, turning the proposition around, the old-fashioned official moralities, obsolete and lost, represented something—though they themselves were not that something—that was needed desperately in the self-indulgent, weak beauty of the shallow personality-world. As Amory emerges within himself as personage, he speaks with the voice of the social puritan the knowledge of the moral puritan: "Inseparably linked with evil was beauty—beauty, still a constant, rising tumult; soft in Eleanor's voice, in an old song at night. . . . Amory knew that every time he had reached toward it longingly it had leered out at him with the grotesque face of evil. Beauty of great art, beauty of all joy, most of all the beauty of women.

"After all, it had too many associations with license and indulgence. Weak things were often beautiful, weak things were never good" (p. 280).

Weak things of that terrible and attractive and deceptive beauty can't and don't make worlds of next moments. Weak things cannot be personages. One needs strength if he is to do work. In personality can be found only the same old selfish emptiness in which courage and imagination defeat themselves and nothing can grow. It is not insignificant that the statement about the evil underlying morally weak beauty should be part of Amory's realization about his own selfishness.

"I am selfish," he thought. . . . "It is by somehow transcending rather than avoiding that selfishness that I can bring poise and balance into my life.

"There is no virture of unselfishness that I cannot use. I can make sacrifices, be charitable, give to a friend, endure for a friend—all because these things may be the best possible expression of myself; yet I have not one drop of the milk of human kindness" (p. 280).

Fitzgerald, having fought himself to self-understanding and hatred of his own vain personality in the act of writing the book, was *now* ready to begin to understand the nature of his morality by understanding the nature of his experience. It's in inexperience that the real fault in this first book lies. It is not in the imaginative drive, or even in the pretentiousness of action, dialogue, and materials. It's in Fitzgerald's own pretentiousness of inexperience. He had to invent too much experience to fill in the gaps of what he either had not yet known or did not yet understand. Later in life he would categorize parts of his first two novels and most of his fiction for the slick magazines as "trashy imaginings," to indicate the difference between his imagination's frivolousness and pretentiousness and its true labor in the transmutation of experience. Consider, for "trashiness," the world in which Amory's mother moves. It is an unrealized world insofar as it is material for the fiction. Fitzgerald had had his Newman and Princeton (almost) and St. Paul, but he had not yet really inhabited the world that great wealth represented to him. Consequently, his feeling about it is exactly what Amory's early sense of success was —a dramatized instinct that has an imaginative validity, or at least an imaginative strength, but not an experiential one. The reader does not feel the density of experience in the pictures the feeling created.

In this first book, Fitzgerald is forced to cheat. Because he cannot yet really give us the *materials* of his imaginative vision, he can only present an abstraction of the vision itself. Consider the non-existence of (Fitzgerald's non-experience with) the angel, Clara. We are told, for instance, that Clara delights everyone, tames everyone, uplifts everyone. We take this to be true because, for example, Amory saw "one of the greatest libertines in [Philadelphia], a man who was habitually drunk and notorious at home and abroad, sitting opposite her for an evening, discussing *girls' boarding-schools* with a sort of innocent excitement. What a twist Clara had to her mind! She could make fascinating and almost brilliant conversation out of the thinnest air that ever floated through a drawing-room" (p. 138).

But in this representative instance, we never really hear the conversations or see the taming and uplift in process. We are *told* that they are in process. We are only told what Amory says she said or what she says she says or what everyone believes she is or says. When we do hear Clara for a few direct sentences, she is never so brilliant and original as she is mildly fatuous. Fitzgerald almost gets away with it because he specifies the generalization: he does supply the concrete instances of the libertine in the parlor. But the almost-trick doesn't quite work. The reader feels a thin quality in the pages that is a result of the fact that the conception of the use and function of a character from a never-never world Fitzgerald imagines is stronger in Fitzgerald the young writer than any experience of such material is in Fitzgerald the young man. If the failure of *The Plastic Age* indicates that Fitzgerald's power lay in his imagination rather than his materials, the failures in *This Side of Paradise* indicate that, inseparable from his vision, his materials had to exist in personal experience before his imagination could work on them successfully. I suppose that I am suggesting that Fitzgerald would have been dismal as a writer of fairy tales, say, of works that are purely products of the imagination. And in fact, his trashiest stories are exactly those (like "The Off-Shore Pirate") that have the least to do with his experience. One of his most successful tales, "The Diamond as Big as the Ritz," is not so much a fairy tale as an allegorical re-creation of his peculiar materials completely experienced. All his work is not by any means his literal autobiography but is the composite restatement that his imagination makes of his autobiography.

The consequences of the disparity between the resources of the imagination and the resources of experience are nowhere seen more clearly than in the Beatrice episodes. Unfortunately, it is in those episodes that Amory is first presented, and the reader never quite escapes the fog of spuriousness that surrounds the one character who has to be believable. The Amory who, as a little boy, is brought up in Minneapolis is not brought up in the Beatrice-world of wealth, leisure, and superfine, theatrical sensitivities. He is simply a vain, eager little middle-class boy whose pretensions are indicated in his acceptance of a party invitation:

My dear Miss St. Claire:
    Your truly charming envitation for the evening of next Thursday evening was truly delightful to receive this morning. I will be charm and inchanted indeed to present my compliments on next Thursday evening.

Faithfully<br>Amory Blaine

But when he comes from his life in Minneapolis to the world of Beatrice, suddenly for a page and a half he wanders around the estate saying things like, "I adapted myself to the bourgeoisie. I became conventional," and prefacing statements to his mother with, "Dear Beatrice." Of course he knows it's a self-conscious pose, but the pose itself is all that Fitzgerald can manage. We can

see no *real,* at-home, posing Amory such as we do in Minneapolis.
Suddenly this youth, we are asked to believe, is cosmopolitan,
charming, and brilliant beyond his years. At dinner with Monsignor and the Honorable Thornton Hancock ("of Boston, ex-
minister to The Hague, author of an erudite history of the Middle
Ages and the last of a distinguished, patriotic, and brilliant family"), "Amory talked with an ingenious brilliance of a thousand
impulses and desires and repulsions and faiths and fears" (p. 26).
Thornton Hancock thinks to himself, "He's a radiant boy."

Then off goes the radiant boy to prep school. And when he
returns to Minneapolis, " 'Oh, I was sort of fresh at first,' he [tells]
Frog Parker patronizingly, 'but I got along fine—lightest man on
the squad. You ought to go away to school, Froggy. It's great
stuff' " (p. 28). Fitzgerald is engaged again in his favorite bluff.
We actually see the Minneapolis Amory, see only a pose in the
Beatrice Amory, and recognize that the dinner-table Amory is like
Clara and her libertine. "Impulses, desires, repulsions, faiths, and
fears" make up a very general set of words at best. Fitzgerald offers
the particulars of none. You wonder indeed what is supposed to
be so "radiant" about this boy that he could leave brilliant men
like Monsignor Webster Sigourney Fay and Henry Adams "charm
and inchanted" at the dinner table, shaking their heads in appre-
ciative wonder. Of all the very young Amories we get, clearly the
middle-class Minneapolis faker of an Amory is the only one that
the yearningly pretentious middle-class St. Paul Fitzgerald knew
experientially. The unwitting disclosure that his early characters
conform not to the actualities demanded by characterization, but
to the energy of Fitzgerald's imaginative vision of the settings of
the moment (*the* cosmopolitan world, *the* aristocratic world), is
not a source of unmixed censure, however. The cheating is also
one more indication that Fitzgerald's adolescent visions are the
source of his energy, and he needed only for his experience to catch
up with them.

"You see," Fitzgerald wrote in 1939, "I . . . announced the birth of my young illusions in *This Side of Paradise*. . . ."[55] The Fitzgerald who developed out of those young illusions did indeed come to the center of the golden world. But he never was merely the man who, out of the exuberant impulse of the moment, jumped into Plaza fountains with his golden girl and who rode down Fifth Avenue on the top of a taxi. He could now observe and evaluate what before he could only imagine and evaluate. With the merger of the adolescence and the experience, the personality and the personage finally merged too, and pencil in hand at the desk, the romantic egotist Fitzgerald entered the world of next things. The emergence is dramatized in the last chapter of *This Side of Paradise*, aptly titled, "The Egotist Becomes a Personage." The world of next things is vaguely envisioned as some sort of social service, or socialism, or social reform, or whatever else might seem to be the worthy work of a socially dedicated personage in the loose world of personalities. Amory looked about him and saw "a new generation [in] . . . a revery of long days and nights; destined finally to go out into that dirty gray turmoil to follow love and pride; a new generation dedicated more than the last to the fear of poverty and the worship of success; grown up to find all Gods dead, all wars fought, all faiths shaken" (p. 282). What the fundamental Amory knew at the end of the book was that washed clean of pretenses he was born anew into a recognition of values other than his generation's. Aware of the meaning of the meretriciousness of his own expectations and aspirations, when his adolescent visions found their concretions in his experience he became aware of the meretriciousness of the dreams his society inspired. Finally, Amory was aware of the moral choices open to him. He might well have been that narcissus-become-priest, F. Scott Fitzgerald, welcoming the excitement of the golden life ahead, yet aware that he could only count on himself in combat

[55] *Letters*, p. 588.

with those excitements. "And [Amory] could not tell why the struggle was worth while, why he had determined to use to the utmost himself and his heritage from the personalities he had passed. . . .

"He stretched out his arms to the crystalline, radiant sky.

" 'I know myself,' he cried, 'but that is all' " (p. 282).

Fitzgerald was to come to know in fact the evils, virtues, hells, and moments he had envisioned. He was to become himself the personality, American, personage, artist whose later books were to be the fulfillment of all the intimations that lay just this side of a paradise to be regained. The knowledge that the expected Utopia was lost in the golden moment in which it was obtained changed a boy brummagem god, through pain and anticipation and nostalgia, into a man and a writer.

# CHAPTER II
# THE BEAUTIFUL AND DAMNED
## *The Ironical-Pessimistic*

IT SOMETIMES HAPPENS that there are some American lives—Twain's and Whitman's are cases in point—that are so deeply rooted in their culture that their very accidents of circumstance seem to be representative of their nation and parallel to it. Fitzgerald, too, soared and fell in his personal and professional career as the nation did. "The Jazz Age," he mused. ". . . I claim credit for naming it . . . it extended from the suppression of the riots on May Day 1919 to the crash of the stock market in 1929—almost exactly one decade."[1] Fitzgerald, along with the Republic, entered modern cosmopolitan consciousness in the era of World War I, and both began the "greatest, gaudiest spree in history" in that annus mirabilis, 1920.

As he knew he would, he awoke one morning to find himself a famous darling. His career began with the age he named, with all the pyrotechnics of a fast-rising rocket, riotously, in a May moment of life—the fact that it was September when Scribner's accepted *This Side of Paradise* was quite beside the point. Scott *knew* it

[1] May 1931, in *The Letters of F. Scott Fitzgerald*, ed. Andrew Turnbull (New York, 1963), p. 225; hereafter referred to as *Letters*.

was May. He was like his own Anthony Patch: "the fire was bright
and the breeze sighing in through the curtains brought a mellow
damp, promising May and the world of summer. His soul thrilled
to remote harmonies; he heard the strum of far guitars and waters
lapping on a warm Mediterranean shore—for he was young now
as he would never be again, and more triumphant than death."[2]
Yet, as always with Fitzgerald, at the moment of splendor some
darker prescient knowledge in his bones guessed that May turned
into the damp and drizzly Novembers of the soul, and that the
flight of the rocket flashed down as precipitously as it did up. Isn't
it odd, after all, that in that sweet morning of his brilliant new
success, having suddenly attained all that made his heart beat
high—fame, authorship, money, centrality, and The Girl—he
should write a book called *The Flight of the Rocket* (later he re-
named it *The Beautiful Lady without Mercy,* and finally, *The
Beautiful and Damned),* concerned not with the bright joys of
attainment but with the musty and claustrophobic smell of failure
and decay? Why couldn't he rest content with the good the gods
provided? What made him scent October 1929 in the 1920 morning of early spring when *This Side of Paradise* was published?

One answer lies, of course, in the "circumstantial events" of
Fitzgerald's personal life, and is suggested by one of his biogra-
phers, Andrew Turnbull:

Fitzgerald, with the instinct that distinguishes the artist from the
self-repeating hack, had tried something new. In a sense, *The Beautiful
and Damned* was a repudiation of the Younger Generation thesis that
had brought him to power; Gloria and Anthony Patch—young, glamorous, emancipated—live selfishly and hedonistically after the mode of
rebellious youth and end up desperate and degraded. The bleakness
of the theme put off many readers and caused somber speculations

---

[2] F. Scott Fitzgerald, *The Beautiful and Damned* (New York, 1950), p. 126. All
further references to the novel will be indicated by parentheses in the body of this
chapter.

about the author's private life. Gloria and Anthony, however, were not literal renderings of Scott and Zelda. "Gloria was a much more trivial and vulgar person than your mother," Fitzgerald wrote his daughter in after years. "I can't really say there was any resemblance except in the beauty and certain terms of expression she used, and also I naturally used many circumstantial events of our early married life. However the emphases were entirely different. We had a much better time than Anthony and Gloria had."

Still, an imagined kinship remained. *The Beautiful and Damned* was a projection of what Fitzgerald had come to consider the decayed part of their lives, and his amazing prescience, as we read the book today, gives a touch of heartache to its brassy prose. The jaunty epigraph—"The victor belongs to the spoils"—might have been the epigraph for Fitzgerald's whole career, while the final glimpse of Gloria with her looks gone and Anthony sunk in alcoholism is all too pathetic. After a fight in which Anthony breaks Gloria's spirit, he muses that "it was yet problematical whether Gloria without her arrogance, her independence, her virginal confidence and courage would be the girl of his glory, the radiant woman who was precious and charming because she was ineffably, triumphantly herself." Gloria recovers from the fight, but what if her spirit were permanently submerged in mental illness? So much of what Scott loved in Zelda depended on verve.[3]

It is indeed unquestionable that much of Zelda went into the novel, as so much of Fitzgerald's life went into everything he wrote. "She frequently pointed out Scott's indebtedness to her; in a review of *The Beautiful and Damned* she had said, 'Mr. Fitzgerald—I believe that is how he spells his name—seems to believe that plagiarism begins at home.' Scott didn't deny it."[4] Zelda criticized the novel, and was effective in persuading Fitzgerald to make changes, such as the deletion of the concluding paragraphs of the

---

3 Andrew Turnbull, *Scott Fitzgerald* (New York, 1962), p. 131.

4 *Ibid.*, p. 177. The review Turnbull refers to is "Friend Husband's Latest," New York *Tribune*, April 2, 1922, p. 11. Zelda went on to say that "on one page I recognized a portion of an old diary of mine [Gloria's diary] which mysteriously disappeared shortly after my marriage, and also scraps of letters which, though considerably edited, sound to me vaguely familiar." For an example of one of Zelda's original letters, rewritten for the novel, see Turnbull, p. 112.

serial publication of the book.[5] A glimpse of the nature of Zelda's influence during the time that Fitzgerald was writing the novel is provided by the diary of Alexander McKaig, a Princeton classmate who saw the Fitzgeralds "every day" during the year before *The Beautiful and Damned* was published:

April 12 [1920]. Called on Scott Fitz and his bride. Latter temperamental small town Southern Belle. . . . I do not think marriage can succeed. Both drinking heavily. Think they will be divorced in three years. . . . June 13 Visit Fitz at Westport. . . . Terrible party. Fitz and Zelda fighting like mad—say themselves marriage can't succeed. Sept. 15 In the evening Zelda—drunk—having decided to leave Fitz & having nearly been killed walking down RR tracks blew in. Fitz came shortly after. [This scene was recast in *The Beautiful and Damned*.] They continued their fight while here. . . . Fitz should let Zelda go and not run after her. . . . Trouble is, Fitz absorbed in Zelda's personality—she is the stronger of the two. She has supplied him with all his copy for women. . . . Oct. 12 Went to Fitzgerald's [in New York now]. Usual problem there. What shall Zelda do? I think she might do a little housework—[apartment] looks like a pig sty. If she's there Fitz can't work—she bothers him—if she's not there he can't work—worried of what she might do. . . . I told her she would have to make up her mind whether she wanted to go in the movies or get in with the young married set. To do that would require a little effort & Zelda will never make an effort. Moreover she and Fitz like only aristocrats who don't give a damn what the work thinks or clever bohemians who don't give a damn what the world thinks. . . . April 17 [1921] Fitz confessed this evening at dinner that Zelda's ideas entirely responsible for "Jelly Bean" & "Ice Palace."[6] Her ideas largely in this new novel.[7]

As were her laziness, her housework, her aimlessness, her beauty, her vague desire to go into the movies.

[5] The original paragraphs appeared in *Metropolitan Magazine*, LV (March 1922), 113.

[6] "The Ice Palace" first appeared in the *Saturday Evening Post*, May 22, 1920, and was included in *Flappers and Philosophers* (New York, 1921); "The Jelly-Bean" first appeared in the *Metropolitan Magazine*, October 1920, and was included in *Tales of the Jazz Age* (New York, 1922).

[7] Turnbull, *Scott Fitzgerald*, pp. 112, 113, 115.

Zelda's "ideas" introduce another consideration, however: the nexus between Fitzgerald's "circumstantial events" and his American milieu. The snobbery, racism, and ultra-"sophisticated" boredom that the Scott-Zelda personae present in the novel are partly a result of their times. Granted, Fitzgerald still had his eye on what he thought of as his "personal" audience. And very probably, conscious of his "artist's desire for flattery and influence,"[8] he was playing to what he thought were the received attitudes of the "right" people. And certainly the tiresome attitudes and attitudinizing in the novel are merely what Fitzgerald thought was profitably *au courant*. Still his sense of *de rigeur* reflects the literary and cultural milieu of the Younger Generation as well as his own vanity, ambition, and marriage. "Have you been reading the great controversy about the Younger Generation?" Edmund Wilson asked Fitzgerald three months after *The Beautiful and Damned* was published. It is

carried on by Spingarn, Nock, Seldes, Rascoe, Rosenfeld, the *New York Times*, and myself. It is weltering around in a great slough of confusion, growing more and more hopeless all the time. Both sides have revealed themselves—if we may judge by their utterance in the debate—utterly incompetent to engage intelligently in the simplest sort of controversy; it is all a great mass of misunderstandings and general inability to deal accurately with ideas—of accusations answered without being read and explanations gone astray amid the "buzz" of the Algonquin (see last week's Freeman), of insults, insinuations, recantations and curses. Instead of picking out the opponent's vulnerable spots and taking careful aim at them, the combatants are in the habit of loading heavy artillery pieces with nails, beer-tops, old pairs of scissors and fragments of broken glass and firing them broadcast at the enemy. Everybody makes generalizations and every generalization is worse than the last; every member of the Younger Generation identifies the Younger Generation with himself and ascribes his own private virtues and preferences to a whole movement and the Older Generation does the same thing. I am sick of the whole business and have just per-

[8] *Ibid.*, p. 113.

formed a great phlebotomy on Rosenfeld's article for *Vanity Fair* on the subject, reducing it to three thousand words from about a million."[9]

The warfare of the generations included the counterattacks of the new humanists against the naturalists and the frontal assaults of Mencken against Philistia. Mencken had replaced Compton Mackenzie as a candidate for God in Fitzgerald's mind during the time he was writing *The Beautiful and Damned*. When arguing with Maxwell Perkins about Maury Noble's contention that the Bible was written by cynical and self-seeking superstitious old men, Fitzgerald defended the section by saying that "I would hate to cut it out as it's very clever in its way and Mencken—who saw it— and Zelda were very enthusiastic about it."[10] The significance of Mencken's influence is discussed by James E. Miller:

Mencken's discussion of "the fundamental defects of American fiction" . . . revealed what he thought to be the mark of great writing. American fiction, Mencken said, "habitually exhibits, not a man of delicate organization in revolt against the inexplicable tragedy of existence, but a man of low sensibilities and elemental desires yielding himself gladly to his environment. . . . The man of reflective habit cannot conceivably take any passionate interest in the conflicts [American popular fiction] deals with." . . . This rare man is passionately interested in the "far more poignant and significant conflict between a salient individual and the harsh and meaningless fiats of destiny, the unintelligible mandates and vagaries of God. His hero is not one who yields and wins, but one who resists and fails." . . . Since this philosophical attitude (belief that the "fiats of destiny" are meaningless and the "mandates and vagaries of God" are unintelligible) results in an inner struggle which, "nine times out of ten," ends in failure in real life, "the theme of the great bulk of superior fiction," Mencken concluded, is "character in decay."[11]

[9] July 31, 1922, the Fitzgerald papers, Princeton University Library.
[10] Before December 12, 1921, *Letters*, p. 150.
[11] James E. Miller, *Fitzgerald, His Art as Technique* (New York, 1964), p. 47. The Mencken essay is "The National Letters," *Prejudices: Second Series* (New York, 1920). For a brief general discussion of the significance of Mencken for Fitzgerald,

The aspect of Mencken associated with the war against the "boo-boisie" is as apparent in *The Beautiful and Damned* as is that associated with the war against the optimism exhibited in popular American fiction—a sentimentalism that Fitzgerald himself catered to in his fiction for the slick magazines. When Fitzgerald cutely presents Beauty as an eternal essence about to be visited upon Gloria, he satirically presents the visitation in unmistakably Menckenesque terms, which clearly indicate that Fitzgerald's national materials were at least as present and influential as his own personal history:

BEAUTY: (*Her lips scarcely stirring, her eyes turned, as always, inward upon herself*) Whither shall I journey now?

THE VOICE: To a new country—a land you have never seen before.

BEAUTY: (*Petulantly*) I loathe breaking into these new civilizations. . . .

THE VOICE: It is the most opulent, most gorgeous land on earth—a land whose wisest are but little wiser than its dullest; a land where the rulers have minds like little children and the law-givers believe in Santa Claus; where ugly women control strong men—

BEAUTY: (*In astonishment*) What?

THE VOICE: (*Very much depressed*) Yes, it is truly a melancholy spectacle. Women with receding chins and shapeless noses go about in broad daylight saying "Do this!" and "Do that!" and all the men, even those of great wealth, obey implicitly their women to whom they refer sonorously either as "Mrs. So-and-so" or as "the wife."

BEAUTY: But this can't be true! I can understand, of course, their obedience to women of charm—but to fat women? to bony women? to women with scrawny cheeks?

THE VOICE: Even so. . . . At first it was thought that you would go this time as an actress in the motion pictures, but, after all, it's not advisable. You will be disguised during your fifteen years as what is called a "susciety gurl."

BEAUTY: What's that?

(*There is a new sound in the wind which must for our purposes be interpreted as* THE VOICE *scratching its head.*)

see Miller, pp. 45–50. See also Robert Sklar, *F. Scott Fitzgerald* (New York, 1967), pp. 60–62, 93–96, *et passim*.

THE VOICE: (*At length*) It's a sort of bogus aristocrat.

BEAUTY: Bogus? What is bogus?

THE VOICE: That, too, you will discover in this land. You will find much that is bogus. Also, you will do much that is bogus.

BEAUTY: (*Placidly*) It all sounds so vulgar.

THE VOICE: Not half as vulgar as it is. You will be known during your fifteen years as a ragtime kid, a flapper, a jazz-baby, and a vamp. You will dance new dances neither more nor less gracefully than you danced the old ones (pp. 28–29).

If in *This Side of Paradise* the hero is a quester after the meaning of life, the hero and the "beauty" of *The Beautiful and Damned* are examples of the meaninglessness of life. And in both cases, Fitzgerald's exploration is inextricably interwoven with his particular and personal American materials. The subjects and even some of the attitudes change, but the essential materials do not. The change is what Edmund Wilson referred to when he said, "Since writing *This Side of Paradise*—on the inspiration of Wells and Mackenzie—Fitzgerald has become acquainted with a different school of fiction: the ironical-pessimistic."[12] It is perfectly true that in 1921, when writing *The Beautiful and Damned*, the "meaninglessness" that an "ironical-pessimistic" view finds in life, leading to the "decay of character," is something that Fitzgerald modishly picked up in his aspiring attempt to be "in" on things. Yet the fusion of his personal life and his literary and social milieu does not have a merely fortuitous connection with his materials and themes.

Of course in one sense this is all fruitless: writers write about what they can. As Henry James argued, they needn't explain the why of their *donnée* even if they could. Yet insofar as the relationship of Fitzgerald's materials to his attitudes creates the total theme that is his examination of America, the problem of failure is very relevant indeed. "My new novel, called *The Flight of the*

12 Edmund Wilson, "F. Scott Fitzgerald," *The Shores of Light* (New York, 1952), p. 32. Reprinted from *Bookman* (March 1922).

*Rocket*," Fitzgerald wrote to Charles Scribner, "concerns the life
of one Anthony Patch between his 25th and 33rd years (1913–
1921). He is one of those many with the tastes and weaknesses of
an artist but with no actual creative inspiration. How he and his
beautiful young wife are wrecked on the shoals of dissipation is
told in the story."[13] Anthony Patch, the romantic egotist, is hardly
the avatar of Amory Blaine, the personage; his career is not the
one promised by the materials and life-story introduced in *This
Side of Paradise*.

Yet, where could they go, those materials and that life, given
the directions that were foreseen for them in the anlage of Fitzgerald's growing, prophetic knowledge? Mencken's call for "tragedy" was much nearer to Fitzgerald in its closeness to his sense of
America than in its mere fashionableness. The near side of paradise, after all, offered very few basic alternatives; it is not insignificant that Fitzgerald is vague about the better something that
Amory goes forward to in the world. When all of the excitement
of self-discovery was finished, one of the truths that Amory had
found was that there was no gate to paradise. There were only
doors either to destructive dissipation and personality or to work
and next things. The transcendent world of American expectation,
Fitzgerald discovered in his first book, exists only in the imagination of the artist or in the delusions of the naive believer, the one
feeding the other. Given the problem of creating a fictional character *in the recognizable social setting which furnished Fitzgerald's most productive materials*, and given the temperament
and personality that needed the experience observed before the
imagination could work it successfully into the desired composite
shapes, Fitzgerald could not persevere as a literary fantast. He
needed composite characters in a social, a historical context in
order to give flesh and bone to the otherwise ectoplasmic creations
of his ceaseless and heuristic memory. What he knew about his

[13] August 12, 1920, *Letters*, p. 145.

materials taught him that all denouements would have to be
enacted within the very mortal world of conditions and circumstances that his materials—American youth, wealth, and the adolescent expectations of innocence—tried to pretend could be
transcended. What career, what clothing, what action, then, are
suitable for the responsible personage who must enact his responsibility in mundane terms? What profession for Amory after *This
Side of Paradise* ends and it's time to begin the new book which
enacts the protagonist's life? Clearly, a new book cannot be begun
on the basis of the ending of *This Side of Paradise* without going
over to the *other* side. Fitzgerald is faced with an old problem for
the American writer: if the new man (or child) learns that the
New World (or West) is the redeemable and redeeming world,
superior to the debasing historical actualities of experience, his
setting off for the new world's new life necessarily must be enacted
in a supra-experiential world. What comes after the book is over
is, implicitly, to be the redemption. The hero must return to
paradise, the good place, the territory ahead, the lost land of innocence, where he will live according to all the goodness he has
learned by negative example in the fallen and betraying world
of gilded sham, devils, and circumstances. Having been conceived
in Eden, the only direction for the American hero is Nodward or
eastward. Going back home, westward to paradise, turns out to
be impossible as long as man is to live in or be defined by the
society in which he acquired his non-utopian experience.

So, like the heroes of Twain and James, Ellison's invisible man
says goodbye to the reader at the moment that he promises to
come back into society redeemed by his sojourn in the wilderness
of the coal-cellar. Malamud's *A New Life* ends at the moment the
hero's new life is about to begin. And Faulkner knew that Ike
McCaslin, try as he might, surrounded with images and auras of
Christ, would not be able to resign from history, to repudiate the
sins of his heritage, to redeem at least himself, to begin anew.

There is, in short, a direct relationship between the plots hatched in the American adolescence of Fitzgerald's imagination and the themes hatched in the American moral insistence of that same imagination and its most productive materials. Fitzgerald's only alternative for a protagonist is the denial of a successful redeeming hero precisely because his materials are a denial of the excited and exalted Utopian expectation.

In this consideration there is a further and larger relationship, that between modernism and the American literary thematic history to which Fitzgerald's work belongs. *The Beautiful and Damned,* in its paralysis of hope and action, looks forward, through Gatsby and Diver, to the literary hero's existential resignation from society altogether. The premodern hero, in his traditional requirements, not only represented his society, but he redeemed it. In the world of the premodern hero, evil, usually representative of some kind of moral or theological aberration, under which the social aberrations were subsumed, is vanquished by the hero after he passes through a mythico-ritualistic series of tests and struggles. Thereafter things are changed. History is different, for the redeemed nature of society is different: everything returns to the stability of the happy status-quo before it was shaken. In the basic conservatism (reaction, perhaps?) of the premodern hero's struggle, the past is reattained and the good time is here again. "They all lived happily ever after." This wish, buried in the deepest recesses of human fears, works in premodern social conditions to create a quest literature in which the quest ultimately is directed toward stasis rather than flux or development. It is in this sense that most of Fitzgerald's magazine fiction, sentimentalized for the pages of *The Saturday Evening Post, Redbook,* and *Metropolitan Magazine* (despite the fact that Lorimer, the great editor of *The Saturday Evening Post,* gave Fitzgerald latitude for far more artistic integrity than one would condescendingly expect) was cheaper, less truly modern, and less significant than his novels. It is often fiction after the genteel model of Booth Tarkington, who represented one pole toward which Fitzgerald was pulled, as Norris, Dreiser, and Conrad in differing ways represented another, more serious pole.

Fitzgerald felt deeply the dividing line that Romanticism marked between the premodern and the modern worlds, at least as far as the direction of quest in literature is concerned. The modern existential hero finds self-development despite or beneath or outside society and circumstance. But the premodern hero not only attained some transcendent condition superior to circumstances, but in the personal success of his rites de passage he also brings his world into his paradisiac condition. The literary possibility for character, given the possibility for the hero, is immense as far as action and stature are concerned. Character can be tremendous, like the American folk hero and the West he inhabits. It can, in will or act, be superior to history. One essential condition for this literary possibility is a society united enough in its beliefs to provide a communal background of agreed values against which the hero and evil antagonist can act. The Romantic and existential heroes, however, have societies that are unified not in belief but in respectability and sham, so that the hero must discover and create belief as he progresses in experience. If in will or act he can be superior to history it is not as a spokesman for his society that he does so. But Fitzgerald, in his serious fiction, and particularly in *The Great Gatsby,* marks a mid-point at which the energies of the American fictional hero are impelled by a Romantic dream of the possibilities of the Self and yet are energies that represent and sum up his society. It was in the merger of these mutually repelling tendencies that Fitzgerald mirrored modern America and made his unique impact upon its reading public.

Fitzgerald, like most American writers, was confronted with particular insistence by the problem of the hero, for his heritage of literary and cultural assumptions demanded the transcendent possibility of character. Christianity insists upon this possibility for the European as well as the American writer; but for Fitzgerald the possibility was enlarged considerably by the inborn, often unconscious, but nonetheless prevalent American expectation of the golden moment. The very nature of America as a metaphor constantly suggests to the imagination the belief that the history of the hero *is* an enactment of the history of America, which *is* an enactment of freedom from history through its redemption.

In "character in decay," or rather the Romantic dream in decay, Fitzgerald resolved a very real dilemma that Mencken could only attack frontally, at the surface of its manifestations. On the one hand Fitzgerald had the America of an older generation, a passing status quo. It represented to him established morality and manners which seemed not entirely unlovely in contrast to contemporary disillusion, cynicism, hedonism, and moral uncertainty. On the other hand, it was precisely that America that was debasingly ideologized by a status quo which had become a philistine commercialism against whose cant and smugness Fitzgerald and his whole generation, from Mencken to Edmund Wilson, rebelled. There was an enormous disparity between the idea of limitless American possibility, the belief which Fitzgerald found so gorgeous, and the genteel Babbittocracy that so loudly mouthed that very belief. In the disparity, the stature of the national everyman's character shrinks enormously as Pathfinder turns out to be only the chairman of the Mohican Falls Chamber of Commerce. On the other hand, the Emersonian stance remains a viable heritage in that the character of the disaffected and lonely active man becomes fate, becomes a vehicle for a moral assessment of the culture from which he is expatriated either in geography or in spirit. Fitzgerald and his debunking contemporaries were acutely aware that the legatee of the monumental expectations of the past, Georgie Babbitt with his corn-fed paunch and Booster's Club pep

and patriotism, could scarcely be expected to carry into actuality
the enormous visionary burden of millenialism that the Republic
had heaped up behind his own moment in time. For the Younger
Generation the removal of Emersonian toughness from the historical actuality reduced that millenialism to an unexamined
Vision of Happiness, changing the script for *Walden* to a vehicle
for Shirley Temple. The ridicule in *Tender Is the Night* inherent
in Rosemary Hoyt's national success, *Daddy's Girl,* is a synthesis
of the contact made in the American artist's consciousness between
the sense of loss and the deflating attitudes of literary naturalism.
The discrepancy between the idealized and the debunked America
resulted inevitably in the discrepancy between the idealized and
debunked American as hero, and resulted in a rich sense of irony
in American fiction since the Civil War. Until he could create a
character who aspired to what the status quo announced as desirable, but who was yet an outcast who imaginatively re-created
for himself the meaning of what was desirable—not in terms of
Main Street but in the gorgeous sense of infinite possibility of a
vanished America—Fitzgerald could only present characters whose
imaginative potential could never be energized into actuality.
Until he got Anthony Patch out of the way, he could not create
Gatsby. To get Anthony Patch out of the way was to be done with
the dead end of a sense of closed possibilities that never went beyond disillusionment and cynicism; it was also to point toward
the American who was at once representative of the scorned actualities and yet imaginatively outcast as a living continuation of
the Romantic millenial vision before it had become vitiated by
what was scorned. In the meantime Fitzgerald needed the composite character who indicated that Amory Blaine was only a
preparation for the creation of the national hero; that the true
hero would have to be very representative of his society. Yet, if
the potential hero, no matter how clever and liberated from commercialism in his culture, wanted money, like the rest of his so-

ciety, ultimately for the material condition of wealth, he would turn out to be no hero at all. In his failure of nerve and imagination would be dramatized the gilded decay of the Romantic dream of self. Both Anthony Patch and Jay Gatsby enact the death of possibility, but as Gatsby is the hero, Patch is just the corpse.

Because he could write about "the American character" or about anything else only by writing about his own character and internal history, Fitzgerald's composite "heroes" of failure are necessarily exemplars of American expectation personified in the personal fears of his own demise as a gilded youth among the golden girls. "Whether it's something that happened 20 years ago or only yesterday," he once said in a *Saturday Evening Post* article, "I must start with an emotion—one that's close to me and that I can understand." What he understood, along with his own generation of denuded and angry young men, was the hollow knock when the golden idol was tapped. As William Goldhurst has demonstrated, Fitzgerald was not merely a sensitive playboy who wrote intuitively (an old myth, now gratefully laid to everlasting rest), but he was a conscious member of a literary community and was influenced in his ideas and his work by people all of whom participated in the Younger Generation's sense of betrayal and rebellion. Even those who were of slightly older vintage contributed to disaffection. Every name was associated with iconoclasms of one kind or another: George Jean Nathan, H. L. Mencken, James Branch Cabell, Sinclair Lewis, Floyd Dell, Sherwood Anderson, Edmund Wilson, John Dos Passos, Donald Ogden Stewart, Theodore Dreiser; and of those whose influences he would feel after he had written *The Beautiful and Damned,* E. E. Cummings, Ernest Hemingway, William Faulkner, Harold Stearns, Hart Crane, Malcolm Cowley, Matthew Josephson, the entire contemporary set of "exiles," who did or did not return. To project Amory Blaine into the future was to project him into an America that no longer existed on the literary horizon and could be found only in the imaginative expectations of the past. To have a *representative* social man, but one without private and fantastic reserves of imaginative energy, was to have a failure in morality and in stature. To many contemporary readers who misunderstood Fitzgerald's use of his materials and saw only his personal history without the conscious craftsmanship and art that made the history something so very much more than "just personal," the material itself seemed terribly one-dimensional. "But, my God!" Fitzgerald exploded at his critics, "it was my material, and it was all I had to deal with." The "all" that he had to deal with was the entire complex of nostalgia that explains why, at the moment of his most joyous beginning, Fitzgerald, true to his vision of his materials, created not a Peter Pan but an Anthony Patch.

Two cultured contemporary readers, Paul Rosenfeld and Edmund Wilson, disagreed about *The Beautiful and Damned*. Although they saw many of the same shortcomings in the novel, Wilson, with his constant, lovely penetration, arrived at this conclusion:

There is a profounder truth in *The Beautiful and Damned* than the author perhaps intended to convey: the hero and heroine are strange creatures without purposes or method, who give themselves up to wild debaucheries and do not, from beginning to end, perform a single serious act; but you somehow get the impression that, in spite of their madness, they are the most rational people in the book: wherever they touch the common life, the institutions of men are made to appear a contemptible farce of the futile and the absurd; the world of finance, the army, and finally, the world of business are successively and casually exposed as completely without dignity or point. The inference is that, in such a civilization, the sanest and most creditable thing is to forget organized society and live for the jazz of the moment. And it is not altogether a personal confusion which has produced the confusion of such a book. It may be that we must not expect too much intellectual balance of young men who write books in the year 1921; we must remember that their environment and their chief source of stimulation have been the wars, the society, and the commerce of the Age of Confusion itself.[14]

Van Wyck Brooks seemed "anti-American" to the Younger Generation because his insistence that the American writer's roots should be nurtured in his national culture assumed, as the definition of that culture, the continuing absorption of the high-minded purpose of an aristocratic, bygone era. Wilson parodied both Brooks and the Younger Generation by confronting Brooks's insistent morality with the insouciant oh-well-what-the-hell of Scott Fitzgerald. Yet, despite the very funny imaginary dialogue ("The Delegate from Great Neck" in *The Shores of Light*), Wilson nonetheless arrives at a Brooksian statement in his review of *The Beautiful and Damned*. For Fitzgerald, given a hero who is representative of society, a citizen dwelling among citizens, the representative man is a character who reflects what he can *not* redeem. The book's irony exists where irony usually exists in modern American fiction—precisely in the gap between the metaphor and the actuality, the expectation of redemption and the nature of society, the Adamic heroism of *the* American and the homunculus he became in the suburbs. What I insist on, in short, is what Wilson hints at in his closing lines: the book's irony is a rejection of its characters *and* materials, not a celebration of them. Paul Rosenfeld, representative of many readers of the book, made the mistake of missing the irony:

But the world of his subject matter is still too much within Fitzgerald himself for him to see it sustainedly against the universe. Its values obtain too strongly over him, and for that reason he cannot set them against those of high civilization, and calmly judge them so. Hence, wanting philosophy, and a little overeager like the rest of America to arrive without having really sweated [how close to the bone Rosenfeld was *there!*], he falls victim to the favorite delusions of the society of

14 Wilson, *The Shores of Light*, pp. 34–35.

which he is a part, tends to indulge it in its dreams of grandeur, and misses the fine flower of pathos. He seems to set out writing under the compulsion of vague feelings, and when his wonderfully revelatory passages appear, they come rather like volcanic islands thrown to the surface of a sea of fantasy. By every law *The Beautiful and Damned* should have been a tragedy, the victims damned indeed; yet at the conclusion Fitzgerald welched, and permitted his pitiful pair to have the alleviations of some thirty millions of dollars, and his hero tell the reader he had won out.[15]

Rosenfeld's comment is a bit like accusing a pathologist of being fascinated by diseases. For one thing, the thirty millions of dollars clearly are the spoils of a Pyrrhic victory, and one can read Anthony's statement of triumph only with an ironic recognition that he has really lost everything except the money and the sycophants it buys, and that he will forevermore be lost. "The victor belongs to the spoils," reads the novel's epigraph. (It is astonishing that readers could have thought otherwise, but Rosenfeld had much company.) Fitzgerald puts up gaudily obvious signposts. Anthony and Gloria, at the beginning of the novel, are characterized as neat, trim, and clean by nature. "Tell me all the reasons why you're going to marry me in June," says Anthony. "Well," replies Gloria, "because you're so clean. You're sort of blowy clean, like I am. There's two sorts, you know. One's like Dick: he's clean like polished pans. You and I are clean like streams and winds. I can tell whenever I see a person whether he is clean, and if so, which kind of clean he is." "We're twins," answers Anthony (p. 131). Gloria insistently equates the "good" people with cleanliness: "Always intensely sceptical of her sex, her judgments were now concerned with the question of whether women were or were not clean. By uncleanliness she meant a variety of things, a lack of pride, a slackness in fibre and, most of all, the unmistakable aura of promiscuity" (pp. 234–35). Gloria continually reasserts

15 *F. Scott Fitzgerald*, ed. Alfred Kazin (New York, 1951), p. 76. Reprinted from Rosenfeld's *Men Seen* (1925).

for the reader her knowledge that her identity, her very life, is bound up in the fresh and clean glow of her physical beauty, in which exists the independence of her "soul." (Fitzgerald calls it "soul," but never gets beyond the concept of "personality," which is what he obviously means, and in the most commonly popular use of the word at that.) To lose her beauty, her fresh cleanliness, is to lose her golden moment and any chance of happiness she might ever again expect. It is, in short, to lose her youth, in which is the only existence of the abstraction, Beauty, that has come to her from the Voice among the stars. "It's your world, isn't it?" Anthony had once asked Gloria.

" 'Well—' she said with a quick upward glance, 'isn't it?' As long as I'm—young.'

"She had paused slightly before the last word and Anthony suspected that she had started to say 'beautiful.' It was undeniably what she had intended" (p. 66).

At the end of the novel, after Gloria and Anthony have won the money, dependence on which has debased them and ruined their physical appearances and conditions, their youth, cleanliness, and beauty are all gone. Fitzgerald's "trick" is so heavy-handed that one must work at missing it. One last sees Gloria and Anthony through the eyes of a handsome young couple, newly in love, and a reminder of what Anthony and Gloria have once been and will never be again. Commenting on Gloria, the "pretty girl in yellow" says, "I can't stand her, you know. She seems sort of—sort of dyed and *unclean*, if you know what I mean. Some people just have that look about them whether they are or not" (p. 448). And as for Anthony's self-congratulation, it is made in a wheel chair; his physical independence is gone and his mind has snapped, and he is incapable of distinguishing between friends who really think he had been "right" all along and the leeches who tell him what he obviously wants to hear. Lest there be any doubt about the "consolation" offered by the thirty millions of dollars, the last scene is introduced by an explicit statement about the irony of the victory, a statement that Fitzgerald, with his quick dramatic sense, immediately activated in a fitting shift in point of view to that of the young couple.

That exquisite heavenly irony which has tabulated the demise of so many generations of sparrows doubtless records the subtlest verbal inflections of the passengers of such ships as the *Berengaria*. And doubtless it was listening when the young man in the plaid cap crossed the deck quickly and spoke to the pretty girl in yellow.

"That's him," he said pointing to a bundled figure seated in a wheel chair near the rail. "That's Anthony Patch. First time he's been on deck."[16]

The quality of the irony at the end of the book, contrasted with that at the beginning, together with the device of the shift in point of view, tells the whole story. The first two sentences in the book are, "In 1913, when Anthony Patch was twenty-five, two years were already gone since irony, the Holy Ghost of this later day, had, theoretically, at least, descended upon him. Irony was the final polish of the shoe, the ultimate dab of the clothes-brush, a sort of intellectual 'There!'—yet at the brink of this story he has as yet gone no further than the conscious stage." It's the modish irony that Fitzgerald is ironic about at the very moment he is Menckenized. Anthony begins as the trim and dapper man-about-town, wearing his mannerisms and attitudes in the same high

16 As Wilson's *Bookman* article makes clear, Fitzgerald's intention had always been firm in the destruction of Gloria and Anthony. In an earlier draft of the novel even Maury Noble and Richard Caramel were destroyed more completely than they were in the finally published version. Furthermore, Fitzgerald's intention was to destroy them *as representatives of their particular culture and way of life*. Responding to Wilson's first draft of the *Bookman* article, Fitzgerald wrote, "But one more carp before I close. Gloria and Anthony *are* representative. They are two of the great army of the rootless who float around New York. There must be thousands. Still, I didn't bring it out" (*Letters*, p. 331). If he was not successful in bringing out their representative qualities (and many sections of the book, such as the descriptions of the city getting ready for the new social season are successful in this respect), still the book leaves no doubt that Fitzgerald finally rejects what they stand for. To claim, as Rosenfeld correctly does, that Fitzgerald identified and even over-identified with his main characters is to tell only half the story.

fashion with which he wears his clean, clean clothes. He is actively up to the minute; no man in a wheel chair he. What catches up with him is the irony implicit in the fact that what Anthony dons as a Younger Generation suit of armor turns out to be the shirt of Nessus. The shift from Anthony to the young man in the plaid cap and the pretty girl in yellow is a dramatic device that creates a sense of how fallen Anthony is at the end of the novel, removed in fact and action from the central place that he had occupied as actor, as consciousness, and as man-about-town. Fitzgerald uses the same method at the end of *The Great Gatsby,* when Gatsby is so lonesomely removed from his house and parties, his dreams and his life. That last car, coming to Gatsby's house one dark and empty Saturday night for yet one other party, when the driver was unaware that the parties were over forever, was one of Fitzgerald's consummate touches. It created an intensely nostalgic sense of how lost and gone was all the vitality that Gatsby had both represented and generated. And at the end of *Tender Is the Night,* the shift in point of view to Nicole's casual observation that Dick, who once so glitteringly and centrally occupied the romantic places of Europe, now had a buried and tiny life in one or another of those little upstate New York towns, creates an overwhelming and choking sense of how lost, fallen, and removed from life is all the promise that Dick once represented. So too, Fitzgerald's plans for *The Last Tycoon* indicate something similar for the death of Monroe Stahr. In *The Beautiful and Damned* the technique doesn't really work because Fitzgerald had not yet fully experienced, in his materials of high success, a character whom the reader could mourn. But the intentions of "character in decay" are unmistakably clear.

For Rosenfeld or anyone else to accuse Fitzgerald of welching on his repudiation of his characters' lives and values in *The Beautiful and Damned* is an indication of one further irony—Rosenfeld, as an American reader, is at least as impressed by those thirty

millions as ever Fitzgerald was. It is not simply that Fitzgerald
was so wonderfully successful in evoking the glitter and fascination of the gilded world (indeed, in this book *he has not yet so
succeeded*), but his audience, in and of itself, is also fascinated
and can ill afford to sneer at Fitzgerald for his announcement that
what fascinates Americans in the upward climb to money-heaven
is the richest lode of his literary materials, the "all" that he had
to deal with. Rosenfeld could overlook the obvious irony of Anthony's "victory" only by saying in effect, "but gosh, he *does* have
all that *money*." Fitzgerald's magic can not be blamed, for he has
not yet succeeded in casting the spell of wealth over his novels,
which is to say that the further irony, in short, is that Fitzgerald
could repudiate those millions more easily than many of his representative and critical readers. What a puissant American siren
Fitzgerald's golden moment is, after all. As *This Side of Paradise*
warned, to accuse Fitzgerald of an adolescent identification with
his materials and let one's pronouncement rest there, is to see
only part—and the lesser part—of Fitzgerald's mastery and significance, his aesthetic and his moral judgment.

Anthony begins not where Amory Blaine left off but where
Amory would have liked to be had he maintained his yearning to
be Humbird. Anthony is "cheerful, pleasant, and very attractive
to intelligent men and to all women . . . a distinct and dynamic
personality, opinionated, contemptuous, functioning from within
outward." He believes that "he would one day accomplish some
quiet subtle thing that the elect would deem worthy, and, passing
on, would join the dimmer stars in a nebulous, indeterminate
heaven half-way between death and immortality." He is not lazy,
really, but afraid to support actively a sustained effort toward any
worthy, quiet subtle thing lest he show the marks. He wants "to
arrive without having really sweated." The present is a pleasant
limbo between a family past which doesn't interest him and a
future when he will inherit his grandfather's money. On his seven

thousand a year, left to him by his mother, he floats in a world which is a quiet drift away from next things. The world of next things, the sweaty world of the bourgeoisie and the proletariat, is never visited by Anthony without a faintly contemptuous condescension (a continuation of Amory's condescension in *This Side of Paradise*) to the greyness, boredom, and perspiration that he sees as its leading characteristics. The inheritance of Adam "Cross" Patch's millions becomes the dimly looming guarantee of eternal immunity from that world. The future legacy is comfortably associated in Anthony's mind with that day in which he shall attain that quiet subtle thing indicative of his high and delicate sensibilities. From Fitzgerald's overview, Anthony is bitched from the begining. He has mind enough, or at least education enough to desire an exquisite personal intellectual accomplishment; yet because his life is aimed at a rare and elegant use of the legacy, that accomplishment, a triumph of the personage, is vaguely defined in dollars, the necessity of the personality. For both Adam and Anthony Patch, their lives are made meaningless by the very wealth that they thought would guarantee the freedom and value of those lives. In Fitzgerald's consistent use of his materials, *The Beautiful and Damned* is more than a story of modish meaninglessness in exactly the same theme that makes *This Side of Paradise* more than a modish "gesture of indefinite revolt."

The original Adam, founder of the family wealth, lives a story of the fallen American whose wealth is a disguise for his fall. Adam does not amass riches in proof of a divinely sponsored new man in God's Eden. Rather, he is a ruthless opportunist. "Early in his career Adam Patch had married an anemic lady of thirty, Alicia Withers, who brought him one hundred thousand dollars and an impeccable entré into the banking circles of New York." She bore him a son and then Alicia Withers withered. But Adam, "more familiarly known as 'Cross Patch,' having left his father's farm in Tarrytown early in sixty-one to join a New York cavalry regiment

... came home from war a major, charged into Wall Street, and amid much fuss, fume, applause, and ill-will ... gathered to himself some seventy-five million dollars" (p. 4). Having grabbed his money in the actualities of his society, Adam then sanctimoniously cloaked his life and history in a hypocritical mask of increasingly simple-minded mildness, manners, and meliorism. He became a prohibitionist, a champion of temperance societies and young men's associations. He began to reek with Godliness. Most significant, as he became senile, he began to remember his history as a statistication of the Horatio Alger myth, as an American saga of patriotism and virtue rewarded. His increasing identification with "sinlessness" and "innocence" is his increasing identification with what he thinks is the real version of America as Eden.[17]

The heritage of the fathers, the Adam-sires, receives full treatment in *Tender Is the Night*. In *The Beautiful and Damned*, the theme is as yet but sketchily adumbrated. History itself is for Adam a vague adjunct of nationalism or else it is bunk. The total past, the very heritage of human history he hands down by virtue of the fact of procreation, is not understood by the American Philistine, who sees himself as the defender of purity, civilization, and Protestantism. In a conversation with Anthony, Adam insists that "you ought to *do* something . . . accomplish something."

Anthony waited for him to speak of "leaving something done when you pass on." Then he made a suggestion:
"I thought—it seemed to me that perhaps I'm best qualified to write—"
Adam Patch winced, visualizing a family poet with long hair and three mistresses.
"—history," finished Anthony.
"History? History of what? The Civil War? The Revolution?"

[17] For a statement about Fitzgerald's awareness of the anti-Business-God-Country stand that the iconoclastic writers of his generation adopted, see William Goldhurst, *F. Scott Fitzgerald and His Contemporaries* (Cleveland, 1963), pp. 19–42 and pp. 74–104.

"Why—no, sir. A history of the Middle Ages." Simultaneously an idea was born for a history of the Renaissance popes, written from some novel angle. Still, he was glad he had said "Middle Ages."

"Middle Ages? Why not your own country? Something you know about?"

"Well, you see I've lived so much abroad—"

"Why you should write about the Middle Ages, I don't know. Dark Ages, we used to call 'em. Nobody knows what happened and nobody cares, except that they're over now" (p. 15).

Certain of his own impeccable canonization in America's legend of pious virtue, he is certain of his own place in world history and has all the perspective of his gilt-edged bonds. On the other hand, of course, the sudden inspiration about the Renaissance popes is as much a sign of Anthony's phony and precious dilettante's inability for next things as "your own country" is a sign of Adam's obtuse and heavy philistinism.

The actual legacy of Adam's memory in the world he departs is not a testament to American virtue but a bitter lawsuit between his ultra-respectable secretary, who is a former skidrow rummy named Edward Shuttleworth, and his increasingly debauched and dirty grandson, Anthony. Both sides lie, remake and confuse the past, and together with the courts, ironically reduce the Patch fortune to the business it was in the first place—the result of grubbing and grabbing and anarchic self-aggrandizement. The myth is sandwiched between two layers of ugly actuality in time, and, as he is to indicate more successfully in the family histories of *The Great Gatsby* and *Tender Is the Night*, Fitzgerald suggests that the history of American success is of a constant sameness: it is a revelation of the function of the myth of America as a misused and misunderstood gilded convenience used to cloak rapacious and anarchic irresponsibilities.

On this element of the book, Rosenfeld and Wilson, the polar representatives of the readers of Fitzgerald, agree. True, Rosenfeld implies a desire to see Fitzgerald turn his attention to "social issues," by which he seems to have in mind a type of the "proletarian artist" that was to be championed in the 1930's. Before he was stirred by the Sacco-Vanzetti case, Wilson did not advocate any such thing, but he too saw the Anthony-Scott and Gloria-Zelda existence as a heartless and very funny farce that is at once a parody and abnegation of American social values and institutions:

His characters—and himself—are actors in an elfin harlequinade; they are as nimble, as gay and as lovely—and as hard-hearted—as fairies: Columbine elopes with Harlequin on a rope ladder from the Ritz and both go morris-dancing amuck on a case of bootleg liquor; Pantaloon is pinked with an epigram that withers him up like a leaf; the Policeman is tripped by Harlequin and falls into the Pulitzer Fountain. In the end, Harlequin puts on false whiskers and pretends he is Bernard Shaw; he gives reporters an elaborate interview on politics and history; a hundred thousand readers read it and are more or less impressed; Columbine nearly dies laughing; Harlequin buys another case of gin.[18]

Both Rosenfeld and Wilson see what Fitzgerald tried so hard to convey along with the fairy-tale enchantment of wealth: his characters and the world they inhabit are either inhuman or corrupt, and in either case their histories indict the values of a nation. Missing the fact that Fitzgerald does not do what he accuses him of doing, Rosenfeld also misses the fact that Fitzgerald does do exactly what Rosenfeld accused him of not doing and wanted him to do: "Should Fitzgerald finally break his mold," predicts Rosenfeld, "and free himself of the compulsion of the civilization in which he grew, it might go badly with his popularity. It will be a pathetic story he will have to tell, the legend of a moon which never rose; and that is precisely the story a certain America does not wish to hear. Nevertheless, we would like hugely to hear him tell it. And Fitzgerald might scarcely miss his following."[19] To be

---

18 Wilson, *The Shores of Light*, p. 32.
19 Kazin, ed., *F. Scott Fitzgerald*, p. 77.

free of the compulsions would be, for Fitzgerald, to be "free" of
the "all I had to deal with." And with the exception of *This Side
of Paradise*, where the moonrise is problematical at best, the moon
Rosenfeld talks about *never does* get above the horizon: Anthony
and Gloria are doomed (it was *supposed* to "be a pathetic story"),
Gatsby is doomed, Diver is doomed, Stahr is doomed. The Diamond as big as the Ritz is demolished, the winter dreams never
do turn to May, and the rich boy never succeeds as a human. In no
single instance of the novels or the serious stories does the glitter
of New York turn to real gold; in no instance does the moral,
naive, and hardworking believer, lured by the glitter, get anything
more than the flight of the rocket, in which the seeker finds not
the extension of the golden moment but only the momentary
glory of its memory and death. In 1925, the same year that Rosenfeld's critique was collected in *Men Seen*, Fitzgerald, in a letter
to Marya Mannes, was quite explicit—even in his imagery—about
what Rosenfeld failed to see in his fiction: "You are thrilled by
New York—I doubt you will be after five more years when you are
more fully nourished from within. I carry the place around the
world in my heart but sometimes I try to shake it off in my dreams.
America's greatest promise is that something is going to happen,
and after a while you get tired of waiting because nothing happens to people except that they grow old . . . because America is
the story of the moon that never rose."[20] Rosenfeld's friendly animosity is typical of the many readings in which Fitzgerald stands
accused of what he condemns. And even at that, because he misses
the personage in Fitzgerald and sees only the personality, it is
surprising that Rosenfeld should be wrong about one thing more
when he suggests that "Fitzgerald might scarcely miss his following." No one could miss it more.

As the argument between Wilson and Rosenfeld suggests,
*The Beautiful and Damned* is entirely about personalities, with

[20] *Letters*, p. 488.

no doomed personage or questing new-man or moral commentator to lend value to the actions of the personalities. It is the only such novel Fitzgerald wrote and it is his dullest, largely because the action is unrelieved by the moral contrast created by the characters who provide commentary, in history, action, or overt judgment, upon the irresponsible personalities and their values. The rocket ride is downtrip only, for the characters are introduced at the peak of their potential and decline steadily in their vision and attractiveness. All the commentary is provided only by those who participate in and stand out in no way from the drift and pointlessness and irresponsibility of the lives commented upon.

The most explicit commentator, Anthony's collegemate and friend, Maury Noble (partly modeled after George Jean Nathan), is characterized as hopelessly cynical. His cynicism is a consequence of his feeling very, very old. His sense of age, in turn, is a consequence of his certainty that there is nothing to believe in because there is no teleological purpose either in the universe or in society. The scene in which Maury comments upon the Bible, as he sits on the roof of a railroad depot during the night of a drunken party, is his explicit speech of self-explanation. It is also Fitzgerald's explicit attempt to follow up the self-conscious, lost-generation vision of all wars fought, all faiths shaken, and all gods dead that made Fitzgerald a "spokesman" for his Younger Generation at the end of *This Side of Paradise*. Here, through Maury, he continues (with maudlin delight) the modish attitudes of cynicism that would be well received by the readers of *Vanity Fair* and of *The Smart Set*, which was edited by Nathan and Mencken. (If Mencken had advocated "tragedy" and character in decay, Edmund Wilson, it will be remembered, had also advised Scott to "cultivate a universal irony.") It is a speech, in short, in which Fitzgerald tried to capitalize upon his reputation as a spokesman, and except for one paragraph it is a jumble of Fitzgerald's own early racism, snobbery, and adolescent pretentiousness. Fitzgerald is unsuccessful in making the reader feel Maury's "suffering" because neither Maury's life nor his party-smarty lingo, with all its clever, shallow cadences, ever gets far from mere fashionableness. The speech is one more revealing instance of what happens to Fitzgerald's art when the personality-participant, showing off for his "private audience," gets in the way of the personage-writer.

There is one paragraph in Maury's "emancipated" speech that is the key to Gloria, Anthony, and the dissipation of any possible, lasting human value, which is Fitzgerald's intentional subject for the book. "I could quote you the philosophy of the hour," says Maury, " 'but, for all we know, fifty years may see a complete reversal of this abnegation that's absorbing the intellectuals today, the triumph of Christ over Anatole France—' He hesitated, and then added: 'But all I know—the tremendous importance of myself to me, and the necessity of acknowledging that importance to myself—these things the wise and lovely Gloria was born knowing, these things and the painful futility of trying to know anything else.' " ("I know myself, but that is all," cried Amory at the end of *This Side of Paradise,* in a summing up not so much of existential nausea as of the inner vanity and selfishness he has come to terms with.) And what was the wise and lovely Gloria born knowing? In her own words, "there's only one lesson to be learned from life . . . . That there's no lesson to be learned from life."

As Monsignor Darcy taught Amory, self-knowledge is essential for the personage. It would seem that Maury is echoing Amory's closing cry, but there is a crucial difference in intention. Clearly, in *This Side of Paradise* the emphasis is on a young man's awareness of self rather than on society, and on the fashionable postwar attitudes of disenchantment rather than on social service. There are no external values except money one can know or believe in. Amory's last words are the logical ones to close the book, fitting as they do the book's emphasis; but fitting as they are, they indicate why "social service" is out of focus, not quite believable for the reader. Yet, as though warned by instinct that he had to take his persona out into the world of the society which provided him his materials, Fitzgerald tried to force Amory's direction outward, not so much into further discovery of himself as into further discovery of the meaning of his society's values and history. At conflict in Fitzgerald in this early stage are what will be, in the 1950's and 1960's, existential social fiction (the work of writers like Mailer, Styron, Bellow, Ellison) and existential asocial fiction (the work of writers like Capote, Purdy, McCullers). If the split is conveniently formed by urban Jews and Negroes on the one hand and Southern "gothicists" on the other (this is a pattern rather than a formula, for it certainly does not account for many individuals who cross "sides" or who inhabit both), Fitzgerald prefigured the pattern in his own psyche. He identified with the South and with his father's aristocratic genealogy. He also identified with Manhattan and the Younger Generation. Amory is his "northern" self as Maury is his "southern," regardless of geography. That is, Maury's statement exists apart from and in repudiation of any exploration but the labyrinths of the self. That inflates it too much. Rather, Maury's statement exists in a context which insists that because self-knowledge is the only possible knowledge, all exterior values are impossible and all action, consequently, meaningless. Amory's independence of society is like that of a Thoreau, who insists that you must know yourself in order to know the world and to act in it. Maury's independence, however, is like that of a soft, gutted, and castrated Hemingway character—if such a thing can be imagined—whose private world, established to replace the disintegrated public one, is devoid of the codes of courage and discipline. All that Maury acknowledges are the imperatives of the self, a gratification of desires that are themselves meaningless except as subjects of gratification. Like Gloria, Maury too is characterized as an "ancient soul," old in the sense of the "stranger" whose companionship with the uni-

verse exists only in his recognition of its benignly indifferent
meaninglessness. Although it is suspiciously chic to discuss Fitzgerald in the overworked terms of irony and existentialism, it is
true, nevertheless, that in this one book Fitzgerald unwittingly
and sophomorically (if only he had had more intellect when he
was younger!) tried to create what comes close to existential characters. The asocial existential man is all that is left to him when
his character who is both moral *and social* is absent, and the tedium
of the novel is in itself an index of the extent to which Fitzgerald had to have his "adolescent" materials of social success or
die as an artist. In *The Beautiful and Damned* there is no interest
in the characters as there is, say, in the characters of Mailer or
Bellow when they are pushed out of a context of manners and into
the imperatives of a self which attempts to create new manners
rather than imitate the surrounding ones. Gloria, Maury, and
Anthony are in decay, but they are not decayed heroes. They are
neither tragic nor agonized. They are merely slobs.

The disagreeable ooze into which his characters settle when the
moral actor is removed from Fitzgerald's indispensable materials
is most evident in the character of Gloria. In *The Beautiful and
Damned,* as in all the novels, the golden girl is dramatized primarily in her effects upon the male hero. But in this book Fitzgerald offers the fullest development of the golden girl as an independent character. Isabel, Rosalind, and Eleanor were not so
much developed characters as they were impingements upon
Amory, as in fuller measure Daisy is upon Gatsby. Even Nicole,
when she is cured and belatedly takes on her liberated, golden-
girl heritage, finds little space remaining in *Tender Is the Night*
in which to enjoy her independent amours. But in *The Beautiful
and Damned,* the golden girl *as person* advances through all the
dramatized events coequally with the central male; and in that
sense, in the wider context of all of Fitzgerald's novels, she is central in *The Beautiful and Damned.* Fitzgerald was too full of the

just-married sense of having won "Rosalind," after all, to keep her from entering more fully into this book than into the others.

Anthony and Gloria have in common the zestful selfishness of Wilson's hard-hearted fairies, which makes them mirrors of each other in the same way that Eleanor and Amory were in *This Side of Paradise*. With some differences in character (Gloria has the courage of the spoiled girl who knows she is desirable to men, Anthony has the physical cowardice of the neurotic child), they are, as Gloria's Bilphist mother pronounces them and Amory ecstatically acknowledges, "twins." The sources, within their own characters, of their dependence on money, and the revelation of those sources together with the effects of that dependence, are the decay of human relationships and character that is the subject of the novel. Those sources are exactly the hearty and chill selfishness that Maury speaks about. The accumulating specifications of Gloria's pampered laziness and self-centered drifting that Fitzgerald offers the reader bring him back to the condemned values already made familiar in the first novel.

The specifications (as McKaig's diary, among many other sources, suggests) were taken in large measure from Gloria's prototype, Zelda. Replying to Wilson when Wilson sent him a pre-publication copy of his article for the *Bookman*, Fitzgerald wrote, "Now your three influences, St. Paul, Irish (incidentally, though it doesn't matter, I'm not Irish on father's side—that's where Francis Scott Key comes in) and liquor are all important I grant. But I feel less hesitancy asking you to remove the liquor because your catalogue is not complete anyhow—the most enormous influence on me in the four and a half years since I met her has been the complete, fine, and full-hearted selfishness and chill-mindedness of Zelda."[21] The full-heartedness is the pampered, zestful, and free courage to seize the moment that Fitzgerald marvelled at in his golden girls. The chill-mindedness gradually became trans-

[21] January 1922, *Letters*, p. 331.

lated from hard honesty to something else in his "heroines": that careless irresponsibility which coldly reasoned out a simple catechism of selfishness: love what gives you ease, youth, and fun, avoid what gives you responsibility and care. The golden girls' self-absorption and selfishness are prerequisites for the characterization of Gloria, even seven years before she is introduced into the story.

Gloria first appears as that essence of "Beauty" to whom the cosmic Voice announced her next avatar as a "susciety gurl," in a section entitled "A Flash-Back in Paradise." The appearances of Beauty are her essence, and her essence is her self-absorption. "She was incomprehensible, for, in her soul and spirit were one—*the beauty of her body was the essence of her soul.* . . . In this outdoor waiting room of winds and stars she had been sitting for a hundred years, *at peace in the contemplation of herself.* . . . Her lips scarcely stirring, her eyes turned, as *always, inward upon herself*" (pp. 27–28, italics mine). Maury recalls that the conversation he had in his initial meeting with her was centered upon that beautiful body: "Mostly . . . we talked about legs. . . . Hers. She talked a lot about hers. . . . She talked a lot about skin too—her own skin. Always her own" (pp. 48–49). And when he, in turn, meets her, Anthony too discovers that she "talked always about herself as a very charming child might talk. . . ."

" 'I must confess,' said Anthony gravely, 'that even *I've* heard one thing about you.'

"Alert at once, she sat up straight . . . 'Tell me. I'll believe it. I always believe anything anyone tells me about myself . . .' " (p. 60). When she talks to people, she catches "quickly . . . as she always did at any unexplained allusion to herself, however faint" (p. 97). She yawns when conversation veers away from the subject of herself, particularly when it comes close to any consideration of work and goals and next things. " 'I've told you I don't know what anybody ought to do,' she said ungraciously ["What'll we plan?" Daisy is to ask Nick Carraway in *The Great Gatsby*, "What do people plan?"], and at her indifference . . . [Anthony's] rancor was born again.

"'Aren't you interested in anything except yourself?'

"'Not much'" (p. 97).

The self-centered, coddled littleness of Gloria's world is one in which beauty, by its very essence, is childish selfishness and youth is babyish pettiness. The childishness of Gloria is repeatedly accented, not only by the gumdrops she "simply must" have and always eats, but by any of the numerous tantrum scenes, such as the waspish fit she permits herself at a restaurant during their honeymoon. Gloria simply must have a tomato sandwich and a lemonade as a midmorning snack. She simply must have a light lunch with a stuffed tomato. The tomato simply must be stuffed with celery. No one must dare jostle Gloria in her gustatory routine. But alas, the waiter brings a tomato stuffed with chicken.

No baby in a high chair faced with spinach responds more petulantly than she. She bangs her fist on the table, glares at the waiter, stamps her feet, insults Anthony, complains about the injustice of the universe and the provincialism of Los Angeles, where they are staying at the moment. And no baby in a high chair is more pampered, petted, and imperially crowned than she in a youth-centered world where the golden baby rules. This glowing babe finally subsides into a sulky silence and picks at the chicken. Will the heifer kick up her heels? All hold their breath while the idol poutingly tastes her food. O glorious golden calf! Snookums eats! All salaam in relief. Anthony quietly exhales. The universe resumes its development.

Fitzgerald moves on to other scenes, but not before he makes it clear that the analogy to a spoiled baby must be noted. Yet even at that, he insists that the golden girl, in her self-indulgence, does have a kind of glory—like Nicole Diver on her shopping sprees—that comes from the very wanton willfulness that nourishes the verve and grand gesture of the golden moment.

Anthony caters to his babywife because, given an allegiance to golden moments that is "twin" to hers, he knew that "it was yet problematical whether Gloria without her arrogance, her independence, her virginal confidence and courage, would be the girl of his glory, the radiant woman who was precious and charming because she was ineffably, triumphantly herself" (pp. 201–2). The streak of cheap sentimentality in Fitzgerald allowed him to think that his golden girl really was radiant, glorious, precious, and charming; but it is revealing that despite his explicit and implicit allegiances to her, what comes through is not her radiant and precious charm but the fact that she is ineffably, triumphantly, a spoiled bitch. The virginal independence and babyish courage of *Baby* Warren, like the virginal whiteness of Daisy and Jordan, whose eyes, like their dresses, show the impersonal absence of all desire, is prefigured in the virginal meanness of the early golden girls. Virginal meanness is not on the side of large life, with its fecundity, earth, sweat, and the consequences of next things. The beauty of the golden girl, like the beauty of Humbird, is deadly sterile. When Gloria thinks she is pregnant, her reaction is predictable and quite in character, for her whole shallow life is merely her appearances.

"I value my body because you think it's beautiful," she wails to Anthony. "And this body of mine—of yours—to have it grow ugly and shapeless? It's simply intolerable. Oh, Anthony, I'm not afraid of the pain."

He consoled her desperately—but in vain. She continued:

"And then afterward I might have wide hips and be pale, with all my freshness gone and no radiance in my hair."

" . . . You'd think you'd been singled out of all the women in the world for this crowning indignity."

"What if I do!" she cried angrily. "It isn't an indignity for them. It's their one excuse for living. It's the only thing they're good for. It *is* an indignity for *me*" (pp. 203–4).

[And when Gloria discovers that she is not going to have a child,

the kind of life she shares with Anthony is saved]: "It's all right," she
announced, smiling broadly. "And it surprised me more than it does
you."

"There's no doubt?"

"None! Couldn't be!"

They rejoiced happily, gay again *with reborn irresponsibility* (p.
209, italics mine).

Gloria is made for play, not creation, for appearances, not "next
things." As in *This Side of Paradise*, in *The Beautiful and Damned*
Fitzgerald continues to equate the beauty of the "hot cats on top"
with sham, illusion, and irresponsibility, and therefore with immorality, or evil. Indeed, Gloria's glory is in illusion and she
knows it, identifies with it, intensifying her beauty in the fact of
cheap sham. Anthony takes Gloria to a cabaret where pathetically
pretentious clerks take their pathetically pretentious dates and
middle-aged, middle-class book-keepers take their middle-aged,
middle-class wives. It is a cabaret where conventional people can
respectably go and pretend to an illusion that they fancy that there
is an appearance of illicit excitement, promiscuity, abandoned
gayety, and the high living of high society folk. But the passionate
pretense is punctured by the shabby decor, the gray food, the dirty
table cloths, and the careless familiarity of the waiters. The air is
thick with the hot, sticky hopefulness of social striving, with
economy-sized aspirations enveloping all illusions, and with the
sad and palpitating belief that all illusions will be found real—
at least for tonight. It is a world of show, sham, and tinsel, of paper
lanterns and a numbly squeaking orchestra. To Anthony's amazement, Gloria revels in this world, loves it, identifies with it, and
outshines all its tinny glitter as the embodied summation of all
the scintillation and radiance it can muster. "She was a sun . . .
growing, gathering light and storing it—then . . . pouring it forth
in a glance . . . to that part of him that cherished all beauty and
all illusion" (p. 73).

Gloria expects that the world will revolve around her, and she delights in the flurry of attention and the envy that centers upon her wherever she goes, taking it as her due, as a matter of course. The only meaning in life for her is fun suited to her beauty, and fun is whatever sensation will keep her from boredom and age. The insistent emphasis on tired middle-class expectations of a sudden change in financial identity (it is, after all, what Gloria and Anthony spend their lives at the center of the book representatively waiting for), together with attendant illusion and pretentiousness, points forward undeviatingly to *The Great Gatsby*. The appearances are all. The action of life for Gloria is to maintain the golden moment of her centrality: her beauty is but a means to itself, which is its own end. Being what she is, therefore, she is always and fully and "heartily" selfish. Her selfishness, irresponsibility, love of novelty, childishness, and chill-mindedness are, for her, honest expressions of her beauty, her courage, and her cruel egotism. "It was in her angers with their attendant cruelties that her inordinate egotism chiefly displayed itself. Because she was brave, because she was 'spoiled,' because of her outrageous and commendable independence of judgment, and finally because of her arrogant consciousness that she had never seen a girl as beautiful as herself, Gloria had developed into a consistent, practising Nietzschean" (p. 161).

The fact of age, which is the fact of the loss of beauty, is damnation. To be beautiful in terms of the golden moment is necessarily to be damned by the facts of earth. When Gloria is told that she is not quite young enough for the motion-picture part of a young wife, her entire world collapses:

*My dear Gloria* [reads the note from Bloeckman]:
   *We had the test run off yesterday afternoon, and Mr. Debris seemed to think that for the part he had in mind he needed a younger woman. He said that the acting was not bad, and that there was a small part supposed to be a very haughty rich widow that he thought you might—*

Desolately Gloria raised her glance until it fell out across the area-way. But she found she could not see the opposite wall, for her gray eyes were full of tears. She walked into the bedroom, the letter crinkled tightly in her hand, and sank down upon her knees before the long mirror on the wardrobe floor. This was her twenty-ninth birthday, and the world was melting away before her eyes. . . .

She strained to see until she could feel the flesh on her temples pull forward. Yes—the cheeks were ever so faintly thin, the corners of the eyes were lined with tiny wrinkles. The eyes were different. Why, they were different! . . . And then suddenly she knew how tired her eyes were.

"Oh, my pretty face," she whispered, passionately grieving. "Oh, my pretty face! Oh, I don't want to live without my pretty face! Oh, what's *happened?*"

Then she slid toward the mirror and, as in the test, sprawled face downward upon the floor—and lay there sobbing. It was the first awkward movement she had ever made (pp. 403–4).

Until she ages in fact, her age had been the agelessness of eternal youth. When Anthony first looked into her eyes, he saw that she is, like Maury Noble (the ageless essence of cynicism), an ancient soul indeed. "He saw, at length, that her eyes were gray, very level and cool, and when they rested on him he understood what Maury had meant by saying she was very young and very old" (p. 60). Her oldness is what her silly, Bilphist mother keeps referring to as "an ancient soul": the present incarnation is but one of an infinite number of avatars. As "A Flash-Back in Paradise" had explained, Gloria is only the momentary rebirth of the essence of eternal beauty in finite form. Gloria's "age," in short, is exactly that of the golden moment, and the essence of her love, as of her beauty, is measured—as it was in *This Side of Paradise*—in the sweet nostalgia of loss, which is the inevitable result of her "age": "Always the most poignant moments were when some artificial barrier kept them apart: in the theatre their hands would steal together, join, give and return gentle pressures through the long dark; in crowded rooms they would form words with their lips

for each other's eyes—not knowing that they were but following in
the footsteps of dusty generations but comprehending dimly that
if truth is the end of life happiness is a mode of it, to be cherished
in its brief and tremulous moment" (p. 137). In her diary, Gloria
lists various types of husbands, and chooses Anthony *because* he
too is a creature of moments only: "And Anthony—a temporarily
passionate lover with wisdom enough to realize when it has flown
and that it must fly. And I want to get married to Anthony." Further down the diary page, she adds (in phrasing Fitzgerald took
from Zelda), "Blowing bubbles—that's what we're doing, Anthony
and me. And we blew such beautiful ones to-day, and they'll explode and then we'll blow more and more, I guess—bubbles just
as big and just as beautiful, until all the soap and water is used
up" (p. 147). "Age," for Fitzgerald's major characters, *has* to be
the moment of youth, and though it is just to laugh at his sixteen-
year-old "speeds" and his "used-up" women of nineteen, it is
equally important to understand the crucial relevance of his
characters' youthfulness to his materials. The "next things" of
responsible maturity have no place in the values he repudiates:
"It was vaguely understood between . . . [Gloria and Anthony]
that on some misty day he would enter a sort of glorified diplo-
matic service and be envied by princes and prime ministers for
his beautiful wife.

"  'Well,' said Gloria helplessly, 'I'm sure I don't know [what
work she and Anthony will do]. We talk and talk and never get
anywhere, and we ask all our friends and they just answer the way
we want 'em to. I wish somebody'd take care of us' " (p. 171).

The damnation of the beautiful moment begins to be apparent
in Anthony's discovery that in his wedding to the spirit of beauty,
he has also wed a mortal incarnation of it. Marriage to the golden
moment translated into flesh is also a marriage to the necessity for
next things; *The Great Gatsby*'s theme of the discrepancy between
the ideal and the actual, between dream and history, is the logical

subject to occupy Fitzgerald's mind upon completion of *The Beautiful and Damned*. It is significant that as Anthony increasingly discovers Gloria's mortal shortcomings in the world of next things —she is *totally* irresponsible and cannot even take the trouble to send out the laundry to be cleaned—he feels the golden moment die out of their marriage. In turn, as Anthony demands next things and Gloria protests that they are not what she has been made for, she too feels the glow fade. Subject to male worries about contingencies, Anthony does not share Gloria's "existential" courage. One night, investigating a noise in their hotel room, Anthony discloses himself to be a coward who lies about his fears, his pretense about physical danger indicating his general inability to meet the demands of the actual. Had he been a Dawson Ryder or a Tom Buchanan, one of those stalwart, moneyed, beefy, stolid "backgrounds" of a man against whom Gloria could scintillate, there would be no problems—as, indeed, there never really are any problems for Tom and Daisy, for Rosalind and Dawson. They are too selfish to be morally or profoundly touched by the consequences of their irresponsible insistence upon uninvolvement in time and events. Money preserves butterflies and flashing ephemerae. But Anthony, anything but beefy and solid, has himself a "heightened sensibility to the promises of life," and without Gatsby's toughness and ability to use the world of next things in order to attain the golden moment, his sensitivities turn out to be merely bad nerves. He cannot provide the freedom from conditions and actualities that the golden girl requires. Further, dedicated to the golden moment to which his sensitivities respond, Anthony is himself "female" in his own need to be provided for. (This aspect of his own personality Fitzgerald referred to directly, as well as obliquely in the characterization of his fictional personae, as feminine.) Anthony's inability to fulfill his "male" role, which demanded that he preserve a carefree insouciance for Gloria, in turn makes it impossible for her to preserve that essence

for which he married her. Increasingly they discover that sensitivity, excitement, and the lightheartedness of fairies demand money.
As the money fades, so do Gloria's "Neitzschean" nerves, until
she becomes as jumpily aware of vulnerability as Anthony had
been. Even at the very beginning of their married life, soon after
they had first begun to smell their own mortality, they displayed
the overprotected sensitivities that help reduce them to the
wrecks they become. In the chapter named "The Radiant Hour,"
in a section significantly named "The End of a Chapter," their
high-strung fearfulness is given center stage:

Gloria's penchant for premonitions and her bursts of vague super-
naturalism were a surprise to Anthony. Either some complex, properly and scientifically inhibited in the early years with her Bilphistic
mother, or some inherited hypersensitiveness, made her susceptible
to any suggestion of the psychic, and, far from gullible about the
motives of people, she was inclined to credit any extraordinary
happening attributed to the whimsical perambulations of the buried.
The desperate squeakings about the old house on windy nights that
to Anthony were burglars with revolvers ready in hand represented to
Gloria the auras, evil and restive, of dead generations, expiating the
inexpiable upon the ancient and romantic hearth. One night, because
of two swift bangs downstairs, which Anthony fearfully but unavail-
ingly investigated, they lay awake nearly until dawn asking each other
examination-paper questions about the history of the world (p. 187).

Their fearful reaction to their imagined ghosts and burglars, to
swiftly unsnapping window shades in hotel rooms and knocks in
the night in the old house in Marietta (in both cases the noises
represent actions that threaten their cozy and hidden isolation
from the outside world, from the history to which they respond
with "examination-paper questions"), is symptomatic of the fear
of intrusion from the mundane world of necessities. In the snug
and sterile cocoon of their irresponsible world, however, if they
are saved from the ugly necessities of sweat, they are also cut off
from the vitality of life (the book badly needs Myrtle Wilson of

*The Great Gatsby),* and that is the real damnation of the golden people. Their impending loss of the youthful moment is encapsuled in the instants that they are aware of the inescapable boredom of their isolation from life, the dull smoothness of their protected routines.

As the conversation [between Anthony, Gloria, and Bloeckman, the movie magnate] continued in stilted commas, Anthony wondered that to him and Bloeckman both this girl [Gloria] had once been the most stimulating, the most tonic personality they had ever known—and now the three sat like overoiled machines, without conflict, without fear, without elation, heavily enamelled little figures secure beyond enjoyment in a world where death and war, dull emotion and noble savagery were covering a continent with the smoke of terror.

In a moment he would call Tana [the Japanese servant] and they would pour into themselves a gay and delicate poison which would restore them momentarily to the pleasurable excitement of childhood, when every face in a crowd had carried its suggestion of splendid and significant transactions taking place somewhere to some magnificent and illimitable purpose. . . . Life was no more than this summer afternoon; a faint wind stirring the lace collar of Gloria's dress; the slow baking drowsiness of the veranda. . . . Intolerably unmoved they all seemed, removed from any romantic immediacy of action. Even Gloria's beauty needed wild emotions, needed poignancy, needed death . . . (pp. 213–14).

And so the dilemma that damns the beautiful. To work for money is to enter the world of next things, and that entrance blunts both the beauty and the sensitivity to beauty—it "shows the marks." Anthony refuses to sweat. The refusal means less money. Less money means an increased hysteria in the face of the palpably increasing speed with which the golden glow fades. As that fades, all identity, purpose, and meaning fade. In order to cling to identity, beauty's personality needs more money. The increased need for money increases the blunting effects of need, and so on and on to the damnation in which all the blowy cleanliness of youthful freshness is totally and irretrievably lost. Finally, the

theme of the golden moment leads back to its beginning in Fitzgerald's vision of his essential materials: as wealth is its own re-
ward, it is for that very reason its own damnation. Their essence
lost by the time they win the lawsuits, Anthony and Gloria no
longer have anything that the money at one time was supposed to
have preserved and made meaningful. Literally, the money cannot buy back the joy of which it was supposed to have been the
invulnerable guarantee. And yet—if they only had had the money . . . . The reader, like Paul Rosenfeld, is ironically left desiring
the very vulgarity of wealth which was supposed to have been the
foundation supporting the essence of beauty. The romance of
money, as Malcolm Cowley called it, is given its poignancy by its
irony, which is exactly what Fitzgerald saw and wanted his reader
to see.

Yet it is in the very success with which Fitzgerald details his view
of the ironical interrelationships of money, beauty, joy, and betrayal in America, that Fitzgerald's novel fails. In order to make
meaningful the damnation of the beautiful, Fitzgerald should
have introduced some contrast between the betraying force and
the beauty-lover, with his heightened sensitivity to the promises
of life. But in this novel beauty and the love of it are figured in a
couple which is both personification of its essence and its betrayer.
Fitzgerald had made Anthony and Gloria too much the "twins,"
had not yet seen that he had to separate Gatsby and Daisy, and
then underscore the difference with the perspective of the moral
commentator, the Nick Carraway. *The Beautiful and Damned*
follows too closely Fitzgerald's sense of identification with his
newly won Zelda, and in the composite character of the "twins,"
Anthony-Gloria is the golden girl only, without even the unsuccessfully dramatized differences between Amory and his succession
of golden girls. As *Tender Is the Night* will demonstrate, when
Fitzgerald gains control over and artistic distance from the materials he is buried in up to his ears, he will know beautifully well

what to do with the merged identities that destroy the differences
between the boys and the girls. But in this early novel, there is as
yet no controlling differentiation between any of the actors, which
means that the very world the actors inhabit is only an extension
of their lives. Edmund Wilson comes at this point when he says
that "in spite of their madness . . . [Anthony and Gloria] are the
most rational people in the book." There is no alternative universe of values anywhere in the novel, so that Anthony and Gloria
and Richard Caramel and Maury Noble and Joseph Bloeckman
never offer any alternatives to each other, and the society they live
in is, if anything, even worse than they are.

The lack of alternatives marks the end of the *Bildungsroman*
for Fitzgerald. Anthony's decay is jazz-age America's coming of
middle age. The Younger Generation does not find itself *in society*
in Fitzgerald's books, for the vocations of its representative young
man have nothing to do with the social promise implicit in the
last view of Amory Blaine. In point of fact, in Fitzgerald's fiction
Jay Gatsby is a bootlegger, and in his integration into the world
of next things he is integrated into gangsterism; Dick Diver is
a doctor who doesn't practice: as a psychiatrist he loses his ability
to reconcile people to the actual as he loses his ability to believe
in the values of the society to which he would reintegrate his
patients; Monroe Stahr is a movie tycoon who no longer controls
his own industry: he is a fading celestial luminary in a world
which has outlived him and to which he no longer belongs. As
one of our disillusioned romantics, Fitzgerald looks forward, like
*Huckleberry Finn* before him, to the outcast and outlaw as hero
when "sivilization" proves to be filled with what the journeying
hero is escaping from. Fitzgerald's perennial appeal is essentially
the same as Twain's: both writers evoke a particular vernacular
in speech and in manners through their sharp eye for representative detail, and make their materials a microcosm of the history
of a nation. Old-fashioned as he is in the context of the hip litera-

ture and heroes of this present moment, Fitzgerald, again like Twain, connects the social hero of genteel American fiction to the underground man of post–World War II fiction.

All of his main characters are damned as non-belongers, reflecting his own sense of never really belonging to the rich world he observed; furthermore there is no vantage point of moral perspective on the part of anyone involved in the action of *The Beautiful and Damned*. Consequently, in order to provide a measure for his characters' damnation, Fitzgerald had to revert to the trick of the devil-figure, used to better advantage in *This Side of Paradise*, from which he copied even such details as the devil's conspicuously odd feet.[22] In *The Beautiful and Damned* the "devil" is a dirty man named Joe Hull. Significantly, the "devil" appears at one of the endless, pointless, drunken parties, as he did when Amory met him. Joe Hull is brought to the Patches' house by Maury Noble and Richard Caramel, both of them silly with drink. He is small, dirty, unshaved, menacing, and appears oddly ominous to Gloria and Anthony. His dirtiness seems somehow total and is the opposite of the blowy cleanness the Patches are rapidly losing. His feet repel Gloria, for his queer toes seem visible through the soft white material that encases them. Gloria is both angered and frightened by the strangely easy familiarity he displays toward her, and her feelings are intensified by the insidious insistence with which, against her will, Hull (Hell?) tempts others to drink more and more.

Retiring to her room in disgust, Gloria lies on her bed.

She became rigid. Some one had come to the door and was standing regarding her, very quiet except for a slight swaying motion. She could see the outline of his figure distinct against some indistinguishable

---

22 From his early childhood, Fitzgerald associated feet with something shameful or even fearful in his own mind. In his "Ledger" entry for August 1901, Fitzgerald wrote of himself that "Again he went to Atlantic City—where some Freudean [sic] complex refused to let him display his *feet*, so he refused to swim, concealing the real reason. They thought he feared the water. In reality he craved it." And again

light. There was no sound anywhere, only a great persuasive silence—
even the dripping [of the rain from the trees] had ceased . . . only this
figure, swaying, swaying in the doorway, an indiscernible and subtly
menacing terror, a personality filthy under its varnish, like smallpox
spots under a layer of powder. Yet her tired heart, beating until it
shook her breasts, made her sure that there was still life in her, desperately shaken, threatened. . . .

The minute or succession of minutes prolonged itself interminably,
and a swimming blur began to form before her eyes, which tried with
childish persistence to pierce the gloom in the direction of the door.
In another instant it seemed that some unimaginable force would
shatter her out of existence . . . and then the figure in the doorway—it
was Hull, she saw, Hull—turned deliberately and, still slightly swaying, moved back and off, as if absorbed into that incomprehensible
light that had given him dimension.

Blood rushed back into her limbs, blood and life together. With a
start of energy she sat upright, shifting her body until her feet touched
the floor over the side of the bed. She knew what she must do—now,
now, before it was too late. She must go out into this cool damp, out,
away, to feel the wet swish of grass around her feet and the fresh
moisture on her forehead (pp. 242–43).

There is, repeated from *This Side of Paradise*, the identification
of the menace as "personality," the repeated need to re-contact
simple and earthy things, the repeated unearthly illumination of
the threatening horror. But even though Amory's flight is also
repeated, in this book the golden girl is not changed by the flight.
The visitation is not explicitly supernatural, as it was in *This Side
of Paradise*, where it was as out of place as it would be in this novel.
But Joe Hull disappears from this novel as swiftly as he entered it,
as swiftly as the devil disappears from *This Side of Paradise*, and
the intrusion, though thematically functional, is sadly mechanical.

Not only does a dramatic lack of moral alternatives in characterization drive Fitzgerald to mechanical methods, but—even

---

in the entry for July 1903: "There was also a little boy named Arnold who went
barefooted in his yard and peeled plums. Scott's freudian [sic] shame about his
feet kept him from joining in." Quoted in Turnbull, *Scott Fitzgerald*, pp. 9, 11.

though he condemns what he describes—the very similarity between authorial attitudes and those of the characters further narrows the range of the book. Still loathe to abandon the supposed
attitudes of the "right" people, Fitzgerald shares with them the
snobbery that he shared in *This Side of Paradise*. He presents the
top two layers of elite society as the new season begins. Then he
uncovers

... a third layer from the skirts of the city, from Newark and the Jersey
suburbs up to bitter Connecticut and the ineligible sections of Long
Island—and doubtless contiguous layers down to the city's shoes: Jew-
esses were coming out into a society of Jewish men and women, from
Riverside to the Bronx, and looking forward to a rising young broker
or jeweller and a kosher wedding; Irish girls were casting their eyes,
with license at last to do so, upon a society of young Tammany pol-
iticians, pious undertakers, and grown-up choir-boys.

And, naturally, the city caught the contagious air of entré—the
working girls, poor ugly souls, wrapping soap in the factories and
showing finery in the big stores, dreamed that perhaps in the spectacu-
lar excitement of this winter they might obtain for themselves the
coveted male—as in a muddled carnival crowd an inefficient pick-pocket
may consider his chances increased (pp. 31–32).

The authorial attitudes explicit in the identification of the city's
"shoes" and the class status of "poor ugly souls" are as schizo-
phrenically allied with those of the major characters as they were
in *This Side of Paradise*.

And what has become of the exalted "social service" among
the "poor ugly souls" that Amory Blaine was to save? It has become fashionably Menckenized. Richard Caramel (whose works,
except for the *Demon Lover*, are as stickily sweet as his name)[23]

---

23 *The Demon Lover* was one of the titles that Fitzgerald earlier had in mind
for his own second book. Evidently Fitzgerald liked his titles and associated them
with literary quality: *The Demon Lover*, Caramel's first book, was his only good
one. As he deteriorated into the self-deceived hack that Fitzgerald was afraid he
himself might become, Caramel showed his own shallowness and obtuseness to
literary quality by scorning a new book named *This Side of Paradise*.

is a writer, the young man of hopes and goals and social sense and
next things. But even though he is the only character in the book
who actually and laboriously works, his works become increasingly
fraudulent and trashy. It is as though Fitzgerald were trying to
write out of himself and exorcise both his own optimisms and his
own facile ability to write trash—which he was so afraid he could
too easily do—and yet to remain modishly sophisticated at the
same time. The spirit of social service is all right as a temperance
lecture for "farmers' wives and pious drug clerks," but it has no
real place in the life of one of the smart set. For a while that spirit

. . . was strong enough to wind a sinuous tentacle about Richard Caramel. The year after his graduation it called him into the slums of
New York *to muck about with bewildered Italians* as secretary to
an "Alien Young Men's Rescue Association." He labored at it over a
year before the monotony began to weary him. *The aliens kept coming
inexhaustibly*—Italians, Poles, Scandinavians, Czechs, Armenians—with
the same wrongs, *the same exceptionally ugly faces and very much the
same smells,* though he fancied that these grew more profuse and diverse as the months passed. His eventual conclusions about the expe-
diency of service were vague, but concerning his own relation to it they
were abrupt and decisive. Any amiable young man, his head ringing
with the latest crusade, could accomplish as much as he could with *the
débris of Europe*—and it was time for him to write.
    He had been living in a down-town Y.M.C.A., but when he quit *the
task of making sow-ear purses out of sow's ears,* he moved up-town
and went to work immediately as a reporter for *The Sun* (pp. 74–75,
italics mine, and for obvious reasons).

Again the snobbery is at least as much Fitzgerald's as Caramel's,
and it is constant for every character. When Gloria—to whom the
"common" people are so many "chattering apes" and "lice," and
who says that she would let millions of them die to preserve one
beautiful thing—explodes into furious contempt at the sight of
"hot, unprosperous people" visiting General Lee's mansion and
trailing peanut shells (the old, lovely America debased again), it

is Fitzgerald rather than Anthony who agrees. Anthony serves only as a foil for Gloria's patrician righteousness, and it is the author's, not the character's, choice to close the scene with the following corroborative detail: "A small boy appeared beside them and, swinging a handful of banana-peels, flung them valiantly in the direction of the Potomac" (p. 167).

The crucial difference between the hot unprosperous people and the cool prosperous ones is significantly one of appearances. The poor are always old and ugly, the rich are graceful and young, and without the accustomed fact of wealth, the poor cannot possibly imitate the rich: "A simple healthy leisure class it was—the best of the men not unpleasantly undergraduate . . . the women, of more than average beauty, fragilely athletic, somewhat idiotic as hostesses but charming and infinitely decorative as guests. Sedately and gracefully they danced the steps of their selection in the balmy tea hours, accomplishing with a certain dignity the movements so horribly burlesqued by clerk and chorus girl the country over" (pp. 191–92).

Fitzgerald's snobbery and early racism are integral parts of his vision of his materials, those parts that composed the adolescent hunger for the "personality" identity of the very different rich hot cats on top. As his awareness of the shallowness of the adolescent dream grows more profound in his later use of his materials, so his snobbery and racism cease to exist as such, and in *The Great Gatsby* and *Tender Is the Night* the attitudes of snobbery become functional rather than pretentious. Which is only another way of saying that as Fitzgerald felt himself coming closer and closer to the failure of the dream he became more of an artist. And as the contrast between his early and later letters shows, he also became richer in sympathy as poorer in pocket, more tender as more weary, more human as less facile. *The Beautiful and Damned* is Fitzgerald's last act of apprenticeship as a novelist as he moves closer to a full moral awareness of his materials. It is not insignificant that in this book even those values—or at least postures—in which Fitzgerald concurs are unexceptionably associated with a world in which there are no alternatives to human failure. Most significant, those postures were associated with identification with the aristocracy of an older, more homogeneous America. Like Wilson, who, in *I Thought of Daisy*, recognized that the new heterogeneous American "folk" were the reality that the old identities and manners no longer were, Fitzgerald was to come to see that they, with names like Gatz, had to be the subject of the fiction of democratic cosmopolitanism. Until one wrestled sympathetically with the aspirations of the new, there could be no alternatives to mere decay in the fictional presentation of the death of the old. If the lack of alternatives forced mechanical techniques, like the way in which the devil-figure was used, the very mechanical quality of the techniques in *The Beautiful and Damned* was a sign that Fitzgerald had come to the end of the mere chronicling of his materials and was forced by those materials to a growing awareness of his theme. With a bit more experience of the incipient failure of his own golden moment, he would be able to control both his materials and his attitudes in order to weld them into a coherent theme. The end of apprenticeship, as always, called for experience.

The essential fault of *The Beautiful and Damned* is that of *This Side of Paradise:* the density is that of the imagination not yet ripened by experience. Fitzgerald's materials led to manic elations and depressions. At first they led to the expectation of American tawdry innocence, a tinsel Eden. So *This Side of Paradise* rides the upswing of adolescent hope, and because Fitzgerald had not yet himself experienced the objective facts of success and the big world of money, his accounts of them ring false. So the companion piece, *The Beautiful and Damned*, rides the downswing of the rocket and because Fitzgerald himself had not yet experienced the objective facts of failure and the ruin of health

through dissipation, the events have the tinny sound of intellectual fashion rather than the richness of the tragedy of character in
decay. Indeed, the only account of degeneration that does ring
true is the kind of detail that seems to be borrowed vicariously
from life through Dreiser.[24] By the time he wrote *The Great
Gatsby*, Fitzgerald had experienced the gaudy spree of success,
and one never doubts the specifications of experience imaginatively reconstructed there. So too by the time he wrote *Tender Is
the Night* he had experienced the facts of failure and dissipation
and one never doubts the experience rendered with "the authority of failure," as Fitzgerald put it. In the web of connections that
relate the novels to each other, *The Great Gatsby*, one may say, is
the romantic readiness of *This Side of Paradise* experienced, as
*Tender Is the Night* is the dying fall of *The Beautiful and Damned*
experienced. But as long as *The Beautiful and Damned* remains
in its main lines (not in its specifics of the parties and tea dances
actually experienced, which give the book whatever life it has)
solely an act of the imagination, it is oppressively tedious in its
musty tale of failure as *This Side of Paradise* was often oppressively
giddy in its youthful tale of anticipation. Also, because the possibility of human failure as well as the prescription for it had been
foreshadowed in *This Side of Paradise*, Fitzgerald is not in the
process of discovering as much about himself or his materials in
his second novel as he was in his first. *The Beautiful and Damned*
is an act of consolidation rather than discovery. Certainly it is a

---

24 The close parallel between the decay of Anthony in his apartment and the
decay of Hurstwood in his makes one suspect that the specific model was *Sister
Carrie*. Fitzgerald was very conscious of the "naturalistic" school, especially
Dreiser and Norris. In a letter to James Branch Cabell he offers one of many statements of literary debt, although the statement of debt to Cabell smacks more of
Fitzgerald's constant desire to be favored by those who have arrived than of literary actuality: "I have just finished an extraordinary novel called *The Beautiful
Lady Without Mercy* [the title was later changed to *The Beautiful and Damned*]
which shows touches of your influence, much of Mencken, and not a little of Frank
Norris. Up to now such diverse writers as you, Mencken, Dreiser, and so forth have
been held together more or less by the common enemy, philistia. . . ." Christmas
1920, *Letters*, p. 464.

more controlled, less self-indulgent novel than was *This Side of Paradise*,[25] but perhaps that fact only indicates that for some subjects—most probably for the subject of the young man finding himself—excitement is worth at least as much as control. Despite its significance in the development of Fitzgerald's main themes, *The Beautiful and Damned* is the least successful of all his books in general energy and in the growth of Fitzgerald's phrases and rhythms of evocation. Yet, in its themes and characters it also carries the forward motion of pointing inevitably toward *The Great Gatsby*. It was an absolutely necessary book, for only from the consolidation of both aspects of his materials, the anticipation as well as the failure, and from the artistic control the consolidation gave him could he move forward to his high creations. *The Beautiful and Damned* was the end of the golden moment.

Later, when he was all too well educated in the "authority of failure," in his retrospective view of life with Zelda his memory occasionally tried to submerge the specific agonies of experience in nostalgic grief, remorse, and kindness:

> Do you remember, before keys turned in the locks,
> When life was a close-up, and not an occasional letter,
> That I hated to swim naked from the rocks
> While you liked absolutely nothing better?
>
> Do you remember many hotel bureaus that had
> Only three drawers? But the only bother
> Was that each of us got holy, then got mad,
> Trying to give the third one to the other.
>
> East, West, the little car turned, right or wrong
> Up an erroneous Alp, an unmapped Savoy river.
> We blamed each other in cadences acid and strong
> And, in an hour, laughed and called it liver.

[25] For a study of the differences between *This Side of Paradise* and *The Beautiful and Damned* in terms of "control" *vs.* "saturation," see James E. Miller, Chapters I, II, and III.

> And, though the end was desolate and unkind:
> To turn the calendar at June and find December
> On the next leaf; still, stupid-got with grief, I find
> These are the only quarrels that I can remember.

Haunted by memory as he was, if only, for his own sake, that had really been true; for what created the art helped destroy the man. He remembered so much more.

# CHAPTER III

# THE GREAT GATSBY

## *A Willingness of the Heart*

HE REMEMBERED THIS: Zelda Sayre's house in Montgomery, Alabama, had been a world-center for him once, when he had been a lost and ambitious young second lieutenant in nearby Camp Sheridan. Fitzgerald changed the locale to Louisville, and the name to that of the Kentucky camp where he had trained, Camp Taylor, but the description of Daisy and her house in *The Great Gatsby* was at least as much an act of memory as of invention: "She was just eighteen . . . and by far the most popular of all the young girls in Louisville . . . and all day long the telephone rang in her house and excited young officers from Camp Taylor demanded the privilege of monopolizing her that night. 'Anyways for an hour!' "[1] Fitzgerald had not sprung from a low caste as had Gatsby, but his own sense of middle-class placelessness, his own hunger for self and fame among the hot cats on top in the world of his imagination, his own identification of the golden girl as the key and sign of that world, give Gatsby's response to Daisy

---

[1] *The Great Gatsby,* in *Three Novels of F. Scott Fitzgerald,* ed. Malcolm Cowley and Edmund Wilson (New York, 1953), p. 57. All further references to this text are indicated by parentheses in the body of the chapter.

and her house an essential community with Fitzgerald's sense of Zelda and hers:

> He found her excitingly desirable. He went to her house, at first with other officers from Camp Taylor, then alone. It amazed him—he had never been in such a beautiful house before. But what gave it an air of breathless intensity was that Daisy lived there—it was as casual a thing to her as his tent out at camp was to him. There was a ripe mystery about it, a hint of bedrooms upstairs more beautiful and cool than other bedrooms, of gay and radiant activities taking place through its corridors, and of romances that were not musty and laid away already in lavender, but fresh and breathing and redolent of this year's shining motor-cars and of dances whose flowers were scarcely withered. It excited him, too, that many men had already loved Daisy—it increased her value in his eyes. He felt their presence all about the house, pervading the air with the shades and echoes of still vibrant emotions.
>
> But he knew that he was in Daisy's house by a colossal accident. However glorious might be his future as Jay Gatsby, he was at present a penniless young man without a past, and at any moment the invisible cloak of his uniform might slip from his shoulders (p. 113).

However glorious might be his future as F. Scott Fitzgerald, the writer, he was at present a penniless young man, and both Zelda and her letters became increasingly "nervous" as Scott failed to come through with fame and fortune, while all the time there was the pressure of other beaus, more solid young men— "backgrounds," like Rosalind's Dawson Ryder.[2] Finally, Zelda was unwilling to continue the tension of remaining out of action while waiting for Scott to amass money, and she broke off the engagement, disappearing back into her gay world of parties and dances and attractive young men exactly as Daisy was to do in the novel. But then Fitzgerald triumphed with *This Side of Paradise*, so Zelda changed her mind, and he won his girl, too. But he never

---

[2] For Zelda's "nervousness" see Arthur Mizener, *The Far Side of Paradise* in the Vintage edition (New York, 1959), pp. 87–100, especially p. 87; and Andrew Turnbull, *Scott Fitzgerald* (New York, 1962), pp. 84–105 and pp. 150–51.

forgot what he had grown up knowing in his bones: the American dream and American wealth are inseparably related. The rich will take as a matter of course what the poor can't win. Scott was always nagged by a repressed knowledge of what would have happened if he hadn't hit the jackpot, and he exorcised that alternative—but real—losing self by naming him Jay Gatsby. So, as Daisy waits for Gatsby to come home from the war, increasingly she resents her seclusion and finally cuts it short. Gatsby

was worried now—there was a quality of nervous despair in Daisy's letters. She didn't see why he couldn't come. She was feeling the pressure of the world outside, and she wanted to see him and feel his presence beside her and be reassured that she was doing the right thing after all.

For Daisy was young and her artificial world was redolent of orchids and pleasant, cheerful snobbery and orchestras which set the rhythm of the year, summing up the sadness and suggestiveness of life in its new tunes. All night the saxaphones wailed the hopeless comment of the *Beale Street Blues* while a hundred pairs of golden and silver slippers shuffled the shining dust. At the gray tea hour there were always rooms that throbbed incessantly with this low, sweet fever, while fresh faces drifted here and there like rose petals blown by the sad horns around the floor.

Through this twilight universe Daisy began to move again with the season; suddenly she was again keeping half a dozen dates a day with half a dozen men, and drowsing asleep at dawn with the beads and chiffon of an evening dress tangled among dying orchids on the floor beside her bed. . . . She wanted her life shaped now, immediately— and the decision must be made by some force—of love, of money, of unquestionable practicality—that was close at hand.

That force took shape in the middle of spring with the arrival of Tom Buchanan. There was a wholesome bulkiness about his person and his position and Daisy was flattered (p. 115).

Later, in "Handle with Care," one of the three articles that Edmund Wilson edited as *The Crack-Up*, Fitzgerald summed it all up in one of the passages that, perhaps more than any other passage he ever wrote, has attracted commentators to quote and requote it. Talking about what went into making his psyche, Fitzgerald said,

"The other episode [the first was also one of toppling from the heights of the golden moment, at Princeton] . . . took place after the war, when I had again over-extended my flank. It was one of those tragic loves doomed for lack of money, and one day the girl closed it out on the basis of common sense. During a long summer of despair I wrote a novel [*This Side of Paradise*] instead of letters, so it came out all right, but it came out all right for a different person. The man with the jingle of money in his pocket who married the girl a year later would always cherish an abiding distrust, an animosity, toward the leisure class—not the conviction of a revolutionist but the smouldering hatred of a peasant. In the years since then I have never been able to stop wondering where my friends' money came from, nor to stop thinking that at one time a sort of *droit de seigneur* might have been exercised to give one of them my girl."

"That was always my experience," he wrote near the end of his life, "—a poor boy in a rich town; a poor boy in a rich boy's school; a poor boy in a rich man's club at Princeton. . . . I have never been able to forgive the rich for being rich, and it has colored my entire life and works." He told a friend that "the whole idea of Gatsby is the unfairness of a poor young man not being able to marry a girl with money. This theme comes up again and again because I lived it."[3]

Gatsby's cry to Tom, when he thinks that finally he will remake his past, comes from the depths of Fitzgerald's imaginative memory: " 'She never loved you, do you hear?' he cried. 'She only married you because I was poor and she was tired of waiting for me. It was a terrible mistake, but in her heart she never loved any one except me!' " (p. 99).

So Fitzgerald remembered this, too: the girl is wealth's accomplice and possession. As the product and symbol of the desired world of wide green lawns and exciting white houses and romantic lives she is inevitably what Isabelle, Rosalind, Eleanor, and Gloria

[3] Turnbull, *Scott Fitzgerald*, p. 150.

were in their promising allurement. She belongs to the highest
bidder, the man who most controls the actualities at the center of the world of the imagined future. The story is a repetition
of what the earlier books pointed toward: to win the king's daughter, the golden girl, who lives high in the white palace, was to win
a fraud because her actualities are never equal to, and so are a betrayal of, the enormously imagined golden world she represents to
the innocent, hungry seeker. In *The Great Gatsby*, Fitzgerald
made out of his life with Zelda and his dream a moral history of
the gnawing and murderous disappointment attendant upon discovering that the gorgeousness of America exists not in her glittering actualities, past or present, East or West, but in the fantastic
sense of possibilities that drives the imagination of the archetypal
American, the eternal pioneer in search of the golden moment
dreamed in the past and to be recaptured in the imagined future.
"That's the whole burden of [*The Great Gatsby*]," Fitzgerald
wrote to a friend during the summer he was writing the novel,"—
the loss of those illusions that give such color to the world so that
you don't care whether things are true or false as long as they partake of the magical glory."[4] The instant that the illusion is wedded
to an actuality of experience—for Fitzgerald it was always the
representative golden girl—the dream seems to split in two. Half
of its energy goes on trying to believe that the girl *is* the realization of the magical glory, half goes on trying to express the right
to that glory in the materials at hand. For Gatsby the materials
were wealth through phoney stocks and through bootlegging,
were parties, were a house, a car. For Fitzgerald the materials
were the "all" of "But, my God! it was my material, and it was all
I had to deal with" that he referred to in his introduction to the
Modern Library edition of *The Great Gatsby*, when he defended
himself against critics who complained that he could only write
about people of wealth, parties, houses, and cars.

[4] *Ibid.*, p. 342, n. 151.

But the dream never really divides. The creative energies that
go into the materials are those that try to make the real world the
imagined one. For Gatsby the goal was the ecstasy of Daisy, for
Fitzgerald the ecstasy of art; for both it was the expectation, and
momentary realization—expressed in the excitement of wealth
and parties—of ecstasy in life. Daisy and art were the entrances to
the rapturous, transcendent state of being of the dream, and the
materials—wealth or art—but a means to the entrance.

It is important here to specify the idea of "the American dream,"
for the term is used continually, and, unless it is understood clearly, becomes too inclusive and vague a generalization. Except for
special (and very natively American) Utopian concepts, the dream
is a dream of self rather than community. Whether one confronts
the Jeffersonian insistence that the purpose of the state's existence
is to guarantee and extend the private and independent liberty of
the individual, or one confronts the ideas in *Walden*, "Self Re-
liance," or "Song of Myself," one reads concepts in which the
liberated individual is the measure of value. And in all cases,
short story or novel, the dream of Fitzgerald's characters is a dream
of self at the lustrous moment of emergence from wanting greatness to being great—Amory's dream. The state of yearning is an
expectant present tense dictatorially bound by the future, a repudiation of the present as a state of impatient placelessness in being
less than the imagined self, a state of loss to be replaced in the future by being the sublime self whose name everyone knows. It
is a dream of self, however clothed, that the history of American expectations—from the conquistadores' greedy vision merged
with eighteenth-century ideas of perfectibility and with nine-
teenth-century Romantic ideologies of the self—developed into an
American heritage of the possibility of total transcendence. (Like
Fitzgerald, I think that the real history of America, written so far in
the literature rather than in the history books, is the history of its
expectations.) The dream of self is one of absolute liberation from

the conditional world of circumstances, from the world of sweat, and of next things, and showing the marks. A secular ecstasy, it is nothing less, in its naive splendor, than what must be called liberation from mortality. Having much in common with American Ahab, Fitzgerald's characters, unlike Ahab's creator, do not read Emerson or Thoreau or Whitman or the continua of thought that channeled into them from the past and out of them into the future; but they do have a sense of the self as a "god in ruins" to be liberated in the future, as a radiant butterfly emerging from the grub, as a "kosmos." In Fitzgerald's mind, the characteristically American idea is an amalgam of feelings, romantic and adolescent emotions, bound up with the historical idea of America as the released new world, and, therefore, with the old promise of the vast Golden West. But Fitzgerald was acutely aware that the idea of the self had been relocated, from the 1880's on, in the shining wealth of the growing, magnetic cities in the East. For Dreiser, Chicago had been the dream city in the making—"It sang, I thought, and I was singing with it"—and for the younger midwesterner, like Fitzgerald, that dreamworld had already moved further eastward, to New York.

He had long dreamed of "the Far-away East," as he wrote in one of the Basil Duke Lee stories, "Forging Ahead," "the faraway East, that he had loved with a vast nostalgia since he had first read books about great cities. Beyond the dreary railroad stations of Chicago and the night fires of Pittsburgh, back in the old states, something went on that made his heart beat fast with excitement. He was attuned to the vast, breathless bustle of New York, to the metropolitan days and nights that were tense as singing wires. Nothing needed to be imagined there, for it was all the very stuff of romance—life was as vivid and satisfactory as in books and dreams."[5] Fitzgerald knew that the stuff of American wealth was the city sign of the American promise—attainment of the gold

[5] *Afternoon of an Author*, ed. Arthur Mizener (London, 1958), p. 47.

was to be attainment of the golden moment. To be rich, for Fitzgerald's characters, and to have the appearances of wealth, were
in and of themselves not important. Gatsby was perfectly willing
to "turn off" his gaudy house the moment he sees that Daisy
disapproves of it. Yet Fitzgerald also knew that for most of American society, the highly imagined Emersonian sense of possibilities
had deteriorated to vague and discontented desires for wealth
and the commodities and identity of wealth—in short, that the
appearances of wealth are at once all there is and are yet empty to
the fulfillment of the dream of self beyond wealth. Like Emerson
and Thoreau, Fitzgerald knew that in America there had been
an enormous displacement of the possibilities of self by the possibilities of wealth, and consequently, that American society, impelled by an undefined heritage of unlimited possibilities, had
become a highly mobile, tentative, and obscurely unfulfilled and
omnivorous energy directed toward power and luxury, but with
no sensitively or clearly defined human ends. Looking about him
in the modern moment of the "Younger Generation," even the
man of "heightened sensitivity to the promises of life," if he lacks
the advantage of an educated understanding of the idea of America, sees only the attractiveness of wealth with which to articulate
his unique American response. The energy of the dream is its
romantic expectation, but the actuality of the dream is merely its
appearances. So the true American, the Columbus of the self,
the rare individual within the American mass, is betrayed by
his belief in America, by his belief that the appearances are the
fulfillment. At this point in his understanding of the American dream, Fitzgerald, in *The Great Gatsby* and *Tender Is the
Night*, does the same thing that seventeenth- and eighteenth-
century writers had done on both sides of the Atlantic. He used
America not as a specific location or nation, but as a metaphor
for the deepest longings of the human race, and his "Americans" become Mr. Every Newman. In the specifics of the Ameri-

can locale, however, Fitzgerald saw most Americans, like most men everywhere, desiring merely the substance of respectable wealth, having no imaginative sensibility of anything beyond the identities of money; yet uniquely propelled by a sense of national promise they no longer understand, they remain wistfully perplexed by the feeling that after everything is attained, they are still missing "something." And they drift in an indefinite discontentment, ever seeking "a change." The true believer seems to sum up all the others in his striving for the appearances he believes in, but he stands out from all the rest in his consuming devotion to his goals, the actualization of his certitude of a released and dazzling self to be achieved through the appearances. "The American dream" for Fitzgerald is the continuing story of the rare, true American's total commitment to the idea of America, and the inevitability of his betrayal by what he identifies as the actualization of the ideal. It is in this conflict that Fitzgerald's materials and experience combined to make the composition of *The Great Gatsby*.

Of course, because the true "American" is a naive, pretentious, brilliant fool, he is doomed. Time, mortality, history doom him in his own American demands on life. Yet, bootlegger that he is, he is not to be dismissed as having gotten what he deserves, for his vision is "the magical glory" of the world. He pays for his demands by giving everything—everything—of his central, secret existence to The Girl, laying at her feet every labor and hope and wish that ever impelled him. His romantic blood-knowledge of the significance of America's opulence and America's insistence upon the new and the future and the young is expressed in his adolescent, creative eagerness. In one of his short stories, "The Swimmers," Fitzgerald summed up his Gatsby-sense of aspiring openheartedly toward the beloved of his dream vision: "The best of America was the best of the world. . . . France was a land, England was a people, but America, having about it still that quality

of the idea, was harder to utter. . . . It was a willingness of the
heart."[6] As the idea of America is sumptuously greater even than
the lavish actuality, the idea of The Girl is stupendously greater
than her alluring existence. In *The Great Gatsby* as in *This Side
of Paradise,* the object of the heart's will can not sustain the loving
heart's eagerness.

Both Fitzgerald and Gatsby were broken by the extravagance of
the emotional expenditure. Both were willing to enter the world
of next things, and to try to keep the sweat and marks from showing, old sport, in order to earn the appearances that would permit
them to win the dream girl. Gatsby knew full well that when he
made Daisy the receptacle of his dreams he would be forever
wedded to her. It would henceforth be emotionally and spiritual-
ly—if I may say so, *nationally*—insupportable to find the basket
broken and shabby after he had put all his East and West Eggs in
it. Putting one's self into the American dreamgirl was much more
than a genital action for the dreamer. Gatsby "took Daisy one
still October night, took her because [in his present identity] he
had no real right to touch her hand. . . . He knew that Daisy was
extraordinary, but he didn't realize just how extraordinary a
'nice' girl could be. She vanished into her rich house, her rich full
life, leaving Gatsby—nothing. He felt married to her, that was all"
(pp. 113–14). The imagined self up there in the transcendent
heavens was made manifest in walking flesh, and what flesh can
bear the burden? Nick learns what Daisy meant to Gatsby:

One autumn night [that "still October night" when Gatsby put himself into Daisy] they had been walking down the street when the leaves
were falling, and they came to a place where there were no trees and
the sidewalk was white with moonlight. They stopped here and turned
toward each other. Now it was a cool night with that mysterious
excitement in it which comes at the two changes of the year. The quiet
lights in the houses were humming out into the darkness and there was

6 *The Saturday Evening Post,* CCII (October 19, 1929).

a stir and a bustle among the stars. Out of the corner of his eye Gatsby saw that the blocks of the sidewalks really formed a ladder and mounted to a secret place above the trees—*he could climb to it if he climbed alone,* and once there he could suck on the pap of life, gulp down the incomparable milk of wonder.

His heart beat faster and faster as Daisy's white face came up to his own. He knew that when he kissed this girl, and *forever wed his unutterable visions to her perishable breath, his mind would never romp again like the mind of God.* So he waited, listening for a moment longer to the tuning fork that had been struck upon a star. Then he kissed her. At his lips' touch she blossomed for him like a flower and the incarnation was complete,

the incarnation of the romping dream of self among the stars (p. 84, italics mine).

Gatsby knew what he knew only because Fitzgerald knew it in the same "unutterable" way. "When I was your age," Scott wrote to his seventeen-year-old daughter,

I lived with a great dream. The dream grew and I learned how to speak of it and make people listen. Then the dream divided one day when I decided to marry your mother after all, even though I knew she was spoiled and meant no good to me. I was sorry immediately I had married her but, being patient in those days, made the best of it and got to love her in another way. You came along and for a long time we made quite a lot of happiness out of our lives. But I was a man divided—she wanted me to work too much for *her* [the magazine fiction, the jazzy need for money and a hot-cat life] and not enough for my dream. She realized too late that work was dignity and the only dignity, and tried to atone for it by working herself, but it was too late and she broke and is broken forever.[7]

The letter was unfair, written toward the end of the 1930's, in which he lived through horror after horror. For at the beginning he had plunged as gleefully as Zelda, more wonderingly than she, into the whirl of success. And Zelda paid hideously and pathet-

[7] July 7, 1938, in *The Letters of F. Scott Fitzgerald*, ed. Andrew Turnbull (New York, 1963), p. 32; hereafter referred to as *Letters*.

ically for all the golden girl selfishness and wastefulness and laziness and, above all, irresponsibility, that made her at once so zestful and so much less than Fitzgerald's dream of her. But autobiography is beside the point if it is considered as a set of historical facts. For all the similarities between Fitzgerald's life and Gatsby's, the novel is hardly a point-by-point recapitulation of history. The amazing pool of source materials in Fitzgerald's life for the fiction he wrote, and the countless and obvious parallels between the two, have misled some readers into reading the fiction as autobiography. But those who have reacted against misreadings occasioned by the parallels between the fiction and the biographical facts often react too strongly when they discount considerations of such relationships as a critical mistake. For Fitzgerald's fiction *is* autobiographical in the deepest sense, a sense that goes beyond facts. It is the autobiography of Fitzgerald's imagination, of his own ecstatic impulses and his imaginative reaction to the exciting American promise of life, whether in St. Paul society, at Princeton, in the expatriate's Europe (Fitzgerald never became Europeanized like Hemingway, never learned the language of the country, remained an unregenerate American and admitted it), or in the ever-beckoning glamour of New York. As Harry Levin has pointed out, the history of the realistic novel shows that fiction tends toward autobiography.[8] Because the realistic novel attempts to create a sense of "what it's really like," it will necessarily depend upon details that evoke that sense, and nowhere, of course, are those details more clear to an author than in his own memory of the experience out of which that sense arises. In America, the realistic novel has been almost unexceptionably a statement of exposé because of the discrepancy between the romantic New World vision—"the Dream"—and the American details in which that vision is supposed to have been enacted. The American autobiographical memory since the Civil War generally has been

---

[8] *James Joyce* (New Directions, New York, 1960), p. 41.

stocked with revelations of the extent to which American life falls
short of the transcendent vision. A sense of cheat and defeat is
particularly characteristic of the fiction of Norris and Dreiser, a
school of realism that early struck Fitzgerald as an example of
what courageous, serious fiction should be.

Because the details of the writer's memory have their own fidel-
ity to history, to social actuality, the very materials of memory
tend to substantiate intimations of mortality and to preclude the
triumph of the dream. Consequently, the American novel, trying
to find a locale in which to dramatize the transcendent vision,
has had a consistent and strong tendency toward the Romance
rather than the realistic novel, for the realistic use of the American scene has tended to be a motion toward defeat. This is not to
say that the American Romance is sponsored by a vision of the
triumph of the New Adam—witness *Moby-Dick*—but rather that
a dramatization of the meanings of scene, of the moral fable inherent in scene, the writer's truth, in short, could not be found in
scene when the culture generally insisted that the scene be identified as the dream realized. As so many American writers have complained, American fascination with the statistics of progress has
tended to blur any distinction between the transcendent vision
and American scene and has fostered the vague, popular assumption that in the details the vision is found. Fitzgerald was acutely
aware that most of the reading public would insist on its Booth
Tarkingtons, and as much as his popular fiction was impelled by
his awareness of Tarkington's characters, situations, and success,
he polarized Tarkington and Dreiser, distinguishing between
them in terms of what is merely successful and what is art. Hawthorne's complaint about America's terrible insistence on actualities continued as a dilemma for the writer in Fitzgerald's century.
One could complain, as Nathanael West and Philip Roth have
done, that American actualities, in their absurdity, extravagance,
and violence, outrun the fictive imagination. In order to make

any impact at all, the writer is forced to super-extravaganza, a surrealistic view of the details of scene, as was West. Or, like Bellow he may complain that too many American writers are so intimidated by the need for "reality" that they will not release their imaginations enough to overcome their most inhibiting fear: that their details of scene might not be technically convincing enough to create a sense of verisimilitude. Rather than overwhelm realistic detail with super-detail, when he wishes to give his seeking American innocent archetypal national qualities, Bellow creates the highly "removed," non-realistic setting of the kind of Africa one sees in *Henderson the Rain King*.

But Fitzgerald's way was something different yet again. For any American writer who still finds in the details of the American scene a reminder as well as a betrayal of the dream vision, the great necessity will be a balance between a nostalgic re-creation of the vision and a careful selection of just those details in which the vision, no matter how cheapened or debased, may still be made dramatically visible in a *realistically recognizable American setting*. In order to balance between Nathanael West and Booth Tarkington—which is, in effect, the almost impossible feat that Fitzgerald brought off—the details experienced will be an absolute necessity if the autobiography as moral fable of the vision is to find voice in dramatically valid fiction in a recognizable world. It becomes especially important to remember Fitzgerald's insistence that it was the details of such a world—as he lived it—that furnished the only materials he could work into art. He was both trapped and made into an artist by his materials.

The trap inevitably becomes the trap of narrative voice. Because he was necessarily consuming his life and his self in his fiction, it becomes almost inescapable that the voices of narrators in the fiction should slip into the voice of the true narrator, the author. There are a few writers who escaped the trap and, like Joyce, "flew by the nets." And it is not insignificant that Fitzgerald worshipped Joyce—when he met Joyce he drunkenly but seriously offered to throw himself out the window in a totally self-abnegating token of Joyce's mastery—as a controlling genius of narrative point of view. Although, faced with almost the identical problems that Joyce met as a "realistic" and alienated Irishman and writer, Fitzgerald did not rise to Joyce's mastery in narrative voice, still it is astonishing that in *The Great Gatsby* and in *Tender Is the Night* Fitzgerald slipped so few times. When Jordan Baker, for instance, describes her walk to Daisy's house in Louisville and says that on that windy, bright day, as her skirt was whipped high, the fluttering flags all said "tut, tut, tut," the description is too adroit to be Jordan's. The language is a bullseye hit on the national target of outmoded genteel respectabilities as the background against which Fitzgerald so consciously played out the drama of the even more disintegrated morality of the Younger Generation. When Daisy buries her face in Gatsby's shirts and blubbers her appreciation of all his struggles, the emotional insight is Fitzgerald's, not Daisy's. She should not be seen as capable of ever deeply being one with Gatsby's dream. When Gatsby says that the part of the Middle West he comes from is San Francisco, Fitzgerald allows parabolic force (for symbolically it is perfectly fitting that Gatsby be from the Golden Gate West) to collide with the rigorous probability of the fable's surface. After all, Gatsby has been around by the time of "that summer," around Europe and around the United States setting up bucketshops and bootleg clearing houses and gambling rooms, and his ignorance couldn't be quite so easy. We wince at Gatsby's silly pretensions but understand their meanings, yet here we wince at Fitzgerald's expense. In sum, the three or four small points at which the realistic surface dissolves because of what the narrative voice of the moment says, are all offsprings of the indescribable tension Fitzgerald managed—and which is, I think, the source of our admiration—between the details of scene and of the moral

fable, between his materials and his vision, between the realistic
novel and the Romance, forging a coalition that surpassed Edith
Wharton's achievement with similar materials. The point at
which the voices of the ostensible and true narrators merge most
overwhelmingly is reached in the epilogue provided by Nick, the
musing soliloquy in which he broods over the meanings of the
scene of the novel at the very end of the book. But at this point
the merger is not loss of control, for Nick, in his recounting the
completed events, has learned by then all that the *author* knew
about the materials of the action. The merger is the unification of
the language of the author's romantic vision and the re-educated
language of the most realistically observant character in the book.[9]
There is not an echo of Nick's occasional, early smartness to be
heard in the final paragraphs. Those closing cadences, which have
moved the vast majority of the book's readers, and will continue
to do so as long as the book is read, are, in fact, the clue provided
in narrative point of view to how, in the deepest and most consummate sense, Nick is indeed a reliable narrator. The point is
that Fitzgerald always wrote about *himself* in a way that makes
him a chronicler of one view of America and its history. He and
those around him were always aware of his need to begin with an
emotion that was close to him, of his need to turn his historically
composite characters into himself. Alexander McKaig noted the
fact in his diary: "Oct. 13 Fitz made another true remark about
himself . . . cannot depict how anyone thinks except himself and
possibly Zelda. Find that after he has written about a character
for a while it becomes just himself again."[10] That was written by
someone outside Fitzgerald himself, and early in Fitzgerald's
career. But Fitzgerald, a year after he finished *The Great Gatsby*,
had this to say to John Peale Bishop: "Also you are right about

[9] Irving Pitman Cummings of the University of Connecticut, in a careful, creative
reading of the manuscript of this book, has made immeasurably helpful suggestions. This discussion of narrative voice is but one of many debts to him.

[10] Turnbull, *Scott Fitzgerald*, pp. 113–14.

Gatsby being blurred and patchy. I never at any one time saw him clear myself—for he started as one man I knew [an underworld character Fitzgerald met at Great Neck, Long Island], and then changed into myself—the amalgam was never complete in my mind."[11]

Fitzgerald believed that Gatsby was not a clear character because it was a commonplace among his friends to say so even though in revising the manuscript he sharpened Gatsby successfully. But few contemporaries recognized the book for what it was and none completely saw its full significance. They never seemed to expect that a crook of the bootleg era, the era of Fitzgerald, and in the fiction of Fitzgerald, could have the proportions of American—which is to say mythic—history. They expected the verisimilitude of a police or sociology report, in which Fitzgerald would finally and "maturely" photograph his age, and not offer one more redaction of his romantic American memory. The passage of time has justified Fitzgerald's autobiographical "composite" instinct. The important point is that if Fitzgerald was repeating the story he had told already in two novels, he was also going beyond them.[12] He was combining the expectation of triumph that underlay the writing of *This Side of Paradise* with the premonitions of defeat that underlay *The Beautiful and Damned*. Because his prescient imagination had always sensed that the instant of the golden moment was also the plunge into the failure of its actualities, what he remembered was the future; what he looked forward to was the imagined and lost past. In short, some-

11 August 9, 1925, *Letters*, p. 358.

12 Commentators have often speculated about how it was possible for Fitzgerald, who had written two popular novels that were hardly great, to have leaped to the heights of *The Great Gatsby* only three years after *The Beautiful and Damned*. In *F. Scott Fitzgerald: The Last Laocoon*, Robert Sklar presents the evidence of the short stories to show how Fitzgerald had progressed through the technical problems of working out his fiction's themes. My conclusions are in complete agreement with Mr. Sklar's, but, as is evident, the terms I choose are the coalescence of experience and imagination in Fitzgerald's life. See Sklar (New York, 1967), Chapter Six.

where within his composite and autobiographical use of his materials was the dark knowledge that in the end was the beginning and in the beginning was the end. That knowledge grew within him toward self-awareness and articulation, drawn toward the light of consciousness by the first two novels and the short stories, and arriving into artistry in *The Great Gatsby*. As I will suggest shortly, the coalescence of all his previous fiction and all his life in his own self-awareness of his dream of glory, the dark knowledge, was deep enough by 1924 to influence the very structure of his third novel.

Fitzgerald paired his books by comparing structures and intentions.

My books have alternated between being selective and blown up. *Paradise* and *Gatsby* were selective; *The Beautiful and Damned* and *Tender* aimed at being full and comprehensive. . . . The difference is that in these last two I wrote everything, hoping to cut to interest. In *This Side of Paradise* (in a crude way) and in *Gatsby* I selected the stuff to fit a given mood or "hauntedness" or whatever you might call it, rejecting in advance in *Gatsby*, for instance, all of the ordinary material for Long Island, big crooks, adultery theme and always starting from the *small* focal point that impressed me—my own meeting with Arnold Rothstein [who was to become transmogrified as Meyer Wolfsheim] for instance.[13]

It is difficult to understand Fitzgerald's assessment, for of all his books, *This Side of Paradise* was more of a catch-all than the others. He threw in much of his previous writing, poetry and prose, that he had liked, and tried, in a very young man's first book, to say everything about his times. However, it is true that *The Beautiful and Damned* has less of Fitzgerald's nostalgic sense of "hauntedness" than any of his other books. But the youthful and gleeful hope behind the writing of *This Side of Paradise*

---

[13] To Corey Ford, early July 1937, *Letters*, p. 551. For a discussion of the selective and comprehensive in Fitzgerald's fiction and in his literary antecedents, see James E. Miller, *F. Scott Fitzgerald: His Art and His Technique* (New York, 1964).

kept the "hauntedness" from evoking true nostalgia in the reader because though the materials were aimed at the re-creation of an immediate past the essential stance of the book faces futureward in a young sense of possibilities. The talk about an old, dying, hypocritical world and its replacement by a new unattractive one is talk that reflects one of Fitzgerald's lasting and constant concerns, but the talk is too often shallow cynicism because the experience of loss had not yet become part of Fitzgerald's own character. The books can be paired in a slightly different perspective than that provided by selectiveness and comprehensiveness. As I have suggested earlier, *This Side of Paradise* is the imaginative expectation of the golden moment, and *The Great Gatsby* is the imagination working on the experience, already past, of having attained it. *The Beautiful and Damned* is the other side of the golden moment, the imagined expectation of defeat and failure, and *Tender Is the Night* is the imagination working on the experience, already past and still present, of having fallen in it. *This Side of Paradise* looks forward to *The Great Gatsby* as *The Beautiful and Damned* looks forward to *Tender Is the Night*. *The Great Gatsby* begins and continues in heightened expectation, and the loss of illusions—the logical culmination of events—comes swiftly at the end. The process of the book's actions is the energizing of the visions of glory. *Tender Is the Night* begins in heightened expectation, but that is quickly destroyed and the process of the book's actions is the gradual annihilation of creative energy and the degradation of character following the loss of romantic illusion. Both books are about "the loss of those illusions that give such color to the world so that you don't care whether things are true or false as long as they partake of the magical glory." But *The Great Gatsby*, like *This Side of Paradise*, is the process leading up to that loss, and *Tender Is the Night*, like *The Beautiful and Damned*, is the process leading down from it. Both *The Great Gatsby* and *Tender Is the Night* have the density of experience gone through, which gives them a unifying hauntedness, a real sense of so much potential glory already lost in the past, and which results in the sigh of real nostalgia and sadness that both books evoke. For these latter books, the composite characters and incidents were completed and set in Fitzgerald's life, ready for his imagination to act upon. The longing sense of loss was summed up for Fitzgerald by Roger Burlingame, one of the editors at Scribner's, and Fitzgerald was quick to seize on the summation: "Dear Roger," he wrote. "I think that's about the nicest letter I ever received about my work. I was tremendously pleased that it [*The Great Gatsby*] moved you in that way—'made you want to be back somewhere so much'—because that describes, better than I could have put it myself, whatever unifying emotion the book has, either in regard to the temperament of Gatsby himself or in my own mood while writing it."[14]

If *The Beautiful and Damned* was a consolidation of Fitzgerald's materials and themes, *The Great Gatsby* was a consolidation of the sense of life those materials and themes were to express. And Fitzgerald knew it, felt it in his bones despite his uneasiness about the sharpness of Gatsby as a character, despite his uncertainty about the success of the confrontation scene at the Plaza, despite his despair that the advertising could only present it as "one more book about New York society."

The first draft of *The Great Gatsby* received criticism indicating that Gatsby was a fuzzy character. Fitzgerald worried about it. He wrote to Maxwell Perkins that "Gatsby's business affairs I can fix. I get your point about them. . . . His vagueness I can repair by *making more pointed*—this doesn't sound good but wait and see. It'll make him clear."[15] Fitzgerald then implicitly gave Gatsby an occupation, bootlegger and stocks-sharper, and made a deliberate mystery out of him in the reactions of people to him, and

[14] April 19, 1925, *Letters*, p. 479.
[15] About December 1, 1924, *ibid.*, p. 170.

thus solved the problem of characterization. He wrote to Perkins
a few days later,

*I myself didn't know what Gatsby looked like or was engaged in* and
you felt it. If I'd known and kept it from you you'd have been *too
impressed with my knowledge to protest.* This is a complicated idea
but I'm sure you'll understand. But I know now—and as a penalty for
not having known first, in other words to make sure, I'm going to
tell more.

It seems of almost mystical significance to me that you thought he
was older—the man I had in mind, half-unconsciously, *was* older (a
specific individual) and evidently, without so much as a definite word,
I conveyed the fact. . . .

Anyhow, after careful searching of the files (of a man's mind here)
for the Fuller Magee case [the source of Gatsby's business intricacies
and "gonnegtions"] and after having had Zelda draw pictures until
her fingers ache I know Gatsby better than I know my own child . . .
Gatsby sticks in my heart. I had him for awhile, then lost him, and now
I know I have him again.[16]

And two months later, these conclusive statements: "(1) I've
brought Gatsby to life. (2) I've accounted for his money."[17]

As for his uncertainty about the scene in the Plaza Hotel
(Chapter Seven), Fitzgerald wrote to Perkins in November 1924,
"By now you've received the novel. There are things in it I'm not
satisfied with, in the middle of the book—Chapters 6 and 7." A
month later he wrote that "Chapters VI and VII I know how to
fix." Later in December he wrote, ". . . I can make *Gatsby* perfect.
The Chapter 7 (the hotel scene) will never quite be up to mark—
I've worried about it too long and I can't quite place Daisy's reaction. But I can improve it a lot. . . . It's Chapter VII that's the
trouble with Daisy. . . ." And finally, in February, as the final
revised proofs went to press, "I've fixed up the two weak chapters
(VI and VII)." Yet, a month after the book appeared, he wrote to

16 About December 20, 1924, *ibid.*, pp. 172–73.
17 About February 18, 1925, *ibid.*, p. 177.

Mencken in May that "There is a tremendous fault in the book—
the lack of an emotional presentment of Daisy's attitude toward
Gatsby after their reunion (and the consequent lack of logic or
importance in her throwing him over). Everyone has felt this but
no one has spotted it because it's concealed beneath elaborate
and overlapping blankets of prose."[18]

But because he was aware of how *The Great Gatsby* consolidated in art everything he had dreamed and lived and written,
he was most concerned about the advertising. He wanted it made
clear that this book was *different,* and was not to be referred to
his other writings or to the literary groups with which he was
associated. On October 27, 1924, as he sent Perkins the very first
draft of the novel, which was to undergo continuous revision in
manuscript and—even up to the last minute—in proof, he wrote,
"This time I don't want any signed blurbs on the jacket—not
Mencken's or [Sinclair] Lewis' or [Sidney] Howard's or anyone's.
I'm tired of being the author of *This Side of Paradise* and I want
to start over." In December: "Please have *no blurbs of any kind
on the jacket!!!* No Mencken or Lewis or Sid Howard or anything.
I don't believe in them *one bit* any more." In January 1925, two
months before the book was due for publication, he warned again
that "This is very important. Be sure not to give away *any* of my
plot in the blurb. Don't give away that Gatsby *dies* or is a *parvenu*
or *crook* or anything. It's a part of the suspense of the book that
all these things are in doubt until the end. You'll watch this,
won't you? And remember about having no quotations from
critics on the jacket—*not even about my other books!*" After advance copies had already been distributed, and a few days before
the official release date, he wrote Perkins:

I had, or rather saw, a letter from my uncle who had seen a prelimi-
nary announcement of the book. He said: "It sounded as if it were
very much like his others."

18 *Letters,* pp. 169, 170, 172–73, 177, 480.

This is only a vague impression of course but I wondered if we could think of some way to advertise it so that people who are perhaps weary of assertive jazz and society novels might not dismiss it as "just another book like his others." I confess that today the problem baffles me—all I can think of is to say in general to avoid such phrases as "a picture of New York life," or "modern society"—though as that is exactly what the book is it's hard to avoid them. The trouble is so much superficial trash has sailed under those banners. Let me know what you think.[19]

Fitzgerald himself knew very well what to think. He knew the book was not a "trashy imagining"—as he called some of his previous work—of modern American society, but was a serious literary indictment of it. Ever afterward, in the depths of his defeat, he knew that he had been a conscious, deliberate, and successful artist in *The Great Gatsby,* and he mourned the book's oblivion in his own lifetime. In May 1940, just a few months before he died, he wrote to Perkins, that faithful and wonderful friend and editor, in brave and plaintive tones: "Would the 25-cent press keep *Gatsby* in the public eye—or *is the book unpopular?* Has it *had* its chance? Would a popular reissue in that series with a preface *not* by me but by one of its admirers—I can maybe pick one—make it a favorite with classrooms, profs, lovers of English prose—anybody? But to die, so completely and unjustly after having given so much! Even now there is little published in American fiction that doesn't slightly bear my stamp—in a *small* way I was an original."[20] A month later, looking back over the wreck of his life in a letter to his daughter, he said, "What little I've accomplished has been by

---

[19] *Ibid.*, pp. 168, 173, 176, 178–79.

[20] *Ibid.*, p. 288. If only he had lived to see how completely *that* wish has been fulfilled. In one five-year period alone (1961–66), of the approximately 110 articles and 16 books and monographs published about Fitzgerald, all of the books and monographs and approximately 30 of the articles have given special attention to *The Great Gatsby*. These figures of course do not include the hundreds of essays written about Fitzgerald before 1961, since the beginning of the Fitzgerald revival in the late 1940's, or since 1966. Since 1950 there has hardly been a course in modern American fiction anywhere in the world that has not included the novel.

the most laborious and uphill work, and I wish now I'd *never* re-laxed or looked back—but said at the end of *The Great Gatsby:* 'I've found my line—from now on this comes first. This is my im-mediate duty—without this I am nothing."[21] He had come to measure on his very pulses the difference between the personality and the personage and how the former came close to killing the "fundamental Amory," and he had always known it, even at the height of the battle between the two, when the personality of the "gaudiest spree in history" came close to unconditional victory. In April of 1924, when he was working on the first complete draft of *Gatsby,* he asked Perkins to

have patience about the book and trust me that at last, or at least for the first time in years, I'm doing the best I can. I've gotten in dozens of bad habits that I'm trying to get rid of
  1. Laziness
  2. Referring everything to Zelda—a terrible habit; nothing ought to be referred to anybody until it's finished
  3. Word consciousness and self-doubt, etc., etc., etc., etc.
I feel I have an enormous power in me now, more than I've ever had in a way. . . .
So in my new novel I'm thrown directly on purely creative work—not trashy imaginings as in my stories but the sustained imagination of a sincere yet radiant world. So I tread slowly and carefully and at times in considerable distress. This book will be a consciously artistic achieve-ment and must depend on that as the first books did not.
If I ever win the right to any leisure again, I will assuredly not waste it as I wasted this past time.[22]

As the work neared completion, he wrote in euphoria to Perkins in August that "I think my novel is about the best American novel ever written." When he sent the novel to Scribner's, he said that "I think that at last I've done something really my own, but how good 'my own' is remains to be seen."[23]

21 *Ibid.,* p. 79.
22 *Ibid.,* p. 163.
23 *Ibid.,* pp. 166, 168.

But Fitzgerald's sure sense of the book was hardly merely a matter of euphoria. He earned his momentary elation by *really* learning from his dissipation, for the first time, that "work was dignity and the only dignity." He knew what he was doing as clearly as, in the leisure of retrospect, any "classrooms, profs, lovers of English prose" know today. He knew, for instance, that the newness of his work in *The Great Gatsby* was the product of his replacing the sense of the dream that lacked the feel of experience, "trashy imaginings," with sustained imagination working on the deepest composite experiences of his life. *He* knew—as those critics who consider it fallacious to talk about his work in the context of his life still do not—that for him this was what accounted for style more than any aesthetic theory or influence, more than any recapitulation, in sterile isolation of works from life, of the techniques of separate works of fiction. He knew that style was an author's attempt to solve a problem—about himself, about his life, about his time; that style, as Emerson had suggested, was the measure of the extent to which a man addressed himself to his human existence. Writing to his daughter, Fitzgerald said:

Let me preach again for a moment. I mean that what you have felt and thought will, by itself, invent a new style, so that when people talk about style they are always a little astonished at the newness of it, because they think that it is only *style* that they are talking about, when what they are talking about is the attempt to express a new idea with such force that it will have the originality of the thought. It is an awfully lonesome business, and, as you know, I never wanted you to go into it, but if you are going into it at all I want you to go into it knowing the sort of things that took me years to learn.[24]

The admonition was useless, for the one thing a personage cannot pass on is the experience, the life—the very process—of the completed accomplishment. All he can pass on (all!) is the art of the perfected thing.

[24] October 20, 1936, *ibid.*, p. 11.

But Fitzgerald knew what he was passing on. Statement after
statement in his letters make it clear that he was conscious of the
relationship between "idea" and detail. Was he dissatisfied with
the scene at the Plaza (Chapter VII)? He was stuck with it. He
knew that he had to keep the detail in which it is the essentially
bloodless Daisy who causes the death of the animal vitality that
Myrtle Wilson represented. When he talked about revising the
Plaza scene, he added, "It isn't imaginary energy that's lacking—
it's because I'm automatically prevented from thinking it out
over again *because I must get all those characters to New York* in
order to have the catastrophe on the road going back, and I must
have it pretty much that way. So there's no chance of bringing the
freshness to it that a new free conception sometimes gives."[25] Was
there a contextual idea in Myrtle's panting, sexual energy? He
opposed Perkins in order to preserve the representative detail:
"I *want* Myrtle Wilson's breast ripped off—it's exactly the thing, I
think, and I don't want to chop up the good scenes by too much
tinkering." Was there significance even in so small a detail as the
fact that the book available for Carraway to read in Myrtle's vulgar apartment is *Simon Called Peter?* "Max," he asked Perkins,
". . . in Chapter II of my book when Tom and Myrtle go into the
bedroom while Carraway reads *Simon Called Peter*—is that raw?
Let me know. I think it's pretty necessary." It is necessary when one
thinks that the book for Fitzgerald (and Fitzgerald knew that the
contemporaries he cared about would agree) was an example of the
sniggering and saccharine and sensationalistic piety that, like
the copies of *Town Tattle* lying on the table in Myrtle's apartment,
indicates the ubiquitous, obscene vulgarity to which respectabilities and pretensions reduce life, regardless of the social stratum to
which the artifacts of one's circumstances indicate one belongs. A
year before he began working on the complete first draft of *Gatsby*,
Fitzgerald wrote to the editor of *The Literary Digest*, "The clean-

25 About December 20, 1924, *ibid.*, p. 172.

book bill [a pending censorship statute] will be one of the most immoral measures ever adopted. It will throw American art back into the junk heap . . . [and] the really immoral books like *Simon Called Peter* . . . won't be touched . . . ." In every correspondence Fitzgerald proved he was earning this book as he hadn't his earlier ones. Strikingly important details like this one come to light in the correspondence: the next to last paragraph in *The Great Gatsby* says, "Gatsby believed in the green light, the *orgiastic* [italics mine] future that year by year recedes before us." But Fitzgerald knew that what he was after in Gatsby's career was not an orgy (" 'The dance?' [Gatsby] dismissed all the dances he had given with a snap of his fingers. 'Old sport, the dance is unimportant.' ") but an orgasm, the intense, ecstatic golden moment of the instant of rapturous triumph extended indefinitely as the imagined future we all beat after, "boats against the current." That's what he *wanted* to write, and lost out, reluctantly. "Orgastic," he wrote to Perkins, explaining the word he had originally and deliberately used, "is the adjective for 'orgasm' and it expresses exactly the intended ecstasy. It's not a bit dirty."[26] He knew what he was doing, and no wonder he was elated. Of all the explanations offered for Fitzgerald's sudden rise to the artistry of *The Great Gatsby*, none appears so meaningful to me as the simplest and most mysterious. Dependent as he was for the actual to create composite materials for his imagination to work over—as contrasted to the "trashy imaginings" that drift without the anchor of achieved experience—and having worked the trashy imaginings into his experience in his previous novels and most of his magazine stories, at some magic time in 1923, for whatever wonderful reasons such a thing ever happens to a man, Fitzgerald's memory, materials, and imagination finally coalesced in the only lasting golden moment—his "beautiful talent, baby"—Fitzgerald was ever to know. He was consciously aware that his "style" lay in

26 *Letters*, pp. 175, 170–71, 476, 175.

his deepening humanity, and that the expression of his "own" experienced vision was real as his pretentiousness, smartness, and flip, modish cynicism in his earlier books were not. He knew that it was not a few years but a decade in enriched humanity that separated *The Beautiful and Damned* from *The Great Gatsby* and it is interesting that he expressed his repudiation of his earlier work in exactly those terms: "My new novel appears in late March [actually it appeared in April]: *The Great Gatsby*. It represents about a year's work and I think it's about ten years better than anything I've done. All my harsh smartness has been kept ruthlessly out of it—it's the greatest weakness in my work, distracting and disfiguring it even when it calls up an isolated sardonic laugh. I don't think this has a touch left."[27]

Both image and incident, language and plot, indicate the centrality and firmness of Fitzgerald's ideas for the book, ideas about American wealth, identity, and beauty. Even the barest plot precis, constructed chapter by chapter, demonstrates how tightly Fitzgerald structured the concerns that had been loose and pre-experiential in his first two books. The story is organized around a series of parties which serve as vehicles that allow the imagery and relationships of characters to present the ideas—the evaluation of materials—that Fitzgerald wished to offer. Chapter One focuses on the Buchanans' dinner party, which demonstrates the nature and quantity of the Buchanan fortune as well as how it is used. Chapter Two, immediately in contrast, opens with the Valley of Ashes, which demonstrates the nature and effect of the Wilsons' poverty. This chapter revolves about a party in Tom's and Myrtle's clandestine apartment, a party which insists upon the grossness of middle-class affectations when wealth is added to coarsening poverty. Chapter Three explores a party that is a culmination of the

27 To Ernest Boyd, February 1, 1925, *ibid.*, p. 478.

first two chapters. Here Gatsby's party is the center of the action, and all the pretentiousness, ostentation, and energy hinted at in Myrtle's party is brought to the highest summary pitch in the introduction of Gatsby. Chapter Four opens with a recapitulation of the cast of characters at Gatsby's parties and proceeds to a luncheon party with Nick, Gatsby, and Wolfsheim. The introduction of Gatsby via parties in Chapter Three is completed here in the suggestion that there is something shady about Gatsby's wealth and in the connection between the Buchanan fortune and Gatsby's money: "Gatsby bought that house so that Daisy would be just across the bay," Jordan tells Nick. For Nick, the reason for Gatsby's money suddenly becomes stunningly clear, and Gatsby "came alive" for him, a Gatsby "delivered suddenly from the womb of his purposeless splendor." Chapter Four, then, ties together all levels of American wealth—or lack of it—in the same web of aspiration and meretriciousness, and spins a strong but gossamer thread of connection between Gatsby and Daisy. That connection is made by the party-sequence plot, in swift consequence of the parties that preceded it, in the party in Chapter Five, the tea party in Nick's bungalow. The reunion of Daisy and Gatsby at this party brings the flashbacks of the first four chapters up to date and so allows Fitzgerald to talk about the consequences of the histories of his characters in the present, allows him to prepare the denouement that caps his evaluation of those histories. Chapter Six, the party at Gatsby's attended by Daisy, is a transitional statement that hints at the impossibility of a real and final reunion between Gatsby and his dream, and which foreshadows the death of that dream's energies at the hands of the dream's object—in effect, Daisy "turns off" Gatsby's house. The chapter prepares the expectation that the consequences of the histories and their interrelationships will be death. Chapter Seven presents the party that fulfills the prophecies of the novel so far. In the party at the Plaza, on that baking day of perspiration and boiling tempers, the impossibility of Gatsby's dream is announced, and the action leading away from this last party, which is accompanied ironically by the strains of a wedding march, eventuates in precisely what the story has promised—death. Daisy and Myrtle have never met—neither even knows what the other looks like, and Daisy doesn't even know Myrtle's name or who or where she is, and yet, logically, with the logic of his symbolism, Fitzgerald has Daisy kill Myrtle during the drive away from the Plaza. No one is unrelated to anyone else in the web of hopes and money. All are tainted, and only Gatsby is exempt from the moral condemnation which is Fitzgerald's central idea of the relationships. No more parties now. Only missed connections and broken promises. Chapter Seven closes with a non-party "party" in which Tom and Daisy sit alone over a bowl of cold chicken and two bottles of ale, "and neither one of them had touched the chicken or the ale," and with Gatsby alone, "standing there in the moonlight—watching over nothing." Chapter Eight opens with a non-party breakfast "party" in which Gatsby and Nick participate and during which Nick hears from Gatsby the rest of the story of his aspiring, dreaming attempt to regain Daisy. A meeting between Nick and Jordan is missed—for life, Wilson kills Gatsby and then himself, "and the holocaust was complete." The non-party party of Chapter Nine, the funeral, is some "party" indeed. There are no guests, and the one exception, Owl Eyes, brings home the point when he hears that no one visited Gatsby's house to pay respects: " 'Go on!' He started. 'Why, my God! they used to go there by the hundreds.' " The final fleshing out of the history of Gatsby's dream grows from the presence of Gatsby's father and the Gatsby juvenilia he brings, while, in contrast, the carelessness and irresponsibility of American wealth, the deceit and hollowness of its appearances, its jewels, its parties, lives on. It is Jordan, ironically, who reintroduces the charge of "careless driving," and Tom and Daisy continue on as always, rid of Nick's judgment, his "provincial squeamishness, forever." All that remained for Fitzgerald at the end of Chapter Nine were those magnificent seven closing paragraphs in which to make it clear that this has been a story of the Golden West, after all, a story of America from the beginning. The fate of Gatsby, the romantic, had been the test of his society, and his society had been found wanting. The wealth, the appearances, the parties continue; the history of America as a continual party, as the "greatest gaudiest spree in history," is the irresponsible actuality into which the dream of America has deteriorated. The history of the dream continues, too, but always doomed, always located in the past, where the transcendent expectations of youth were, "borne back ceaselessly into the past."

Before an examination of *The Great Gatsby* can specify the relationship of the book's details to the book's ideas about America, it is necessary to pay some attention to the consciousness through which the book's events are presented, Nick Carraway. Ordinarily this would not be necessary. Most readers have found Nick to be a reliable narrator, one whose evaluations of the events are a voice for Fitzgerald's ideas. But there has been a persistent minority which demands that we see Carraway as an unreliable narrator, a prig. This view arose from two sources. One is the critical mode of the moment, in which all first-person narrators are presumed guilty until proven innocent. The other is Fitzgerald's debt to Conrad. Fitzgerald had been reading Conrad before he wrote *The Great Gatsby,* and in a letter to Mencken, a month or two after the novel was published, he said, "By the way you mention in your review of *Sea Horses* that Conrad has only two imitators. How about . . . me in *Gatsby* (God! I've learned a lot from him). . . . But his (Conrad's) approach and his prose is naturally more imitated than his material. . . ."[28] The critics who see Carraway as

28 May or June 1925, *ibid.*, p. 482.

unreliable assume that because Fitzgerald learned a lot from
Conrad about narrators, and because Conrad's favorite narrator,
Marlow, sometimes does not understand what he reports, Carraway is unreliable. For proof they point to the fact that at the beginning of the novel Nick boasts about his advantages, that he is
everyone's buddy, and they assume that he is never really involved
in Gatsby's story. Nick emerges as a dishonest priss. Yet when the
reader looks at Nick's behavior with two open eyes rather than
"closely" with one, it becomes difficult to assume such a point of
view without destroying the total intention of the novel itself.[29]
Most generally there cannot really be any argument about the
fact that the Buchanans are "careless people—they smashed up
things and creatures and then retreated back into their money or
their vast carelessness, or whatever it was that kept them together,
and let other people clean up the mess they had made" (p. 136).
There can be no real argument about the fact that *despite* his
underworld activities, Gatsby is, after all, a sympathetic character,
and that it is the energy and purity of his dream, within the vulgarity and corruption that clothes it, that gives the story its *raison
d'être*. There can be no real argument about the fact that the
total effect of the book condemns irresponsibility as it mourns
the loss of the dream. There can be little real argument that the
Buchanan world, including Jordan Baker, a cheat and a "careless
driver," represents part of what is condemned and that Gatsby, at
the same time that he is scorned, is admired and represents what
is mourned. Finally, there can be little real argument about the
fact that Nick sides with Gatsby and repudiates the Buchanan
world, that he does take responsibility seriously and will not lie to
himself. In a general consideration of what the book is "about,"

[29] One of the fullest arguments for the view of Nick as cold, unreliable, dishonest,
and priggish is an influential and powerful essay by R. W. Stallman, "Gatsby and
the Hole in Time" (1955), reprinted in *The Houses That James Built* (East Lansing,
1961), pp. 131–50.

after all, the "aboutness" falls apart—the book makes no sense—if Carraway is repudiated.

In particulars, Carraway's boasting turns out to be something quite other than priggishness. He tells us certain key things about himself, primarily about his tolerance. " 'Whenever you feel like criticizing anyone,' he [my father] told me, 'just remember that all the people in this world haven't had the advantages that you've had.' . . . In consequence, I'm inclined to reserve all judgments, a habit that has opened up many curious natures to me and also made me the victim of not a few veteran bores." Of course one should not take as evidence the statements of the person whose character is on trial; let's assume, therefore, for the moment that we cannot take Nick's word. Why, then, of all things possible that any man can boast about, should Fitzgerald have Nick talk about tolerance—especially that tolerance which will not immediately scorn those whose actions betray a lack of social and educational and economic "advantages?" Why should Fitzgerald make the intolerant character who does do precisely what Nick does not, Tom Buchanan, into an unsympathetic boor whose snobbishness is a sign of hypocrisy, maudlin sentiment, self-deceit, and arrogant cruelty? And what will a narrator who can see through Gatsby's pretensions, pretensions formed of all the vulgarity Gatsby has never been able to evaluate because of his own lack of advantages, what will such a narrator need if not exactly the tolerance that will not leap to snobbish conclusions? If we are to conclude that Nick does not have tolerance, but prurient curiosity, why, then, should Fitzgerald, so conscious of what he's doing in this novel, insist strongly on having Nick tell us that he does not seek confidences? "The abnormal mind is quick," says Nick, "to detect and attach itself to this quality [of tolerance] when it appears in a normal person, and so it came about that in college I was unjustly accused of being a politician, because I was privy to the secret griefs of

wild, unknown men. Most of the confidences were unsought—
frequently I have feigned sleep, preoccupation, or a hostile levity
when I realized by some unmistakable sign that an intimate revelation was quivering on the horizon . . ." (p. 3). If there is reverse
speed here and Carraway is covering up for the fact that he *was*
a politician, Fitzgerald would have had to show this somewhere—
at least *once*—in the novel. But he never does. Indeed, as the story
progresses, Nick is let into Gatsby's secrets unwillingly at first,
and later through sympathy—significantly at the time that Fitzgerald has created sympathy for Gatsby *in the reader* as well as in
Carraway. (There is no arguing against the claim that the reader
is not supposed to sympathize with Gatsby. Such a claim is down-
right insensitivity and obtuseness and the only answer is to tell
the critic to go read the book once more—once more with feeling.)
In short, it becomes clear that Carraway is not a man of duplicity,
but a man of "advantaged" experience: he is educated into the
meanings of Gatsby's life step by step, as the reader is, and his
moral conclusions come precisely as the *reader* is ready for them.

Further, Carraway's tolerance is not the gossipy sentimental
intimacy of the bull-session. His abhorrence of that is his tough-
mindedness, not his priggishness: "for the intimate revelations of
young men, or at least the terms in which they express them, are
usually plagiaristic and marred by obvious suppressions." What
he wants is honesty, not mush. The very quality of his desire for
honesty is presented in language that subtly unites him with
Gatsby: "Reserving judgments is a matter of infinite hope." He
is aware that the advantages given him by his father (the heritage
of the fathers will become much more central in *Tender Is the
Night*) have opened him, in his aloofness, to a selective appreciation of human possibility, and he is self-conscious enough to see
that his awareness of his own advantages seems snobbish. "I am a
little afraid of missing something if I forget that, as my father
snobbishly suggested, and I snobbishly repeat, a sense of the funda-

mental decencies is parcelled out unequally at birth" (p. 3). He is afraid of missing not the bull-session intimacy but the real thing, the rare person, the glimpse of human possibility in unlikely places, knowing that in the sensibilities of decency—just as in romantic readiness—all men are not created equal. The important point is that there is no need to sneak up behind Carraway and "expose" him: it is *he* who deliberately and self-consciously uses the word "snobbish" twice in his insistence upon distinguishing between people.

Carraway is also clear in his awareness that his own announcement of his own advantages is boasting. Wryly, he calls it just that. "And, after boasting this way of my tolerance, I come to the admission that it has a limit" (p. 3). In the announcement of the limit is Fitzgerald's final preparation of Carraway as exactly the kind of man to view Gatsby's story. Those who would criticize Nick would do better to pick up his occasional flipness of tone. For instance he refers to World War I as "that delayed Teutonic migration. . . . I enjoyed the counter-raid so thoroughly that I came back restless" (p. 4). When Daisy asks him if she's missed in Chicago, Nick replies, "The whole town is desolate. All the cars have the left rear wheel painted black as a mourning wreath, and there's a persistent wail all night along the north shore." There are two references (to haughty "negro bucks" and "the short upper lip" of Eastern European immigrants when Carraway and Gatsby drive over the Queensboro Bridge into New York) in which Fitzgerald comes close to the "harsh smartness" of *This Side of Paradise,* but in all cases the effect is functional. Nick's "smartness" is always either wry self-deprecation, or momentarily the "sophisticated" manner of the Buchanan world he moves in, or a refusal to be either dramatic or maudlin. But it is the nature of the limits of Nick's tolerance that gives the most compelling clue to his character. "Conduct may be founded on the hard rock or the wet marshes, but after a certain point I don't care what it's

founded on," he says. Conduct may have firm justification or only
the marshy excuses of sentiment and "flabby impressionability,"
but after a certain point, Nick insists, one must judge the results
of conduct. Beyond a certain point of badness the justifications
make no difference. Fitzgerald presents Nick as the heir to his
father's advantages—an older America of duty and honor and
good manners to which Fitzgerald was increasingly more devoted
than to his new world of flaming youth. Again, it is *Tender Is the
Night* in which this theme receives full treatment; but here, at
the very beginning of *The Great Gatsby*, Nick is aligned with old-
fashioned virtues of honesty and a sense of moral responsibility
manifested at the very least in decent behavior. At the very beginning of the novel, we don't yet know dramatically why Nick
should insist on honesty and decency and responsibility. But his
insistence is immediately joined to a hint about the moral quality
of the events of the story he is *about* to tell, to a hint that what he
learned only reinforced his impulses toward the "advantages"
he inherited from his father. In short, what he is about to tell us
is bad, a story of dishonesty, indecency, and irresponsibility.
"When I came back from the East last autumn I felt that I wanted
the world to be in uniform at a sort of moral attention forever; I
wanted no more riotous excursions with privileged glimpses into
the human heart." As Fitzgerald knew that the consequences of
his materials were in their accumulation, so Nick gives the moral
judgment of those materials at the beginning before the story is
told. The arch-representative of those materials—wealth, success,
the pretense that one is one of the hot cats on top—is Gatsby, and
yet "Only Gatsby, the man who gives his name to this book, was
exempt from my reaction," says Nick—"Gatsby who represented
everything for which I have unaffected scorn." Nick, in his "advantages," aristocratically scorns the spurious, the vulgar, the
ostentatious, all of which are summed up in Gatsby's gaudy dis-

play of wealth. But it is just because of his tough-minded tolerance and his sense of infinite hope that Nick is able to see that what he scorns in Gatsby is mere clothing, clothing borrowed from the values of a world that Gatsby—and Nick himself—is impelled to join by all of that world's false promise. Gatsby chases the dream and, lacking all advantages, is naive enough to believe that the actualities of wealth are the protoplasm of his vision. It is not Gatsby but the actualities of Gatsby's society that are on trial for Nick. The real Gatsby, Nick discovers, is the innocent seeker and believer. He was misled enough to think that the trinkets he worked for would be the state of being that his imagination told him he could call into being. And how he worked to transform the world!

If personality is an unbroken series of successful gestures, then there was something gorgeous about him, some heightened sensitivity to the promises of life, as if he were related to one of those intricate machines that register earthquakes ten thousand miles away. This responsiveness has nothing to do with that flabby impressionability which is dignified under the name of the "creative temperament"—it was [like Nick's] an extraordinary gift for hope, a romantic readiness such as I have never found in any other person and which it is not likely I shall ever find again. No—Gatsby turned out all right at the end; it is what preyed on Gatsby, what foul dust floated in the wake of his dreams that temporarily closed out my interest in the abortive sorrows and short-winded elations of men (p. 4).

Nick stands outside the circle of the events as he tells the story, for the story is already all over when he begins it. Yet he is a central observer during the events themselves, but not all things to all men. He comes to dislike Tom, tells him so, and repudiates him. In the face of the scorn and indifference and callowness of others he begins to participate in Gatsby's story, and finally the undeniable fact is that he alone takes responsibility for Gatsby's funeral. Through sympathy he does become involved in Gatsby's attempt to regain Daisy. No—Nick turned out all right at the end. It is what nauseated him, what foul behavior that was disclosed in the dream of success, that removed him from the East and the circular tale of the end in the beginning. For what educated and disgusted him during that riotous summer was what educated and destroyed Gatsby.


Nick's move to West Egg village introduces the connection between American time and American identity. The Middle West which Nick leaves "seemed," after the War, "like the ragged edge of the universe—so I decided to go East and learn the bond business. Everybody I knew was in the bond business . . ." (p. 4). The West had become a dull and settled place, and the Middle West had, by 1925, come to represent Babbitt on Main Street in his repressive Winesburg, Ohio. "Everybody" is East, where the excitement is. As Fitzgerald had learned from Dreiser, the glamorous place where new life could be made for the taking changed in locus at the turn of the century from the West to the big city, and what had been the golden place became the dull and settled land of conformist and respectable towns. America's golden past had become dull bronze, and for Nick and Gatsby as for Fitzgerald the glittering dream of the future had moved East. So too, in "the great, wet barnyard of Lond Island Sound" (whose animals we shall see later at Gatsby's parties), it is East Egg that beckons with its green lights and rich glistening houses, and West Egg that is "the—well, the less fashionable of the two." The hint that the setting is a metaphor for a partial social history of America is strengthened in the statement that in this "most domesticated body of salt water in the western hemisphere," the two Eggs "are not perfect ovals—like the egg in the Columbus story, they are both crushed flat at the contact end." The distinction between these two proximal eggs, these sources of continuing existence that Columbus discovered, is wholly unnatural and rests upon "the bizarre and not a little sinister contrast" between established wealth and parvenu wealth: the "physical resemblance" between the two Eggs "must be a source of perpetual confusion to the gulls that fly overhead. To the wingless a more arresting phenomenon is their dissimilarity in every particular except shape and size" (pp. 5–6).

Yet even at the beginning of the novel, the distinctions between East and West are deliberately blurred. If the West Nick flees has become dull and conformist, still it is in the gaudy middle-class pretentiousness of West Egg that the energy of Gatsby's dreams and parties is manifested. If the older East with its established wealth has become gay and glittering, still it is in the pale pointlessness of the upper-class wealth of East Egg that the hypocrisies of bourgeois respectabilities are insisted upon. It is Tom, who owns the East Egg world, who ignorantly and pretentiously mouths the racist rant about "civilization's going to pieces" under a "Rise of the Colored Empires" which will destroy "we Nordics" who have "produced all the things that go to make civilization—oh science and art, and all that. Do you see?" (pp. 11–12). It is adulterous Tom, who, with his own series of married and unmarried mistresses, frets about how women run around these days, asserts with smug and righteous anger that "I suppose the latest thing is to sit back and let Mr. Nobody from Nowhere make love to your wife. Well, if that's the idea you can count me out. . . . Nowadays people begin by sneering at family life and family institutions, and next they'll throw everything overboard and have intermarriage between black and white. . . . I know I'm not very popular. I don't give big parties. I suppose you've got to make your house into a pigsty in order to have any friends—in the modern world."

"Angry as I was," thinks Nick as he listens, "I was tempted to laugh whenever he opened his mouth. The transition from libertine to prig was so complete" (p. 99).

Not only can one not distinguish East from West in the stereotypes of hypocritical respectabilities, but even in the origins of the inhabitants the two are intermeshed. Tom of East Egg is the Easterner. " 'Oh, I'll stay in the East, don't you worry,' he said. . . . 'I'd be a God damned fool to live anywhere else' " (p. 10). And he does stay, after Nick leaves the East. Yet there is no unique identity or purpose in Tom's being an Easterner. He's the Easterner from the Middle West. "His family were enormously wealthy . . . but now he'd left college and come East in a fashion that rather took your breath away; for instance, he'd brought down a string of polo ponies from Lake Forest. It was hard to believe that any man in my own generation was wealthy enough to do that.

"Why they came East I don't know. They had spent a year in France for no particular reason, and then drifted here and there unrestfully wherever people played polo and were rich together" (p. 6). The actualities of people's lives are unchanged by region. The "unrestful" drift that characterizes the purposelessness and uneasiness of the Buchanans' rich Eastern life is sharply different from the Middle West *in its manners*. The life Fitzgerald shows us in the glamorous and rich East is a series of "continually disappointed anticipation," but the easy irresponsibility of cosmopolitan wealth allows one to move effortlessly and with casual sophistication from one nothing to another. The Middle West, however, in its provincialism, never quite acquires the "advantages," the manners, which teach it how to handle hope and disappointment. So, says Nick of his first dinner at the Buchanans, "It was sharply different from the West, where an evening was hurried from phase to phase toward its close, in a continually disappointed anticipation or else in sheer nervous dread of the

moment itself" (p. 11). But Nick is new to this eastern society.[30]
He is to discover that beneath the manners, the actuality that
makes West and East indistinguishable from each other is that in
both places the fact of life is emptiness caused by the elusiveness
of undefined dreams and even, in many cases, the absence of desire. In fact, at the same time that Nick is aware of the difference
in surfaces between himself—the middle western "new" Easterner
—and the Buchanans—the middle western "old" Easterners
(" 'you make me feel uncivilized, Daisy,' Nick "confessed on . . .
[his] second glass of corky but rather impressive claret. 'Can't
you talk about crops or something?' ")—he is immediately aware
of the "unrestful" drift of the lives of the people about him. The
first introduction to the interior of the Buchanan house, in one of
Fitzgerald's finest passages of descriptive prose, begins with a
sense of richness and drifting in which the inhabitants—richly
drift.

We walked through a high hallway into a bright rosy-colored space,
fragilely bound into the house by French windows at either end. The
windows were ajar and gleaming white against the fresh grass outside
that seemed to grow a little way into the house. A breeze blew through
the room, blew curtains in at one end and out the other like pale flags,
twisting them up toward the frosted wedding-cake of the ceiling, and
then rippled over the wine colored rug, making a shadow on it as
wind does on the sea.

The only completely stationary object in the room was an enormous
couch on which two young women were buoyed up as though upon an
anchored balloon. They were both in white, and their dresses were
rippling and fluttering as if they had just been blown back in after a
short flight around the house. I must have stood for a few moments
listening to the whip and snap of the curtains and the groan of a picture on the wall. Then there was a boom as Tom Buchanan shut the
rear windows and the caught wind died out about the room, and the

[30] "In those days the contrasts between East and West, between city and country,
between prep-school and high school were more marked than they are now, and
correspondingly the nuances of dress and manners were more noticeable. Fitzgerald
quickly grasped the prevailing code and adapted himself to it." (Turnbull, p. 46).

curtains and the rugs and the two young women ballooned slowly to the floor (p. 8).

The rich, fragile languor in the imagery of the house is immediately tied to the directionless and precarious lives lived within it in the imagery and dialogue of the characterization:

The younger of the two was . . . extended full length at her end of the divan, completely motionless, and with her chin raised a little, as if she were balancing something on it which was quite likely to fall. . . .

The other girl, Daisy, made an attempt to rise—she leaned slightly forward with a conscientious expression—then she laughed, an absurd, charming little laugh. . . .

"I'm p-paralyzed with happiness" (p. 8).

. . . [Jordan Baker] yawned and with a series of rapid, deft movements stood up into the room.

"I'm stiff," she complained, "I've been lying on that sofa for as long as I can remember." . . .

"No, thanks," said Miss Baker to the four cocktails just in from the pantry, "I'm absolutely in training."

Her host looked at her incredulously.

"You are!" . . . "How you ever get anything done is beyond me."

I looked at Miss Baker . . . . Her gray sun-strained eyes looked back at me with a polite reciprocal curiosity out of a wan, charming, discontented face (p. 10).

(Fitzgerald is so conscious of the sense of spiritual inanition conveyed by the imagery, that he will repeat the scene at the beginning of the Plaza Hotel confrontation in which Gatsby's dream is destroyed.)

Slenderly, languidly, their hands set lightly on their hips, the two young women preceded us out onto a rosy colored porch. . . . "In two weeks it'll be the longest day in the year," [said Daisy]. "Do you always watch for the longest day of the year and then miss it? I always watch for the longest day in the year and then miss it."

"We ought to plan something," yawned Miss Baker, sitting down at the table as if she were getting into bed.

"All right," said Daisy. "What'll we plan?" She turned to me help-lessly: "What do people plan?" . . .

Sometimes she and Miss Baker talked at once, unobtrusively and with a bantering inconsequence that was never quite chatter, that was as cool as their white dresses and their impersonal eyes in the absence of all desire. They were here and they accepted Tom and me, making only a polite pleasant effort to entertain or to be entertained. They knew that presently dinner would be over and a little later the evening, too, would be over and casually put away (pp. 10–11).

Discontentment, missed connections, no-party parties charac-terize the Eastern evening, but the more Nick discovers about this world, the more he is educated into the recognition that beneath its cool manner is the same sweat and vague desire for "plans" and something "new" that characterizes, in more ner-vous, vulgar striving, the lives of the aspirants from the West, who all wish to seem like East Eggers. In the amorphous, yearning nervousness of American life, there is no distinction between East and West. Even at the bottom of the social ladder, George B. Wilson's discontented yearning, his desire to buy and sell cars to attain the necessary gold, is aimed at the long-cherished hun-gering to "go West." All the people in this novel come from the same America. "I see now," says Nick at the end of the book, "that this has been a story of the West, after all—Tom and Gatsby, Daisy and Jordan and I, were all Westerners, and perhaps we possessed some deficiency in common [the lost heritage of "The West"] which made us subtly unadaptable to Eastern life [the present actuality]" (p. 134). It is the *idea* of the West which is summed up in the appearances of exciting Eastern city money, the idea of the transcendent life in the gay place of the orgastic future. So all Americans, in the boom of the bond business, "go East" to find their "West." Gatsby, the one character exempted from the flabby impressionability that only vaguely believes in the golden moment, the one man who has defined that moment sharply and directed his life's energies toward it, is most associated with the West. In his innocent and "disadvantaged" pretensions he is associated with the Westernmost West. When he tells Nick that his people were a wealthy family from the Middle West, Nick inquires casually, "What part of the Middle West?" "San Francisco," Gatsby replies. All the characters, like Gatsby, have the wistful sense of a past dream-state to be recaptured. But Gatsby, like Fitzgerald, sums them all up in the sharp definition of what that dream self is and how to work toward and overtake it. So Jordan goes on trying to maintain the "Golf Champion," balancing precariously in her discontented and uneasy lie of a life the "lie" of the golf ball she had illegally moved in order to attain that championship. So Nick goes East to find what he cannot in his ragged edge of the universe in the Middle West. So Daisy watches for the longest golden moment in memory of her glowing romance with Jay Gatsby—and always misses it. Even Tom Buchanan, that hard side of beef, drifts wistfully in memory of his golden moment when he was Saturday's hero as Yale's greatest end: "I felt," says Nick, "that Tom would drift on forever seeking, a little wistfully, for the dramatic turbulence of some irrecoverable football game" (p. 7). The actuality of the West was not the dream of the West, but none of them realize that in leaving their forward-looking, expectant Middle Western youth, they were leaving in the past, in that youth, the only place where the desired America exists—in the yearning desires of that youthful imagination.

In two contrasting set-pieces, Fitzgerald makes clear that the West is the dream of the American future in the past, the excitement of newness and youth, when we and America and the Golden West were young, and that the East is the present fact of the impersonal wealth so passionately dreamed of and in which we cannot find our expected identities, places, or names. Nick reminisces:

"Even when the East excited me most, even when I was most keenly aware of its superiority to the bored, sprawling, swollen towns beyond the Ohio, with their interminable inquisitions which spared only the children and the very old—even then it had always for me a quality of distortion. West Egg, especially, still figures in my more fantastic dreams. I see it as a night scene by El Greco: a hundred houses, at once conventional and grotesque, crouching under a sullen, overhanging sky and a lustreless moon. [Recall the flight from the devil in *This Side of Paradise*.] In the foreground four solemn men in dress suits are walking along the sidewalk with a stretcher on which lies a drunken woman in a white evening dress. Her hand, which dangles over the side, sparkles cold with jewels. Gravely the men turn in at a house— the wrong house. But no one knows the woman's name and no one cares" (p. 134).

But the West is the idea that was to have been realized in "Eastern" achievement. It is the past, youth, and the sense of excitement to come—it is that which is the Westerner in Americans and that gives Americans, "Easterners" all, an unutterable awareness of their belonging to the land of Columbus. In the contrasting set-piece Nick says:

"One of my most vivid memories is of coming back West from prep school and later from college at Christmas time. Those who went farther than Chicago would gather in the old dim Union Station at six o'clock of a December evening, with a few Chicago friends, already caught up into their holiday gayeties, to bid them a hasty good-by. I remember the fur coats of the girls returning from Miss This-or-That's and the chatter of frozen breath and the hands waving overhead as we caught sight of old acquaintances, and the matchings of invitations : 'Are you going to the Ordways'? the Herseys'? the Schultzes'?'[31] and the long green tickets clasped tight in our gloved hands. And last the murky yellow cars of the Chicago, Milwaukee & St. Paul railroad looking cheerful as Christmas itself on the tracks beside the gate.

[31] Turnbull points out that the "St. Paul families referred to by name . . . were not old Eastern aristocrats but the newly rich" in a town where "there remained more of a sense of hierarchy . . . than in other Midwestern cities. St. Paul was a 'three-generation town'; Minneapolis, Kansas City, Milwaukee could boast of only two." See p. 26 and p. 338, n. 26.

"When we pulled out into the winter night and the real snow, our snow, began to stretch out beside us and twinkle against the windows, and the dim lights of small Wisconsin stations moved by, a sharp wild brace came suddenly into the air. We drew in deep breaths of it as we walked back from dinner through the cold vestibules, unutterably aware of our identity with this country for one strange hour, before we melted indistinguishably into it again.

"That's my Middle West—not the wheat or the prairies or the lost Swede towns, but the thrilling returning trains of my youth. . . . I see now that this has been a story of the West after all . . ." (pp. 133–34).

Not the fact of the land, but the thrilling expectation of it. Nostalgia. All human beings miss their youth, but in that universal fact of the psyche, Fitzgerald found a clue to what is uniquely American.

Just as the difference between the fact (the East) and the dream (the West) is ubiquitous in the lives of the novel's people, regardless of region, so too in time and nationality Fitzgerald sees that what has become of the dream of the past is inescapably present, and that almost all Americans are indistinguishable from each other in the irresponsible betrayal of the idea of America by the wealth of America.

The West to which Nick has retired is future to the events of the story: it is the narrator's present moment after the narrative has been finished, and from which he looks back at events. He has gone back "West," not to the dream he knows is finished with Gatsby's death, but to the second best he can find. Although it is provincial, smug, philistine, and landlocked away from the excitement on the seaboard, the West of the present moment holds for Nick the memory of what it was once supposed to have been. For Nick at least it is a place of some identity and not the sea-change of lights, faces, names and places that characterize the swift mobility of identity in the East. Nick says, "I am part of that ["my Middle West . . . the thrilling returning trains of my youth"], a little solemn with the feel of those long winters, a little complacent from growing up in the Carraway house in a city where dwellings are still called through decades by a family's name. I see now that this has been a story of the West after all. . . ." Nick knows that his moral choice is in part squeamish provincialism, for the realities beneath the apparent regional differences are the same. But it *is* a moral choice in that Nick chooses the memory of the manners of an older America that was supposed to have provided the dream, even though it did not, chooses that memory over the absolute limbo of the haunted El Greco night-scape— chooses, in short, moral nostalgia over immoral present fact. He has learned the necessity for a "Western" identity by observing how "the East" has cheated Gatsby out of his imagined place, house, region, home. Gatsby has been so robbed of his identity that he can never go "home" again. The burial of the dream is real. "—Mr. Gatz," says Nick to Gatsby's totally uncomprehending father, "I thought you might want to take the body West."

"He shook his head.

" 'Jimmy always liked it better down East. He rose up to his position in the East' " (p. 127).

A man, Nick knows, must be responsible for the identity he claims, and not trust to the drift of wealth and standing. It is exactly that sense of responsibility that is one more of the ties, like hope and wonder, between Nick and Gatsby. The stability of the Western identity that Nick claims is a constancy of commitment, a sign of an old-fashioned, lasting sense of responsibility. He doesn't drift off to let others clean the mess he might have made. He had left home earlier to maintain the honesty of his feelings and the honorableness of his relationships. He would not be stampeded by gossip into leading into engagement a girl he didn't love. "I am slow-thinking," Nick says, "and full of interior rules that act as brakes on my desires, and I knew that first I had to get myself definitely out of that tangle back home. . . ."

"Everyone suspects himself of at least one of the cardinal vir-

tues, and this is mine: I am one of the few honest people that I
have ever known" (p. 46). So too, when he had finally had a belly-
ful of Jordan and the Buchanans, instead of merely avoiding
Jordan, he insists on meeting her to break clean in the honesty of
his feelings. "I wanted to leave things in order and not just trust
that obliging and indifferent sea to sweep my refuse away" (p.
134). (The critics who call Nick unreliable never note the constant counterpoint that is part of Fitzgerald's technique in differ-
entiating Nick and Gatsby from everyone else in the novel.) So,
in a choice of false appearances Nick chooses those, the West,
that at least hold for him the memory of a promised land peopled
by *identities*. "After Gatsby's death the East was haunted for me
like that [the El Greco night-scape], distorted beyond my eyes'
power of correction. So when the blue smoke of brittle leaves
was in the air and the wind blew the wet laundry stiff on the line
I decided to come back home" (p. 134), and the Buchanans, the
East, were "rid of my provincial squeamishness forever" (p. 136).
Like Gatsby, for Nick the one incorruptible centrality of his life
is his sense of his self.

In the metaphor of bad driving that threads its way through
the novel, a metaphor for the irresponsibility of the world Nick
repudiates, Nick accuses Jordan, the cheating champion, of being
careless.

"Jordan Baker instinctively avoided clever, shrewd men, and
now I saw that this was because she felt safer on a plane where
any divergence from a code would be thought impossible. She
was incurably dishonest. She wasn't able to endure being at a
disadvantage and, given this unwillingness, I suppose she had
begun dealing in subterfuges when she was very young in order
to keep that cool, insolent smile turned to the world and yet
satisfy the demands of her hard, jaunty body" (p. 45). She demands
and expects that others will assume responsibility for her so that

she will remain unencumbered. When she almost knocks down a workman with her car, she laughingly cuts off Nick's protests about what a rotten driver she is by insisting that the good drivers will give way to her. Her selfish irresponsibility needs and uses the dependability of others. "That's why I like you," she tells Nick.

The relationship between Nick and Jordan is not merely a sub-plot that gives Nick something to do in the story: in the moral parallel between the Gatsby-Daisy relationship and the Nick-Jordan relationship, Nick is initiated firsthand into what he also learns through Gatsby. The reader is prepared for Nick's repudiation of Jordan, especially when Jordan abandons Tom and Daisy, after having lived with and off them, in order not to be involved in their troubles. It was a very Tom-and-Daisyish thing to do, and is paralleled again, in Gatsby's household, by the callous Ewing Klipspringer and his concern for his tennis shoes. Nick, who insists on judgment, always does so within the context of his tolerance. He forgets, for a while, that Jordan is a cheat, and is willing to allow for hope. But he will put up with only so much bad driving: "conduct may be founded on the hard rock or the wet marshes, but after a certain point I don't care what it's founded on." When Nick breaks off his relationship with Jordan, she would put the blame on him, lying to herself about the possibility that it might have been her own callous and totally selfish irresponsibility that finally repelled Nick. "You said a bad driver was only safe until she met another bad driver?" says Jordan. "Well, I met another bad driver, didn't I? I mean it was careless of me to make such a wrong guess. I thought you were rather an honest, straightforward person. I thought it was your secret pride." Nick's knowledge that not everyone can drift, that someone must assume responsibility if the whole world is not to be out of "moral uniform," a place of mess and ashes and destructive collisions, is based upon his own sense of identity which will not allow himself to lie to himself for whatever appearances of "honorable intentions." Like Huck Finn, he has the deepest kind of integrity, and his answer is a simple and direct denial of self-deception: " 'I'm thirty,' I said. 'I'm five years too old to lie to myself and call it honor.' . . . Angry, and half in love with her, and tremendously sorry, I turned away" (p. 135).

Although the dissimilarities of identity between the East and the West are wiped out in the underlying realities, the surface distinctions that are supposed to indicate real differences are clear. The remembered West still calls a dwelling through decades by a family's name. But the East is a constant and endless catalogue of namelessness and mistaken identities and missed connections. The time it takes to establish a self in the fluid world of wealth is speeded up until history is annihilated. The suddenness by which Gatsby, "Mr. Nobody from Nowhere," can appear on the scene with a house that pretends to ancient establishment is repeated in endless minor details throughout the book. The repetition makes a panorama of the sense of placelessness and yearning that the "damned middle class" Fitzgerald had grown up with and that he came to learn was the transcendent identity-hunger that, unarticulated, is the real meaning of American mobility and fluidity and informality and repudiation of any bounds imposed by the past in the perennially "new" world of perennially "flaming" youth.

History is wiped out at a stroke, identities grow like mushrooms after a rain. When Nick first came to West Egg, he "was lonely for a day or so until one morning, some man, more recently arrived than I, stopped me on the road."

> "How do you get to West Egg village?" he asked helplessly.
>
> I told him. And as I walked on I was lonely no longer. I was a guide, a pathfinder, an original settler. He had casually conferred on me the freedom of the neighborhood.

And so with the sunshine and the great bursts of leaves growing on the trees just as things grow in fast movies, I had that familiar conviction that life was beginning over again with the summer (p. 5).

The promise of sudden and possible new worlds is immediately related to the excitement of money. In the "young breath-giving air," Nick "bought a dozen volumes on banking and credit and investment securities, and they stood on my shelf in red and gold like new money from the mint, promising to unfold the shining secrets that only Midas and Morgan and Maecenas knew" (p. 5). Gatsby's house, the central symbol of the American distortion of history that annihilates time and creates new "established" identities overnight, was a "*factual imitation* of some Hotel de Ville in Normandy, with a tower on one side, *spanking new* under a *thin beard of raw ivy*, and"— the wealth that makes it all possible —"a marble swimming pool, and more than forty acres of lawn and garden" (p. 6). Never missing a touch, Fitzgerald later recounts the history of the house. It had been built by a parvenu brewer, who in the "fast-movie" time of America wanted to consolidate appearances of old establishment. He had "agreed to pay five years' taxes on all the neighboring cottages, if the owners would have their roofs thatched with straw" so that the brewer's house would appear to be the manor amidst the peasants' dwellings. Like all the pretensions of wealth in the novel, the attempt to turn back the clock is an idiocy that ignores the very actualities of American time that have made pretend-identity possible in the first place. (And as always, Gatsby as central representative of American time makes the most concerted effort—no drifter, he—to turn back the clock.) Fitzgerald firmly believed that the debasement of the dream into the possibilities of money, ignoring the human identity that the dream was to have created in the first place, created a totally inorganic sense of America in Americans, so that the nation becomes filled with a populace which in tasteless and yearning sentiment endeavors to re-create the imaginary pastoral, idyllic past out of the fluid and identityless wealth that turns into a fast movie the very never-never past that is sought. Writing to Perkins about the idealization of the American "INARTICULATE, FARMER, WHO, IS, CLOSE, TO, SOIL, AND [IS], 'STRONG! VITAL! REAL!' " in an idealized pioneer past, Fitzgerald runs through the history of the "beautiful farmer" novel that had great vogue in the 1920's. Fitzgerald concludes:

As a matter of fact the American peasant as "real" material scarcely exists. He is scarcely 10% of the population, isn't bound to the soil at all as the English and Russian peasants were— and, if [he] has any sensitivity whatsoever (except a most sentimental conception of himself, which our writers persistently shut their eyes to), he is in the towns before he's twenty. Either Lewis, Lardner, and myself have been badly fooled, or else using him as typical American material is simply *a stubborn seeking for the static in a world that for almost a hundred years had simply not been static.* Isn't it a fourth rate imagination that can find only the old property farmer in all this amazing time and land?[32]

Gatsby, in his desire to turn back the clock, "represented everything for which I have an unaffected scorn," says Nick. But Gatsby's dedication to the meretricious and adolescent American belief in Eden, his dream of himself, is his Nick Carraway-like integrity amidst the "foul dust" of the debasement of the dream that is made by the population of "discontented" and drifting money seekers in the fast-movie fairyland of American wealth. In every case, Gatsby is dissociated from American identity at the moment he sums it up.

So, in the irresponsible and irrepressible world of changing

[32] *Letters*, pp. 186–87. For the most coherent discussion of the longing for the idealized pastoral in the American imagination, see Leo Marx, *The Machine in the Garden* (New York, 1964) and Charles Sanford, *The Quest for Paradise* (Urbana, 1961).

namelessness, only Gatsby knows and cares about the people who affect his dream. The high point of the presentation of the non-caring, non-knowing, no-names who inhabit both East and West Egg is at Gatsby's party. It is not surprising in the land where anybody is somebody and nobody knows nobody that when Nick introduces the world of parties to which he drives on his way to the Buchanans he should say that he was going "to see two old friends whom I scarcely knew at all" (p. 7). In his introduction of West Egg parties, in three superb pages Fitzgerald studs his description with intensifying details of contact all organized around the idea that there are no identities contacting each other:

> . . . chatter and laughter, and casual innuendo and introductions forgotten on the spot, and enthusiastic meetings between women who never knew each other's names. . . . Laughter is easier minute by minute, spilled with prodigality, tipped out at a cheerful word. The groups change more swiftly, swell with new arrivals, dissolve and form in the same breath; already there are wanderers, confident girls who weave here and there among the stouter and more stable, become for a sharp, joyous moment the center of a group, and then, excited with triumph, glide on through the sea-change of faces and voices and color and the constantly changing light. . . . There is a burst of chatter as the erroneous news goes around that [one of the wanderings girls] is Gilda Gray's understudy from the *Follies*. . . . People were not invited— they went there. . . . Somehow they ended up at Gatsby's door. Once there they were introduced by somebody who knew Gatsby, and after that they conducted themselves according to the rules of behavior associated with an amusement park. . . .

People are presented namelessly as "two girls in yellow" who announce that "you don't know who we are." Their three escorts are each introduced as "Mr. Mumble." Groups of guests mistake the identities of other groups, yet there are no real groups for the people huddled together don't know each other. And nobody gives a damn.

As always, it is Gatsby who is the center of this world while yet
not of it. His is the most concealed and contrived identity. And
on the surface, as in the deepest sense, if nobody knows anybody
else, it is Gatsby that everybody doesn't know most of all. (Also,
as always, Nick is differentiated from the rest. Not only is he the
only guest who earnestly inquires everywhere about his host, seeking him out to pay his respects, but also he "was one of the few
guests who had actually been invited . . . I had been actually
invited.") When Nick asks after Gatsby, people deny knowing
their host with such amazement and vehemence that Nick slinks
off. The Miss and Mr. Nonames report reliable rumors from dependable friends who heard from trustworthy people who know
responsible sources who said that Gatsby. . . . All the bits of "news"
are mutually contradictory, yet that stops no one from believing
all of it. Gatsby killed a man. No, Gatsby was a German spy. No,
he was in the American army. Yes, he killed a man. Well, somebody knew somebody who grew up with Gatsby in Germany. But
in the constant contrast between Gatsby and the irresponsible
world he represents, Fitzgerald takes care to keep his counterpoint going and show that, unlike the others, Gatsby does his high-
bouncing homework—Gatsby knows even the fractional pieces of
information about the necessary identities. In the midst of the
brawl of know-nothing nobodies speaking misinformation, he
leans toward Nick and says, "Your face is familiar. . . . Weren't
you in the Third Division during the war?" (p. 37).

Only one of the drunken guests—who also had not been invited
(" 'Who brought you?' he demanded. 'Or did you just come? I
was brought. Most people were brought.' ")—sees the extent of
Gatsby's attempt to be something other than "Mr. Nobody from
Nowhere." Identified as an owl-eyed man with spectacles, he is
impressed by the fact that the books in the library are real books.
" 'This fella's a regular Belasco,' " says Owl Eyes of Gatsby. " 'It's
a triumph. What thoroughness! What realism! Knew when to

stop, too—didn't cut the pages. But what do you want? What do you expect?'

"He snatched the book from me and replaced it hastily on its shelf, muttering that if one brick was removed the whole library was liable to collapse" (p. 36).

The owl-eyed man, who sees through the appearances to the magnitude of Gatsby's attempt, who mixes admiration with his contempt for the show, is the only one of all the hundreds at the parties in the summer who attends Gatsby's funeral in the fall.

Nothing is needed more desperately in this world of blind nonselves than seeing and being selves. But the ability to see, like the ability to be, is thwarted by the foul dust that blinds and kills. The owl-eyed man with spectacles, in the context of his society, recalls the spectacles that preside over the valley of foul dust and ashes, the eyes of Dr. T. J. Eckleburg. In the abandoned nightmare of the El Greco world, he is the non-existent God to whom the lost souls pray. The eyes are "blue and gigantic" but "they look out of no face." Insisting on the omniscience, omnipotence and justice of God, Wilson, to Michaelis's shock, stares at the eyes of Eckleburg. "God sees everything," he repeats, to which Michaelis makes a rejoinder more apt than he knows: "That's an advertisement."

Yet what other God is there in the novel? The God of the valley of ashes, the valley of dead or obscure identities, is himself the history of those identities. Once upon a time there was a promise of new vision, of one who would make us see. But The Great Oculist Himself either "sank down himself into eternal blindness, or forgot [his promissory advertisement] and moved away." But the memory remains, constant tarnished reminders remain of what is past: "But his eyes, dimmed a little by many paintless days under sun and rain, brood on over the solemn dumping ground" (p. 19). I will discuss more fully the relationships of "sun" and "rain" and "vision" to "dumping ground" a bit later in this chapter. For the moment it is necessary only to recognize that in terms of time and history, a promise out of the past, a promise long since lost and dimmed, the "vision," broods on, debased, misplaced, and crazily misunderstood. For, after all, the very name indicates the bathos of the potential hugeness of the symbol. Old God? America? The vision of the dream? Why sure, that's only old T. J. Eckleburg, "a wild wag of an oculist . . . in the borough of Queens." What could be less romantic? What could be better fitted to the world of ashy identities characterized by the irony that an owl-eyed man with thick spectacles sees better than the animals with twenty-twenty vision in the El Greco night-scape?

Eckleburg is God, but of course he's not God, he's only an advertisement. Eckleburg is the sign of the dead vision of the American dream, but of course he's not that, he's only the sign of a sightless oculist. The essence of the symbol is its irony, in which the bathetic connection of the name to the dramatic quality of the advertisement brooding over the valley of ashes, does what the entire "history of that summer" does to Gatsby: reverses expectations in images of nonexistent selves blind to others, in images of something past, lost, dead in sun and rain. Jordan's cheat's eyes are always described as "sun-strained," and when Nick refers to his El Greco memory of "the East," he recalls it as "distorted beyond my eyes' power of correction." For what is real is the paintless lusterlessness and distortion, seen through the distorting obscurity of foul dust. Owl Eyes, unlike the blind, bespectacled eyes of Our Lord and our vision of our national dream-promise, are the eyes of an animal that is supposed to be wise and to see through obscuring darkness. But what of the other animals who inhabit "the great wet barnyard of Long Island Sound?" Their names, first cousin to the name of the oculist, are reductions to absurdities.

The names of those who fill the world around Gatsby significantly denote either animals or vegetables; or the immigrant
newness (mainly Polish, Irish, Jewish, Italian) of fast-rising identities as Americans, the new "old established" Americans significantly associated with the movies; or they are names that indicate
the opposite, the debasement of the greatness of established names
of the past. An implicit sociology and history of America is played
out to a background strain at the party, amid the tossed-off names
and the tossed-off identities, of a piece of music that is itself a
tossed-off debasement of the idea of history, "Vladimir Tostoff's
*Jazz History of the World.*"

Nick calls attention to the names, insisting that in themselves
they suggest the quality of the "people" who inhabit Gatsby's
world. Appropriately, Fitzgerald has the names written on something that suggests a dead past and defunct time, and the names
in the jazz history of the new world are those of creatures blind
to Gatsby's real identity. "Once I wrote down on the empty spaces
of a timetable the names of those who came to Gatsby's house that
summer. It is an old timetable now, disintegrating in its folds,
and headed 'This schedule in effect July 5th, 1922.' But I can still
read the gray names, and they will give you a better impression
than my generalities of those who accepted Gatsby's hospitality
and paid him the subtle tribute of knowing nothing whatever
about him" (p. 47).

Chester, a name already reduced to pretentious idiocy in the
name of the photographer at Tom's and Myrtle's party, comes
with the animals and vegetables from East Egg.

From East Egg . . . came the Chester Beckers and the Leeches . . . and
Doctor Webster Civet . . . . and the Hornbeams . . . and a whole clan
named Blackbuck, who always gathered in a corner and flipped up
their noses like goats at whosoever came near. . . . And Edgar Bea-
ver . . . the Cheadles . . . and the Fishguards . . . and S. B. Whitebait . . .

and the Hammerheads . . . and Cecil Roebuck . . . . And the Catlips . . . and James B. ("Rot-Gut") Ferret . . . . A man named Klipspringer was there so often and so long that he became known as "the boarder"— I doubt if he had any other home . . . and Francis Bull.

(When Meyer Wolfsheim is interrupted in his conversation at lunch, he is talking about a flunky named Katspaugh.)

The vegetables at the party were "Clarence Endive . . . and Newton Orchid, who controlled Films Par Excellence . . . and Ernest Lilly . . . . Of theatrical people there were Gus Waize and George Duckweed." In the catalog of debased "greatness" there were "a man named Bunsen . . . and the Willie Voltaires [Willie!] . . . and the Chrysties (or rather Hubert Auerbach and Mr. Chrystie's wife) . . . and the Stonewall Jackson Abrams . . . and . . . Mrs. Ulysses Swett . . . and Mr. P. Jewett, once head of the American Legion . . . and a prince of something, whom we called Duke, and whose name, if I ever knew it, I have forgotten" (pp. 47–49). Owl Eyes was brought to Gatsby's party "by a woman named Roosevelt . . . Mrs. Claude Roosevelt. Do you know her? I met her somewhere last night" (p. 36). There are princes called duke, but generally the "great" names of these no-names from somewhere work reductively, like T. J. Eckleburg, to diminish the associations held with American history. Even the gray old shuffler selling dogs outside the railroad station "bore an absurd resemblance to John D. Rockefeller." The confusion of identities extends to the very four-footed animals themselves.

"I'd like to get one of those police dogs; I don't suppose you got that kind?" says Myrtle to "Mr. Rockefeller."

The man peered doubtfully into the basket, plunged in his hand and drew one up, wriggling, by the back of the neck.

"That's no police dog," said Tom.

"No, it's not exactly a po*lice* dog," said the man with disappointment in his voice. "It's more of an Airedale." . . .

The Airedale—undoubtedly there was an Airedale concerned in it somewhere, though its feet were startlingly white—changed hands . . . .

"Is it a boy or a girl?" [Myrtle] asked delicately.
"That dog? That dog's a boy."
"It's a bitch," said Tom decisively.

And then the possibility for purchasing whatever "identity" is demanded: "Here's your money. Go and buy ten more dogs with it" (p. 22).

Among the other people at Gatsby's parties were those of new "American names," the "Poles, the Mulreadys . . . and Cecil Schoen and Gulick the State senator . . . and Eckhaust and Clyde Cohen and Don S. Schwartze (the son) and Arthur McCarty, all connected with the movies in one way or another . . . and the Bembergs and G. Earl Muldoon . . . Da Fontano the promoter . . . and Ed Legros. . . ." And of other theatrical people, there were "Horace O'Donovan and Lester Myer."

[And there were the] Corrigans and the Kellehers . . . the Dewers and the Scullys . . . Henry L. Palmetto . . . the young Quinns . . . Benny McClenehan arrived always with four girls. They were never quite the same ones in physical person, but they were so identical with one another that it inevitably seemed they had been there before. I have forgotten their names—Jacqueline, I think, or else Consuela, or Gloria or Judy or June, and their last names were either the melodious names of flowers and months [of vegetable life and of time] or the sterner ones of the great American capitalists whose cousins, if pressed, they would confess themselves to be . . . Faustina O'Brien . . . the Baedeker girls [a superb touch!] . . . young Brewer [another!] . . . Mr. Albrucksberger . . . Miss Haag . . . Ardita Fitz-Peters.

And of the others, the names are suggestive of their own categories. There were "a bum named Etty . . . the O. R. P. Schraeders . . . and the Ripley Snells." (The snells came with the fishguards. There were whitebaits and hammerheads with them, too.) There were "the Dancies . . . Maurice A. Flink . . . Beluga . . . and Beluga's girls . . . and there were the Chromes and the Backhyssons . . . and S. W. Belcher and the Smirkes. . . ."

"All these people came to Gatsby's house in the summer."
These "people." And none came to his funeral in the fall.

Like the names, the dwellings and cars detail Fitzgerald's idea
of the betrayal of appearances by combined wealth and sham.[33]
At the top of the social ladder, "the white palaces of fashionable
East Egg glittered along the water." The Buchanans' palace is
"even more elaborate than [Nick] expected, a cheerful red-and-
white Georgian Colonial mansion overlooking the bay. The lawn
started at the beach and ran towards the front door for a quarter
of a mile, jumping over sun-dials and brick walks and burning
gardens—finally it reached the house drifting up the side in bright
vines as though broken by the momentum of its run . . . the front
vista [included] in its sweep a sunken Italian garden, a half acre
of deep, pungent roses . . ." (pp. 7–8). The delicate, lovely rose
and whiteness of the house is intensified in the description of the
interior, with its fragile, light, airy, rosy space and its frosted
wedding cake of a ceiling. Here is the appearance of the desired
world for which Gatsby, leading the pack, and all West Egg and
all New York and all the Valley of the Ashes and all the world
yearns. But when Fitzgerald turns from the appearances, he makes
an immediate connection between wealth and arrogant brute
power. Tom's enormous wealth is immediately associated with
pointless drift, and the description of the fragile house is immediately associated with images of hard power and dominant
ownership:

The front was broken by a line of French windows, glowing now with
reflected gold and wide open to the warm windy afternoon, and Tom
Buchanan in riding clothes was standing with his legs apart on the
front porch. . . . Now he was a sturdy straw-haired man of thirty with

---

[33] I am elaborating here on an idea that has been often noted and that was given
one of its first and best statements in "The Romance of Money," Malcolm Cowley's
introduction to *The Great Gatsby* in *Three Novels of F. Scott Fitzgerald*. The
fabulous qualities of the names in the time-table were first suggested, but incompletely, by R. W. Stallman in "Gatsby and the Hole in Time." See note 29, above.

a rather hard mouth and a supercilious manner. Two shining arrogant eyes had established dominance over his face and gave him the appearance of always leaning aggressively forward. Not even the effeminate swank of his riding clothes could hide the enormous power of that body—he seemed to fill those glistening boots until he strained the top lacing, and you could see a great pack of muscle shifting when his shoulder moved under his thin coat. It was a body capable of enormous leverage—a cruel body.

His speaking voice, a gruff, husky tenor, added to the impression of fractiousness he conveyed. There was a touch of paternal contempt in it, even toward people he liked . . . .

"Now, don't think my opinion on these matters is final," he seemed to say, "just because I'm stronger and more of a man than you are." . . .

"I've got a nice place here," he said, his eyes flashing about restlessly.

Turning me around by one arm, he moved a broad flat hand along the front vista. . . .

"It belonged to Demaine, the oil man." He turned me around again politely and abruptly. "We'll go inside" (pp. 7–8).

All the old established loveliness of America and all that wealth can buy of connection with the great past—it is a Georgian Colonial mansion—is owned by a series of people of strength, which is wealth, and goes from the rich man of main strength (de maine), who like Cody tore wealth up out of the resources of the land, to the main strength of enormously powerful, enormously wealthy Tom Buchanan. Tom's taking the house is a parallel to his taking the pink-and-white fragile beauty of Daisy, who, like the rose-and-white house, is the object of everyone's desire. Buchanan, with his series of houses, his Daisy, and his series of other men's wives, personifies, as he exercises his *droit de seigneur*, what Fitzgerald distrusted and hated with the smoldering anger of the peasant.

One rung down the ladder—it is, after all, only "a courtesy bay" that separates East and West Egg—is the tremendous new wealth of the parvenu who has found the main strength of wealth to push himself into the stream of constantly changing identity. From a distance, the differences between East and West Eggs, be-

tween great old wealth and great new wealth (with all the regional suggestions) is invisible. Even New York City itself—the
craziest of all amalgams of western, eastern, immigrant, old established, wealthy, poor identities, the place where all the bond-
business wealth is obtained in the fast-movietime culture—appears the same as elite and exclusive East Egg: "Over the great
bridge, with the sunlight through the girders making a constant
flicker upon the moving cars, with the city rising up across the
river in *white heaps and sugar lumps all built with a wish out of
non-olfactory money. The city seen from the Queensboro Bridge
is always the city seen for the first time, in its first wild promise of
all the mystery and the beauty in the world*" (p. 52, italics mine).
The city and its society is a microcosm of the nation: it is for
Gatsby's and Nick's eyes in this passage exactly what the newly
discovered continent itself was for Dutch sailors' eyes, and like
everything else in the novel extends the significance of "the history of that summer" in New York.

The crazy instability of identity means that no American appearances can be trusted to be the fulfillment of that golden dream
identity they wildly promise in hints of all the mystery and beauty
in the world. Immediately upon presenting the East-Egg-dream-
vision of New York, Fitzgerald reverses expectations and does so,
significantly, in terms of identities. All the mystery and beauty in
the world is immediately followed by a dead man who passes "in
a hearse heaped with blooms," which is followed by mourning
European immigrants.

Indeed, Gatsby's house and identity fully belong in America
as much as Buchanan's. It is only close up in the dreamlight that
one can see the differences between it and the appearances with
which East Egg wealth condescends to the appearances of West
Egg wealth. It is, as I have indicated earlier in the discussion, a
difference in manners, not in moral realities. It is West Egg that
fears "showing the marks," fears the sweat it so necessarily pro-

duces in its strivings. So West Egg must out-appear East Egg in every show of belonging, in every show of manners and wealth.[34] Gatsby's politeness is as much a part of his cheap-fiction show as Tom's fractiousness is part of his *droit de seigneur*. Gatsby's house out-performs and outshines in its gaudiness the lovelier house of the Buchanans. The melodramatic and hilarious clinquant of Gatsby's invented history (the dream person to go along with the dream girl and the dream house and the dream car) is created because, as Mr. Nobody-from-Nowhere-Gatsby tells Nick, "I didn't want you to think I was just some nobody" (p. 51). The cars are like the houses. The new great Belasco wealth of the parvenu must stage the ornate show that choruses "I belong! I am! I belong! I am!" with every action.

East Egg has the huge limousine in which Daisy appears at Nick's cottage. But the casualness of long belonging to the old American elite is evidenced in the blue coupé the Buchanans drive with the drifting easiness in which they have no need to prove the validity of their address. Gatsby's famous car, on the other hand, "was a rich cream color, bright with nickel, swollen here and there in its monstrous length with triumphant hat-boxes and supper-boxes and tool-boxes, and terraced with a labyrinth of wind-shields that mirrored a dozen suns. Sitting down behind many layers of glass in a sort of green leather conservatory, we started to town" (p. 49). The Buchanans never deign to drive anyone anywhere—indeed, going to the Plaza Tom commandeers

[34] It is not improbable that Fitzgerald was conscious of using East and West Egg, *as names*, as signs for human behavior. In 1923, at Great Neck, the model for the "Eggs," when he was beginning *The Great Gatsby*, Fitzgerald insistently used the "good and bad eggery" language of *Sinister Street*. He constantly referred to people as "eggs," with qualifying adjectives that made explicit the kinds of eggs they were. See Turnbull, p. 136. As late as eight years after he finished *The Great Gatsby*, Fitzgerald still used the word "egg" as a representation of an uncompleted stage of human life. He wrote to his daughter, "my come-back to your calling me Pappy is christening you by the word Egg, which implies that you belong to a very rudimentary state of life and that I could break you up and crack you open. . . . 'Egg Fitzgerald.' How would you like that to go through life with—'Eggie Fitzgerald' or 'Bad Egg Fitzgerald' . . ." (August 8, 1933, *Letters*, p. 4).

Gatsby's car, and coming from the Plaza Daisy commandeers it. But in the ill-bred ostentation of Gatsby's necessary and loud display of lavish generosity, all of his motor vehicles serve the same function as the appearances of his silvery-gold car with its money-colored leather: Gatsby's "*two* motor-boats [the Buchanans only have one] slit the waters of the Sound, drawing aquaplanes over cataracts of foam. On week-ends his Rolls-Royce became an omnibus, bearing parties to and from the city between nine in the morning and long past midnight, while his station wagon scampered like a brisk yellow bug to meet all trains" (p. 31). "I thanked him for his hospitality," says Nick. "We were always thanking him for that—I and the others" (p. 117).

The next rung down in the ladder of social appearances is occupied by the same middle-class pretentiousness that characterizes Gatsby's world, but only in complete dependence upon the noblesse of those who can exercise the *droit de seigneur*. Here again, Myrtle Wilson has, beneath the appearances and manners, a oneness of identity with East and West Egg. The more differences in money between classes, the more visible the differences between caste. But just as the differences between West and East Egg are sinister and bizarre non-differences of appearances only, so too in Myrtle's life there is the same wistful yearning, the same misplaced power and energy that characterizes Tom's as much as it does Gatsby's world.

Myrtle Wilson becomes the vehicle for Fitzgerald's idea about the vast energy generated by American yearning for the world of the hot cats on top. But unlike Gatsby, Myrtle has no unifying dream. She represents the energy of desire in the actuality of America as Gatsby represents the energy of desire in the idea of America. Like Gatsby, she too comes from Nowhere, a halfway point between the getting and spending of American wealth— which is precisely where geography puts the Valley of Ashes as a metaphor of placelessness. The place of gray ashes has none of the fragile, airy, rose-and-white spaciousness of East Egg, and represents East Egg's opposite color down at the "shoes"of American society, as Fitzgerald termed it in *The Beautiful and Damned.*

"About halfway between West Egg and New York the motor road hastily joins the railroad and runs beside it for a quarter of a mile, so as to shrink away from a certain desolate area of land. This is a valley of ashes—a fantastic farm where ashes grow like wheat into ridges and hills and grotesque gardens . . ." (p. 19). Wilson's car-lessness and grotesque "gardens" and garage typify him as Buchanan's and Gatsby's cars and gardens and houses do them—there are no half acres of "deep and pungent roses" in this "fantastic farm" near the "great wet barnyard of Long Island Sound." The valley is the limbo of utter poverty, and the lack of wealth produces the same difficulties of identity that opulence does. The houses and cars on West and East Egg do not equal the enlarged human identity they are supposed to represent. But in the absence of *any* wealth in wealthy America, it is hard even to *see*, let alone define, a house or—more important—a human "where ashes take the forms of houses and chimneys and rising smoke and, finally, with a transcendent effort, of men who move dimly and already crumbling through the powdery air" (p. 19). Sweating and showing the marks in poverty does not produce even the show of identity, but only more sweat and powdery ash. The terrible irony of the valley's poverty is that the efforts of work, the sources of income, are as obscure in providing true human definition as are the bootlegger or "oil man" sources of wealth on the Eggs. "Occasionally a line of gray cars crawls along an invisible track, gives out a ghastly creak, and comes to rest, and immediately the ash-grey men swarm up with leaden spades and stir up an impenetrable cloud which screens their obscure operations from your sight" (p. 19). In the *luftmensch* world of Fitzgerald's fiction, sources of income are sometimes named, but they are never really seen. Moneygetting remains an obscure and invisible business, whether at the "gold hat" or at the "shoes" of society. No one really knows where anyone else's money comes from and no one really cares about the relation of the money to the name unless one's own station is threatened. In this fictive world of money-selves, Fitzgerald presents a system in which men with money receive no true human identity from their riches, and men without money receive no such identity from their labor. Although Fitzgerald's sense of economics derives from his own sense of himself rather than from Marxist theory, and though he was never really a Marxist, it is easy to see why he came to think of himself as one and to make the description of the working day in *Das Kapital* recommended reading for his daughter. If the valley of ashes is an Eliotic wasteland, it is as economic deprivation rather than as fallen Christian faith that it is a sign of the spiritual deprivation that pervades the entire geography, coast to coast, Egg to Egg.

Life in poverty is neither the garish multicolor of West Egg nor the gleaming rose-and-whiteness of East Egg, but an ash-gray identity that is the denial of any color in life. George B. Wilson, the denizen of the valley, is a "spiritless man, anaemic" and "dim and already crumbling." When he moves in his garage he is seen "mingling immediately with the cement color of the walls" (p. 21). Whatever vitality exists in this place is aimed at getting away from the labor that poverty makes anything but "the only dignity." Myrtle emulates West Egg with the same vibrant passion that the *nouveaux riches* aim at East Egg, continuing down to the full length of the social ladder the emulous discontentment of American life. In her energy she "carried her surplus flesh sensuously as some women can. Her face . . . contained no facet or gleam of beauty, but there was an immediately perceptible vitality about her as if the nerves of her body were continually smoldering. . . ." She "wet her lips . . . and spoke . . . in a soft coarse voice" (p. 21). When she is killed she lies in the road with her mouth "wide open and ripped at the corners, as though she had choked a little in giving up the tremendous vitality she had stored so long" (p. 105). In her un-East Egg energy she is Gatsby without the gorgeousness of his imagination. Measured against the pale anemic lethargy of her husband, of Jordan Baker, of Daisy, she offers the energy of satisfaction to Tom. But Tom's American energy is that of brutalizing wealth and power, Myrtle's that of coarse and vulgar aspiration. Where can American energy go, Fitzgerald asks, what can it produce, what can it aspire to but commodities and pretentious appearances without the gorgeous dream of the *idea* of America to give it human purpose and identity? It can only go back to its beginnings, duplicating itself in the death of the dream, in the purchase of more baubles. Tom bought Daisy with a $350,-000 pearl necklace, bought her away from her love of Gatsby's dream of her, away from Gatsby's love. At the end of the book Tom is last seen going "into a jewelry store to buy a pearl necklace—or perhaps only a pair of cuff buttons" (p. 136).[35] Without the dream of America, the dream of American wealth can only eventuate in the murder of human identity. "Myrtle Wilson, her life violently extinguished, knelt in the road and mingled her thick dark blood with the dust" (p. 105). Myrtle never leaves the valley of ashes any more than George goes "West" or Tom or Gatsby ever leave "the East" or Nick ever *really* goes "home." Her life prefigures Gatsby's, and Fitzgerald created her to serve a double purpose. First she indicates the debasement of expectation that is visited by the fever for wealth—fed by the uniquely American ubiquitous possibility of it—upon the sense of all that America promises and upon the undeniably vibrant American

---

[35] One of the many revealing glimpses of Fitzgerald's defensive fight for the golden girl against the *droit de seigneur* of money is seen not only in the fact that he tried to establish his identity by wanting to give all his money to cabdrivers when he was drunk or by keeping a plate of money on a table in his hotel room so that bellboys could help themselves, but also in the fact that after he published *The Great Gatsby*, he spent an entire publisher's check on—a pearl necklace for Zelda. See Sylvia Beach, *Shakespeare and Company* (New York, 1959), pp. 116–17, 119.

energy that tries to rise to the top in pursuit of it. There is even a hint—too subtle to be followed with absolute certainty that here again the names work as they did in the list of those who attended Gatsby's parties. There is no positive similarity between "Myrtle" and "Martha" except the initial, and no positive similarity between "Wilson" and "Washington" except the initial. But *George* and Myrtle are introduced "a few days before the Fourth of July" and, in the same reversal of identities that characterized the view of the dream city of New York, "a gray, scrawny Italian child was setting torpedoes in a row along the railroad track" (p. 21). This speculation will not bear pursuit, but what is certain, though, is that American energy in this book is coarsened by wealth's exercise of *droit de seigneur* over it, and, finally, is killed by the irresponsible carelessness of wealth's uses of all that tremendous energy. The careless rich are not hurt by their irresponsible use of power, but the striving poor are. Tom's strength exercised on Daisy results only in a black-and-blue bruise on her little finger. "That's what I get for marrying a brute of a man, a great, big hulking physical specimen of a—" (p. 11). But the parallel to it, the net result of Myrtle's "marrying" the same brute, is a torn breast. Daisy repeats what Tom won't have—"hulking"— and gets only a sulky frown. Myrtle repeats what Tom won't have ("Daisy! Daisy! Daisy!") in an assertion that the social gulf of identity has been closed between them, and she gets a broken nose. Daisy's affair with Gatsby results in a few tears for Daisy and in total loss and death for Gatsby. Tom's affair with Myrtle results in a few tears for Tom and in total loss and death for Myrtle.

Fitzgerald's second use of Myrtle in the parallel he makes between her and Gatsby is the further separation of Gatsby from the foul dust that floated in the wake of his dreams. Gatsby uses the tawdry appearances for further ends; Myrtle sees them as ends in themselves and finds her very being in them. By implication and association, she thereby indicates Gatsby's superiority to East Egg and the valley of ashes as well as to West Egg. Well mated to East Egg Tom, Myrtle is, in her sparse "disadvantaged" proletarian life, the same coarse, sentimental barbarism that he is at the top. The mixture of the two creates all over again the gaudy, smutty trumpery of the West Egg between East Egg and the valley of ashes. Fitzgerald couldn't give indigent Myrtle her own car with which to continue his symbolic parallels, but he does contrive to continue them through the irony of the association of her car-lessness and her husband's occupation. He does contrive to have Tom flag a taxi for her and in this way shows the kind of car she would own if she could: "she let four taxicabs drive away before she selected a new one, lavender colored with gray upholstery" (p. 22).

Similarly, she has a flat above a garage, not a house, but Tom does secure an apartment for her: "The apartment was on the top floor—a small living-room, a small dining room, a small bedroom, and a bath. The living room was crowded to the doors with a set of tapestried furniture entirely too large for it, so that to move about was to stumble continually over scenes of ladies swinging in the gardens of Versailles . . . . Several old copies of *Town Tattle* lay on the table together with a copy of *Simon Called Peter*" (p. 23). Myrtle's sister, Catherine, is an artificial girl made up to the eyes, and she makes pretentious comments about Europe on the strength of one three-week stenographer's vacation visit. Chester McKee, who comes to Myrtle's party, is a photographer, but he announces that he's in "the artistic game"; his equally pretentious wife keeps insisting that this or that, he or she, would make a good "subject" and that Chester "could make something of it." The dress and the conversation are like the people and the furnishings and follow the revelatory function of the motif of dwellings and cars: Mrs. Wilson changes into an elaborate dress the color of Gatsby's car, and she becomes more haughty and "more violently affected" by the moment. She seems to fill the smoky room with her gestures, her shrieking laughter, her noisy and ungrammatical talk about the rapacity and undependability of service people. She condescends to her guests and pretends to a wardrobe in which the most expensive clothes are to be casually used but once or twice. Her shopping plans, a Valley-of-Ashes debasement of what Nicole Diver will do with such elan, are symptomatic of her life.

And later, " 'My dear,' she cried, 'I'm going to give you this dress as soon as I'm through with it. I've got to get another one tomorrow. I'm going to make a list of all the things I've got to get. A massage and a wave, and a collar for the dog and one of those cute little ashtrays where you touch a spring, and a wreath with a black silk bow for mother's grave that'll last all summer' " (p. 29).

Tom is bored by the talk; Nick is amazed. Both have "belonged" and have the sophistication that the "disadvantaged" do not have in their vulgarity. The belongers can make jokes about pretentious appearances, as when they enter the suite at the Plaza. " 'It's a swell suite,' " whispered Jordan respectfully, and every one laughed" (p. 96). But except for Nick, the advantages prove to be advantages of sophistication and manner only, not of moral responsibility or heightened human decencies. Nick's father, in fact, was quite correct, for dehumanization is visible on all levels. Fitzgerald introduces into the scene in Myrtle's apartment, hand in hand with the vulgarity, the same non-contact with meaningful truth, the same rumor and identitylessness that he introduced at Gatsby's huge West Egg parties and in the wistful purposelessness of Jordan's, Tom's, and Daisy's East Egg lives. The announcements of blurring of real identity are the obbligato against which the repulsive scene is played: the "artistic game" here results in "an over-enlarged photograph, apparently a hen sitting on a blurred rock. Looked at from a distance, however, the hen resolved itself into a bonnet, and the countenance of an old lady beamed down into the room." Catherine's false face, so full of makeup, was one in which "the efforts of nature toward the old alignment gave a blurred air to the face." McKee, who can only make blurred photographs of hens on rocks, talks about changing the light to "bring out all the modelling of the features" of Myrtle's coarse face. The conversation about Gatsby is a preview of and a parallel to the conversation at Gatsby's parties. The conversation about Daisy, too, is a complete misrepresentation of the facts. Nick "wanted to get out and walk eastward toward the park through the soft twilight, but each time I tried to go I became entangled in some wild, strident argument which pulled me back, as if with ropes, into my chair" (p. 28). Drunk as he is, he is yet dimly aware of his revulsion toward the society in which he participates, aware at once of the vulgar actuality within the room and yet of the appearance of excitement the energy-lit windows of the party-room must make to the outsider who does not belong: "Yet high over the city our line of yellow windows must have contributed their share of human secrecy to the casual watcher in the darkening streets, and I was him too, looking up and wondering. I was within and without, simultaneously enchanted and repelled by the inexhaustible variety of life" (p. 28). Voicing Fitzgerald's own repelled, attracted, fascinated attitude of the outsider-belonger, Nick presents a scene of total loss of identity and sea-change of existence as the strident screaming of the women announces their pretentious sense of personal and social superiority to their husbands: "The little dog was sitting on the table looking with blind eyes through the smoke, and from time to time groaning faintly. People disappeared, reappeared, made plans to go somewhere, and then lost each other, searched for each other, found each other a few feet away. . . . 'Come to lunch some day,' " suggested McKee as he and Nick "groaned down in the elevator.

" 'Where?'

" 'Anywhere' " (p. 29).

No matter where one looks, in whatever social level, all one finds are non-people who have lost their dreams and don't know where to find them, non-identities wheeling and wandering and colliding carelessly in a wistfully desperate attempt to overtake a self. Everyone wants to turn the clock back. Pretentiousness is an attempt to regain the imagined glory of a lost and totally inapplicable past—Myrtle's West-Eggish apartment decorated with scenes of Versailles—and to maintain a sentimental hold on the past into the future—a wreath for Mother's grave that'll last all summer. None of these disintegrating non-people, already crumbling in the smoky, powdery air, knows that in the loss of the useful past, the dream, is the loss of the vaguely desired future and that their Nowhere lives are also Never-Never lives. And like the "Baedecker girls," the "guides" to the past are always drunk. Only Gatsby never drinks.

Fitzgerald's manipulation of the car motif is to associate cars with mobility, mobility with change of identity, change of identity with identitylessness. At the same time, the cars, used as showpieces of social identity, make the same comment on the dehumanizing emphasis on money, for money is the key to mobility. Consolidating the idea of cars as showfronts and mobility—the same thing, in essence—Fitzgerald then weaves through the idea of the motif another idea, that of combined excitement and irresponsibility. Daisy, who performs the ultimate murder of identity by committing manslaughter with a car, is the owner of that whispering promise of a voice which hints at fulfillment of all the most exciting hopes America offers in its availability of fast-movietime magicolored showplace life. "It was the kind of voice that the ear follows up and down, as if each speech is an arrangement of notes that will never be played again. . . . There was an excitement in her voice that men who had cared for her found difficult to forget: a singing compulsion, a whispered 'Listen,' a promise that she had done gay, exciting things just a while since and that there were gay, exciting things hovering in the next hour" (p. 9). Gatsby,

who cares more than anyone for what she represents, best understands what the key to that enlarged life is. He has learned what
his society has taught him—how he has learned from the very beginning!—about money-mobility. Gatsby identifies that promise
in Daisy's voice and ties the idea of money as identity to all the
alluring promise of identity.

"She's got an indiscreet voice," [Nick] remarked. "It's full of—" I
hesitated.
   "Her voice is full of money," [Gatsby] said suddenly.
   That was it. I'd never understood before. It was full of money—
that was the inexhaustible charm that rose and fell in it, the jingle of
it, the cymbals' song of it. . . . High in a white palace the king's
daughter, the golden girl . . . (p. 91).

The promise of a new life that Nick feels in leaf-bursting, mon-
eyland summer is associated repeatedly with cars: "Already it was
deep summer on roadhouse roofs and in front of wayside garages,
where new red gas-pumps sat out in pools of light . . ." (p. 17). To
Gatsby, one of the exciting attractions about the Daisy Fay he
courted was her "little white roadster." When Gatsby asks Nick
to his party, he sends the invitation with his spring-colored chauffeur in "robin's egg blue." Daisy's advent to the exciting reunion
tea party with Gatsby is made in blues and lavenders in her
limousine, and with reference to her chauffeur's nose. The book
is peppered with images and bits of conversation and incident that
make cars representative of the same exciting promise that Daisy's
voice offers, creating a parallel—if not an equation—between that
voice and the treacherous murderousness of cars irresponsibly
used. Nick, with his own heightened sensitivity to the mystery
and intoxication of romantic possibility, is constantly aware of
the connection. He most feels his singleness when New York
excitement begins and he is not wheeling in a car toward entranc-
ing "insideness": ". . . at eight o'clock, when the dark lanes of the
Forties were five deep with throbbing taxicabs, bound for the

theater district, I felt a sinking in my heart. Forms leaned together in the taxis as they waited, and voices sang, and there was
laughter from unheard jokes, and lighted cigarettes outlined
unintelligible gestures inside. Imagining that I, too, was hurrying
toward gayety and sharing their intimate excitement, I wished
them well."

Nick once more is the commentator for Fitzgerald, the belong-
ing-outcast man who, like the Nick at Myrtle's party, knew full
well what the inside life was like, yet who, as the outsider, could
never be insensible (in his romantic readiness) to the promising
allurements of the movie-set fascinating appearances of American
life. He loved America sadly. He repudiated it more sadly still.
Within his own memories, Fitzgerald had recurrent images of
taxis in New York as embodiments of arrival at the rosy center.
". . . I remember riding on top of a taxicab along deserted Fifth
Avenue on a hot Sunday night. . . . I remember riding in a taxi
one afternoon between very tall buildings under a mauve and
rosy sky; I began to bawl because I had everything I wanted and
knew I would never be so happy again."[36]

The prescient Nick, who sees through the very appearances
that stimulate and entrance him, knows their phoniness because
he has already learned about the phoniness in that "car" voice
of the moneyed golden girl. Daisy boasts to Nick about her sophistication. But "the instant her voice broke off, ceasing to
compel my attention, my belief, I felt the basic insincerity of
what she had said. It made me uneasy, as though the whole evening had been a trick of some sort to exact a contributory emotion
from me. I waited, and sure enough, in a moment she looked at
me with an absolute smirk on her lovely face, as if she had asserted her membership in a rather distinguished secret society
to which she and Tom belonged" (p. 15).

The party-excitement of the promise is one with falseness and

36 "My Lost City," The Crack-Up (New York, 1956), pp. 27, 28–29.

irresponsibility. The car images are related constantly to party irresponsibility not only in the "careless driver" conversation between Nick and Jordan, but in subtly repeated details that plant the idea in the reader's perceptions. People "got into automobiles which bore them out to Long Island, and somehow they ended up at Gatsby's door. Once there . . . they conducted themselves according to the rules of behavior associated with an amusement park." The young Englishmen who want to grab what they can get are selling "bonds . . . or automobiles." What first reminded Nick of Jordan's identity as a cheat was that "she left a borrowed car out in the rain with the top down and then lied about it." The scene that at once relates Gatsby to "cars" and yet isolates him from them, which sums up the relationship of "car" to blind irresponsibility and makes Owl Eyes the one animal innocent of the irresponsible world he lives in, is the hilarious scene of the exodus from Gatsby's party.

Drunk drivers cluster about a car which had shed a wheel against a wall. As Owl Eyes climbs out of the car, he is accused of bad driving by all the righteous drunks who are staring at the car in the ditch. But Owl Eyes was not driving. The man who was driving was so drunk he didn't know he was driving. His response to the fact that the wheel had come off was to look up into the sky as though the wheel had dropped from above, and then to suggest that they get some gas, and then to suggest that they put the car in reverse. And all the time the comic show goes on, the line of cars from Gatsby's driveway grows longer and louder as drunk driver after drunk driver leans on his horn, creating a cacophony that is an auditory metaphor for everything summed up by the total irresponsibility of rotten driving. The man whose booze befuddled the drivers who were corrupt before they came to the party, Gatsby himself, though source and symbol of the loud and jazzy night, is sober, polite, cool, and not a participant in the comic rot that flows from his party. Innocent of all he participates in, Gatsby remains pure in his isolation from the very show that he believes is the necessary clothing of his incorruptible dream.

The caterwauling horns had reached a crescendo and I turned away and cut across the lawn toward home. I glanced back once. A wafer of a moon was shining over Gatsby's house, making the night fine as before, and surviving the laughter and the sound of his still glowing garden. A sudden emptiness seemed to flow now from the windows and the great doors, endowing with complete isolation the figure of the host, who stood on the porch, his hand up in a formal gesture of farewell (pp. 41–43).

The moral parallels in all Eggs are touched again by shorn car wheels: soon after Tom's honeymoon, his adulterousness is exposed by the fact that he "ran into a wagon on the Ventura road one night, and ripped a front wheel off his car. The girl who was with him got into the papers, too, because her arm was broken [noses or arms, it's all the same]—she was one of the chambermaids in the Santa Barbara Hotel" (p. 59).

Even after Gatsby's death "those gleaming, dazzling parties of his were with me so vividly," says Nick, "that I could still hear the music and the laughter, faint and incessant, from his garden, and the cars going up and down his drive. One night I did hear a material car there, and saw its lights stop at his front steps. . . . Probably it was some final guest who had been away at the ends of the earth and didn't know that the party was over" (pp. 136–37).

Summing up a history of party sprees and the excitement of cars and the gilt identity of resplendent houses in the pandering whisper of Daisy's promising voice, Fitzgerald personifies in Daisy a metaphor for the history of America that, in the moment it was touched by actuality, was a betrayal of the transcendent idea. Nick muses over the history of that summer:

And as the moon rose higher the inessential houses began to melt away until gradually I became aware of the old island here that flowered once for Dutch sailors' eyes— a—fresh, green breast of the new world. Its vanished trees, the trees that had made way for Gatsby's house, had once pandered in whispers to the last and greatest of all human dreams; for a transitory enchanted moment man must have held his breath in the presence of this continent, compelled into an aesthetic contemplation he neither understood nor desired, face to face for the last time in history with something commensurate to his capacity for wonder (p. 137).

The history of the idea is the history that—without even knowing it—Gatsby thinks he is following. The history of the actuality is all that he gets in every level of his journey towards Daisy's green light. How precious, then, is Nick, who sees through appearances at the moment he is among them. How infinitely precious and doomed is Gatsby, who exercises to the full his capacity for wonder in the presence of this magic land. How lost and dehumanized are "all the others" who glut themselves blindly at Gatsby's energies, who have only appearances as their hope of being, whose only idea of self is owning things and going places and putting on the dog—a blind "Airedale" with white feet.

No mechanic can fix a car that has no direction. *"Repairs. GEORGE B. WILSON. Cars bought and sold."* Enough cars and he can "go West." He looks hopefully and wistfully to Tom O'Money Buchanan, pleading with him to sell him a car so that he can "move" somewhere better. Nick, associated with Gatsby, Owl Eyes, and the pioneering Dutch sailors in his unusual sense of hope and wonder, at first associates even the dwellings of poverty with the possibilities of gay excitement. "It had occurred to me that this shadow of a garage must be a blind, and that sumptuous and romantic apartments were concealed overhead" (p. 20). But he quickly learns that at the moneyless bottom of American society, poverty erases the chances of fulfilling the possibilities of the self; again, the dwelling epitomizes the state: "The only building in sight was a small block of yellow brick sitting on the edge of the wasteland . . . and contiguous to absolutely nothing"

(p. 20). The values of the society say that life means money or annihilation. The desperate attempt to reach East Egg is the desperation of trying to flee death in nothingness and become alive as "somebody." On every social level in the novel, the overwhelming and constant lesson of America is that without wealth one is in the precariousness and peril of constantly being "Mr. Nobody from Nowhere," "contiguous to absolutely nothing." And the parallels between all levels are constantly made visible. Consider the raw vigor of Myrtle Wilson, contiguous to absolutely nothing, and the West Egg energy that East Egg disdains: "West Egg," says Nick, "this . . . raw vigor that chafed under the old euphemisms and . . . the too obtrusive fate that herded its inhabitants along a short-cut from nothing to nothing" (pp. 81–82). As one becomes more aware of the moral measure Fitzgerald takes of the society he records, one is struck by the frequency with which he uses the word—"nothing."

George B. Wilson, repairs, cars bought and sold, looks yearningly to the East Egg that promises "the car" and at the same time sardonically withholds fulfillment of that promise.

"Hello, Wilson, old man," said Tom, slapping him jovially on the shoulder. "How's business?"

"I can't complain," answered Wilson unconvincingly. "When are you going to sell me that car?"

"Next week; I've got my man working on it now."

"Works pretty slow, don't he?"

"No, he doesn't," said Tom coldly. "And if you feel that way about it, maybe I'd better sell it somewhere else after all."

"I don't mean that," explained Wilson quickly. "I just meant—" (p. 20).

The total lack of human sympathy in East Egg (Fitzgerald fills the book with instances like that of the unfeeling and coarse snub paid to Gatsby by the equestrians who, with Tom, stop one morning at Gatsby's house, instances that continue to indicate that inhuman non-connection is as prevalent in East Egg as at the worst of Gatsby's or Myrtle's parties) is the selfish irresponsibility that gives money precedence over people and reduces people to objects of use or amusement. So, when Wilson is obviously sick—fittingly, he is sick about his discovery of Myrtle's money-bought betrayal—Tom callously can sport with him about Gatsby's car, that total sign of belief in the promise of money.

With an effort Wilson left the shade and support of the doorway and, breathing hard, unscrewed the cap of the tank. In the sunlight his face was green.
"I didn't mean to interrupt your lunch," he said. "But I need money pretty bad, and I was wondering what you were going to do with your old car."
"How do you like this one?" inquired Tom [indicating Gatsby's car, which he is driving to the Plaza]. "I bought it last week."
"It's a nice yellow one," said Wilson as he strained at the handle.
"Like to buy it?"
"Big chance," Wilson smiled faintly. "No, but I could make some money on the other."
"What do you want money for, all of a sudden?"
"I've been here too long. I want to get away. My wife and I want to go West" (pp. 93–94).

Like Tom and his irrecoverable football game and Jordan and her golf game and Daisy and her longest day of the year, even the nobodies contiguous to absolutely nowhere have their dream: "She's been talking about [going West] for ten years" (p. 94).

The irony is compounded by a recollection of the announcement that Myrtle's sister, Catherine, makes about what she thinks are Tom's plans. " 'When they get married,' continued Catherine, 'they're going West to live for a while until it blows over' " (p. 27).

It takes the shock of discovering the essential sameness of betrayal in their lives, regardless of dwellingplace, to restore what is left of the possibilities of human sympathy. At the moment

Tom and Wilson are in similar positions. Even so, in another parallel to the contrast between Daisy's bruised knuckle and Myrtle's broken nose, wealth makes a crucial difference. Wilson, the victim, is broken and looks guilty, while Tom, the offender, whose money has allowed him a life of adultery, remains hard and well. Wilson "had discovered that Myrtle had some sort of life apart from him in another world, and the shock had made him physically sick. I stared at him," says Nick, "and then at Tom, who had made a parallel discovery less than an hour before—and it occurred to me that there was no difference between men, in intelligence or race, so profound as the difference between the sick and the well. Wilson was so sick that he looked guilty . . ." (p. 94).

Yet, the shock allows Tom to make one of the few statements of human sympathy he is ever capable of, but even then the sympathy is delivered in the only terms available to the inhabitants of the novel's world. " 'I'll let you have that car,' said Tom. 'I'll send it over tomorrow afternoon' " (p. 94). Tom has to repeat his question to Wilson—"What do I owe you?"—and the repetition underscores what the dream of American wealth owes everyone. Tom cuckolds Wilson, indirectly causes Myrtle's and Gatsby's death; Daisy betrays Gatsby, directly causes Myrtle's and indirectly Gatsby's death. The hot cats in control are caught in the same heartless betrayal as those who would change places. "What do I owe you," indeed. Nothing but real existence itself. What should Wilson reply—"My dreams, you bastard"? Yet, recalled to actualities the fitting question is met by the terms of a fitting answer: "Dollar twenty."

In all the unreality of name and place suggested by the dwellings and cars, Nick too has a place. His real place, to which he returns, is the one stable and lasting dwelling in the book, the house in the West that for decades has been known as the Carraway house. As it stands for certainty and the stable expectation of the Western future, it is not so much a place as a state of mind inappropriate to the El Greco world of the East, which has betrayed that future regardless of actual region. In the East, in the actuality of money making, Nick too dwells in a faceless house, an "eyesore" of a cardboard bungalow. But his cottage is a "small eyesore, and it had been overlooked." It is lost among the mansions that surround it. Like his dwelling, his car, "an old Dodge," is unpretentious. His house and car, like Nick himself in the party in Myrtle's apartment, are both "inside" and "outside" the cars and houses which surround him. "I had a view of the water, a partial view of my neighbor's lawn, and the consoling proximity of millionaires—all for eighty dollars a month" (p. 6). Again Nick is like Fitzgerald, the perfect commentator on American society with its fast-movietime wealth and identity. He is innocently fascinated by it, pulled into it, educated into its moral meanings, and remains, while participating in it, outside and able to observe it. In class as in geography, Nick is in the center. He comes from people who are connected to wealth, but not the great wealth of East or West Egg. Yet it is enough wealth so that there is identity—a comfortable stretch of family history between Nick and Wilson's contiguity to absolutely nothing. "My family have been prominent, well-to-do people in this Middle Western city for three generations" (p. 4). Fitzgerald places Nick perfectly. Nick has to "belong," to have the advantages that allow him to scorn the phoney and pretentious appearances. Yet he cannot belong *too* much, or he would then become another representative of all that is East Egg, all that is to be repudiated. He cannot be the "disadvantaged" Mr. Nobody or, like Myrtle Wilson, he could only be the coarse sensibility that could never narrate the events, and could only represent at the lower end of the scale the bankruptcy of morality and imagination that East Egg represents at the other end.

Those who "belong," the established beings like the Carraways and the Buchanans, are, in their established belonging, nonmarginal identities. They have money, "Nordic" names; they are white. They represent everything that Wilson would aspire to, everything that would lead a Jimmy Gatz to change his name to Jay Gatsby, old sport. Yet, like the cars and dwellings and the undefined wistfulness and discontent, the very histories of those who belong, like the histories of those who don't belong, indicate that in time, as well as in geographical and social space, the idea of America has been debased to the actualities of irresponsible wealth and power by its translation into the identities provided by money.

Buchanan's money takes over from Demaine, the oil man— the taking up of America's resources. So too, Carraway's family fortune was begun by a hard-boiled grand-uncle who made a significant choice. The mythic idea of the Civil War—the struggle for liberated human identity, the grandeur of the heritage supposedly transmitted in the established Anglo-Saxon names—was repudiated in favor of a choice of hard cash and selfish safety. The "actual founder of my line was my grandfather's brother," says Nick, "who came here in fifty-one, sent a substitute [one could buy substitutes for money] to the Civil War, and started the wholesale hardware business that my father carries on today" (p. 4). The use that Fitzgerald makes of his Grandfather McQuillan's Middle West wholesale grocery business is one in which the rise to wealth—the past that produced the established identities of today—was, in its turn, the same parvenu pretension that characterizes everything that East Egg scorns in Gatsby. "We have a tradition that we're descended from the Dukes of Buccleuch . . ." (p. 4). But even if one pushes that "right-name" identity back to a mythical past, the uncovered actuality is that the money fever of the present moment is but a continuation of a rapacious past. The Dukes of Buccleuch were Scots border raiders.[37]

[37] "The success of his Grandfather McQuillan was the great social and economic fact in Scott Fitzgerald's background. It was the base he had to work from. For a boy

The revered name that sums up the actualities of the revered past and the history that most represents all that allures the wistful dreamer is the history of Dan Cody. The associations suggested by the name are themselves an aura of the West, and not only the West as region, but as a past golden time when space was open and all wishes were to be fulfilled by grabbing. The corruption of the romantic idea of Buffalo Bill is a degradation of a national dream-memory. It was Buffalo Bill Cody who brought the "Wild West" show to the East and to Europe; Buffalo Bill Cody, the last of the great scouts like Davy Crockett, Kit Carson, Jim Bridger, Daniel Boone, and Wild Bill Hickock, who wrote books about the West and Western heroes; Buffalo Bill Cody who exemplified all that a boy might read and dream about in his Hopalong Cassidy books. In the deterioration of his personal history, Dan Cody serves as an ironic association with Buffalo Bill, and in the novel his name heads the list of those like Mrs. Ulysses S.[wett], "John D. Rockefeller," and Mrs. Claude Roosevelt.

Fitted to the red-white-gold patterns of imagery, colors introduced at the very beginning of the book as representations of copper, silver, and gold money, Cody's heroic Western success is also "a product of the Nevada silver fields, of the Yukon, of every rush for metal since seventy-five. The transactions in Montana copper . . . made him many times a millionaire . . ." (p. 75). Cody's yacht, the sight of which will eventually lead Jimmy Gatz to his golden girl, drops anchor in Little Girl Bay, and its name is the Tuolomee—the name of a California county through which the Mark Twain–Bret Harte trail runs and in which one of history's most fantastic gold strikes was made. California, Nevada,

growing up in the Midwest there was more substance in it than . . . patents of nobility. . . ." When McQuillan's career ended, the obituaries called it "a living romance, for in the brief period of twenty years [McQuillan] passed, by his own unaided exertions, from the humblest beginnings to a place among the merchant princes of the country." Turnbull, p. 4.

Montana, Tuolomee, Cody, the names of romance, become the names of money, and are immediately associated with the "Little Girl" who betrays the Westerner, Ella Kaye. The similarity between Kaye and Fay (Daisy's maiden name) might have been unintentional as had been the similarity between Amory Blaine and Mackenzie's Michael Fane. But it is difficult to believe that Fitzgerald was unaware of the suggested parallel in a novel in which each detail works so subtly and cunningly toward his major ideas about his society. In any case, what might have been the grandeur of the patriarch created out of the successful and hard-handed rapacity of the old, tough, Western dream-time has deteriorated to senility and dissipation. "The transactions in Montana copper that made him many times a millionaire found him physically robust but on the verge of soft-mindedness, and, suspecting this, an infinite number of women tried to separate him from his money" (pp. 75–76). What was to have been the proud American heritage of the dream of the West always comes to the same thing, whether we see it in the hard-boiled present moment of Tom Buchanan, the hard-boiled portrait of Nick's great-uncle, or—the same man, the same face, really—in the portrait of Cody "up in Gatsby's bedroom, a gray, florid man with a hard, empty face—the pioneer debauchee, who during one phase of American life brought back to the Eastern seaboard the savage violence of the frontier brothel and saloon" (p. 76). Ella Kaye, a newspaper woman and a shrewd whore, got all of Cody's money, and the promises of the American past and West and wealth were debauched into the hands of a lovely and ambitious tart. It was the first time in Jimmy Gatz's life that he was betrayed by the lovely girl with all the money, and, significantly, the betrayal of expectations is again reduced to terms of money. It "was from Cody that he inherited money— a legacy of twenty-five thousand dollars. He didn't get it. He never understood the legal device that was used against him, but what remained of the millions went intact to Ella Kaye" (p. 76).

Of course the basic association of "The Girl," the dream, and money is made for Gatsby by Daisy Fay, and in her betrayal of Gatsby the hint of a parallel between "Kaye" and "Fay" is fulfilled. For Daisy too leaves Gatsby with nothing (always he is left "watching over—nothing") and the dream is sold out for money. All the gloriously colored and heightened sense of self that Western, American, Jimmy-pioneer-beachcomber-Gatz summed up in Daisy Fay was expressed in his inestimable love for her. The girl with the pandering voice of promises is left with a choice: that dream, that idea of self—that *love*—or money. Fitzgerald makes the choice clear. Just before her bridal dinner, tormented by the choice, too "nervous" and frail to bear the enormous burden of Gatsby's vision and love, Daisy gets drunk. Her choice is between a letter of love—from Gatsby, who is absent and whose future is uncertain—and the three-hundred-and-fifty-thousand-dollar pearl necklace—from Tom Buchanan—who is very solidly present and whose future is very lavishly certain indeed. Drunk, she can repudiate the actualities for the dream of glory. "She groped around in a waste-basket she had with her on the bed and pulled out the string of pearls. 'Take 'em down-stairs and give 'em back to whoever they belong to. Tell 'em all Daisy's change' her mine. Say: "Daisy's change' her mine!" ' " When she is gotten into a cold bath, she "wouldn't let go of the letter. She took it into the tub with her and squeezed it up into a wet ball, and only let me leave it in the soap-dish when she saw that it was coming to pieces like snow," reminisces Jordan. Sobered to the cold actualities, Daisy is like the Rosalind who cannot continue the grandstand play into the world of next things. She "didn't say another word. We gave her spirits of ammonia [says Jordan] and put ice on her forehead and hooked her back into her dress, and half an hour later, when we walked out of the room, the pearls were around her neck and the incident was over. Next day at five o'clock she married Tom Buchanan without so much as a

shiver, and started off on a three months' trip to the South Seas"
(pp. 58, 59).

What, then, could ever have been expected of Jimmy Gatz,
that rare one? Without the "advantages" that Nick has had, what
could he find in his culture and his history to strive for? Beach-
combing, wandering, dreaming, the food for his dreams are the
Western history of Hopalong Cassidy, presenting all the corrupted virtues of a Franklinian way to wealth. After Gatsby is
dead, his old father "pulled from his pocket a ragged old copy
of [young Jimmy's] book called *Hopalong Cassidy*. . . . On the
last fly-leaf was printed the word SCHEDULE, and the date
September 12, 1906, and underneath:

Rise from bed . . . . . . . . . . . . . . . 6.00        A.M.
Dumbbell exercise and wall scaling . . . . . . 6.15–6.30     "
Study electricity, etc. . . . . . . . . . . . 7.15–8.15     "
Work . . . . . . . . . . . . . . . . . . . 8.30–4.30   P.M.
Baseball and sports . . . . . . . . . . . . . 4.30–5.00     "
Practice elocution, poise and how to attain it . . . 5.00–6.00     "
Study needed inventions . . . . . . . . . . . 7.00–9.00     "

GENERAL RESOLVES

No wasting time at Shafters or [a name, indecipherable]
No more smokeing or chewing
Bath every other day
Read one improving book or magazine per week
Save $5.00 [crossed out] $3.00 per week
Be better to parents

(pp. 131–32)

Gatsby's father continues the bathos of the "great names" and
their mindless association with wealth. All he can see in Gatsby's
"huge incoherent failure of a house" is that if his son "would of
lived, he'd of been a great man. A man like James J. Hill. He'd
of helped build up the country." As indeed Buccleuch Duke
Hill did, as Rockefeller did, as Ulysses S. Grant, as Dan Cody

and Nick's hard-boiled uncle and Demaine the oil man and Buchanan all did "build up" the country. "The poor son of a bitch," Owl Eyes says of Gatsby. The poor, naive, believing son of a bitch. He dreamed of a country in the mind and he got East and West Egg. He dreamed of a future magic self and he got the history of Dan Cody. He dreamed of a life of unlimited possibility and he got Hopalong Cassidy, Horatio Alger, and Ben Franklin's "The Way to Wealth." What else could he imitate? The tawdry movie show of his adolescent imaginings was the only surface he could possibly find to produce as a sign of the real richness he sought. In what else, nursed on the pap of the "moon-pitchers," in what else but that cheap corruption could adolescent and disadvantaged Jimmy Gatz clothe his incorruptible dream, just as he would later clothe himself in his "gorgeous pink rag" of a suit? After all, the movie-picture name is not that of the immigrant actuality, but is the belonging name of the WASP matinee idol. The sight of Dan Cody's yacht simply crystallizes in Jimmy Gatz's mind everything that his culture had taught him to believe. "It was James Gatz who had been loafing along the beach that afternoon in a torn green jersey and a pair of canvas pants, but it was already Jay Gatsby who borrowed a rowboat, pulled out to the *Tuolomee,* and informed Cody that a wind might catch him and break him up in half an hour.

"I suppose he'd had the name ready for a long time, even then. His parents were shiftless and unsuccessful farm people—his imagination had never really accepted them as his parents at all. The truth was that Jay Gatsby of West Egg, Long Island, sprang from his Platonic conception of himself. He was a son of God—a phrase which, if it means anything, means just that—and he must be about His Father's business," which, in the America beckoning, pandering, promising, and whispering all about him, is "the service of a vast, vulgar, and meretricious beauty. So he invented just the sort of Jay Gatsby that a seventeen-year-old boy would be likely to invent, and to this conception he was faithful to the end" (p. 75). Owl Eyes was quite right to see through to complete admiration. It is as though a Dead End kid, with only the cheaper magazines as education, were to vault himself into being *all that he thought it meant to be* if one were Winthrop Quincey Astor, acted by Ronald Colman, and somehow, through a fullness of imagination, should actually carry the trick off. "The man's a regular Belasco!"

Beneath the posing and everything for which Nick has unaffected scorn, Gatsby's "heart was in a constant, turbulent riot. The most grotesque and fantastic conceits haunted him in his bed at night. A universe of ineffable gaudiness spun itself out in his brain while the clock ticked on the wash-stand. . . . Each night he added to the pattern of his fancies until drowsiness closed down upon some vivid scene with an oblivious embrace. For a while these reveries provided an outlet for his imagination. . . ." And then Fitzgerald adds a statement that sums up his love of, fascination with, and condemnation of America. In no human terms are our movietime reveries real, yet they are the actuality of our dream vision of life and become, finally, the actualities of our desires. The gaudy revery of a life that has been fashioned out of American wealth, past, and hope has become the reality of national life. So young Gatsby's "reveries provided an outlet for his imagination; they were a satisfactory hint of the unreality of reality, a promise that the rock of the world was founded securely on a fairy's wing" (p. 75). And when the fairytale movie picture of Cody's yacht appears, Jay Gatsby is ready. His "instinct toward his future glory" and "the drums of his destiny" beat high at the sight: "To young Gatz, resting on his oars and looking up at the railed deck, that yacht represented all the beauty and glamor in the world. . . . A few days later [Cody] took him to Duluth and bought him a blue coat, six pairs of white duck trousers, and a yachting cap. And when the *Tuolomee* left for the West Indies and the Barbary Coast Gatsby left too" (p. 76).

Ella Kaye completes the basic elements of his education. He learns not only that money is the key to the appearances of American life, but that the fact that you have it is more important than how you got it. Get! The history of the country is the history of robber baron wealth! Get! The fact of life is that the winner is the one who gets the money. Get, get! So, though he never "understood the legal device that was used against him" by Ella Kaye, he "was left with his singularly appropriate education; the vague contour of Jay Gatsby had filled out to the substantiality of a man" (p. 76). It does not matter to Gatsby that he makes his money through bootlegging and bucketshopping. What matters is that he must never *appear* to be marginal. The fact of the sources of his wealth cannot generate shame and guilt and fear— that strange yet identifiable look that passes over Gatsby's face when Tom refers to Gatsby's business—but the disclosure of the parvenu and sweaty nature of his wealth can do it. For that matter, Buchanan's East Egg friends, like Walter Chase, are not above making a few dollars through Gatsby—and going to jail as a result. "Everyone" has gone "East," everyone is in "the bond business." Gatsby learned well. He's had more luck and energy than those without his driving imagination, believing all the while in the reality of the cheap substitutes "all the others" held out to him. " 'They're a rotten crowd,' I shouted across the lawn," says Nick. " 'You're worth the whole damn bunch put together.'

"I've always been glad I said that. It was the only compliment I ever gave him, because I disapproved of him from beginning to end. . . . His gorgeous pink rag of a suit made a bright spot of color against the white steps, and I thought of the night when I first came to his ancestral home three months before. The lawn and drive had been crowded with the faces of those who guessed at his corruption—and he had stood on those steps, concealing his incorruptible dream, as he waved them good-by" (p. 117).

For Gatsby, the problem is simple. He merely had not had enough money at the right time to secure that incorruptible dream. He had seen the summation of that world, Daisy, led off by a string of pearls like a halter round her neck, bought by the highest bidder for the *droit de seigneur*. All one need do then is what his nation has taught him. Get rich, and you can turn the clock back, do it all over again, regain the life which existed in the youthful dream. The song that Daisy's voice whispers is the song of America:

> Then wear the gold hat, if that will move her;
>   If you can bounce high, bounce for her too,
> Till she cry "Lover, gold-hatted, high-bouncing lover,
>   I must have you!"

The poet's name, "Thomas Parke D'Invilliers," is the same fictitious name Fitzgerald had used for John Peale Bishop in *This Side of Paradise*, and which in *The Great Gatsby* is another name for F. Scott Fitzgerald, who knew from the inside out why Gatsby seeks the gold hat and bounces high and tries to turn the clock.

In fact, Gatsby does no less than begin all over again, sweating and earning by hook or by crook his second chance. He will buy the house, stage the parties, drive the car, throw all those shirts in profuse and expensive piles on the bed until Daisy, overcome by all the puppy-panting eagerness, all the devotion, energy, belief, and dedication, will blubber into the silken folds of the obviously expensive shirts, which, like the house and car, are "showpieces." "They're such beautiful shirts. . . . It makes me sad because I've never seen such—such beautiful shirts before." For me? . . . this garish display all for me? You mean all these years—just for me? All the labor for this vast, tasteless display just for me? Oh, lover, gold-hatted, high-bouncing lover, I've never seen such—such beautiful shirts before.

All one has to do is remake the past.

Just that, and win the future. "He came back from France when Tom and Daisy were still on their wedding trip, and made a miserable but irresistible journey to Louisville on the last of his army pay. He stayed there a week, walking the streets where their footsteps had clicked together through the November night and revisiting the out-of-the-way places to which they had driven in her white car. Just as Daisy's house had always seemed to him more mysterious and gay than other houses, so his idea of the city itself, even though she was gone from it, was pervaded with a melancholy beauty" (p. 116). The core of what Fitzgerald wanted his readers to see is that Gatsby's demand on Daisy is the demand of the American imagination upon America: nothing less than that the past should be the imagined past, that history should have been the actualization of the ideal, and that the non-ideal actualities of history continuing into the present should not be true. "He wanted nothing less of Daisy than that she should go to Tom and say, 'I never loved you.' After she had obliterated four years with that sentence they could decide upon the more practical measures to be taken. One of them was that, after she was free, they were to go back to Louisville and be married from her house— just as if it were five years ago" (p. 84).

But it is too much to ask that the object of the deepest hunger of the human heart should have remained inviolate and unchanged and untouched in the reality of human weakness, in time's proof that men are creatures smaller than the ideal that some of them can greatly dream. Nick, with his strong sense of this land, and who learns more and more, in the history of that summer, that the swift, thrilling returning trains of his youth don't run anymore, and that they ran on a rail-line as defunct now as the old time-table on which he scrawled the names of those who had come to Gatsby's party, Nick, who learns through Gatsby the meanings of the past, tries gently to warn him.

"I wouldn't ask too much of her," I ventured. "You can't repeat the past."

"Can't repeat the past?" he cried incredulously. "Why of course you can!"

He looked about him wildly, as if the past were lurking here in the shadow of his house, just out of reach of his hand.

"I'm going to fix everything just the way it was before," he said, nodding determinedly. "She'll see."

He talked a lot about the past, and I gathered that he wanted to *recover something, some idea of himself perhaps, that had gone into loving Daisy.* His life had been confused and disordered since then, but if he could once return to a certain starting place and go over it all slowly, he could find out what that thing was (p. 84, italics mine).

As Nick is one with Gatsby and counterpointingly disapproving of him, so too counterpointing Gatsby's obsession with the past is Nick's thirtieth birthday, pointing into a diminished future. The apparent difference between Nick and Gatsby is one of "advantages." The real difference is that Nick is willing to "go back home," willing to accept the diminished and diminishing actuality as the inescapable history for which man must settle. He has learned that in the jazz history of the world the golden moment is always one when time's up and that the real name of the tune is "*Three O'Clock in the Morning,* a neat, sad little waltz of that year," played at Gatsby's last party when all the necessity for his stupendous labor is finally gone. But Nick is one with Gatsby in his memory of youthful elation and expectation.

The green light, that money-colored go-light at the end of Daisy's dock, was one more beckoning symbol to Gatsby. There, on the final shore, there on East Egg was the alabaster palace and the golden girl in it, the girl to whom he had "forever wed his unutterable visions," and her light gleamed "Go! Go! Go!" beckoning always to that palatial land. And "Gatsby believed in the green light, the orgastic [I'll use Fitzgerald's intended word] future that year by year recedes before us. It eluded us then [in our past], but that's no matter—tomorrow we will run faster, stretch out our arms farther . . . . And one fine morning—" (p. 137).

Gatsby sums us all up. He sums up our American desire to believe in a release from history, to believe that our early past did indeed establish redemption, to believe that in our founding the *idea* of our superb and hopeful heritage was actualized. He sums up the "vast, vulgar, meretricious beauty" that our wealth has made and in which we dress the romantic sense of self that the idea of American possibilities keeps whispering is at hand. He sums up, too, the fast-movietime we have made of history, wiping out past, present, and future in the whirling certitude that the new, that our wealth and power, will make time do our bidding. Nick, with his fourth decade opening before him, repudiates finally the "Younger Generation" that began as Isabelle and ends up as the Buchanans and Jordan Baker. "I'd had enough of all of them for one day," he says, voicing once more Fitzgerald's sense of the necessity for responsibility, for the "fundamental decencies," for work as meaning and as dignity, for all the ideologies, if not the actualities, of an older America. This is not to say that Fitzgerald prefers that amalgam of puritanism and gentility that went into the Victorianism from which he grew. As his short stories, his letters, *This Side of Paradise* and *The Beautiful and Damned* make clear, he was aware that like all else in American history, those ideologies of work, responsibility, politeness, respect, decency, had been perverted and bastardized in actualities which were the grabbing of wealth and the cloaking of the sweat and the "marks" with gentility and the pretentious manner of a long-established identity. Yet, given the callousness and disrespect of the younger generation, given the childish sense of having the world on a string, given, in short, the existential alternative of value in the intensity of the moment per se, Fitzgerald chooses community and history. In *The Great Gatsby*, he comes to a position in which he says that though the Protestant ethic is to be scorned in its Babbittry, scorn is neither the final nor the only judgment to be offered. In what it could have meant it is the name for human responsibility and decency. Fitzgerald never resolved allegiance to a genteel world whose hypocrisies he repudiated, but he had deep and lasting connections with it. Yet the final choice is empty, too. Nick goes "home," but he can never go "Home," as Fitzgerald makes clear. And like Nick, Fitzgerald repudiates reluctantly the gorgeousness of the romantic sense of self. It was the highest point of human hope, Fitzgerald mourns. How hard to grow up an American, enticed by your nation, only to have to grow up at last and settle for the cold limitations of history. Fitzgerald takes a place in a long continuum of writers, since Fenimore Cooper, who recognize in the passing of an "older America" (even in Cooper's time, as stated explicitly in *Home as Found*), the passing of gorgeous possibilities. They repudiate the "new times and the new generation," not really condemning youth in a perennial warfare of the generations, but they condemn America's peculiar accent on youth, America's irresponsible sense that the power and the glory and the luxury of the Great West will somehow make all come out right in the end and is inexhaustible and will rewrite history the way children would like it. So why not be a child? Demaine is always there. Edwin Arlington Robinson, for one, says it more bitterly than Fitzgerald when, in "Cassandra," he asks Americans what their gay and frantic activities mean:

> You laugh and answer, "We are young;
>    Oh, leave us now, and let us grow;"
> Not asking how much more of this
>    Will Time endure or Fate bestow.

> Because a few complacent years
>    Have made your peril of your pride
> Think you that you are to go on
>    Forever pampered and untried?

What lost eclipse of history,
   What bivouac of the marching stars,
Has given the sign for you to see
   Millenniums and last great wars?

What unrecorded overthrow
   Of all the world has ever known
Or even been, has made itself
   So plain to you, and you alone?

Your Dollar, Dove and Eagle make
   A Trinity that even you
Rate higher than you rate yourselves;
   It pays, it flatters, and it's new.

NEW.

Gatsby never understood that he was trapped by time and human history. Yet even in the only moment he ever had his future—in the past, in his youthful imaginings—the dreamlight was punctuated by the sounds of time. "A universe of ineffable gaudiness spun itself out in his brain while the clock ticked on the washstand and the moon soaked with wet light his tangled clothes upon the floor" (p. 75). And at the moment of triumph, when he meets Daisy in Nick's bungalow, Gatsby is harassed by time, by dead time. He has troubles with a clock whose time he can't control. He thinks he is turning time back, but the point is that the clock doesn't work.

Gatsby, his hands still in his pockets, was reclining against the mantelpiece in a strained counterfeit of perfect ease, even of boredom. His head leaned back so far that it rested against the face of a defunct mantelpiece clock . . . the clock took this moment to tilt dangerously at the pressure of his head, whereupon he turned and caught it with trembling fingers and set it back in place. . . . "I'm sorry about the clock," he said. . . . "It's an old clock," I told them idiotically. I think we all believed for a moment that it had smashed in pieces on the floor (p. 66).

It is inevitable that Nick's premonitory warning about time should be fulfilled in Daisy's final announcement of her inability to fulfill Gatsby's dream. " 'Oh, you want too much,' she cried to Gatsby. 'I love you now—isn't that enough? I can't help what's past.' " An enormous distance has been travelled from *This Side of Paradise* to *The Great Gatsby*. Rosalind had told Amory, "I love you—now," and there were premonitions of the inconstancy of the present as it becomes the future. Now, with Daisy's outcry, there is not even any certainty about the nature of the past. "She began to sob helplessly. 'I did love him once—but I loved you too.'

"Gatsby's eyes opened and closed.

" 'You loved me too?' he repeated" (p. 101).

It would have to be inconceivable to him that a love which had excluded every other reason for existence should have been shared, that he had not been to Daisy what she had been to him. It would have to be inconceivable that a love which had grown infinitely beyond the relations between one male and one female should have been, after all, merely that. Just one more boy-wins-girl, like Tom and Daisy. Inconceivable indeed that the enormous concept of Gatsby's love, transcending time, space, history, and names, should turn out to be just one more affair, no more important than the dance, old sport.

Brooding gloomily over the matter after he had been put "in his place," Gatsby announces his measure of Daisy's marriage. "Suddenly he came out with a curious remark.

" 'In any case,' he said, 'it was just personal.'

" 'What could you make of that,' " asks Nick, " 'except to suspect some intensity in his conception of the affair that couldn't be measured?' " (p. 116).

Every tick of the clock had led up to the stroke that rang, "time's up!" and foreshadowed—significantly at the moment of apparent triumph—what had to happen. When Gatsby had finally won Daisy into his house, he takes her to his bedroom window.

"If it wasn't for the mist we could see your home across the bay," said Gatsby. "You always have a green light that burns all night at the end of your dock."

Daisy put her arm through his abruptly, but he seemed absorbed in what he had just said. Possibly it had occurred to him that the colossal significance of that light had now vanished forever. Compared to the great distance that had separated him from Daisy it had seemed very near to her, almost touching her. It had seemed as close as a star to the moon. Now it was again a green light on a dock. His dream of enchanted objects had diminished by one. . . . I saw that the expression of bewilderment had come back into Gatsby's face, as though a faint doubt had occurred to him as to the quality of his present happiness. Almost five years! There must have been moments even that afternoon when Daisy tumbled short of his dreams—not through her own fault, but because of the colossal vitality of his illusion. It had gone beyond her, beyond everything. He had thrown himself into it with a creative passion, adding to it all the time, decking it out with every bright feather that drifted his way. No amount of fire or freshness can challenge what a man will store up in his ghostly heart" (pp. 70–71, 73).

Never missing a trick, Fitzgerald adjusts the imagery to "time" when Gatsby, at the instant of the golden moment, begins to suspect that the comedown to actualities is all there is: Gatsby "had passed visibly through two states and was entering upon a third. After his embarrassment and his unreasoning joy he was consumed with wonder at [Daisy's] presence. He had been full of the idea so long, dreamed it right through to the end, waited with his teeth set, so to speak, at an inconceivable peak of intensity. Now, in the reaction, he was running down like an overwound clock" (p. 70).

Gatsby strikes a responsive chord in Nick, as in the reader, because the "intensity in his conception of the affair" is the summation of all our unarticulated memories of a time when time was young. When Gatsby recounts to Nick what Daisy had meant to him through all the years, Nick's own memory is stirred by something "unutterable," a ghost of a dream, an unarticulated remembrance of what might have been a dream of what might have been. "Through all he said, even through his appalling sentimentality, I was reminded of something—an elusive rhythm, a fragment of lost words, that I had heard somewhere a long time ago. For a moment a phrase tried to take shape in my mouth and my lips parted like a dumb man's, as though there was more struggling upon them than a wisp of startled air. But they made no sound and what I had almost remembered was uncommunicable forever" (p. 85).

What is there to remember? The discovery of Columbus? The Dutch sailors? The dream of the founding fathers, of great documents believed in by great men in smallclothes? Buffalo Bill Cody and the great expansive spaces and the founding dream knocked into the cocked hats of the fathers? Fitzgerald leaves no doubt that the idea of America, what mankind and the self were supposed to have been in the actualization of that young nation now back there somewhere in the past, is sign and metaphor for human youth itself. The old America in memory's silent rictus is the young America of the past to which we ride on the thrilling returning trains of our youth. The old America is a snap of the mind that flashes us nostalgically back to the last, best hope of mankind when "for a transitory enchanted moment man must have held his breath in the presence of this continent . . . face to face for the last time in history with something commensurate to his capacity for wonder." America is the golden moment in the history of the human race, and it is that instant of history that Gatsby's life re-enacts in modern dress and in all its complex modifications. "As I sat there, thinking of this continent," says Nick, "brooding on the old unknown world, I thought of Gatsby's wonder when he first picked out the green light at the end of Daisy's dock. He had come a long way to this blue lawn, and his dream must have seemed so close that he could hardly fail to grasp it. He did not know that it was already behind him [in time as well as region] somewhere back in that vast obscurity beyond the city, where the dark fields of the republic rolled on under the night" (p. 137).

When Daisy, the dream actualized, betrays Gatsby by letting him take the consequences of irresponsible actualities, she clears out of his life forever. His bewildering doubts at the instant of the golden moment culminated in his new vision of the world and human possibility just before his death, which is the consequence of the betrayal of the dream. All that's left are missed connections and the valley of ashes of dead dreams. Gatsby's death comes when time has caught up with Gatsby through Gatsby's catching up with his dream. The summer is over. The leaves are yellowing. The history of "America" is completed as Gatsby realizes there never will be a phone call from Daisy and that the world of history and limited possibility is all there is to live in. What a terrifying realization it was for him, the *old* sport.

I have an idea [says Nick] that Gatsby himself didn't believe [the phone call from Daisy] would come, and perhaps he no longer cared. If that was true he must have felt that he had lost the old warm world, paid a high price for living too long with a single dream. He must have looked up at an unfamiliar sky through frightening leaves and shivered as he found what a grotesque thing a rose is and how raw the sunlight was upon the scarcely created grass. A new world, material without being real, where poor ghosts, breathing dreams like air, drifted fortuitously about . . . like that ashen, fantastic figure [George B. Wilson, Cars Bought and Sold] gliding toward him through the amorphous trees (pp. 122–23).

He had paid for living a romantically successful life of imaginative possibilities such as Nick will never encounter in anyone again. A single dream. At the outset Nick had warned us, when he introduced the "history of that summer," that—"this isn't just an epigram—life is much more successfully looked at from a single window, after all" (p. 5). The price of belief is death, yet, "if personality is an unbroken series of successful gestures, then there was something gorgeous" about Gatsby. He transcends the history that kills him.

As Cody represented that history in "The West," another name represents it in equal measure in the present, in the East. The animal names, the predatory and callous rapaciousness, belong to the home of the wolf, which is the appellation for Meyer Wolfsheim. The cannibalistic qualities of wealth and power are indicated in his choice of cuff buttons, which "were composed of oddly familiar pieces of ivory.

" 'Finest specimens of human molars,' " Wolfsheim explained." Through Wolfsheim, too, the belief and faith of a nation, the history of ideals and dreams is debased. He turned the *national sport* into money. "He's the man who fixed the World's Series back in 1919. . . . The idea staggered me. I remembered, of course, that the World's Series had been fixed in 1919, but if I had thought of it at all I would have thought of it as a thing that merely *happened*, the end of some inevitable chain. It never occurred to me that one man could start to play with the faith of fifty million people—with the single-mindedness of a burglar blowing a safe" (p. 56). Wolfsheim's reminiscences of the past are reminiscences of the gangster gambler, Rosy Rosenthal. But his reminiscences are sentimental evasions of responsibility for the present. He too fails to come to Gatsby's funeral. His excuse is that we should "learn to show our friendship for a man when he is alive and not after he is dead . . . . After that, my own rule is to let everything alone" (p. 130). What seems like good advice is given in a context of a lost past. "When I was a young man," Wolfsheim said, "it was different—if a friend of mine died, no matter how, I stuck with them to the end. You may think that's sentimental, but I mean it—to the bitter end" (p. 130). But in the dominance of actuality over memory, he will not get involved—his "gonnegtions" are delicate—in the funeral of a man who had made money illegally and who had been shot to death. What Wolfsheim remembers, too, is another history of Gatsby. "My memory goes back to when I first met him . . . ."

" 'Did you start him in business?' I inquired.

" 'Start him! I made him.' "

Showing friendship for a man while he is alive means for Wolfsheim the same debasement of appearances, for money, that characterizes "the whole rotten crowd" on both of Columbus's Eggs and all stops between New York and Gatsby's "San Francisco." It's like fixing the World's Series: "I saw right away," said Wolfsheim, "he was a fine-appearing, gentlemanly young man, and when he told me he was an Oggsford I knew I could use him good. I got him to join up in the American Legion and he used to stand high there" (p. 130).

At first Wolfsheim seems to be created out of the "harsh smartness" of Fitzgerald's earlier novels. He is a cartoon character, an anti-Semite's stereotype. But the portrait is intentional: this man, who would be scorned by East Egg, who hasn't the right name, the right address, or the right appearance, is brother beneath appearances to the human actualities of "the history of that summer" in the white palatial homes that glittered along the Sound. The effect is one of backlash: there can be no contempt for this "kike" gangster without contempt for the history of names like Carraway and Buchanan and Baker. Fitzgerald is Shavian here. He does not say that "the Jew," as conceived in loathing and contempt, is a good man, but that those who so conceive him are him exactly in their established American identities. In a couple of stunning details, Fitzgerald explicitly hints at "gonnegtions" between Wolfsheim and Cody, between Wolfsheim and Buchanan. The name of Wolfsheim's company—created in a novel written five years before Nazism would give it a different connotation— is one that evokes the "old, warm world" of the Great West in the immemorial sign of American Indians. It is "The Swastika Holding Company." When Wolfsheim pretends not to be present in order to avoid involvement in Gatsby's funeral, the town to which he is supposed to have removed is the very Chicago from which Tom came in such great style, and to which Daisy wanted to return to see how much she'd been missed. And when we last see Tom, "he went into the jewelry store to buy a pearl necklace—or perhaps only a pair of cuff buttons." By the time of Gatsby's death, one cannot distinguish between the moral significance of either piece of jewelry. No matter how far back into time the dream is pushed—Meyer Wolfsheim to Buchanan to Demaine to Cody to Nick's grand-uncle to the Dukes of Buccleuch to the Dutch sailors to Columbus to the land of Indian swastikas—the actualized history of the dream has been a journey into obscenity. The dirty word, in sympathy from Owl Eyes or in the callousness of others who refuse to attend the funeral or in the mindless scrawl of a child is all that the fantastic, incoherent, disadvantaged, burning history of Gatsby has been reduced to, and it is the last we see of Gatsby's house. "On the last night," says Nick, just prior to leaving the East in his wish for the "whole rotten crowd" of the world of human history to "be at a sort of moral attention forever," "I went over and looked at that huge incoherent failure of a house once more. On the white steps an obscene word, scrawled by some boy with a piece of brick, stood out clearly in the moonlight, and I erased it, drawing my shoe raspingly along the stone." And then, in the following four famous concluding paragraphs, Nick speaks his vision of the old, vanished America and the meaning of Gatsby's story as an analog for that dream.

The tapestry of what I have called "stunning details" is woven into final wholeness of idea not only by threads of cars, names, houses, regions, and time, but also by image-patterns of flowers, colors, lights, sun, heat, moon, and coolness. Fitzgerald and Zelda had always thought of themselves as night people, who lived in the

night-lit world of quickened excitement, and Fitzgerald associated the "female" part of his imaginative self with the moon, stars,
the night, lamplit windows. The "male" world of next things, in
which he struggled, was the daytime world of sweat and heat, and
it was dominated by the Toms of virile economic strength.

The year before Fitzgerald completed *The Great Gatsby*, he
and Zelda

renewed their friendship with Tommy Hitchcock, the polo star, whom
they had known on Long Island where he had suggested the kind of
glamor Fitzgerald bestowed on Tom and Daisy. . . . Fitzgerald admired Hitchcock . . . 'a woman's idea of a man.' [Hitchcock] . . . had
flown in the Lafayette Escadrille with Hobey Baker [a Princeton idol
in Fitzgerald's day], and after being shot down and made prisoner,
had escaped by jumping from the window of a moving train. Returning to America with the *Croix de guerre* and a great name in
polo, he had the humility to enter Harvard as a freshman. "That combination [of qualities]," wrote Fitzgerald, "is what forever will put him
in my pantheon of heros."[38]

The hero-Tom remained obsessively for Fitzgerald as the dominant male among the hot cats on top. When Gatsby introduces
Tom Buchanan to people at his party, he introduces him as "the
polo player," and the extremely male figure in *Tender Is the
Night* is Tommy Barban.[39] The transmutation of the envied male
into an unsympathetic opponent in the fiction is not important
as a sign of latent homosexuality, or fear of it, for that avenue of
approach offers little that rewardingly illuminates Fitzgerald's
fiction—despite the penchant for psychoanalysis in our current
critical moment. Whatever "normal" means, Fitzgerald was certainly sexually normal, and whatever sexual inadequacies he
might have felt—as illustrated in *A Movable Feast* by Hemingway's

38 Turnbull, *Scott Fitzgerald*, p. 172.
39 "Tommy [Barban]," wrote Fitzgerald ". . . was Tommy Hitchcock in a way
whose whole life is a challenge—who is only interested in realities, his kind . . .
(February 17, 1938, *Letters*, p. 566).

rather boorish account of Fitzgerald's bewailing the size of his penis—are to be examined more profitably in the context of the total insecurity of identity that Fitzgerald found to be the core of his social milieu. Alexander McKaig's diary suggests, once more, the interrelationship of opposites in Fitzgerald's "success complex—artist's desire for flattery & influence—member of financially decadent family—Fitz bemoaning fact [that he] can never make more than hundred thousand a year. . . ."[40] The artistic imagination and the "female" hunger for flattery are aimed at identification with the "male" world of economic power, and that is the real issue, in the "autobiography" of Fitzgerald's fiction, of his male "penis envy." The insecurity of Nick-Fitzgerald as the belonging-outsider was summed up in the Gatsby-Fitzgerald insecurity of the dream "of infinite possibilities."

So you see [wrote Fitzgerald], I looked at myself in two ways. There seemed to have been a conspiracy to spoil me and all my inordinate vanity was absorbed from that. All this was on the surface, however, and liable to be toppled over at one blow by an unpleasant remark or a missed tackle; and underneath it, came my own sense of lack of courage and stability. If I may push it farther still, I should say that, underneath the whole thing lay a sense of infinite possibilities that was always with me whether vanity or shame was my mood.[41]

No doubt someone will write an article demonstrating that sexual insecurity (such an article probably will make much of Fitzgerald's compulsive shame of his feet when he was a young boy) "explains" Fitzgerald's fiction. But all such an explanation can offer is a partial explanation of the private psyche of Fitzgerald the man. The art, however, is to be seen *in its translations,* where, both in shame and vanity, prompted by his sense of infinite possibilities, Gatsby is "toppled over at one blow" as the "indefinable expression, at once definitely unfamiliar and vaguely recognizable" (p. 92), of

[40] Turnbull, *Scott Fitzgerald*, p. 113.
[41] *Ibid.*, p. 35.

shame and guilt and fear passes over Jimmy Gatz's face when " 'Jay Gatsby' had broken up like glass against Tom's hard malice" (p. 112). If it is the fictional uses of autobiography we are really interested in, what is important is not the facts of Fitzgerald's private subterranean psyche, but the way that psyche created national statements about insecurity and identity out of the symbolic colors and flowers and houses of its memories, fashioning them into a picture of a civilization it held in common, as social materials, with its readers. In Gatsby's moonlit dreams, the cool life lived in the rosiness of lots of long green (free of sweat and smell) is the golden world represented by silver and whiteness in the novel's interrelated motifs. The dream of that world is all moonlight and roses, and in Fitzgerald's imagination the remembrance of dreams past was given a context of golden sunheat and silver mooncoolness at the moment he was writing the novel.

Just as Fitzgerald learned the compassionate uses of his memory and became an artist, his storehouse of experience was enlarged by a sexual fact that almost smashed its capacity to hold anything— Zelda's act of infidelity. In the hot glare of the Mediterranean summer, while Scott was working on *The Great Gatsby*, Zelda had a brief, intense affair with a virile tom, Edouard Josanne, an officer of French naval aviation. When Fitzgerald discovered the liaison, it stunned him as a total betrayal. Although he came to recognize it as something less than that, and though the affair was broken off soon after he discovered it, the aura of betrayal remained in his memory of the hot sunlight as a further intensification of his sense of the fragility of human love and hope. He didn't write it into *The Great Gatsby* as an actual incident—he saved it for the relationship between Nicole and Tommy Barban in *Tender Is the Night*—but it gave impetus to his presentation of Daisy, like Isabelle, Rosalind, and Gloria before her, as no man's constant dream. There is no question that he was able to absorb immediate events into the novel, sometimes in startlingly effective ways. For instance, only one month before he mailed the completed (but not yet fully revised) manuscript to Scribner's, he wrote to Perkins, "For Christ's sake, don't give anyone that jacket you're saving for me." The proposed dust jacket for the novel showed Daisy's eyes, blue and gigantic, brooding down solemnly over New York City, and Fitzgerald suddenly conceived of Dr. T. J. Eckleburg. ". . . Don't give anyone that jacket you're saving for me. I've written it into the book."[42] Similarly, he incorporated Zelda's act not as part of the plot, but, in its ambience, as part of the imagery of the book. As Scott was a "moon person," as Zelda often called him, so Josanne was bronzed, lean, and redolent of the sun. Zelda and Scott discussed the infidelity into proportions they could handle, and Zelda must have continued the moon-sun comparison as she talked it all out with Scott, for the contrast remained with her through her writing, seven years later, of her painfully and literally autobiographical novel, *Save Me the Waltz*.[43] The Zelda-persona, Alabama, turns to the Scott-persona, David, and, talking about the French naval flyer, asks, "Do you think he actually *is* a god. . . . He looks like you—except that he is full of the sun, whereas you are a moon person." Again, the Josanne-persona, Jacques, "was bronzed and smelled of the sun; she felt him naked underneath the starched linen. . . . Kissing the whitelinen stranger was like embracing a lost religious rite." And again, "David went home to work till the light changed—

---

[42] Some time in mid-August 1924, *Letters*, p. 166.

[43] Turnbull notes Zelda's imagery in *Save Me the Waltz*. Zelda's novel was auto-biographical in a way Scott's had not been. The events and characters had a thinly disguised one-to-one relationship to those in the Fitzgeralds' actual lives. In its first version (in which the Scott-persona was called Amory Blaine), it was fairly vicious in its attempt at self-justification by way of destructively "exposing" Scott. Zelda apparently had a terrible need to compete with Scott, to beat him, and when her talent proved less than his, she tried to belittle his achievements and methods. Often she publicly accused him of stealing ("Mr. Fitzgerald believes that plagiarism begins at home") from her letters and diary—which he had done a few times, but in ways that were hardly plagiarism. The first version of *Save Me the Waltz* was so cruel and spiteful, in fact, that Scott had to insist on revisions before it was published. See Turnbull, pp. 145, 206–7.

he insisted he couldn't paint anything but exteriors in the noon light of the Midi. He walked to the beach to join Alabama for a quick plunge before lunch. He found her and Jacques sitting in the sand. . . . David was hot from his walk. The sun in the perspiration of his neck stung like a nettled collar. . . ."

"David swam . . . alone, looking back at the two figures glittering in the sun side by side." And again: "Jacques swung along . . . part of the sun and part of the . . . blue and white collar of the beach, part of Provence and the brown people. . . . His golden face and white linen standing off from him, exhaling the gold glow of his body, ran together in a golden blur."[44] Zelda had learned something from Scott's use of light and color imagery in *The Great Gatsby*, just as, in the first place, her infidelity had given him a consolation of that imagery which he had already begun in the first drafts of the novel. Not a memory, not an experience remained unorganized when it went into the book.

Fitzgerald's methods of organization revolved around a series of associations between details and the idea of betrayal, repeated until the idea takes on the life of its own style. So his use of colors, like everything else, is associated with the betrayal of the dream by the object of it, whether in cool whiteness or in golden sun. The "white palaces of fashionable East Egg glittered along the water" across the "courtesy bay" which Gatsby must traverse in his final step to the attainment of his dream, and the place of money-showing is like the place of money-getting, New York City, "rising up across the river in white heaps and sugar lumps all built with a wish out of non-olfactory money." The whiteness is the "purity" of unimpeachable appearances, of established belonging to the dominant class of hot cats on top. Daisy and Jordan almost always wear white, and silvery whiteness becomes a sign of the cool elegance of the alluring world in which the imagined rich

44 Zelda Fitzgerald, *Save Me the Waltz* (The Grey Walls Press, London, 1953), pp. 111, 117, 121, 124.

live in the moonlit dream. All-desiring Gatsby has to learn that
the whiteness in reality is only the valley-of-ashes color that is all
that's left of a burned-out dream in which the placid manners of
the golden girls were "as cool as their white dresses and their impersonal eyes in the absence of all desire." Even in her youth,
when she was "the most popular of all the young girls in Louisville," Daisy "dressed in white and had a little white roadster"
parked outside her big white house (p. 16). The first things Cody
buys Gatsby are six pairs of white duck trousers for him to wear
on that big, white yacht; Daisy's house was "beautiful and cool";
it is in the cool autumn, when "the sidewalk was white with moonlight," during a "cool night," that Gatsby weds Daisy to his dream
among the silver stars "as Daisy's white face came up to his own."
When Gatsby and Daisy meet two days later, Daisy's "porch was
bright with the luxury of bought star-shine . . . and Gatsby was
overwhelmingly aware of the youth and mystery that wealth im-
prisons and preserves, of the freshness of many clothes, and of
Daisy, gleaming like silver, safe and proud above the hot struggles
of the poor" (p. 114). As white is close to silver, so silver, especially
in the context of money, is close to gold, and both white-silver and
gold characterize Daisy's world for Gatsby. When Gatsby says
goodby to Daisy, at a moment of perfect, serene love, before he
leaves for the army, it "was a cold fall day"; but Daisy soon disappears again into her Fay House, her world where "a hundred
pairs of golden and silver slippers shuffled the shining dust" at
society tea-dances (p. 115). Gatsby learns the money colors of the
dream world and Fitzgerald slows down movietime to one perfectly representative still for the gold-hatted high bouncing party
Gatsby throws for Daisy. The still is all "star," moon, and white.
The essence of the "perfect" love in the "perfect" moment is extended through the whole evening as a movie director bends over
his "star" under a "white-plum tree." At the end of the evening,
the "moving-picture director and his Star . . . were still under the

white-plum tree and their faces were touching except for a pale, thin ray of moonlight between. It occurred to me," says Nick, "that he had been very slowly bending toward her all evening to attain this proximity, and even while I watched I saw him stoop one ultimate degree and kiss her cheek" (p. 81). In another of Fitzgerald's encompassing details, Gatsby wears the colors he had learned as he makes the final movement toward the proximity he too had been trying to attain, across that courtesy bay. When he presents himself for the reunion meeting with Daisy, he wears all the colors of belonging and money: "An hour later the front door opened nervously, and Gatsby, in a white flannel suit, silver shirt, and gold-colored tie, hurried in" (p. 64).

The windows of the Demaine house were "gleaming white against the fresh" green that surrounds Buchanan's mansion, and under the "frosted wedding cake of a ceiling" the women inside "were both in white." The white of belonging, of social and economic dominance, is carried out in a repetition of Tom's "scientific" racism. "Have you read 'The Rise of the Colored Empires' . . . ?" he asks Nick. ". . . if we don't look out the white race will be—will be utterly submerged. . . . It's up to us, who are the dominant race, to watch out or these other races will have control of things. . . . This idea is that we're Nordics. . ." (p. 12). Fitzgerald is making a subtle analog for the highly colored energy of West Egg's pushing and straining against that courtesy bay that separates it from the white glittering palaces of East Egg; and in the confrontation scene at the Plaza, when Tom dismisses Gatsby as Mr. Nobody from Nowhere, the dominance of white is reintroduced by Tom. Tom's smug "transition from libertine to prig was . . . complete," and, appropriately, follows a discussion of class presidents, wedding guests, and "belonging"—a belonging that clearly excludes highly "colored" Gatsby. "I suppose," says Tom, "the latest thing is to sit back and let Mr. Nobody from Nowhere make love to your wife. Well, if that's the idea you can count me out. . . . Nowadays people begin by sneering at family life and family institutions, and next they'll throw everything overboard and have intermarriage between black and white."

" 'We're all white here,' murmured Jordan" (p. 99). All except Gatsby, who is purer than "the whole rotten crowd." The irony of white is constantly made apparent. Tom correctly assesses Gatsby as "colored." He had called Gatsby's car a "circus wagon," which it was, and had called Gatsby's house a "menagerie," which it all too often was. The irony is that if white is the color of purity, "white" Tom, of all people, has never earned the right to deprecate "colored" Gatsby any more than he would have the right to deprecate "colored" Wolfsheim. "If you're white you're all right," as the song goes, and as "white" Tom asserts the all-rightness of East Egg dominance, the strains of Mendelssohn's Wedding March explode up from the ballroom below, strains recalling white trains, white veils, white vows at the very moment that white Daisy is in the process of being "divorced" from Gatsby.

So too, what seems to be the cool purity of the virginal white dresses worn by Daisy and Jordan is only the color of their "rightness," hardly of purity, and signifies the leisurely and luxurious drift of their pointless lives. Their whiteness, in contrast to the put-on whiteness of vital Gatsby or the strong-blooded energy of Myrtle Wilson, is the coolness of bloodlessness. The cool silver-white, finally, is a hurtful deception, whether on the level of Gatsby's moonshine dreamlight or Daisy's surface whiteness or, even, on the level of bantering humor: the secret about the nose of the Buchanan butler is that "he used to be a silver polisher for some people in New York that had a silver service for two hundred people. He had to polish it from morning till night, until finally it began to affect his nose" (p. 12). For white Jordan Baker and for white Daisy Buchanan the effect of "silver" on

those without it is simply a slight joke, soon forgotten, as is indicated by Daisy's bewilderment when Nick refers to her chauffeur's nose. Like all the rest of "the whole rotten crowd," the
two young ladies are two of a kind. Daisy explains that Jordan,
too, is "from Louisville. Our white girlhood was passed together
there. Our beautiful white—" (p. 16).

But like the reality beneath cars, houses, names, times, and regions, the significance of the whiteness extends through all classes
and places, from glittering East Egg to sugar-lump New York.
Myrtle Wilson's vulgar apartment is her own pretense at belonging, and it is "one slice in a long white cake of apartment houses."
In the money-making depths of New York, as Nick goes to work
in the morning—in one consummate and sarcastic image—"the
*sun* threw my shadow *westward* as I hurried down the *white*
chasms of *lower New York* to the *Probity* Trust" (p. 43). And
after Gatsby's famous explanation of the secret of money in Daisy's
voice, Nick thinks, "High in a white palace, the king's daughter,
the golden girl . . ." (p. 91). Perhaps the summation of both the
appearance and reality of whiteness as a sign of belonging is the
last view of Gatsby's marble steps. "On the white steps an obscene word . . . stood out clearly in the moonlight. . . ." What
white is *supposed* to be is in the past, "the real snow, our snow"
in the "frosty dark" of our thrilling Western youth. But what it
has come to be is the color of—a very costly string of pearls.

All that can be expected is a continuation of the golden girl's
white world. The combination of gold and white as the "advantages" that East Egg passes on to itself is sketched swiftly in the
introduction of Daisy's child. Giving birth to the baby, Daisy had
wished for nothing more than beautiful, white, golden girl irresponsibility and shallowness for her daughter. " 'All right,' I
said, 'I'm glad it's a girl. And I hope she'll be a fool—that's the
best thing a girl can be in this world, a beautiful little fool' "

(p. 15).[45] And the adult irresponsible dream girls lie in silver-white state as the next generation's gold-and-white dream girl is ushered in. "The room, shadowed with awnings, was dark and cool. Daisy and Jordan lay upon an enormous couch, like silver idols weighing down their own white dresses against the singing breeze of the fans.

"We can't move," they said together. (Fitzgerald's parallel to the introductory scene presenting a motionless, "p-paralyzed" Daisy and Jordan is obvious here.)

"Jordan's fingers, powdered white over their tan, rested for a moment in mine" (p. 88). When the child enters and hugs Daisy, Daisy says, " 'The bles-sed pre-cious! Did mother get powder on your old yellowy hair?' . . . Her face bent into the single wrinkle of the small white neck. 'You dream, you. You absolute little dream.' " The white-and-yellowy pre-cious dream agrees in a perfectly appropriate sense of accord with the others: " 'Yes,' admitted the child calmly. 'Aunt Jordan's got on a white dress too' " (p. 89).

The summation of the idea of the white golden girl, promising the lasting golden moment, is in the name behind the promising voice. A daisy is a cool whiteness radiating from a golden center. The origin of the flower's name, "day's eye," is obvious in its representation of the sun. But the white and the gold promise of the name and voice never fulfills the expectations of the extended golden moment, the moment of most sun. It is, after all, the very representative of the day's eye who always misses the day of most sun. "Do you always watch for the longest day of the year and then miss it? I always watch for the longest day of the year and then miss it." "What'll we do with ourselves this afternoon?" cries Daisy during the summer's hottest day of sunlight, "and

[45] Fitzgerald "plagiarized" the statement, taking it from the mouth of one golden girl and putting it into the mouth of another. The statement was made by Zelda after the birth of the Fitzgeralds' daughter. See Turnbull, *Scott Fitzgerald*, p. 127.

the day after that, and the next thirty years?" (p. 90). Daisy's maiden name, when the day's eye herself was a little bles-sed precious, was also as significant as the WASP name of power, wealth, and belonging she took after she married Tom. It makes no difference whether by "Fay" Fitzgerald intended "fairy," "fate" or "faith." This fairy of the sun, this spirit of the day's eye, is the golden promise, visions of which had convinced young Jimmy Gatz that the "rock of the world was founded securely on a fairy's wing." As "faith," the whispered promise, Daisy is the object of the most heightened and romantic faith possible. As "fairy" or "faith," she is the sum and sign and seal of the fate that our "white" history has visited upon our golden dreams.

Because the gold-and-white object of universal desire is those dreams, the dream is associated with dreamlight. Cool light, coolness, starlight, moonlight, night, are generally the associations clustered around Gatsby and the dreamview of all that Daisy represents. When Gatsby is first introduced he is seen in a significant setting. The hopeful, exciting sounds of a spring night play chorus to the "loud, bright night. . . . The silhouette of a moving cat wavered across the moonlight, and turning my head . . . I saw . . . a figure had emerged from the shadow of my neighbor's mansion and was standing with his hands in his pockets regarding the silver pepper of the stars" (p. 17). Nick can't understand Gatsby's next action, but the immediate juncture of "silver," "moon," and "stars" with what comes next is to become very clear to the reader. Gatsby stretched his arms out under the stars, in a yearning trembling reach. Nick glances at what Gatsby was stretching toward and can't understand. All he can see is a green light at the end of a dock.

Gatsby entertains on his hot beach under the sun, but his entertainments are mostly associated with blue evening hours "as the earth lurches away from the sun" (p. 32). When Gatsby stands isolated from the "careless driving" at the conclusion of one of

his parties, he stands under "a wafer of a moon" that was "shining over Gatsby's house, making the night fine as before and surviving the laughter and the sound of his still glowing garden" (p.
43). Nick most feels the Eastern tug of expectation and romantic
excitement during "the enchanted metropolitan twilight," and
when he tries to struggle out of the actual East of Myrtle's apartment into a more alluring land, he "wanted to get out and walk
eastward toward the park through the soft twilight" (p. 28). When
Daisy packs to run away to Gatsby—and "was effectually prevented"—it was a "winter night." When Nick learns why Gatsby
bought the house and stretched his arms out over the water, Nick
thinks, "Then it had not been *merely* the stars to which he had
aspired on that June night" (p. 60, italics mine), and when Nick
first begins his Eastern romance with Jordan, in the evening,
under "a barrier of dark trees . . . a delicate pale light beamed
down into the park" (p. 61). At night when young Gatz spun out
his ineffable dreams, "the moon soaked with wet light his tangled
clothes upon the floor," and when the young yachtsman grows up
he dresses his burning desire in the "cool" appearances everyone wants. Everyone hungers for something, and Tom gazes wistfully at the blue and white cool of a sailboat going off to a never-
never dreamland: "Slowly the white wings of the boat moved
against the cool blue limit of sky. Ahead lay the scalloped ocean
and the abounding blessed isles" (p. 90). A few brief lines after
this image, Jordan, whose first name promises refreshment, but
whose last name promises heat, says, as the sun-heat proves too
much for her, "Life starts all over again when it gets crisp in the
fall." The statement is, of course, the direct contradiction of Nick's
early expectation "that life was beginning over again with the
summer." (Jordan's cheat's eyes in her white, wan face are always
described as "sun-strained," and Fitzgerald will re-use his imagery
in changed form when he creates Nicole's "white crook's eyes" in
*Tender Is the Night*.) And in that heat, it is Gatsby who stands

out as "fall," as "cool." Fitzgerald has Daisy tell Gatsby she loves him in a very particular way: " 'Ah,' she cried, 'you look so cool.'

"Their eyes met, and they stared together at each other, alone in space. With an effort she glanced down at the table.

" 'You always look so cool,' she repeated" (p. 90), and when Tom and Gatsby, cruelly strong sunlight and cool moonlight, stand ready to go to town to confront each other on the hottest day of the year, "a silver curve of the moon hovered already in the western sky" (p. 91). When Nick discovers Gatsby "under the moon" watching protectively over Daisy's house and learns of Gatsby's innocence, Nick "walked away and left him standing there in the moonlight—watching over nothing" just as before, under the stars Gatsby had stretched out his arms—to nothing. Though time comes full circle with the seasons, and Gatsby goes from the dream to the disillusionment, he remains to the end associated with the coolness of the autumn day he dies, when he uses the pool he had never used once all summer. The irony that kills Gatsby is that the cool silver-white of his hot, burning dreams is not the recapturing of "the warm, old world," but is merely a raw new world's coldness in which "he must have . . . shivered" just before he died. After Myrtle's death, when the nature of the "whiteness" is clear, Nick will not go back into Buchanan's rose-and-white house. "I'd be damned if I'd go in; I'd had enough of all of them for one day, and suddenly that included Jordan too" (p. 108). Now that the silver-cool whiteness of long green money, of fresh red and gold wealth, has been exposed as the cover for "bad driving," it no longer promises the fresh green coolness of the new summer's warm, old world. When Nick throws over Jordan in his last phone conversation with her, he notes that "usually her voice came over the wire as something fresh and cool, as if a divot from a green golf-links had come sailing in at the office window, but this morning it seemed harsh and dry" (p. 118).

The silver-cool appearances of the world of Columbus's Eggs

are the betrayal of the silver-cool starshine, dreamlight, moon-wash of Gatsby's imagination. Gatsby's *real* silver-white, beneath the silver-white-gold appearances he shares with the rest of his society, is the silver-white of Nick's memories of Christmas vacation. The identity-destroying actuality of the history that kills him is captured in Nick's El Greco dream in which all the signs of Gatsby's hopes are distorted nightmarishly by an irresponsible world of wealth in which everything exists "under a sullen, over-hanging sky and a *lustreless moon*," and on a stretcher "lies a drunken woman in a *white* evening dress. Her hand, which dangles over the side, *sparkles cold* with *jewels*." She is brought into a house—"the *wrong house*. But no one knows the woman's *name and no one cares*" (p. 134).

Fitzgerald makes the money-color of gold glow like its silver companion. It is at once a companion to silver and, as a sun-color, an opponent to the cool light of Gatsby's moondream. In both cases, the moral result of the color is the same. As would be expected, it is first associated with the golden girl at the center of the world. One of Nick's introductory and admonitory descriptions of Daisy is one in which "for a moment the last sunshine fell with romantic affection upon her glowing face; her voice compelled me forward breathlessly as I listened—then the glow faded . . ." (pp. 12–13). The yellow windows of Myrtle's apartment are explained by Nick, and the glowing windows and gardens of Gatsby's parties are multicolored backgrounds for gold. His "station wagon scampered like a brisk yellow bug"; there are crates and "crates of oranges and lemons," and "pastry pigs and turkeys bewitched to a dark gold," as they are served to "yellow cocktail music," while "two nameless girls in yellow" talk to Jordan, whose "slender golden arm" rests on the arm of white-flanneled Nick (pp. 31, 32). When Daisy meets Gatsby at Nick's house, she comes out into the golden "twinkle-bells of sunshine" after the rain and "two rows of brass buttons on her dress gleamed in the sunlight." She looks at Gatsby's garden, which rivals Tom's burning and pungent rose-lawns. Gatsby's flowers include "sparkling jonquils . . . and the pale gold odor of kiss-me-at-the gate" (p. 69). The flowers are early spring flowers (rosy hawthorn and white plum blossoms as well as yellow jonquils) and impossible in July, when the reunion takes place. The point is not that Fitzgerald is an ignorant gardener, which is quite irrelevant. The point is that his mind was consumed by *certain* kinds of flowers and colors in the creation of Gatsby's house, and he carries the detail through to Gatsby's own bedroom, which, unlike the others, is not full of rose and lavender, but is "the simplest room of all—except where the dresser was garnished with a toilet set of pure dull gold" (p. 70).

When golden girl day's eye attends Gatsby's party, she says in reference to her life with her adulterous Tom, "and if you want to take down any addresses here's my little gold pencil." Again, Gatsby is set off in purity from what the money-colors hide in the lives of others. Gatsby's colors, again, provide the same *surfaces* as those of everyone else. His car is a "nice yellow one," and when the "front of his house catches the light" the house is filled at earliest dawn with "gray-turning, gold-turning light" (p. 115). And, again, the yellow debasement of what the gold is supposed to mean is given concreteness in the lack of it, in the yellow brick of Wilson's garage, and, above the ash-white anemic color of his face, his blond hair. Always, region, class, and name provide no moral differentiation among people in the meaning of colors. The difference is provided in memory: as the analog for Gatsby's white is the white of Nick's "real snow," so the analog for Gatsby's gold is what was promised by the "murky yellow cars of the Chicago, Milwaukee & St. Paul railroad," "the thrilling returning trains" of Nick's youth, "looking cheerful as Christmas itself on the tracks beside the gate" (p. 133). But the dead "great name past" is characterized by "Port Roosevelt . . . lined with the dark, undeserted saloons of the *faded-gilt* nineteen hundreds" (p. 52).

And, of course, the entire golden sun motif, compacted in that
hottest day of brutal summer heat in the Hotel Plaza scene, becomes, like the other colors, a sign of the murderous falseness of
its own appearances. Like all the other details that fit so well,
it is fitting that the premonitory rain that fell during Gatsby's
reunion with the day's eye should promise that the golden moment
will not last. So gold as betrayal is at once the harsh sun as a sign
of the power of the money actualities that oppose the fragile coolness of Gatsby's moonlight. It is "roaring noon" on a hot day in a
restaurant with "Presbyterian nymphs on the ceiling" when Nick
is introduced by Gatsby to Wolfsheim. The very history of Gatsby's
decline and death in the triumph of the golden moment begins
with the warming weather and increasing sun. Gatsby woos Daisy
in the cool fall, and she almost joins him on a winter night. He
takes her in cool October. But when Daisy and Tom marry, their
honeymoon is associated with sun and heat, as they took "a three
month's trip to the South Seas" (p. 59). Gatsby seems to join the
sunlight world in triumph when the sun breaks through the rain in
his reunion with Daisy, and when "he realized . . . that there were
twinkle-bells of sunshine in the room, he smiled like . . . an ecstatic
patron of recurrent light. . . . 'My house looks well, doesn't it?' he
demanded. 'See how the whole front of it catches the light' " (p.
68). But the irony is that in the world of sweat and actuality,
where Gatsby can triumph in his energy and effort, he is doomed
because he cannot really assume the identity of that triumph.
Conversely, those who appear to be silvery white, but who betray
the coolness of their appearance, are triumphant in the gold-light
world of sun. And they don't earn it or even deserve it, betraying
their very name-function, like Daisy and her longest day of the
year. The day of the Hotel Plaza confrontation was "broiling . . .
certainly the warmest of the summer" (p. 87). There follows a
full page of details of overwhelming heat and sun, continued
throughout the trip to the hotel and the stay there, and punctuated

by conversation in which East Egg again shows itself irresponsibly ignorant of the nature of the very power it represents. In "watching for the sun" there is no difference between delicately lovely Daisy and harsh, powerful Tom: " 'I read somewhere that the sun's getting hotter every year,' said Tom . . . . 'Or wait a minute— it's just the opposite—the sun's getting colder every year' " (p. 89).

At the hotel the talk of mutual "belonging" and of pretenders is introduced by Jordan's reaction to the strains of the Wedding March: "Imagine marrying anybody in this heat!" Daisy's rejoinder is to identify herself and Tom with the heat and sun that characterized their honeymoon: " 'Still—I was married in the middle of June,' Daisy remembered, 'Louisville in June!' " In the burst of reminiscence, Gatsby's carefully prepared "white" world comes apart under the power of the gold that *really* owns the whiteness. With every word with which Gatsby desperately attempts to rebuild his appearances, to "belong," Daisy drew "further and further into herself, so that he gave up, and only the dead dream fought on as the afternoon slipped away" (p. 102).

Gatsby's first taste of the loss of the dream was one of sunlight and heat when he revisited Louisville after Tom had married Daisy. The golden center he loved had been bought by someone else, and what he lost in a city whose very means of mobility are yellow-colored was the day's eye itself, which receded further and further from him, like the afternoon slipping away, until all that would be left would be his dreams of the cool past.

He left feeling that if he had searched harder, he might have found her—that he was leaving her behind. The day-coach—he was penniless now—was hot. He went out to the open vestibule and sat down on a folding-chair . . . . Then [the train went] out into the spring fields, where a yellow trolley raced them for a minute with people in it who might once have seen the pale magic of her face along the casual street.

The track curved and now it was going away from the sun, which as it sank lower, seemed to spread itself in benediction over the vanishing

city where she had drawn her breath. He stretched out his hand desperately as if to snatch only a wisp of air, to save a fragment of the
spot that she had made lovely for him. But it was all going by too fast
now for his blurred eyes and he knew that he had lost that part of it,
the freshest and the best, forever (p. 116).

Gatsby's moonlight dreams were dreams of the sun. It was "the
old warm world" that his cool-light dreams were to regain. When
his betrayal is final, and he walks toward his pool and his death, he
becomes aware of "how raw the sunlight" is, how raw after a
moonlit dream of what the sunlight would be on that "one fine
morning" when—.

The sunpower of money calls fast-movietime, lush growth from
the American soil. The most prominent flower, besides the obvious daisy and the slightly less obvious myrtle, is the rose. The
rose is used as the rosiness of the rich world, and in its first introduction redness is associated with money. Fitzgerald manipulates
the Montana-copper-red of the red-and-gold bindings of Nick's
Morgan, Mycaenas, Midas, Money books into the same ironic
deployment of appearances that silver, white, gold, coolness, and
heat underwent. The "burning gardens" of Tom's glorious gold
and red and green world are capped by the "cheerful red-and-white
Georgian Colonial mansion." The sweep of the gardens includes
"a half acre of deep, pungent roses." Beneath the white frosted
wedding cake of a ceiling ripples a "wine-colored rug," referred
to again later as a "crimson carpet," whose cool shadows, like
"wind . . . on the sea," are seen after one walks into a "bright rosy-
colored space." All appears rosy in this world, and Nick reminds
Daisy "of a—of a rose, an absolute rose. Doesn't he? . . . An absolute rose?" (p. 13). The actuality makes no difference ("This
was untrue," says Nick. "I am not even faintly like a rose") as long
as appearances are fun. But beneath the appearances of rosy fun
is the reality of Tom's adultery. The whole house is like a rose
flower, and in the evening when the lights are turned on over the

wine-colored rug, "the crimson room bloomed with light" (p. 15). The rose-colored world is part, naturally, of Gatsby's gaudy dream of self in the absurdly wild and "disadvantaged" story he tells Nick about himself: "After that I lived like a young rajah . . . collecting jewels, chiefly rubies . . . ." And Nick thinks, "I saw him opening a chest of rubies to ease, with their crimson-lighted depths, the gnawings of his broken heart" (pp. 50, 51). The colors of Gatsby's rooms take on the imagined colors of the dreams, the gaudy colors of wealth, of Tom's house and Myrtle's taxicabs: "We went upstairs through period bedrooms swathed in rose and lavender silk and vivid with new flowers . . ." (p. 69). When Daisy and Gatsby, reunited in Gatsby's house, look out the window in their newly rediscovered dreamworld, "there was a pink and golden billow of foamy clouds above the sea.

" 'Look at that,' she whispered, and then after a moment: 'I'd like to just get one of those pink clouds and put you in it . . .' " (p. 71). As white Tom will not allow intruders into white East Egg life, he resents the colors of money on colored Gatsby. "An Oxford man! . . . Like hell he is! He wears a pink suit." Gatsby can no more help wearing a "pink" suit than he can help wearing a white suit, silver shirt, and golden tie, any more than he can help wearing the gold hat and bouncing high. On the night of Myrtle's death, Gatsby watches over Daisy's house in "the luminosity of his pink suit under the moon," merely echoing what he had been following from the moment he had first seen Daisy Fay's white house. On this night too, "there were two or three bright windows downstairs and the pink glow from Daisy's room on the second floor" (p. 110). It is fitting that when Nick says his final farewell to Gatsby that Gatsby's "gorgeous pink rag of a suit made a bright spot of color against the white steps" as Gatsby "stood on those steps, concealing his incorruptible dream" (p. 117). It is fitting that when Gatsby is denuded of that dream he should find "what a grotesque thing a rose is."

As with the other colors, what Gatsby conceals beneath his own appearances of rosiness is pure. What the "whole rotten crowd" conceals is the corrupting nothingness of the appearances themselves, and that's all—the "nothing" that Gatsby so naively and pathetically guards. So as the white finally is the white of the woman in the El Greco dream, and as it has its final dirty shade in the pale ashes of the valley, so rose, also the sign of money, has its ironically exposing presentation. It is, like the other colors of moral irresponsibility, merely part of the identity-destroying talk of the animals and vegetables and great names in the book. " 'One time [Gatsby] killed a man,' " says one of the "young ladies, moving somewhere between his cocktails and his flowers . . . 'he killed a man who had found out that he was nephew to Von Hindenburg and second cousin to the devil. Reach me a rose, honey, and pour me a last drop into that there crystal glass' " (p. 47). The "rose" that is reached is a flower as Meyer Wolfsheim's cuff links are "jewels": the memories of the "Old Metropole" are memories of the gangster, Rosy, Rosy, Rosy, Rosenthal. Flowers like cars and clothes—white, rose, silver, lavender, gold. No one sends them to Gatsby when he's dead. In the crazy inversion of all appearances and expectations it is not even too much—in a world "where even Gatsby can happen"—that as Meyer Wolfsheim hides in the office of his Swastika Holding Company, the tune he whistles is "The Rosary."

The exotic growth that gold-power calls up out of the fresh green breast of the new world is paralleled to "rose" in the verdant lushness that begins with the bursting leaves of the new life Nick thinks he will find in the money-summer of the East.

The green follows exactly the same betrayal of excitement and anticipation of the other colors. The central green, of course, is Daisy's green light. Gatsby wears the green hat, too—any color, all colors, bounce! bounce! bounce!—and won't have Daisy come to Nick's cottage before Nick's grass can be clipped to the same "well-kept expanse" of Gatsby's glowing gardens and emerald lawns. And, fittingly, and in premonitory fashion again, the talk of the lawns (p. 63) is immediately followed by talk of money and favors and corruption and Wolfsheim. Perhaps it is an accident that when Jimmy Gatz first sights Cody's yacht he is wearing "a torn green jersey," perhaps it is an accident that when Gatsby offers a liqueur to Nick and Daisy to celebrate the reunion he offers Chartreuse, but it is certainly not mere luck on Fitzgerald's part that when Daisy whispers about her excitement in her promissory voice at Gatsby's party, she says, "If you want to kiss me at any time . . . just let me know and I'll be glad to arrange it for you. Just mention my name. Or present a green card. I'm giving out green—" (p. 79). In the heat of the summer, coolness and luxury are constantly associated with deep shade, deep foliage, the sprigs of mint in long cool drinks, the fresh promises of a new world, and they are absolutely constant.

In consistent control of his colors, Fitzgerald announces the treacherous actualities beneath alluring green appearances by shifting the context to a reversal of the promise. The absence of money at the moment of his discovery of betrayal turns Wilson's face the color of what he lacks and needs, a lack and need which gold-light only makes the more obvious. "In the sunlight his face was green" (p. 93). The mis-identification of Gatsby in the surfaces of money colors is continued when his golden-white car is at first identified by one witness as "light green"—a near miss and an understandable confusion which Fitzgerald uses symbolically, especially in the context of "the green leather conservatory" of the car's interior beneath windshields that *mirror* a dozen suns. As Gatsby, betrayed, discovers how "grotesque a thing a rose is" he also sees not sumptuous green lawns but the thinness of "the scarcely created grass." Again and always, the true green of Gatsby is the dream-green, the pure green, different from the actualities of the money-colors he wears. It is, once more, the same green as

that in Nick's memory, the memory of "the long green tickets"
that admitted one to the yellow cars of the Christmas-cheerful
thrilling trains of our youth. It is the last memory of the greatest
promise "that flowered once for Dutch sailor's eyes—a fresh green
breast of the new world."

As Gatsby is deserted by all colors in actuality, and is innocently
the ideal dream-meaning of all colors beneath the surface, so he is
the emulation of corrupt all-color on the surface. Too gaudy for
condescending "white" East Egg, he will wear any hat. "In his blue
gardens" caterers "came down with . . . enough colored lights to
make a Christmas tree of Gatsby's enormous garden." Together
with the dark gold pastry pigs and turkeys, there are "baked hams
crowded against salads of harlequin designs . . . ." Soon "the halls
and salons and verandas are gaudy with primary colors . . . . The
lights grow brighter . . . through the sea-change of faces and voices
and color under the constantly changing light" (pp. 31–32). He
wears white suits, he wears silver and gold, he wears pink, he wears
caramel-colored suits, he has chauffeurs in spring-toned "robin's
egg blue." When he spills his shirts out for Daisy to see, "they fell
and covered the table in many colored disarray. . . . He brought
more . . . shirts with stripes and scrolls and plaids in coral and
apple-green and lavender and faint orange, with monograms of
Indian blue" (p. 70). But, again, the reality beneath the gaudy
surface differentiates Gatsby from the multichrome of Columbus's
Eggs and relates him, despite his Christmas tree-lit parties to the
Christmas cheerfulness of the yellow and green and white night-
time of Nick's Christmas memories. Red and green, white, silver
and gold, the colors of America are indeed the colors of Christmas.

The relationship between Christmas (the genesis of *The Great
Gatsby* was in one of Fitzgerald's famous short stories, "Winter
Dreams") and summer flowers is the same as the relationship between moon-coolness and sunheat: they are all one as the multicolor of promise and new life. What Fitzgerald brings his motifs

down to is this: the very burst of new life, always beginning anew
in a perennial American summer of always-Christmas, is as mis-
leadingly false as the riotous colors of wealth that are immediately
related to the new green leaves at the very beginning of the book.
Nick's money-books and the "great bursts of leaves" in West Egg
are duplicated in the descriptions of Tom's and Gatsby's gardens,
in the colors and lushness of the vegetation. Daisy-flower's "crimson room bloomed with light." She surprises Nick "by opening
up again in a flower-like way" with that promise-laden voice of
hers (p. 17). When she arrives at Nick's bungalow, she arrives
like a hyacinth girl, associated with the rain and the lavender-blue
of spring flowers, in colors that are vulgar when associated with the
parvenu. She arrives "under the dripping bare lilac trees . . .
beneath a three-cornered lavender hat . . . . The exhilarating
ripple of her voice was a wild tonic in the rain. . . . A damp streak
of hair lay like a dash of blue paint across her cheek, and her hand
was wet with glistening drops . . ." (p. 65). And when Gatsby "forever wed his unutterable vision to her perishable breath . . . at his
lips' touch she blossomed for him like a flower and the incarnation
was complete." The extension, by continuous parallels of imagery,
from the characters to national history is one of Fitzgerald's triumphs. The very fresh, green breast of the new world, pandering
in whispers, once *flowered* for the eyes of Dutch sailors. The rain
at Gatsby's funeral is not the flower-making rain of a spring-green
world, but the cold autumn rain of death.

When Gatsby has the grass manicured around Nick's cottage so
that the setting will be attractive for his "flower," Nick thinks to
go to West Egg to search for lemons and flowers for the tea. "The
flowers were unnecessary, for at two o'clock a greenhouse arrived
from Gatsby's, with innumerable receptacles to contain it" (p.
64). Gatsby wears the flower hat, too, with the "spring" garden by
his big postern and with the bedrooms "swathed in rose . . . and
vivid with new flowers" that someday his Daisy might see. Even

on the night in which the daisy killed the myrtle, the world of the rose-and-white Buchanan house offers lovely, flower appearances to Daisy, for her "two [bedroom] windows bloomed with light." From the beginning, back in Louisville, in Gatsby's eyes Daisy's house had been "ripe," "beautiful and cool," and "redolent . . . of dances whose flowers were scarcely withered." But the reality of the golden life into which Daisy finally disappears is that of "dying orchids on the floor beside her bed" (p. 115).

So—the flowers are like the colors, and Daisy again sums up everything in which Gatsby was mistaken. Benny Mclenahan's girls, in that old time table of Nick's, all had "names of flowers," and in all the cheap obviousness of what Daisy, beneath appearances morally is, too, there are no moral differences in effect between Benny's girls and Daisy, as there are no eventual differences, in life and hope, between the flowers Gatsby sends and the heaps of flowers covering the hearse that Nick sees as he and Gatsby slide across the bridge into the sugar-lump city. The flowers are for the dead, or they are dying themselves, or they are cheap imitations of fresh beauty. The "Star" beneath the white-plum tree in Gatsby's party is a "gorgeous, scarcely human orchid of a woman" (p. 80), and all that Gatsby is left by his "flower" Daisy, who scorns the creatures at his party, is all that he's left by those very creatures: crushed flowers, rinds, and pulp. "I love New York on summer afternoons when everyone's away. There's something very sensuous about it," says Jordan, "—overripe as if all sorts of funny fruits were going to fall into your hands." Jordan should know. The flowers that East Egg supposedly represents result in the "funny fruits" and are as monstrous as the vegetables who mingle with the animals and the "great names" at Gatsby's party. No real flower exists. Daisy never really "flowers" for Gatsby, in life or in death. She only retreats into her vast carelessness or wealth or whatever it is that holds her and Tom together. Nick orders flowers for Gatsby's funeral, and "could only remember . . . that Daisy hadn't sent a message or a flower" (p. 133).

In pointing out the relationship of details to ideas, I have been insistent on the context of the betrayal of the American dream by American history, of American expectation by American wealth. It is not insignificant that of the many titles Fitzgerald thought of for the novel—*Gold-Hatted Gatsby, The High-Bouncing Lover, Among Ash-Heaps and Millionaires, On the Road to West Egg, Trimalchio in West Egg*—the one he most wanted, after it was too late to change the plates—was *Under the Red, White, and Blue.* I have insisted that the dream is a Romantic dream in which the self replaces the very universe, in which the possibilities of self transcend any things that are needed to identify it. Yet it is precisely the identifying "things" that time, with its constant lesson of mortal limitation, has substituted for the Romantic possibility. The energy of the dream is its Romantic expectation; the actuality of the dream is merely its appearances.

In commenting upon what has happened to those appearances, Fitzgerald does two things at once. Wistfully, reluctantly, he bids adieu to the old dream of America as a gorgeous impossibility. Inevitably time figures prominently as a force in fiction that says goodbye to Romantic vision. Even Daisy is dimly aware of the relationship between golden moments, dreams, and time. She is tugged by "Three O'clock in the Morning." "What was it up there in the song that seemed to be calling her back inside? After all, in the very casualness of Gatsby's party there were romantic possibilities totally absent from her world. . . . What would happen now in the dim incalculable hours? Perhaps some unbelievable guest would arrive, a person infinitely rare and to be marvelled at, some authentically radiant young girl who with one fresh glance at Gatsby, one moment of magical encounter, would blot out those five years of unwavering devotion" (p. 83). Fitzgerald suggests that the definition of human realities is not to be found in existential albeit gorgeous isolation, but in the social dimensions of history and place and class. Yet, at the same time, he finds that in America those dimensions have been so defined by appearances alone that they have no underlying reality of the human spirit and provide no discovery of the realities and potentialities of that spirit. The Romantic vision to which he says farewell remains more attractive than the actualities for which he knows he must settle. American but placeless; desiring the lovelier manners and sense of work of an older American ethic, yet repudiating the hypocrisy that the older generation made out of its own ideologies; finding in the Younger Generation the necessary rebellion against old hypocrisies yet finding also in the brave new world every dehumanizing debasement of the old one, Fitzgerald remains as "placeless" at the end of *Gatsby* (to what Middle West *does* Nick return?) as at the end of *This Side of Paradise* or *The Beautiful and Damned.* Yet he had arrived somewhere very firmly. One need only compare Gatsby's dreams and debasement with Nick's memories and set them, as Fitzgerald does, against the closing, "nationalizing" paragraphs of the book. Fitzgerald arrives at no "answers," but it is not his purpose to write a sociological program. The moving and lyrical prose, in which the narrator's voice is finally a song of the significance of the author's life, indicates how compellingly and cohesively Fitzgerald had finally merged his vision, his memory, and his materials into a moral history of the meaning of America. In the earlier books the fragments had provided squeaking Isabelle or the embarrassing cynicism of Maury Noble and the Patches. In *The Great Gatsby* they were united into a sorrowful, lovely realm of coherent meaning.

To this "place," at least, his art had brought him.

# CHAPTER IV
# TENDER IS THE NIGHT
## *Broken Decalogues*

December, 1940. Dearest Scottie:

... I am still in bed—this time the result of twenty-five years of ciga-rettes. You have got two beautiful bad examples for parents. Just do everything we didn't do and you'll be perfectly safe. But be sweet to your mother at Xmas despite her early Chaldean rune-worship which she will undoubtedly inflict on you at Xmas. Her letters are tragically brilliant on all matters except those of central importance. How strange to have failed as a social creature—even criminals do not fail that way—they are the law's "Loyal Opposition," so to speak. But the insane are always mere guests on earth, eternal strangers carrying around broken decalogues that they cannot read.[1]

At the most, this letter could not have been written more than twenty-one days before Fitzgerald died; up to the moment his heart tightened behind its cigarette-hardened arteries he thought of the failures in his life as the moral consequence of his being the "beautiful bad example" of self-indulgent apostasy from "good-ness." "I am [crippled] by my inability to handle money," he wrote, and by "my self-indulgences of the past. . . . What little I've accomplished has been by the most laborious and uphill work,

1 *The Letters of F. Scott Fitzgerald*, ed. Andrew Turnbull (New York, 1963), p. 100; hereafter referred to as *Letters*.

and I wish now I'd *never* relaxed or looked back—but said at the
end of *The Great Gatsby*: 'I've found my line—from now on
this comes first. This is my immediate duty—without this I am
nothing.' "[2]

The broken decalogues, disobeyed and trampled on, led to
nights of despair, days of the locust—always Fitzgerald felt that
his generation's departure from the good, gone world of the old
commandments of work and discipline and politeness was a
symptom of a general breakdown and insanity in Western civilization. Intrigued as he was by Spengler's *Decline of the West*,
which he had begun to read in 1926, he had come to see Zelda's
insanity and his own alcoholism as private, painful symbols of
the disintegration of a time and a nation. His own jazz-age golden
moment was a brief, insular American idyll that turned out to be
a sordid corruption of its own promise. "It's odd that my talent
for the short story vanished," he wrote wistfully to Zelda two
months before he died. "It was partly that times changed, editors
changed, but part of it was tied up somehow with you and me—
the happy ending."[3]

"Often I have encouraged [your being an old-fashioned girl],"
he told Scottie, "because my generation of radicals and breakers-
down never found anything to take the place of the old virtues of
work and courage and the old graces of courtesy and politeness.
But I don't want you to live in an unreal world or to believe that
the system that produced Barbara Hutton can survive. . . ."[4] The
broken decalogues. The old virtues and the old graces, work and
courage, courtesy and politeness, came from a dream-filled past
that also somehow produced "Barbara Hutton." In the history of
an entire people the golden commandments from a lost Sinai were
replaced by gilded calves in the promised land. That's what *Ten-*

---

[2] To Scottie, written six months before his death, June 12, 1940, *ibid.*, p. 79.
[3] October 23, 1940, *ibid.*, p. 128.
[4] July 1938, *ibid.*, p. 36.

*der Is the Night* is all about, and to see it as a "psychological novel"
is to miss what Fitzgerald himself meant when he said, using confusing terminology, that the book is a "philosophical, now called
psychological novel."

He meant by that term that unlike *The Great Gatsby*, which
he called a "dramatic" novel, *Tender Is the Night* is not a lyrical
organization of dramatic moments, but a Jamesian, scenic arrangement of dramatic moments, a visual novel whose scenes are
to suggest a philosophy of history. The history of manners, in what
Fitzgerald meant by the "philosophical novel," becomes a cultural clue to the meaning, the moral development, of an era. An
entire civilization can be tested and evaluated in the values that
surround the fate of the hero of the novel. Fitzgerald thought of
*Tender Is the Night* as his *Vanity Fair*, even calling it *The
World's Fair* in one draft. In technique, as well as in "classifi-
cation," the novel is one of scenes rather than lyrical, "elaborate
and overlapping blankets of prose." The novel reflects what Fitzgerald learned in Hollywood, and the difference in voice between
his two greatest novels is immediately discernible when you reflect
that you tend to remember great poetic passages, or at least a sense
of poetic prose, from *The Great Gatsby*, but that you don't recall
many, if any, such passages from *Tender Is the Night*. What you
tend to remember is scenes, movie stills almost, of the action. Unquestionably, a "dramatic" novel can also be a "philosophical" or
"psychological" novel, but the extent to which the prose of *Tender
Is the Night* insists upon scene and action creates a question that
provides a most fruitful critical clue to the nature of the novel: in
the development of the book, version after version, what did all
the scenes provide as consistent elements, regardless of change of
characters, plot, and even specific scenes? What kinds of elements
did Fitzgerald keep and re-create in the various changes and de-
letions and rewritings? They were most decidedly not elements
focusing on case history, on psychiatry, on psychological analysis

of behavior, normal or abnormal. Those elements crept into the story with the onslaught of Zelda's illness, but they never became the focus of the story. The elements common to all versions in the development of the plot are exposing scene after exposing scene of high social life, either in Hollywood or on shipboard or among American expatriates in Europe. That life is presented constantly as the flashing world of broken decalogues most likely to unhinge and undo the innocent seeker or whatever is left of the responsible, polite personage in a society in which the old virtues and graces no longer define people, success, or social life itself. Consistently, over the years, as Fitzgerald tried to discover what his book was about— what *story* he was telling—he focused on scenes in which the relationships of characters became vehicles for the delineation of the corrosion of the personage among destructive, significantly expository, social types. Without question, Zelda's emotional collapse provided material for the final version of *Tender Is the Night*, but, as in the earlier versions, disease leads outward to the social heritage which it sums up rather than inward to a causal analysis of individual psyche. Fitzgerald's "philosophical, psychological" novel is a social novel if it is anything, and if it is anything it is a great social novel which demonstrates how the intricacies of psychology can describe, in dramatic form, the effects of an eroded society on human personality.

The development of the novel has been traced exhaustively by Matthew Bruccoli in his book, *The Composition of Tender Is the Night*;[5] therefore, there is no need here for a full account of the evolution of the materials of the novel. To sum up the growth of the book, one need only refer to Mr. Bruccoli's definitive study, which is an analysis of the contents of the seven blue cardboard boxes of the manuscripts of *Tender Is the Night*, stored in the Princeton Library, where the Fitzgerald papers are housed. The boxes contain approximately 3500 pages of the various drafts of

[5] University of Pittsburgh Press (Pittsburgh, 1963).

the novel, together with proofs and tearsheets on which Fitzgerald made further revisions. Mr. Bruccoli has sorted these papers out into three major versions of the novel, which underwent a total of seventeen drafts (eighteen, if one counts the incompletely revised version of the book, published posthumously). The first version, the story of Francis Melarkey, a young Hollywood technician who was to have killed his mother, was revised in five drafts, with a change in title for almost every change in draft: *Our Type, The Boy Who Killed His Mother, The Melarkey Case,* and *The World's Fair.* These drafts occupied Fitzgerald from 1925 through 1930—living high and drinking wildly he began working on the novel in the spring and summer, a few months after he had completed *The Great Gatsby.* Briefly he interrupted the Melarkey story of matricide in 1929 to begin the second, the Kelly version, but he quickly abandoned his new hero and his new start without a title, without a complete draft, without anything, in fact, but two long and tentative scenes on an ocean liner and the introduction of a young actress named Rosemary. The Melarkey versions introduced background characters named (through various rechristenings) Abe and Mary Grant, later to become the Norths, and Seth and Dinah Piper, later to become the Divers.

These various drafts were undertaken during the time when Fitzgerald was beginning his most self-destructive years, whose effects he would endure in the remorse, disintegration, and darkness of his life in the 1930's. The wasteful and increasingly compulsive sprees in Europe in 1925 and 1926 were continued on his return to America. The first sojourn in Hollywood in 1927 did nothing to lessen the Fitzgeralds' intense and unremitting depletion of their physical, emotional, and economic stamina, and the exhausting slide toward the bankruptcy of all their resources was continued during the summer in Paris in 1928. After several months back in the States, at home at the "Ellerslie" estate outside Wilmington, Delaware, the Fitzgeralds moved abroad again, and

ᵣ, when Zelda had her first emotional collapse in the
1930, Scott began to smell the stench of the ruin that he
a.... new had begun to overtake him. What had been the ecto-
plasm of his imagination in *The Beautiful and Damned* had become the protoplasm of his existence as he worked on *Tender Is
the Night*. Under the circumstances, the novel did not write itself
out to a successful conclusion. It floundered while Fitzgerald
learned an old voice anew, the voice that grovels before the kitchen
maids, the voice that speaks with "the authority of failure," and
which, imagined in his would-be author, Anthony Patch, was to
take more dense and lively shape in the character of a psychiatrist
who never finished *his* book, either, and who fatigued himself into
disappearance, like a speck seen through the wrong end of bi-
noculars. That character germinated and grew early in 1932 with
Zelda's second and very severe breakdown, following Scott's unsuccessful second stay in Hollywood. So, early in 1932, the third
version of the novel began to take form under the various titles
of *The Drunkard's Holiday, Doctor Diver's Holiday,* and, finally,
*Tender Is the Night*. With this version, the novel became all Dick
Diver's and Fitzgerald found his story.

Developing through six manuscript drafts—an original set of
notes and five revisions, the third version was revised a sixth time
in the galleys for its serial publication in *Scribner's Magazine*, a
seventh time in the page proof for the serial publication, an eighth
time on tearsheets from the published magazine serial in preparation for publication in book form, a ninth time in the galleys for
the book, a tenth time in the page proofs for the book and an
eleventh time in the published book itself, when Fitzgerald began
to prepare a final revision for the republication of the novel as he
would like to see it. He died before he could complete it.

As I have suggested, what is more important in the growth of
the novel than the chronicle of the materials is a recognition of
what remains unchanged. In all seventeen drafts, it is clear that

what Fitzgerald is concerned with is a presentation of the glittering golden world in its effect on the yearning, searching American, on the bitter arrivist, on the dewy *naif*, on the strong and callous rich, but most of all, on the innocent, expectant idealist. The famous note he wrote to himself as he miraculously hit stride again in the bitter year of 1932 is not so much an explanation of the many complex changes in the various versions of the novel as it is an explanation of what increasingly summed up the revisions as they undulated and surged toward the final draft: "The novel should do this," the note said: "Show a man who is a natural idealist, a spoiled priest, giving in for various causes to the ideas of the haute bourgeoisie, and in his rise to the top of the social world losing his idealism, his talent and turning to drink and dissipation. Background one in which the leisure class is at their truly most brilliant and glamorous."[6]

The dedication of the novel,

To

GERALD AND SARA

Many Fêtes

is a dedication to people who were near, dear, and very valuable to Fitzgerald, and who, for him, were sparklingly representative members of "the leisure class" at its "truly most brilliant and glamorous." Gerald and Sara Murphy, among the most cultured and gracious of the American expatriates in Europe, were, for Scott, living examples of the old virtues and the old graces, of civilization wrought to an exquisite turn through work and courage, courtesy and politeness. They were the older, vanished, promising America. At the same time, they were representative to him of the new world that emerged from the ruin of the Victorian time that in self-deluded ways opened the doors to "Barbara Hutton," to gaudy cosmopolitanism, graceless money, and callous power that sup-

[6] Fitzgerald's "General Plan" for the book is given in full as "Appendix B" in Mizener's *The Far Side of Paradise*.

planted and destroyed—paradoxically was fostered by—the graciousness the Murphys personified.

Gerald Murphy constantly displayed an attentive charm that nourished the egos of his companions. His Irish features shone politely and intelligently above his elegant sartorial finesse as he lavished sensitive responses upon his guests. A superb party giver and host, he made for his own group of friends a private Riviera while the conventional haut monde spent more orthodox summers up north at Deauville. In both basic and small ways the Murphys provided part of the model for the composite Dick Diver. For instance, not only was Dick's essential and delicate "civilization" and "taste" derived from Gerald, but, to come to minor concrete particulars, the Murphys talked the proprietor of the Hôtel du Cap d'Antibes (which sat for Fitzgerald's portrait of Gausse's Hôtel des Étrangers) into leaving part of the hotel open for guests in the summer of 1922. In the brilliant white sunshine, among the empty villas, Gerald cleared a strip of beach with a rake and a mattock, as Dick was to do, while Sara sunned and swam, wearing a string of pearls to set off her brown back, as Nicole was to do. The rest of the "leisure class" soon caught on, and the Murphy's garden-bejewelled Villa America, overlooking the Golfe Juan, became a central part of a crowded and fashionable summer watering place for artists, writers, and famous hot cats on top. The Murphys epitomized the world Fitzgerald wanted to capture in all the versions of his novel, and in his relationship to them of envy and belonging, of hostility and love, and of constant fascination, Fitzgerald saw in them everything that his underdog sense of "work as the only dignity" repudiated and to which his romantic sense of life's charmed possibility as an extended golden moment drew him. As the Murphys dispensed grace and fun to the new, young postwar world and were, in turn, sustained within it, Fitzgerald, wistful and envious, saw that what was needed was a touch of the ruin which, neglected in the sunny world of money

and culture and gaiety and independence, was the personal and
international reality which alone could turn fairyland into a
paradigm of the actuality of human limitations. Dick Diver was
to know "that the price of his intactness was incompleteness.

" 'The best I can wish you, my child,' so said the Fairy Black-
stick in Thackeray's *The Rose and the Ring*, 'is a little misfortune.' "[7] One part of the Murphys that went into Dick Diver was
the association between taste and ruin, charm and lesions of vitality, civilization and defeat. It was hardly that the Murphys'
charming life was also a charmed one. They had deep and real mis-
fortunes of their most personal own. It was that they *seemed* to
live in grace because they lived in graciousness, and Fitzgerald
wished to capture them in all the tensions and ambivalences of
"the old virtures and the old graces" and the "Barbara Hutton"
world of broken decalogues. His immersion in ruin (and his often
being ostracized by it) was, finally, what set Fitzgerald off from the
Murphys and gave him a full, evaluative overview of the world
that, for him, they represented. He analyzed and analyzed them,
straining his relationship with them to the breaking point and
causing them to assert, by gesture and by direct statement, that
they could not tolerate Fitzgerald's company as long as he was
either drunk, rude, and sophomoric or analytic, "objective," and
probing. In his own identification of himself as both failure and
outcast on the one hand, and on the other hand both spiritual descendent of the Murphy's world and crown prince of the world of
broken decalogues, he fashioned his most problematical and complex composite self, Dick Diver. By injecting his own increasingly
chaotic and catastrophic experience, as an index to the morally
chaotic state of the new young world, into Gerald Murphy's impeccable and apparently enviable life on the Golfe Juan, he was

[7] *Tender Is the Night*, ed. Malcolm Cowley, in *Three Novels of F. Scott Fitzgerald* (New York, 1953), p. 5. All further references to the novel are to this text
and will be indicated by parentheses in the body of the chapter.

once more able to turn his autobiographical impulse into the im-
personality of an art which allowed him to express his most personal statements. Drunk or sober, on a spree or remorseful, he
found the meaning of his own experience in his novel and its
hero. And though he said more than once that he was sometimes
drunk when he wrote ("I would give anything if I hadn't had to
write Part III of *Tender Is the Night* entirely on stimulant"),[8] he
insisted fully as often that his constant revising made writing for
him not merely an act of alcoholic sensibility but also, and finally,
a sober, disciplined, and rational act of will. Anyhow, he concluded, anybody who thinks that one can write a book on booze is
crazy.

The quick and easy flow of feelings and his expressive need for
it were among the reasons he began to drink. Also, he found that
when he was high, his volatile senses gave him a warm, euphoric,
emotional gratification that sprang from a passionate—sometimes
sentimental—desire to flatter and win people. With high-octane
liquids he found that he could please people with a sure and fluid
ease. His old charm floated to the surface of his anxieties and oiled
the troubled waters. Even when he had been young and successful,
liquor heightened his sense of being everybody's darling, of being
the bright, gay, sought-after Mr. It. Drink aimed right at the vital
center of his insecurities and ambivalences of identity: when you
please people they like you. You belong. So hard to love, Dick
Diver muses, and so easy to be loved. And so necessary. The deep
need was something that Fitzgerald associated with his own identification with his national "race," his "times," his "generation,"
his "age." He was continually aware that the desire to be liked and
loved has a queer national parallel with his most personal self.
From the moment the United States took on a separate and equal
identity among nations, they were torn between a sense of themselves as America—the new, different, superior, envied, liberated

8 To Maxwell Perkins, March 11, 1935, *Letters*, p. 260.

golden state in which men's dreams are realized regardless of their lost pasts, the new Kid who made it biggest and best, the late arrival who was the hottest cat on top at the apex of history, the old dream of the young republic that "rolled on under the night"— and a sense of themselves as a chunk of real estate, internally divided and various, subject to compromises with institutional techniques and the world of "next things," and culturally and technologically and militarily inferior to the parent civilization from which they had separated. At the beginning, the nation found itself in the condition of the adolescent country boy in urbane adult society. He thumps his chest, screws up his eyes in his handsome but pimply face, and says that he is *so* a man—and at the moment of declaration his voice breaks. Part of him, like Fitzgerald, grovels before the kitchen maids. Our Brother Jonathan from the hinterlands, our Yankee, Uncle-Sam, shrewd and hungry rube, is afraid that the sophisticated reaction of the hot cats will be a politely controlled snicker behind a dazzling and spotless sleeve. On the other hand, the handsome, vain boy with millennial dreams is romantically aware of the extent to which the future of the Western world is in his growing bones.

The political assumptions of the American eighteenth century were unexceptionably those of a separate nation whose separateness was taken as a metaphoric indication, in geography as in political language, of a differentness in newness and superiority. If newness and youth were a momentary embarrassment, they would become a permanent and envied characteristic of the country of utopia. They would become all-important. The sense of youthful promise, of the potential realization of an enormous selfhood, a lasting golden moment bigger and better in every way than the biggest and best the snickerers can produce, results in that part of the eternally young comman-man country-boy of a nation that insults the great. The confusions of anti-intellectualism, snobbish anti-snobbishness, and suspicious egalitarian dislike of any de-

parture from the common norm have filled many books and anal-
yses of American culture, and they have no full, convenient
place in this book. Most particularly, the role of the peculiarly
American millennial impulse in American literature, so obvious
in Fitzgerald's creation of his fictional selves, is the subject of a
separate book. Suffice it to say here, in a brief consideration of
Fitzgerald-as-American, that the grovelling before the kitchen
maids is never done without an angry and bewildered sense of
being too greatly destiny's darling to indulge in such nonsense,
and that insulting the great is never done without an uneasy sense
of most comfortably belonging, after all, among the folks in the
democratic kitchen. Our foreign policy, like our literature, is of
a piece with a representative "Fitzgerald." It has been a confused
mixture of power politics in which, in the world of next things,
America builds its empire better than the rest of the world, and
of the undefined millennial idealisms, from Thomas Paine through
Woodrow Wilson to the present moment, in which, acting as a
personification of Salvation, according to what we think the rest
of the world expects from our self-image, we try to remake the
world in that image and wonder why nobody loves us as we ache
to be loved. Are we not millennial redemption? But of course it
would be silly to do more than mention the subject here. I can
only refer to America's sense of itself as the golden moment and
suggest that its need to be liked and loved is a total national summation of the uncertainty of identity that Fitzgerald microcosmi-
cally summed up in his most American aspects. With as deeply
national a *good* writer as Fitzgerald, one can no more exhaust
the crucial significance of art as cultural expression than one can
exhaust the tactics of the work itself. I wish to suggest merely that
the uneasiness of personality of a man hailed as representative
by his culture is likely to be, in deeper ways than the contemporaries who hail him suspect, the uneasiness of that very culture
itself. For this reason a dim sense of the vast relationships between

ourselves, the writer, an "identity crisis," and the autobiographical impulse in art leads us to hail the representative as "significant." Fitzgerald hovered between insulting and grovelling,
between biting and flattering, between "trashy imaginings" and
"being the greatest writer who ever lived," as America hovers between boastfully protesting that "made in America" is best and
anxiously turning to Europe for the best that has been thought
and said and made—from philosophy and painting to wine and
clothes. Fitzgerald hovered between a great, unselfish desire to
please, to serve, to be used, and a bewildered and total self-assertion
just as America hovers between what it thinks of its Marshall
Plans, and what it sometimes does with them, what it ideologizes
about Vietnams and what Vietnams actually turn out to be.
Drink, the euphoric sense of making it, the excitement of ever-
promised new chances, both highlighted and mediated between
Fitzgerald's ambivalences as the intoxication of wealth and power
did his nation's. The morning after demanded sober self-examina-
tion as both Fitzgerald and his nation dived from the spree of the
twenties into the cold Depression years in which *Tender Is the
Night* was published. But regardless of these generalizations and
speculations, the plain fact is that as he was caught—often drunkenly—between the ambivalences, Fitzgerald did come to identify his
own disintegration with his nation's disintegration of the old decalogues beneath the weight of its own wealth and power: the
"times" of "the happy ending" have "changed," and "I don't
want you to . . . believe that the system that produced Barbara
Hutton can survive."

By the time he came to the Dick Diver version of *Tender Is
the Night,* working out of the themes implicit in *This Side of
Paradise* and *The Beautiful and Damned* and artistically solidified in the motifs that expressed those themes in *The Great Gatsby,*
Fitzgerald had complete amalgams of associations in his imagination. They were amalgams in which the corrupt new world of soul-

less wealth becomes identified with the new America as the new
America spreads over the world, is internationalized, and loses
its old unique identity; amalgams in which, in a completely contrasting set of associations, the destroyed, old world of our Gatsby-
youth, Dick Diver's lost "safe, beautiful world" of promise, hope,
passion, charm, virtues, and graces, is identified with an older
America that is forever buried as, with Dick, we say goodbye to
all our fathers. In short, in *Tender Is the Night,* Fitzgerald supplied an international setting whose series of scenes allowed him
a Jamesian "philosophical" perspective of the two Americas. His
"philosophical novel" thus allowed him a broader canvas and
more complex contrasts than ever before with which to present a
moral picture of the two Americas that had appeared as "the
actuality" and "the dream" in *The Great Gatsby.* Dick Diver, the
spoiled priest intricately and inextricably associated with both
Americas, like Fitzgerald with his worlds of personage and personality, significantly is not only the drunk ruined by wealth and
power, but is also the potential world-redeemer self-ruined by his
own responses, by his deepest need to be liked and loved. Like
Gatsby, he lives in both worlds and has a real home, "these days,"
in neither. As composite fictive character, he is his creator and his
creator's nation. "I am part of the race consciousness," Fitzgerald
told his secretary. "I take people to me and change my conception
of them and then write them out again. My characters are all
Scott Fitzgerald," fully as much as the characters that Dick "took
to him" and "worked over" were all Diver creations of the composite moment.[9] Fitzgerald restored people to an essential meaning as he remade them into part of a character, as Dick restored
people to an essential identity in his creative moments: "It was
themselves he gave back to them, blurred by the compromises of
how many years" (p. 111). The creation of others is an act of com-

[9] In the journal of Laura Guthrie, quoted in Andrew Turnbull, *Scott Fitzgerald*
(New York, 1962), p. 259.

posite self-creation. Because they were made whole out of the love-need of Diver's eager leap to service, they must reflect goodness, be good, if only for the moment of the perfect dinner in a lovely garden during an exquisite evening on the Golfe Juan. So Dick realizes that he was all the personalities he had loved, and "for the remainder of his life . . . was condemned to carry with him the egos of certain people, early met and early loved, and to be only as complete as they were complete themselves" (p. 263). So Fitzgerald's characters, too, had to illustrate the "goodness" implicit within the destructive impulses, the creative power within the self-doubt and self-debasement. "I'm so bad, such a lousy son-of-a-bitch that I've got to do something good—so good in my work —that it counterbalances the bad."[10] The "good" was the disciplined creation of art, the work he never should have left, as he said after he had found himself with *The Great Gatsby*. The badness is the vanity, the self-love, the need for love, the destructive impulsiveness euphorically sure of second chances—all that he first began to explore in *This Side of Paradise,* out of which came the creative power that repudiated its materials. He felt that *Tender Is the Night* was his most complex and profound creation, his confession of faith in his possibilities of goodness that came so complexly from what was self-destructive. " 'If you liked *The Great Gatsby*,' he inscribed the book for a friend, 'for God's sake read this. Gatsby was a tour de force, but this is a confession of faith.' Into *Tender Is the Night* he put his hard-earned beliefs: that work was the only dignity; that it didn't help a serious man to be too much flattered and loved; that money and beauty were treacherous aides; that honor, courtesy, courage—the old fashioned virtues—were the best guides after all.' "[11]

The goodness of his production was to be a sign of the goodness of his talent; his enduring talent made visible once more was to

10 *Ibid.,* p. 261.
11 Turnbull, *Scott Fitzgerald*, p. 241.

be a sign of the goodness still lasting in the man, still possible in his life—the possibilities still there in the old-fashioned virtues and disciplines. When he showed a visitor the foot-thick pile of the manuscript of the book a year before it was published, Fitzgerald said, "It's good, good, good. When it's published people will say that it's good, good, good."[12] "I've *got* to be good and I *can* be in my work. I must be loved. I tip heavily to be loved. I have so many faults that I must be approved of in other ways . . . I create a world for others. Because of this women want to go away with me, they think the world of delight I make for them will last forever. I make them seem brilliant to themselves and most important."[13] The key to the destruction of Diver, as a person, a talent, an era, and the dream of a nation, is here in his very "goodness" and his creation of a world of delight.

That goodness went into Diver from the life that spoke to Fitzgerald of endurance—in the face of the knowledge that the "fulfilled future and the wistful past" evoked by that life were disappearing irrecoverably into the destructive present. Like his borrowings for *The Great Gatsby*, whatever he borrowed from experience for his tale of annihilated goodness in his new book about America was a borrowing that in each instance he felt in his bones was a reflection of his times and his culture as well as his personal history. In his sense of one aspect of the Murphys that went into Dick Diver, he wrote to Sara Murphy that "I am too moved by what I am saying [about you] to write it as well as I'd like. You are part of our times, part of the history of our race. The people whose lives you've touched directly or indirectly have reacted to the corporate bundle of atoms that's you in a *good* way. *I have seen you again and again at a time of confusion take the hard course almost blindly because long after your powers of ratiocination were exhausted*

12 Quoted in Cowley's introduction to *Tender Is the Night, Three Novels of F. Scott Fitzgerald*, p. iv.
13 Guthrie, quoted in Turnbull, p. 261.

*you clung to the idea of dauntless courage.*"[14] So too, the heritage
Dick takes from his father, the representative of an "older America," is one of honesty, courage, and politeness.

Fitzgerald had already come to feel that romanticism and impulse were parts of his own and his national temperament, and
that though being a romantic had led him and his nation to their
yearnings, their memory, their excitement, and their creativity,
self-indulgence and impulsiveness had led to a dissipation of all
that was valuable in the romanticism. Yet, in his very nerve-fibres
he knew that he would never have had one without the other,
that one was a manifestation in spoiled temperament of what the
other was in creative imagination. The trick of conservation in
his broken tiredness was to channel the destructive impulsiveness, to control rather than deny himself. Yet, he sensed that control would be a loss of the open, feeling charm that had made him
lovable and had intensified his "heightened sensitivity to the
promises of life." He even saw his trick of conservation as something that could only be manifested in a personality which would
be a dull, if not a "bad, son-of-a-bitch." His guilt about his squan-
dered life ate even into his preserving, conserving sense of his
art. If he felt that he was "so bad, such a lousy son-of-a-bitch" in
life and so "good" in his artistic control and creation, he was also
aware of the opposite, in which he was charming, considerate, and
lovable in life and ruthless in his art: "I can be so tender and kind
to people in even little things, but once I get a pen in my hand I
can do *anything.*

"If you want to be a top-notcher, you have to break with everyone. You have to show up your own father. At first they will throw
you out for it, but in the end they will take you back on a different
footing when the world acclaims you. You've got to go a long, lone
path."[15] In either case, good in life or in art, he was aware of

---

[14] August 15, 1935, *Letters*, pp. 423–24.
[15] Guthrie, quoted in Turnbull, p. 260.

"them," and their taking you in or throwing you out; he was always aware of the shoddy, creative vanity that drove him in both life and art: "Some people think I am a son-of-a-bitch and hate my guts. I can't be one of the herd, I have tried. I get on top . . . and then something happens and I come out at the bottom. But I make the curve again every time to the top.

"I had to excel in everything I undertook so *they* would seek me out" (italics mine).[16] If, because he could no longer trust his creative impulsiveness as he had "when life was literally a dream," having learned the long, hard, and indescribably expensive way what it had cost him, he would have to create only out of hard, tight control. He was preserving his goodness at the expense of his gilded moments. He could say, "People are divided into two classes. There are those who think, are sensitive and have some fatal flaw. Then there are those who are good and unimaginative —and uninteresting."[17] And, when he thought of himself as controlling his "interesting" life in order to have at least some creative energies left for interesting art, he thought of himself as a dull son-of-a-bitch indeed: in "Pasting It Together" he announced the practices of hard and stingy self-preservation that would henceforth characterize him (and which, of course, did not). In *The Crack-Up* articles taken together, there is the sad conclusion that "I am just like you now." Significantly, the preservative stance is to be that of the good and uninteresting lifeman Amory came to yearn for in terror in *This Side of Paradise;* in that guise Fitzgerald could remain the interesting artist. That is, whether he is talking about life or art, the preservative goodness (no matter what Fitzgerald calls it in his own sense of personal diminishment) is a repudiation of the bright new world of hot cats. The lesson of preservation was at war with the old sense of safe goodness as philistine dullness. Rational order, the kind Dick imposed upon

16 *Ibid.*
17 *Ibid.*

Nicole's world, became for Fitzgerald the secret whereby romantic creativity was expressed rather than exploded. When he fell away from his control into self-indulgence, he learned horribly all over again the price of trying to regain "those illusions that give such color to the world so that you don't care whether things are true or false as long as they partake of the magical glory." Like the part of Nicole that was Zelda and himself, Fitzgerald would have to learn to recognize the doors to escape into the glorious fantasy of the past and to keep them closed, for they were in fact the doors to destruction. Beneath rational order, therefore, were familiar, uncomfortable friends and aids: the old virtues and graces, discipline, courtesy, work, and courage, that were the opposites and enemies of impulse and waste—whether of money, manners, talent, or lives. What he adored in Sara Murphy was what he missed so injuriously in Zelda: a perfect exercise of control displayed in the manners demanded by the old virtues and graces. For Fitzgerald "the test of human values" had come to be "conformity to the strictest and most unflinching rationality," as he wrote to the old-school Mrs. Bayard Turnbull, "while in your case it is based on standards of conduct. I don't mean that because Rousseau's life was disordered an intellectual should use that to justify his own weakness, nor even that my criteria necessarily subsume yours, but I must *think* they do even though I continually check up by seeing the lives of 'orderly' people, judging what's fake and what's real."[18] Imperceptibly, through ruin, he had long ago come to be a mature romantic—a man of excited imagination but of controlled impulse.[19] "I am a romantic and I can't change

---

18 Spring 1933, *Letters*, p. 436.

19 It should be obvious that my use of the term "romantic" follows Fitzgerald's, and in no way is an attempt at the genus Romantic. Even though there are—necessarily—essential similarities between the two terms, Fitzgerald's is both simpler and less precise. He uses the word in a popular, not a scholarly, historical, or philosophical sense. He aims at an emotional category, and means in small part the man with bedroom eyes, the man who wants to be "popular," but most largely and centrally he means the dreamer with a heightened sensitivity to the promises

that—not now. I am mature—in fact I was mature at thirty, but I didn't know it."[20] By romantic, Scott meant the emotional consciousness that measures its experience and itself by the calibrations of exhilaration connected with the delighted excitement of wonder, of unlimited expectation—always sensibility, feeling, not cold rationality—as well as of the nostalgia of memory. By maturity he meant all that he meant by goodness: in two words, rational responsibility. Responsibility was what he stressed in his novels: the courage and discipline to accept and clean up after the consequences of your own actions, as Carraway did and the Buchanans and Warrens never could. *That* ability required the old virtues articulated consciously: rational order. Only by the imposition of that on the romantic consciousness is the romantic creatively able rather than impulsively destructive. The very writing of *Tender Is the Night* was Scott's long, dogged effort away from impulsive destructiveness and toward goodness, the ripening into being of that functional composite of opposites, a "mature romantic." (And in "The Crack-Up" what was Fitzgerald's definition of "a first-rate intelligence," after all, but "the ability to hold two opposed ideas in the mind at the same time, and still retain the ability to function?") Yet he knew how precarious the hold of maturity was over the destructive impulsiveness of the romantic temperament. Should the intellectual lose his discipline, Dick the doctor lose his rational order, Dick the lover lose his control, then all that had made him, in his need to be loved, would destroy him. But how hard to keep control, how very hard when the object of it was the self-sacrificial creation of something—a wife or an art—out of one's own limited atoms of flesh and spirit.

The outer focus of the scenes in *Tender Is the Night* is on the

---

of life, the man whose temperament is attuned to the illusions whose color gives life a magical glory. He means himself.

[20] Guthrie, quoted in Turnbull, p. 259.

disintegration of an older into a new world, the outward signs of the breaking of all the social and personal decalogues of responsibility. The inner focus is on the disintegration of the disciplined and creative "romantic" within the ruinous world of the selfish and the impulsive. The loss that the story is all about is the loss of all the order and control and "goodness" that Fitzgerald felt he would painstakingly, painfully, and determinedly regain in the writing of the book and which would provide the margin of inextinguishable difference between Richard Diver and F. Scott Fitzgerald, who otherwise were so much alike. Dick's dying fall is the fictional statement of what, two years later, was to be given as straight autobiography in the three parts of the "Crack-Up" article. Dick's "dive" is the all-inclusive, individual summation of the disintegration of the social world, the breakdown of Western civilization that Fitzgerald felt around him and saw articulated in Spengler's *Decline of the West*.

In a letter to Zelda just half a year before his death, Fitzgerald summed up the dying fall, the loss of friendship, charm, and power, that went into the description of Dick Diver's life. In the loss of the good, gone days, the Fitzgeralds' dive (the notebooks indicate that Scott intended the name "diver" to suggest a man who fell from a high place, from great promise) swooped from the rumble of drums in the "orchestra, bingo! bango! playing for us to dance the tango" to the rumble of chaos and the talk of war. "Twenty years ago," Fitzgerald wrote longingly and sadly, *"This Side of Paradise* was a best seller and we were settled in Westport. Ten years ago Paris was having almost its last great American season but we had quit the gay parade and you were gone to Switzerland [broken down, in the Prangins clinic]. Five years ago I had my first bad stroke of illness and went to Asheville [North Carolina, to recuperate]. Cards began falling badly for us much too early. The world has certainly caught up in the last four weeks [the Nazi invasion of Holland, Belgium, and France]. I hope the atmosphere in Montgomery is tranquil and not too full of war talk."[21]

The dying fall and disintegration were not matters merely of the literary influences, Hemingway and Conrad. They were the very marrow of Fitzgerald's life, for which the dying fall became the perfect literary instrument of the exploration of the inevitable ruin of the good man in the barbaric world of unreal new realities. For *Tender Is the Night,* even more than for the preceding books, it would be possible to make an almost complete list of one to one correspondences between the events in the Fitzgeralds' lives (especially during the two and one half years abroad between mid-1924 and late 1926) and events in the novel. Even a small part of such a list offers clear evidence of Fitzgerald's composite uses of his materials. For instance, Charlie MacArthur and Scott drunkenly tried to saw a waiter in half, as Abe North was to do, with a musical saw; the scenes at the film studio in Rome were based upon the sets the Fitzgeralds saw there during the filming of *Ben Hur;* Ramon Navarro, the model for Signor Nicotera, was at the studio when the Fitzgeralds visited; Scott knew a movie director named Earl Brady; Rosemary was fashioned after Lois Moran, a dewy seventeen-year-old blonde actress who fascinated Fitzgerald, who imagined himself in love with her; Scott was roughly handled and jailed for socking an Italian cop, as was Dick; like Dick, Scott went back to the States, and went South, to Maryland and Alabama, when his father died in January of 1931; the Divers' Villa Diana was a composite of the Murphys' Villa America and the Fitzgeralds' Villa Marie. The list can be made quite extensive, from basic, shaping facts like Zelda's affair with the sunbronzed French military pilot and Scott's growing sense of his own emotional bankruptcy and physical diminishment to details of setting, like Sara Murphy's wearing a string of pearls on

21 June 4, 1940, *Letters,* p. 119.

the beach. But one moves from the specifics very quickly to Fitzgerald's process of compositing the materials, from which value
and meaning are created out of the facts themselves. One cannot
dismiss Abe North, for instance, by simply saying that he was
based upon Ring Lardner, for in his obituary essay, "Ring," Fitzgerald makes unmistakable his own sense of Lardner's Americanness. Abe, for instance, is also quite explicitly a hint of a ruined
Lincoln. "His voice was slow and shy; he had one of the saddest
faces Rosemary had ever seen, the high cheek bones of an Indian,
a long upper lip, and enormous deep-set golden eyes" (p. 64).
But when *this* Lincoln becomes involved with black people—
significantly with a Negro named *Freeman*—the result is not eman-
cipation, but murder in the same process of a deteriorating civilization that turns Mary Lincoln into a pretentious "Contessa di
Minghetti." In the book's pervasive metaphor of war, Fitzgerald
uses the Civil War as he uses World War I—as an end to innocence, as an end to the good gone days of graces and virtues dissolved into the corruption associated with U. S. Grant, who had
been so full of promise. So Abe, the "factual" Ring Lardner,
is also Grant (recall that in one version, before his name was
"North," Abe's last name had been "Grant"), the man of promise.
He "was a musician who, after a brilliant and precocious start had
composed nothing for seven years" (p. 91). Grant is used both as a
sign of early national promise and, like Dan Cody, of the debauchery of that promise. So the early, promising Dick, ready to
begin his moment, is likened to "Grant, lolling in his general
store in Galena . . . ready to be called to an intricate destiny"
(p. 6). Talking about the battles fought in the trenches that
Dick's party visits, Abe says, "General Grant invented this kind
of battle at Petersburg in sixty-five." But Dick's reply introduces
the other side of the brilliant, early promise. "No, he didn't,"
Dick answers, "—he just invented mass butchery" (p. 118). Abe,
in the depths of the drunkenness that results in the murder of a

Negro, likens himself to Grant in his debauchery: "But remember what George the Third said, that if Grant was drunk he wished he would bite the other generals" (p. 170). And just as Dick's career opened, like Grant's, on a note of promise, so it closes in the very last sentence of the book, like Grant's in an obscurity of dissolution. Nicole liked to think that Dick's career was still "biding its time, again like Grant's in Galena" (p. 334). What comes of the Abe North promise is what is ushered in at the beginning of the book with Nicole's father. In his hopeless dissoluteness, Abe's eyes, "bloodshot from sun and wine" (p. 121), are like Devereux Warren's, "sun veined" and red with whiskey. The Barban-Warren-Buchanan sun world leaves its marks on the Lincoln-Grant American promise in eyes that are only outward signs of the interior moral collapse, as Abe grows "enthusiastic about being cared for, or rather about prolonging his state of irresponsibility" (p. 164). The gradual and increasing corruption and paralysis of Abe is a complete foreshadowing of the young promise embodied in Dick. As Abe is beaten to death in drunkenness and crawls away to die, so too Dick is beaten insensible in a drunken brawl with the police. Abe is a paradigm of Dick, as Grant is of them both. In short, the Ring Lardner "fact" of Abe North is less important than Fitzgerald's compositing of Grant and Lincoln into a portrait whose national overtones are delicately bound into meaning by association with Lardner's shyness and his urge toward death, combined with Fitzgerald's own drunken self-destructiveness and abuse of his resources and talents and promise.

Or one can say that much of Nicole is Zelda,[22] yet Zelda, in the

22 In his "General Plan" for the novel, intact among Fitzgerald's notes, are the explicit statements that Nicole is a "Portrait of Zelda—that is, a part of Zelda." He specifies that the materials are to come, from among other sources, "Early Prangins [the Swiss clinic where Zelda stayed a while]—to February 1931. . . . From Forel (include Bleuler Consultation)." Forel treated Zelda and consulted with Bleuler. The "General Plan" is reprinted by Mizener as "Appendix B" to *The Far Side of Paradise*. In the unrevised Vintage edition of *The Far Side of Paradise* (New

specifics of her own personality and illness, is not only a model for
the "emergent Amazon" but also for the brave, brilliant woman
dying in the iron maiden of eczema; in neither case can one talk
about Zelda, Nicole, or the anonymous patient without seeing that
in the novel, as far as Fitzgerald was concerned, the importance
of the associations between facts and fictional characters lies in
the book's complex motif of sexual roles and crumbling identities in a world where moral dissolution makes identity increasingly difficult to determine. So too, one cannot examine Tommy
Barban as a composite of his originals, Tommy Hitchcock and
Edouard Josanne, without recognizing that the consequent composite is concerned, again, not with a roman à cléf, but with the
fading of national identity in the hard, male, sun-strong world of
money, of rapacious lusts and of practical power exercised as hard
"realities." Tommy is exactly the same domineering figure that
Tom Buchanan was, and he is used to the same ends. In all his
characteristics, he displays the qualities that marked Buchanan—
the same arrogance, the same physical power, the same boredom
and inability to bear the ennui of drifting pointlessly through life,
the same condescension mixed with the same inability to bear
the unprofitable fretfulness of life without imaginative goals. "He
was tall and his body was hard but overspare, save for the bunched
force gathered in his shoulders and upper arms . . . there was a
faint disgust always in his face which marred the full fierce lustre
of his brown eyes. Yet one remembered them afterward, when one
had forgotten the inability of the mouth to endure boredom and
the young forehead with its furrows of fretful and unprofitable
pain" (p. 74). He is the male figure that Fitzgerald despaired of
being—the rangy defensive end, the powerback, the man of combat who excells in the male sun-world. And except for his desire
for women, he is constantly insensitive to people, especially, of

York, 1959), the edition most commonly available, "Bleuler" (see page 210, *Tender
Is the Night*) is incorrectly transcribed as "Eleuler."

course, to men. "He did not like any man very much or feel men's presence with much intensity—he was all relaxed for combat . . ." (pp. 213-14). Fitted for the war-world that was birthed out of war, even his laugh is a "martial laugh: 'Um-buh—ha-ha! Um-buh—ha-ha!'" (p. 213). His values are only those of physical immediacy. The only time he is frightened is when he is cold, and as for his wars, he doesn't care what he fights for. As Tommy recounts his rescue of the Russian prince, during which he killed three red guards, "Dick decided that his parched papier-maché relic of the past [the prince] was scarcely worth the lives of three young men" (p. 215). In sum, this child of war and of brutal sunlight (black skin, afraid only when he is cold) is the perfect citizen of the world of "emergent Amazons," suited to them, knowing all the old Languedoc peasant remedies for their combative "independence." He is devoid of sensibilities, sophisticated in the ways of the hot cats. That earnest cipher McKisco has no idea, when he argues war and politics with Tommy, of "what he was up against with Barban, neither of the simplicity of the other man's bag of ideas nor of the complexity of his training" (p. 92). The man of Languedoc remedies is a constant in Fitzgerald's fiction, even prefigured in the beefy "diamond in the rough" football hero, Langueduc, who does not appeal to Amory as much as the slim, romantic, more "female" hot cat, Humbird. The closest one comes to the character in *The Beautiful and Damned* is blocky Bloeckman, who knocks Anthony down and who is powerful in the male business world that Anthony cannot crack. Both Toms, Buchanan and Barban, are physically powerful, and one is also powerful in the hard world of hard football and hard money, the other in the hard world of hard combat. None of the avatars of the figure has moonlit dreams, none has any "female" sensibility or sympathy for it, and all are hostile opponents of the various aspects of Fitzgerald's uses of himself in his composite heroes. Barban and Dick dislike each other. Barban, as the hard simplification of values allowed by barbarism, is the enemy of the complex, polite, and imaginative civilization that reached its creative apogee in the virtues and graces of Gerald Murphy-Dick Diver. As always in Fitzgerald's fiction, the disguised autobiography imaginatively composited serves to illuminate the themes, providing the light whereby the inner life of the author illuminates the fiction.

Consistently, in his contrasting composite characters and in his explicit statements, when Fitzgerald is specific about the inner life out of which came *Tender Is the Night*, his point of reference always is the need for goodness, creative sympathy, imaginative sensibility—personal goodness—as the only weapon available to individuals in a world full of "war talk," a world of intensifying disintegration. His letter to Zelda is just one of the countless instances in which one senses his grasp of connections between the war-world of the 1930's and the war-world of his novel and his own past. The private, inner war against his own self-indulgences and the consequences of irresponsible and wasteful impulse aimed toward the self-disciplined morality and responsibility he saw disappearing all around him in the crack-up of not only himself but his generation, which he constantly alluded to. Goodness became his creed and his anchor in his own dissipation. He had learned what he had guessed in *This Side of Paradise:* in goodness is lasting identity. The dean of his generation was anything but its spokesman. The man seen even today as the champion of flaming youth was anything but the advocate of flaming "liberation," and in his attempt to control the remnants of his own life through the discipline of his art and talent, he became—always was—conservatively "old-fashioned" within all his real sympathies for the rebellions of his age against its past. "The utter synthesis between what we want and what we can have is so rare that I look back with a sort of wonder on those days of my youth when I had it, or thought I did," he said in a summation of the center of his fiction.

He was writing to a young married woman who had been in love
with him and whose lover he was a year after *Tender Is the Night*
was published. Breaking off the affair, Fitzgerald wrote,

Your charm and the heightened womanliness that makes you attractive to men depends upon what Ernest Hemingway once called (in an
entirely different connection) "grace under pressure." The luxuriance
of your emotions under the strict discipline which you habitually
impose on them makes that tensity in you that is the secret of all
charm—when you let that balance become disturbed, don't you become just another victim of self-indulgence?—breaking down the solid
things around you and, moreover, making *yourself* terribly vulnerable? . . . I don't belittle your fine intelligence by supposing that
anything written here *need* be said, but I thought maybe the manner
of saying it might emphasize those old dull truths by which we live.
We can't just let our worlds crash around us like a lot of dropped
trays.
    —*You have got to be good.*
    —Your sense of superiority depends upon the picture of yourself as
being *good,* of being large and generous and all-comprehending, and
just and brave and all-forgiving. But if you are not *good,* if you don't
preserve a sense of comparative values, those qualities turn against
you—and your love is a mess and your courage a slaughter.[23]

Doctor Diver had learned all of that.

    Two years later, in an echo of Dick's statement that he was
bringing his daughter up to be a woman, not to be his wife, not to
adore him, Fitzgerald wrote to Helen Hayes about discipline versus "liberty" in a letter about bringing children up, not out.

We can all manufacture our unconventionality when the time comes,
and we have earned the right to it, but this country is filled with gen-
iuses without genius, without the faintest knowledge of what work is,
who were brought up on the Dalton system or some faint shadow of
it. As I told you, it was tried and abandoned in Russia after three

23 Early September 1935, *Letters,* p. 530.

years. It is an attempt to let the child develop his ego and personality
at any cost to himself or to others—a last gasp of the ideas of Jean
Jacques Rousseau. As a practise against too much repression, such as
sending a shy girl to a strict convent, it had its value, but the world,
especially America, has swung so far in the opposite direction that I
can't believe it is good for one American child in a hundred thousand.
Certainly not for one born in comparatively easy circumstances.

. . . The human machinery which controls the sense of right, duty,
self-respect, etc., must have conscious exercise before adolescence, because in adolescence you don't have much time to think of anything.[24]

Doctor Diver had always "been uneasy about what he had to give
the ever-climbing, ever-clinging, breast-searching young" (p. 330),
but he was certain that he was bringing up his daughter not to
the "liberation" of the world his wife was cured to join, but to be
a responsible human being.

Fitzgerald's characters *were* his own best self-expression, after
all. "Again and again," he wrote John O'Hara, "in my books I
have tried to imagize my regret that I have never been as good as
I intended to be (and you must know that what I mean by good is
. . . a personal conscience and meaning by the personal conscience
yourself stripped in white midnight before your own God)."[25]
When his morale beneath the manner had already cracked badly,
all that Doctor Diver, the professional psychiatrist to a morally
incurable world, had to draw on in his total bankruptcy of resources was a very personal testament from an old-fashioned
world: "We must all try to be good."

The young Dick Diver had believed in goodness, in discipline,
in work, in courage, in grace, in courtesy. He was a mature romantic before he was a ruined one in a world that took only the liberation that the romantic had to offer but took none of the struggle
and discipline by which he reached it. He combined with the rational order imposed by his intelligence and education the roman-

24 September 16, 1937, *ibid.*, pp. 553, 554, 555.
25 July 25, 1936, *ibid.*, p. 539.

tic and "very American" (as Franz calls it) sense of total possibility. He could, he would cure a sick world. America, with a disciplined application of the "old virtues" and Old-World experience to its new hopes and young vigor and enormous power, would redeem the Old World and make man new again. Gatsby-like, Dick Diver, the mature and intelligent doctor, felt in his "lucky Dick" bones the possibility of the "utter synthesis between what we want and what we can have," the possibility of mingling "the fulfilled future and the wistful past" into "a single gorgeous moment." The magic key to the romantically imaginative hope was goodness. That's where Dick Diver, like Grant in Galena, began his intricate destiny. A New-World doctor to the brave new world, he is victimized by it through his belief in goodness and service, his need to be loved and used. His decline is the defeat of goodness. His defeat is the decline of that "older America" which was the youthful dream and hope of the world.

Knowing full well by this time of his life how much of his deepest self and relations went into Dick Diver, and how much, therefore (since his art was his only "goodness"), his composite characters were his "only" way to a self he could live with, he knew that whatever might be wrong with his book, the *sources* of characterization were not among them. He always fought the same fight with Hemingway about it:

Next to go to the mat with you on a couple of technical points. The reason I had written you a letter was that Dos [Passos] dropped in in passing through and said you had brought up about my book what we talked about once in a café on the Avenue de Neuilly about composite characters. [Hemingway had argued that multiple sources of identity fed into one character could result only in flawed characterization.]

Following this out a little farther, when does the proper and logical combination of events, cause and effect, etc., end and the field of imagination begin? Again you may be entirely right because I suppose you were applying the idea particularly to the handling of the creative faculty in one's mind rather than to the effect upon the stranger reading it. Nevertheless, I am not sold on the subject, and especially to account for the big flaws of *Tender* on that ground doesn't convince me. Think of the case of the Renaissance artists, and of the Elizabethan dramatists, the first having to superimpose a medieval conception of science and archeology, etc., upon the Bible story; and, in the second, of Shakespeare's trying to interpret the results of his own observation of the life around him on the basis of Plutarch's *Lives* and Hollinshed's *Chronicles*. There you must admit that the feat of building a monument out of three kinds of marble was brought off. You can accuse me justly of not having the power to bring it off, but a theory that it can't be done is highly questionable. I make this point with such persistence because such a conception, if you stick to it, might limit your own choice of materials. The idea can be reduced simply to: you can't say *accurately* that composite characterization hurt my book, but that it only hurt it for you.[26]

Fitzgerald went right ahead with what he had always done, turning his experience, as Hemingway did too, after all, into a spiritual autobiography which was a biography of the *zeit*. The extent to which he found a theme in the materials of his actual experience was the extent to which he was able to discover and assess his own identity. It is not surprising to find Francis Fitzgerald writing to Mencken during the very first drafts of the first version of the novel that "I expect to spend about two years on my next novel and it ought to be more successful critically. It's about myself—not what I thought of myself in *This Side of Paradise*."[27] Indeed not. This version is about a Francis named Melarkey. "What I thought of myself in *This Side of Paradise*" was all involved in charm and illusion and impulse. Part of the tension between the personality and the personage, there was always a tension, for Fitzgerald, between being charming and being good. Being charming was being good insofar as it was a manifestation of being "tender and kind to people in even little things," the disciplined courtesy

[26] June 1, 1934, *ibid.*, pp. 308-9.
[27] May 4, 1925, *ibid.*, p. 481.

of the old-fashioned virtues and graces. But being charming could also be self-indulgent weakness, a romantic impulsiveness insofar as the charm was a vain and uncontrolled response to the need to be admired, sought after, visible, loved. Charm could be phoney flattery. Charm could be irresponsible showoff exuberance. Charm could be melarkey.

It was not always possible for Fitzgerald to sort out his charm according to his real motives at every moment. He knew that his charm might be part of his "flaw," but it was also part of what made him "interesting," and not merely like you and me. But he knew himself well and honestly enough to know that too often his vanity and ambition and self-indulgence resulted in fascinating, funny, and wastefully indiscriminate charm of the wrong sort, like Dick Diver's carnivals of love. And often they resulted in hideous and embarrassing acts. In short, part of the man was moral ramrod, part of the man was weakling and phoney. He often winced inwardly at the part of himself he didn't trust. He called it "romantic," he called it "spoiled," he called it "impulsive," he called it "Irish," and he called it "female." He associated the charm that sprang from weakness and vanity with the "female" aspect of his character, and I suspect that what made him wince most deeply and privately was that he felt that much of his charm, the manipulative shallow kind—precisely because it was always well intended in the full emotions of serving, of using and giving oneself, either under the influence of liquor or romantic excitement—was nothing more than the maudlin whorishness of selfish, mawkish sentiment, a vain and pathetic, girlish, self-protective self-love. Much, much of Fitzgerald, Fitzgerald felt, was Melarkey. Exorcising his weakest self in the discipline of his art, he could understand with terrible clarity the dissipation of talent of a doctor whose real and precious charm of discipline, virtue, and graces was destroyed by the charm which catered to the egos of a world that selfishly never saw more than surfaces or its own irresponsi-

ble fun and games, its Buchanan-like drift. The fun and friendship
that the wrong charm bought reduced a man to destruction.
"Tired of friends," says Abe North in his heavy despair at the
failure of true friendship in his destructive, impulsive alcoholic
charm. "The thing is to have sycophants" (p. 144). The destruction of self, true friendship, and true charm could, at the beginning, be merely the subject of a bad joke: in 1925, Fitzgerald
could call his fictive alter-ego "Melarkey." But in 1934, Dick
Diver, quite another composite self, says with very unfunny slow
sadness, "I guess I'm the Black Death. . . . I don't seem to bring
people happiness anymore" (p. 237). And in 1940, six months before his death and purged of Melarkey by the long years of ordeal
by ruin, Fitzgerald wrote, "Once I believed in friendship, believed I *could* (if I didn't always) make people happy and it was
more fun than anything. Now even that seems like a vaudevillian's
cheap dream of heaven, a vast minstrel show in which one is the
perpetual Bones."[28]

The cheap and tinsel dream was the "romantic," or "Irish," or
"female" part of him that, only when controlled and ordered, was
the imaginative sensibility expressed as the dreamlight "night
person," the moonlit Gatsby so distinct from the sunlit, brutal
Toms. Fitzgerald's sense of maleness and femaleness and of good
and bad is expressed in *Tender Is the Night* in a complex motif of
sexual identity as morality. When exercised by an intelligence
that is self-conscious, the "female" charm makes a radiant world:
it is Dick Diver's "trick of the heart," so distinct, again, from the
hard attractiveness of the Tom-figure, Barban. But when it is
weak and undisciplined or hard and selfish, the "Irish," "romantic," "female" charm is emotional mayhem or chicanery—not a
trick of the heart, but a trick of manners. As Dick came to realize,

[28] To Maxwell Perkins, May 20, 1940, *ibid.*, p. 288.

the manner lasts long after the morale has cracked. The warfare between and breakdown of sexual identities in *Tender Is the Night* is a projection into broken decalogues, disintegrated private and national identities, of the interior war within Fitzgerald—of the "female" that was imaginative artist and the "female" that was pampered irresponsibility. It was a war between the Gatsby-Diver and the golden girl parts of himself. That interior war was a concentration of the entire complex of identity, which was a constant combat between the personage and the personality, the responsible visionary and history's pet, the artist and the hot cat. Fitzgerald always knew it, and the more clearly he knew it the more expert he became in the authority of failure. He said to Laura Guthrie, his secretary:

"I don't know why I can write stories. I don't know what it is in me or that comes to me when I start to write. I am half feminine—at least my mind is . . . . My characters are all Scott Fitzgerald. Even my feminine characters are feminine Scott Fitzgeralds . . . ."

"Women are so weak really—emotionally unstable—and their nerves, when strained, break. They can endure more physical pain than men, and also more boredom. The boredom they endure is incredible, but they can't take nerve or emotional strain. The greatest women of all time are those of conquered passion or no passion. Women like Florence Nightingale, Jane Addams, Julia Ward Howe. [Women who had conquered or completely controlled their impulsive "Irish," their romanticism: women who were "female" no more.] Theirs has been a sublimated and useful work. They had no conflicts as Zelda had."

"This is a man's world," he often said. "All wise women conform to the man's lead."

And yet, despite his emphasis on male superiority, Fitzgerald was essentially a woman's man [and it is instructive here to consider the growing antagonism between Fitzgerald and the obtrusively male Hemingway]. Perhaps one needed to be a woman to catch the feelings, rising and dying like the wind, that flitted across his mobile face. (Men would be more on guard against the vein of weakness in him.) His conversation, too, was the sort that women delight in; it was emotional analysis, people, their nuances, the sparks between them. Fitzgerald,

who could beat a woman at her own game of intuition, would tell her
maddening things about herself, and just as she was about to lose her
temper he would say, "Has anyone ever told you you have a most
expressive mouth?" . . .

As with Rilke or D. H. Lawrence the feminine strain in Fitzgerald,
the extreme delicate sensitivity, went a long way toward explaining his
artistic power, yet he was in no way effeminate. He was normally but
not overly sexed. Perhaps one could say that with him a strong sex
drive had been geared to beauty and creation, while the destructive
side of his nature found an outlet in drink.[29]

In this statement, Turnbull comes close to a central truth. The
real distinction, I believe, is not one between the "female" and
the "destructive" in Fitzgerald, but between the controlled and
the impulsive aspects of his "Irish, female romanticism," between
the imaginative and the destructive aspects of the vision of the
golden moment. The "lousy son-of-a-bitch" was simply the "goodness" exaggerated, spoiled, and sour. The irresponsible golden
bitch was adapted to the hard, sunlit, jazzy world of brute male
power that resides in physical, economic, or social strength; the
disciplined, sensitive "femaleness" was destroyed by it.

Fitzgerald knew the "femaleness" of Irish Dick Diver's world,
and used it deliberately. The hard Irish Diver that was masculine
and imperious was not Barban-masculinity, but was the disciplined
manifestation of the "romantic Irish," or "female" that was all
old graces and virtues, and hard in a good way. "His voice, with
some faint Irish melody running through it, wooed the world,
yet . . . [Rosemary] felt the layer of hardness in him, of self-control
and self-discipline, her own virtues" (p. 75). But the "good"
hardness is placed at the service of the "bad" hardness, the
lousy-son-of-a-bitch irresponsible selfishness that characterizes
the Warren-Buchanan-Melarkey world, male and female, just
as Rosemary's discipline and courage are used for the making
of *Daddy's Girl*. In the bright new world, both male and female

29 Turnbull, pp. 259, 261–62.

break down as identities, and under the impulse and selfishness
of both hot cat toms and hot kitten daisies, who characterize the
world that Dick would cure through his service and discipline,
the "good," the "mature" romanticism breaks down into ruin.
In short, Fitzgerald felt that whether he was writing about men
or women, in writing about the pampered, selfish, impulsive destructiveness of his flaming generation, he was writing about the
vain, impulsive destructiveness of the golden-girl "female" within him. That is, whether his materials demanded male or female
characters, he felt that the post-war world he was writing about
was really a woman's world. What happens, simply, is this: as the
"good" female is out of place, is used, in the brutal sun-world
of the hot cats who exercise their *droit de seigneur*, the "bad female" adapts to it. Adapting, the golden girl finds irresponsible
power in her liberation from the old "man's world." The "emergent Amazon" ends up the female personification of her hot Tom,
and exercising her power over him, she succeeds in the war for
control of the new world of flaming youth. Her triumph signals a
triumph, therefore, of selfishness, vanity, impulse, and irresponsibility. The breakdown of sexual identities is a sign of the breakdown of moral identities, and metaphors of war and combat
become signs of the breakdown of a civilization. Daisy Millers
are used up or become Daisy Buchanans. In the development of
American literary heroes and heroines, the triumph of the shining
bitch is part of Fitzgerald's moral history of America. The crazy and
poisonous competition that Zelda aimed at Scott helped furnish
models. It was as though she were saying, "Well, here I am, free
and independent in the new century, bright and beautiful in my
verve and liberty, and everyone makes such a fuss about *you!* Just
because you're a *man.* Well I'm just as talented, just as much a
somebody, and I'll prove it in my own writing, my painting, my
dancing!" A woman could use a man up, impede him, begrudge
him each victory, resent him unless she were happy as his sup-

porter and follower. And the day when women followed is over. So women compete in the hard male world and either are broken, like Dick's eczema-bound patient, or become "men," triumphant golden girls. Warfare replaces the old identities, the "emergent Amazon" destroys the good "female." Order and identity existed back there, when it *was* a man's world and "wise women conformed to the man's lead"—both men and women had identity. But in the golden girl's world of self-indulgence and vanity, both men and women lose their identities. It is a man's world in the brute hard sunhot world of earning money. But the male power is increasingly at the service of female whim, and in the irresponsible "female" uses of "male" strength is the bad use of the world's energies—bad uses to which wealth lends charm, as is made explicit in the lyrical passage describing Nicole's gorgeous shopping forays.

Nicole bought from a great list that ran two pages, and bought the things in the windows besides. Everything she liked that she couldn't possibly use herself, she bought as a present for a friend. She bought colored beads, folding beach cushions, artificial flowers, honey, a guest bed, bags, scarfs, love birds, miniatures for a doll's house, and three yards of some new cloth the color of prawns. She bought a dozen bathing suits, a rubber alligator, a travelling chess set of gold and ivory, big linen handkerchiefs for Abe, two chamois leather jackets of king-fisher blue and burning bush from Hermes—bought all these things not a bit like a high-class courtesan buying underwear and jewels, which were after all professional equipment and insurance, but with an entirely different point of view. Nicole was the product of much ingenuity and toil. For her sake trains began their run at Chicago and traversed the round belly of the continent to California; chicle factories fumed and link belts grew link by link in factories; men mixed toothpaste in vats and drew mouthwash out of copper hogsheads; girls canned tomatoes quickly in August or worked rudely at the Five-and-Tens on Christmas Eve; half-breed Indians toiled on Brazilian coffee plantations and dreamers were muscled out of patent rights in new tractors—these were some of the people who gave a tithe to Nicole and, as the whole system swayed and thundered onward, it lent a feverish bloom to such processes of hers as wholesale buying,

like the flush of a fireman's face holding his post before a spreading
blaze. She illustrated very simple principles, containing in herself her
own doom, but illustrated them so accurately that there was grace in
the procedure, and presently Rosemary would try to imitate it (pp.
113–14).

The Rosemary female will become the Warren female of capitalist
gorgeousness; the Daddy's Girl created by Devereux Warren will
be what the nation's Daddy's Girl will harden into; the victorious
golden girl in her very destructiveness will most exhibit the charm
and fascinating glitter of a life that all will hunger for. O brave
New World, America, America: the total amalgam in Fitzgerald's
imagination is that of the vastly attractive, powerful, energetic,
voluptuously affluent Beautiful Bitch, the perfection of capitalist
gorgeousness, the desirable, enviable all-American destroyer. What
was adumbrated in the debs and popular daughters of *This
Side of Paradise* is brought in *Tender Is the Night* to much fuller,
more complex use than anything Fitzgerald was capable of in his
first novel.

As moneyed "female" destroys energy (Daisy's killing Myrtle,
her indirect destruction of Gatsby), sucking it up like a vampire
and leaving corpses strewn after her, the hardening, using female
becomes indistinguishable from the predatory male. In *Tender Is
the Night* there is a clear and consistent relationship between
sexual, national, and economic identities, as all identities become
wiped out and merged in a brave new world that flames out of the
destruction of the "lovely" old one. The "men" who are associated
with the world of "white" people one first sees on the Riviera—
the sycophants like Mrs. Abrams, the arrivists like the McKiscos,
the pale, colorless bores—are Dumphrey and Campion, two homo-
sexuals. They introduce the breakdown of sexual identity that
can be expected from the sycophantic world of golden fashion that
will follow them into the private world Dick has made. Tommy
Barban's male world, typified by the hard but predictable code

duello, is marred by McKisco's unfamiliarity with its ways and by the gasping, squealing voyeurism of Campion. Significantly, when the male identifiable as a male can take no more of the civilization he lives in, he wants to get away from women. "This fight's between two men," Abe explains the duel to Rosemary, and adds, "—what Tommy needs is a good war." For Tommy Barban Barbarian, controlled energy in the service of women, of "civilization," of "culture," is emasculating and suffocating. He has absolutely no sense of the strength of disciplined self-sacrifice it takes to "build out some broken side till it was better than the original structure," which is one of Dick's aims as the man of cures. That is, in his own impulsive needs for physical action and violence, he is the self-indulgent male-tom who mirrors the selfish gratifications that the females get in other terms. Blind to the "good" femaleness of Dick's world, and wanting in the female only the most basic complement of his own hard male impulse, he develops dislike and contempt for precisely what is "goodness" in "female" Diver. In moral terms there is no distinction of identity between Tom's extreme maleness and the "bad" femaleness that the world increasingly becomes. So, he says to Rosemary, "When I'm in a rut I come to see the Divers, because then I know that in a few weeks I'll want to go to war . . . they make me want to go to war" (p. 87). And Abe, from the depths of the self-destruction that defeat of the "good" femaleness within him (his artistry, his talent) has brought him to, at the moment he says goodbye to Nicole, says a peculiar thing. Nicole, after all, is the world he tried to make—"he had been heavy, belly-frightened, with love for her for years" (p. 143). And as Abe is, or at least was, promising American creative energy, Nicole is the most beautiful female consumer of that energy. For her sake the world produces, in her service, for the sake of her health and self, Dick labors. A shambling wreck of himself, reduced to deadly defeat by the smashup of his talents in his impulsive self-indulgence in the world of

wealth and hot cats, Abe "spoke up suddenly." What he said
was, "Tired of women's worlds" (p. 144).

Sexual identity as such is perfectly recognizable in the book;
what is not simple is Fitzgerald's use of sexual identities to arrive
at moral identities. There is a hierarchy of values constructed by
these identities. At the top is what Dick Diver represents: a goodness of civilized order and polite decency earned and paid for by
self-sacrificial self-discipline and courage. The effort to produce
it comes from a great expectant capacity for hope not disconnected
from the millenial and radiant hopefulness or infinite capacity
for wonder that characterized Amory Blaine and, in much fuller
measure, Gatsby. Those who benefit from this world of ideals and
visions are the familiar old consuming enemies who misuse and
use up the civilized and ordered goodness created by the romantic.
They do not have a high sense of what life is or could be; they
have no idea of how hard, tough, "male," courageous, virtuous
the civilized "female" is. All they see in it is momentary pleasure
and safety to be taken, but after a while, they want to "go to war."

In moral identity, both Toms and golden girls occupy the brave
new world that has used up and is driving out the imaginative
responsibility of the older world of virtues and graces, the world
represented by the controlled romantic. What the boys and girls
of the new world want is freedom from control, and in this they
find a liberated new identity. They want their pleasures raw, with
no thought of next things. When Tommy Barban and shiny, new,
nickel-hard, nickel-bright Nicole with the "white crook's eyes"
run off for pure sexual release and impulsive self-gratification,
they have a fitting and significant conversation.

" 'All this taming of women!' [Tommy] scoffed.

" 'In any society there are certain—' She felt Dick's ghost
prompting at her elbow but she subsided at Tommy's overtone:

" 'I've brutalized many men into shape, but I wouldn't take

a chance on half the number of women. Especially this "kind"
bullying—what good does it do anybody?—you or him or anybody?'

"Her heart leaped up and then sank faintly with a sense of what
she owed Dick" (p. 311). She doesn't owe much, after all. Only her
life and sanity. Only all the self-sacrifice of controlled and controlling love that took Nicole after she had been destroyed by
sexual release, impulsive gratification, after she had been victimized by the irresponsible moral shabbiness of the Buchanan world
(the name is now spelled Warren) that is the heritage of her
fathers and is seen in "white crook's eyes." Only the love that
took Nicole and rebuilt her, poor "broken side," into civilized
humanity through order, discipline, love, courage, all the virtues
and graces, through all the "kind bullying."

But cured, Nicole is free to be the *impulsive* female, which is
all that Barban in his brutal directness and lack of civilized
morality identifies as female. Nicole is able to take her place in
the sun-gold male world of golden girls, because she too has "become a boy," she too has force and power—not of civilization,
imagination, virtues, and graces, but money. Money, again and
always. What Gatsby recognized in Daisy's voice is what Tommy
knows is true of Nicole. She is too rich, and therefore too free,
to be bound in this brave new liberated world to the kindly,
bullying disciplines that make sanity out of madness, responsibility
out of moral garbage, order out of "the confusion of all values."
When Nicole began to say some lame thing to Tommy, some weak,
mild thing about what she owed Dick, she began to say, "I suppose I've got—"

" 'You've got too much money,' he said impatiently. 'That's
the crux of the matter. Dick can't beat that' " (p. 311).

Indeed he can't, exactly as Gatsby couldn't beat Buchanan.
Dick can no longer be the inseminating male force, the fruitful
creative female, the combination of civilized goodnesses that

change male and female into man and woman. "Lucky Dick" is no longer "the big stiff." Formerly a good diver-swimmer, he discovers on the aquaplane that he no longer has the strength and power to get up. All he's left with are the empty forms of the civilization he built, the manners without morale. Big Dick goes limp with the last effort with which he gives Nicole her freedom in her Warren world. There, the golden-girl female restored, she is a match for and matched by, she is the fitting complement to, her Tom. "It's very hard taking care of white eyes—especially the ones made in Chicago," she says to him. This hard, stiff Tom does not reply with the civilized virtues and graces: "I know all the old Languedoc peasant remedies," says he. So Nicole, naked, primitive, and unrestricted female now, no longer guided woman, is male-free in her sexual identity of irresponsibility. The moment that Fitzgerald portrays Nicole in her new freedom, he at once associates the new Nicole with irresponsibility. "[Tommy's] assertion"—the assertion that Nicole has white crook's eyes, reflecting her restoration to her identity as the golden girl of the Warren clan, ducal family U.S.A.—"seemed to absolve her from all blame or responsibility and she had a thrill of delight in thinking of herself in a new way. New vistas appeared ahead, peopled with the faces of many men, none of whom she need obey or even love," and unable to wait to sample her new identity with the new stiff dick, Tom, beside her, she "drew in her breath, hunched her shoulders with a wriggle, and turned to Tommy.

" 'Have we *got* to go all the way to your hotel in Monte Carlo?' " (p. 312).

Free, free at last from virtues, graces, and responsibility, she is the new female enacting an old female role. "Symbolically she lay across his saddle-bow as surely as if he had wolfed her away from Damascus and they had come out upon the Mongolian plain." Moment by moment she loses the armor that Dick had taught her to wear, deliciously gives up the swords and weapons that had been a defense against anarchic impulse, destructive gratification, unrestricted release, illicit stiff daddy-dicks and bloody sheets leading to madness in the moment of selfish and impulsive irresponsibility. Goodbye to the real Dick's control and order. Goodbye to all that, goodbye to all Dick's fathers. Hello chaos, hello with a sweet, voluptuous swoon. "Moment by moment all that Dick had taught her fell away and she was ever nearer to what she had been in the beginning [O Warren golden girl], prototype of that obscure yielding up of swords that was going on in the world about her. Tangled with love in the moonlight she welcomed the anarchy of her lover" (p. 316).

Identity, in terms of power, is interchangeable. Rosemary's mother advises the young actress to go ahead and have her affair with Dick: you can afford to be irresponsible; you've earned it, the mother advises. What might happen to Dick or Nicole is neither the mother's responsibility nor Rosemary's. Go ahead, golden girl, babydoll, Daddy's Girl, use him, use them, use anyone, because you've got what it takes in the bank: "—go ahead and put down whatever happens to experience. Wound yourself or him—whatever happens it can't spoil you, because *economically you're a boy, not a girl*" (italics mine, p. 98).

In Fitzgerald's treatment of sexuality, there is the same surprise that there was in *This Side of Paradise*—the rediscovery that Fitzgerald was not a champion of the new world of libertine, flaming youth, but, really, something quite the opposite. Many readers have noted that the sexuality in Fitzgerald's novels is fairly chaste, that there are very few bedroom scenes, and even those few, like the scene in the hotel room shared by Nicole and Tommy, are not highly explicit: the focus of interest is not on genital activity as an autonomous subject. Yet, there has been the lingering assumption that Fitzgerald, as dean of the New Generation, was restricted only by the literary mores of his times, that his literary age had not yet achieved the liberation that writers and

publishers know today. Moreover, today there is an automatic
assumption—critical, literary, psychological, even political, that
sexual liberation is of such a nature, in present contexts, that it
is automatically used—especially by a serious writer—as a sign of
something good. He must champion it, be a social ally of it, a
proponent of free sexual gratification as healthy and sane individual identity. Yet, the facts of *Tender Is the Night*, like the
explicit and implicit statements of the earlier books, indicate that
contemporary attitudes are not by any means a complete statement of Fitzgerald's attitudes.[30] Although Fitzgerald was one with
his age in rebelling against a broken down and claustrophobic
gentility, he recoils from the "liberty" of total sexual freedom,
"progressive education," and the priority of individual desires
over social responsibility. It seems self-contradictory to say "F.
Scott Fitzgerald" and "conservative, old-fashioned" in the same
breath, but it is not. But labels must be used carefully. In his
political and social thought, Fitzgerald kept reaching out experi-
mentally and radically. He was hospitable to Marxism and hostile
to Mrs. Grundy. But just as he thought of himself as a modern
man, aligned against philistine middle-class dullness and respectability, so too there always remained dominant in one part

[30] At this point, once more Robert Sklar's study, *F. Scott Fitzgerald: The Last
Laocoon*, is pointed and helpful. Mr. Sklar's study, tracing the literary development
of Fitzgerald, finds as its focus the genteel hero in American letters. Fitzgerald's
heroes, Sklar discovers, are really transmutations of the genteel hero developed
beyond the more sentimental and popular versions that the young Fitzgerald had
grown up with in the works of writers like Booth Tarkington. I think that Sklar is
almost completely right in his identification of the values implicit in Fitzgerald's
heroes. However, the one limitation of the approach is that it is primarily a study
of literary influences and parallels, which tends to reduce the problem of moral
values in Fitzgerald's work to an academic investigation of literary types. Although
I agree with Mr. Sklar's conclusions, quite obviously I think that the genteel hero
is not really a *true* center for an understanding of Fitzgerald, but rather is one
of the most important manifestations of Fitzgerald's trying to work a concept of
himself and of America out of his life. That is, I think the true center is the composite "autobiographical" uses of American history. Therefore, I agree with Sklar's
definitions of the values that Fitzgerald approved of and opposed, but my point of
departure is quite different, and my goal is not the working out of a problem of
literary history and influences.

of his mind and temperament an old-school gentlemanliness that he associated with his father and in which he insisted upon self-disciplined and courteous responsibility to others as a line which marks the distinction between freedom and license, with its immoral selfishness. This aspect of Fitzgerald flows integrally into the characterization of Dick, who becomes as unrecognized in his lifetime as Fitzgerald did in his.

Because everyone in the novel has either plunged—dived—out of Dick's world, like Abe North, or else merely uses Dick's world for its restorative sanity before using the strength thus gained to plunge triumphantly into the Barban-Warren world, nobody really knows what a self-sacrificial (and doomed) redeemer Dick is. All they see, like Rosemary (the importance of whose point of view becomes increasingly apparent), are the surface differences between Dick, the Tommies, and the "light people." Most people, like Rosemary, respond "whole-heartedly to the expensive [and what cost, indeed!] simplicity of the Divers, unaware of its complexity and its lack of innocence, unaware that it was all a selection of quality rather than quantity from the run of the world's bazaar; and that the simplicity of behavior also, the nursery-like peace and good will, the emphasis on the simpler virtues, was part of a desperate bargain with the gods and had been attained through struggles she could not have guessed at" (p. 77). Seeing only surfaces, the rest of the world can not see the *moral* distinction in identity between the hard-female-male Diver and the people around him. When, for a sexual joke, Dick wears the swim trunks Nicole made for him, a garment that looks like "black lace drawers" (but "close inspection revealed that actually they were lined with flesh-colored cloth") McKisco's reaction is merely funny: " 'Well, if that isn't a pansy's trick!' exclaimed Mr. McKisco contemptuously—then turning quickly to Mr. Dumphrey and Mr. Campion he added, 'Oh, I beg your pardon' " (p. 77). But there is nothing funny about the warfare of sexual identities that male-female relationships become when they are merely the clash of desires that Tommy and Nicole demand as she lies symbolically across his saddle. He is literally "in the saddle," subduing her with his Languedoc (with the silent play on all the variations from "tongue-doctor" to "long dick") peasant remedies that provide the only subjugation of women he thinks worthwhile or necessary. That clash makes sexual identities simpler and clearer, but it robs them of all the possible dimensions that Dick tried to create in his careful doctoring of identities. Tommy's simplification of identity is not a liberation of it, but a brutalization of it. As in the novels of Henry James, Fitzgerald's characters gain their fullest and greatest identities in the rare and precious imaginative levels, the multi-levels, of relationship that the virtues and graces can make possible between human beings. Poor Gatsby had only a debased version of those virtues and graces, but how he strove to attain them! Diver, intelligent and educated, with the Carraway "advantages" that Gatsby lacked, becomes Fitzgerald's most complete hero. He tries to cure the sick into civilization, not into barbarism, but he is doomed. The only world left for his patients to emerge into is that of the Barbans and the Warrens.

On the other hand, there is only the squalid and the pathetic in the clash of sexual identities that, removed from the brute simplicity of sex in Tommy's world, can only pretend to civilization without really having it. So the ersatz man and ersatz writer, McKisco, whose name sounds like "a substitute for gasoline or butter," has only an ersatz mind and an ersatz civilization. He too creates his wife's world, but when he prescribes within it, the result is claustrophobia. "Obviously he had created his wife's world, and allowed her few liberties in it." He can only be a pastiche of Dick. Dick confines and prescribes his wife's world in order to try to expand it. He tries to be an emancipator, a doctor. McKisco is merely a jailer, a slaveholder with a subject slave. He is all talk. His "languedoc" treatments doctor nothing. It is inevitable that the pathetic relationship should have within it a large dose of guerilla warfare, and that the uneasy but incessantly nagging rebelliousness of Violet McKisco should practically threaten McKisco's life. In the fruitlessness of that marriage, Violet can be neither female nor woman.

The trouble was I suggested the duel [said McKisco]. If Violet had only kept her mouth shut I could have fixed it. Of course even now I can just leave, or sit back and laugh at the whole thing—but I don't think Violet would ever respect me again.

"Yes she would," said Rosemary. "She'd respect you more."

"No—you don't know Violet. She's very hard when she gets an advantage over you. We've been married twelve years, we had a little girl seven years old and she died and after that you know how it is. We both played around on the side a little, nothing serious but drifting apart—she called me a coward out there tonight" (p. 104).

Fitzgerald's sense of loss—imagined as a loss of Scottie in the person of Honoria in the moving "Babylon Revisited"—and his sense of the cheap hack he might have been, let him project one imagined part of himself into Albert McKisco, even in the loss of the daughter and the constant and wearying domestic squabbles. Violet and McKisco constantly fight. She throws sand in his face; in a misuse of his "maleness" as well as of his "civilization," he sits on her and rubs her face in the sand for revenge. What he needs is a bit of the simpler male brutality of Barban. He gets it in the duel and is, in part, redeemed by it. He comes to respect himself enough to know his true limitations, the real smallness of his talent beneath the pufferies that admiring critics come to pile on him. Dick, always mediating between the civilized effeminate and the direct brutality of the savage, tries to mediate identities into human fullness. Barban needs McKisco's respect for ideas, confused though it is; McKisco needs Barban's strong sunlight. (The duel was "the first thing . . . [McKisco] had ever done in his life. Actually he was one of those for whom the sensual world does not exist, and faced with a concrete fact he brought to it a vast surprise.") Dick by no means denies the sensual. He tries to channel it. He knows that a civilized fullness of relationship between males and females turns them into men and women; in his world of virtues and graces the subordination of women to men, the kindly bullying, is not arrogance or insecurity, but a means toward dependable identity, which will allow both men and women serenity, sanity, and freedom for more than the relationships that are demanded—either in squalid squabbles or in the anarchy of barbarian lust—by the sexes related in oversimplified surrender or in clashing warfare. In Dick's world, the three women, Nicole, Rosemary, Mary North, had a cheerful and refreshing resemblance. "Their point of resemblance to each other, and their difference from so many American women, lay in the fact that they were all happy to exist in a man's world—they preserved their individuality through men and not by opposition to them" (pp. 111–12). Women are frightened by men who, like Abe, are "gigantic" in their "wreck, . . . dominating [them] with his presence, his own weakness and self-indulgence, his narrowness and bitterness." And then civilized "Dick Diver came and brought with him a fine glowing surface on which the three women sprang like monkeys with cries of relief, perching on his shoulders, on the beautiful crown of his hat or the gold head of his cane. Now, for a moment, they could disregard the spectacle of Abe's gigantic obscenity" (p. 145). Abe, indeed, has just proclaimed himself "Tired of women's worlds." It is man's responsibility, Dick feels, to give women the freedom that comes from the reliability of their men. "Up to a point that was right: men were for that, beam and idea, girder and logarithm." Men and women should be "opposite and complementary," and when they become "the drought in the marrow" of each other's bones, when they become the same, "one and equal," identity disintegrates. Even Dick, as he loses control and strength, becomes a "lean chest" at which

Nicole must dry-suckle for nourishment, in a reversal of sexual roles (p. 297).

What Diver envisions for Nicole is an extension of self, *through* reliable sexual identity, to a human, responsible consciousness and not merely to the sexual function that she was in the incest that drove her to madness, and that she becomes again, cured and liberated, with Tommy. It is not the new freedoms of wealth and power and sex that liberate human beings into becoming more than their elementally selfish selves: it is responsibility and dependable identities that give them the security to be more fully human, to have virtues and graces within the "opposite and complementary" order of relationships. The freedom Dick dreams of for Nicole, and for all the sick and broken ones he would re-build, is a free identity that includes sexual identity but is not limited to it. But in the free new world of Buchanans and Barbans and Warrens, that dependable identity is destroyed as all become the same, the girls are economically boys and the boys are girls. "Mamma's girl," Collis Clay calls Rosemary, when she has become a fully sexual female. "I mean she was so carefully brought up and now she's a woman of the world—if you know what I mean." Mamma's girl became mamma's "boy" in the exploitation of *Daddy's Girl*, which was the mindless product of a civilization in which Shirley Temple becomes the national hero, the redeemer, the conqueror of evil, the builder-out of broken sides.

There she was—the school girl of a year ago, hair down her back and rippling out stiffly like the solid hair of a tanagra figure; there she was—*so* young and innocent—the product of her mother's loving care; there she was—embodying all the immaturity of the race, cutting a new cardboard paper doll to pass before its empty harlot's mind . . . .

Daddy's girl. Was it a 'itty-bitty bravekins and did it suffer? Ooo-ooo-tweet, de tweetest thing, wasn't she dest too tweet? Before her tiny fist the forces of lust and corruption rolled away; nay, the very march of destiny stopped, inevitable became evitable, syllogism, dialectic, all rationality fell away (p. 130).

The baby that becomes the queen of *this* nursery rather than of the nursery-like peace under Dick's beach umbrellas is consummately characterized in Baby Warren, who takes over Daddy's fortune. Baby is the "man" of the family, unfulfilled as a woman, unfulfilled even as a female. Everywhere in the world the new children of the corrupting fathers are similar identities. Just as Daddy's Girl becomes Mamma's "boy," so too, Daddy's boy can become daddy's girl: the Chilean counterpart of Devereux Warren, and associated with him even in the similarity of their hotel apartments, is Señor Pardo y Ciudad Real. "Warren was a strikingly handsome man . . . tall, broad, well-made . . . and he had that special air about him of having known the best of this world" (p. 15). Señor Real was "a handsome, iron-gray Spaniard, noble of carriage, with all the appurtenances of wealth and power . . ." (p. 261). Warren had made a "Daddy's Girl" indeed out of Nicole, and left the doctors to clean up the mess he had made. As Warren with his incest had made his child, so Real, with his male, authoritarian bullyings and whippings had intensified his. His boy has become a "girl"; Francisco (the Francis that is Melarkey?) is the "Queen of Chile," and Real calls in the doctors to clean up the mess. In the heritage from *these* fathers (Sid, the founder of the Warren fortune, was a horse-trading crook), the women demand the liberation they had derived from male support in the old relationship, while denying their old subordination that had made the old relationship what it was. They want the men to put the world in place for them, while denying the men the old importance of place, of identity, of selfhood, that had gone with their function. So the men become vulnerable in their pride, the need for which becomes invisible to the obtuse Babies who need only boss and pout and order and demand—and flourish their male checkbooks. Manners change. What had been the good manners of the old virtues and graces become only a pastiche of courtly manners, the frilliest social artificialities, and that's what the Babies demand. Baby, at one point says to Dick—without saying the words:

"We own you, and you'll admit it sooner or later. It is absurd to keep up the pretense of independence."

... Now he lost his temper at Baby and simultaneously tried to coop it up within him, resenting her cold, rich insolence. It would be hundreds of years before any emergent Amazons would ever grasp the fact that a man is vulnerable only in his pride, but delicate as Humpty Dumpty once that is meddled with—though some of them paid the fact a cautious lip-service. Doctor Diver's profession of sorting the broken shells of another sort of egg had given him a dread of breakage. But [unable to contain himself, with the manners barely lasting after the morale had cracked]:

"There's too much good manners," he said on the way back to Gstaad in the smooth sleigh.

"Well, I think that's nice," said Baby.

"No, it isn't," he insisted to the anonymous bundle of fur. "Good manners are an admission that everybody is so tender that they have to be handled with gloves. Now, human respect—you don't call a man a coward or a liar lightly, but if you spend your life sparing people's feelings and feeding their vanity, you get so you can't distinguish what *should* be respected in them" (p. 193).

Defeated by the triumph of the babyboygirl world, Dick is embittered by the futility of his self-sacrifice: to build up Nicole to humanity only to have to turn her loose, in her freedom, to the world which is the triumph of the irresponsible sickness he had spent his life combatting. In his lost war, he turns against the appearances, the manners, of what he had been trying to defend (his manners become increasingly rude and hostile), recognizing the rotten reality beneath the appearances. In describing his own feeding of vanities he is reduced to sounding like Mrs. Abrams among the light people on the beach, complaining of "so darn much formality." Dick's lost battle for a freedom that would preserve identity is echoed in the lost war of his brilliant, courageous

patient dying beneath her torture-sheath of excruciating eczema.
"I'm sharing the fate of the women of my time who challenged
men to battle," she says. There is a hint that she suffers from
emotionally induced symptoms of syphilis, that she is dying beneath a sexually oriented self-punishment for something she
doesn't understand. For a libertine's declaration of freedom? No,
for she has "found nothing to blush for since I cut my wisdom
teeth." She was not attempting to be a golden girl. She was searching for that fuller identity that Dick tries to create and to which
the male Barban is hostile. But she is not strong enough for the
struggle that defeats even Dick Diver. One cannot be specific
about the eczema-bound patient; one can say only that hers was
not the triumphant combat of the babyboygirl. For whatever
reason, she has lost a world she could once rely on, she has lost
in a world where the relationships between the sexes has been
reduced to battles and total surrenders. Like the girls who have
become "boys" and the boys who have become "girls," she too,
unsuccessful emergent Amazon, has lost an identity she once had.
She is not tough enough to survive in the brave new world of new
"identities."

" 'To your vast surprise it was just like all battles,' [Dick] answered, adopting her formal diction.

" 'Just like all battles.' She thought this over. 'You pick a set-up
or else win a Pyrrhic victory, or you're wrecked and ruined—
you're a ghostly echo from a broken wall.' " She voices what is
happening to Dick, who picked nothing less than the redemption
of a world for his battle, neither a set-up nor a Pyrrhic victory.
"I am here," she insists, "as a symbol of something. I thought perhaps you would know what it was." Indeed he does. What she
sought, Dick had sought by being "the greatest psychologist who
ever lived."

" 'You are sick,' he said mechanically.

" 'Then what was it I had almost found?'

" 'A greater sickness.'

" 'That's all?'

" 'That's all.' With disgust he heard himself lying, but here and now the vastness of the subject could only be compressed into a lie." She's not hard enough for independence, not self-deceived enough for the "independence" of the "liberated woman." She lacks a measure of the necessary Barban peasant toughness of those who can adapt to the sun-bright new world or who can oppose it. "Exploration was for those with a measure of peasant blood, those with big thighs and thick ankles who could take punishment as they took bread and salt, on every inch of flesh and spirit." Fellow in arms to Gatsby, she lacks his obsessive endurance; co-warrior to Dick, she lacks his initial strength. She had almost found human greatness, but the new world was too much for her. There is just too much destructive truth—learned out of his own experience—for Dick to be able to tell it to her.

"—Not for you, he almost said. It's too tough a game for you."

But she cannot discount her pain. There was a goodness she sought, and she knows it. Not just another sickness. Her pain " 'is for something,' she whispered. 'Something must come out of it.' " And Dick replies with the only formula left him from the old world, a reply of deepest meaning, unheard by the babyboygirls:

"He stooped and kissed her forehead.

" 'We must all try to be good,' he said."

The only fresh innocence Dick can see anywhere exists only in the youthful past, in the memory of the illusions of the future that existed in the past—and like Rosemary, the sun-bright new world is in the process of shedding its youth. The only person who reminds Dick of the redeemed future imagined in the youthful past is Rosemary, who has not quite yet emerged into the world of male and female, but still, with her sunburn, hovers on the edge of innocent, fresh childhood. Her pinkness is "like the thrilling flush of children after their cold baths in the evening. . . . Her body hovered delicately on the last edge of childhood—she was almost eighteen, nearly complete, but the dew was still on her" (pp. 58–59). And looking "at her with cold blue eyes," Dick "said thoughtfully and deliberately, 'You're the only girl I've seen for a long time that actually did look like something blooming' " (p. 77). Literally meaning "dew of the sea," rosemary suggests youth and memory. Rosemary, the plant, is considered tonic and stimulating and stands for remembrance. But what can blooming rosemary flower into with the nurture of *Daddy's Girl* wealth and a *Daddy's Girl* world? What drives Dick from sweet young love, in his early infatuation with her freshness, that he so desperately needs, to a frenzy of jealous lust as he breaks down faster and faster, is the vision provided by Collis Clay, the vision of Rosemary playing the liberated speed, the pet, the new woman, the golden girl, in the closed Pullman compartment.

("–Do you mind if I pull down the curtain?"

"–Please do. It's too light in here.")

Rosemary brings to this novel in full complexity the golden moment that Isabelle had introduced in *This Side of Paradise*. Her very youthfulness is the means whereby she gains entrance to the bright new world that a nation of movie-star worshippers dreams of. But a world that nourishes itself on dreams like *Daddy's Girl*—what did Gatsby have to feed on, after all?—will create values no more substantial than its movies. Its movies become its reality. The kids—of all ages—inherit a kid's world, and the novel is rife with reference to babies and nurseries. To step from movie-glory into the bright charm of the dazzling "real" world one gains by movie-fame and movie-money is only to step back into the moral immaturity and irresponsibility of the movie, the Señor "Real" world. As far as deep, ripe, conscious, mature, and civilized human reality is concerned, one steps from nothing into nothing. Identities dissolve like movie images—and the novel is also rife with references to movies. Fitzgerald, speaking out of his Hollywood scriptwriter's experience, uses the movies as he did in *The Great Gatsby* as a metaphor for shallowness, tawdriness, dehumanization, and gorgeous illusion. The world given over to the golden girl is a world given over to youth. But the irony is that of *This Side of Paradise*—the golden moment is empty. A world of kids, for kids, by kids is paradoxically the denial and betrayal of all that youth dreams of. *Someone*—poor Dick!—must be maturely responsible enough to give real substance to what, in a world of kids, can only remain wistful yearning. The babies who make it, as *Daddy's Girl* symbols to all the other babies, can make it only into a sun-hardened world in which the dew dries, a poor, empty, brainless world in which the star toughens and darkens and hardens into a debasement of what gave her her appeal in the first place. If the star must preserve anything, it is the appearance of her dewy youth, and maturity in the new world is simply corrupted into the enemy, age. The "woman's world," the baby's world, paradoxically is the destroyer of the responsible maturity that might make youth and its dreams regeneratingly meaningful. So Rosemary goes from mother-worship and "the nursery footing" on which she keeps her babyfirst romance to the hard phoney world of commercialized love, sentiment and tinsel, and becomes one with the corrupt people on the beach. She becomes the star whose reading material is "two novels, one by Edna Ferber, one by Albert McKisco" (p. 227).

("—Do you mind if I pull down the curtain?"

("—Please do.")

The vision of what the liberated golden girl will inevitably become is a final sign that Dick's past, youth, and promise have been taken and changed. They are gone. Frustrated by jealousy and defeat, he sees that others are using up the precious sweetness. Desperately, hungrily, he lusts for what he can get, falling in love with every pretty face he sees, wanting to be restored, to be back "there" where it was all new and good, good, good. But there is no such place or time. All that's left is the new world in which Dick had once so desperately believed, and which turns out to be the boygirl nurserykingdom of Baby. All that Dick gets when he finally gets Rosemary is Daddy's Girl completely grown up into Mama's "boy" (wow, you should see her now!). " 'Are you actually a virgin?' 'No-o-o!' she sang. 'I've slept with six hundred and forty men— if that's the answer you want.' " And tired, out of love, much older than he had been, Dick finally takes a much older Rosemary, amid phone calls, jealousy of Signor Nicotera, moments snatched from gay, brave new world schedules. "She wanted to be taken and she was, and what had begun with a childish infatuation on a beach was accomplished at last" (p. 231).

At last nothing. Exactly that—nothing plus nothing is nothing. There is only the defiant rebellion of women who have lost an old, dependable relationship with men, or the surrender in lust of Rosemary to Dick, Nicole to Tommy, in a simplification of relationships that destroys all the old dreams of what life would be like in the radiant and gorgeous new world of full and independent human personality. The eczema-ridden patient almost found it. Dick almost did. But the only ones who survive are the combatants who toughen and dry like Tommy's skin. What shows through Nicole's madness, as she comes closer and closer to the final sexual transference which will effect her cure, is a growing defiance. Even in the depths of her breakdown at the fair, when she rides hysterically on the small ferris wheel, as she regains an evil composure, her posture is significant. *She* wrecked the car. *She* almost killed Dick and the children. As Dick takes over and assumes responsibility (it becomes harder and harder each time), and gets the children safely out of the way, he and the proprietor of the inn try to right the family car that Nicole has capsized. And as "she watched the *men* trying to move the car her expression became defiant." Her defiance is given more meaningful shape in the scene in which Nicole gives Tommy the jar of camphor-rub for his slight cold. The curative stuff is for the family. It is "extremely rare" and "it's out of stock down here." It is an irreplaceable healing balm that is not often used, but is badly needed. Nicole tosses the whole jar to Tommy, irresponsibly claiming her right to her own desires and gratifications in the new world she owns, disclaiming any claims on her. She throws away Dick for Tommy, throwing away the curative, patient years of rare Dick's self-denial and discipline and ordered care and virtues and graces. What beckons is her liberation, her freedom, her place in the blinding hot sun of the Barban-Warren world. Although there are more moving scenes in the book, the moment with the camphor jar is one of the two or three most crucial. The whole sense of the book is there: the Amory-Gatsby hero, given intelligence, self-consciousness, and discipline, moves into the new world armed with the instruments of an older world of virtues and graces. It is Gatsby's world, in which the imagination promises a realization of millennium. Dick arrives in the world "on fewer Achilles heels than would be required to equip a centipede, but with plenty—the illusions of eternal strength and health, and of the essential goodness of people . . . (p. 5); he used to think that he wanted to be good, he wanted to be kind, he wanted to be brave and wise . . . he wanted to be loved . . ." (p. 23). Tell it to the Warrens. Tell it to the marines. Tell it to the U. S. cruiser that Warren commissioned to get his daughter through the submarine blockade. Tell it to Tommy Barban. The believing, dedicated, innocent seeker, committed to the service of his love, his ideals, his vision, expends himself totally only to discover that the cause he gave his life to is an irresponsible and selfish, gilded corruption. Nicole throws the jar away to Barban. At center, Diver's story is Gatsby's all over again, the central story of Fitzgerald's life and art. So, when Dick cures Nicole that she may go back into the world, what world is there for her to go to? Not Dick's world. That existed only in the memory of young hopes, back there in the glorious dawn, the past. "We're all there is!" cries Mary North Minghetti, representative of the brave new world of "liberated" women. It's the world made by Nicole's fathers, moreover, the world Nicole was born to. "If my eyes have changed it's because I'm well again," says Nicole. "And being well perhaps I've gone back to my true self—I suppose my grandfather was a crook and I'm a crook by heritage, so there we are" (p. 311). The white crook's eyes are her true eyes. When Dick bitterly protests the outrageous, unearned, righteous, Babyish snobbishness of Mary North Minghetti, Nicole replies spitefully, "I like her."

Mary is to be spoken of in a slightly different context, for she is more clearly seen in Fitzgerald's handling of the breakdown of national rather than sexual identities. But it is sufficient to note for the moment that she had existed as sympathetic character, as charming woman, when she dedicated herself to the support and redemption of her man. But with the death of Abe, Mary is finally freed from the world of courage and discipline from which Abe had come and out of which he had been corrupted. And although her role is more noticeable in the motif of dissolved national identities, she too is put in moral perspective by her place in the theme of sexual identity. She finds her liberty in the fantastic wealth of an Asian potentate whose customs are based upon the complete subjection of women, as typified in Hossain's himadoun sisters and Mary's total fealty. But it's a small price to pay, for she is free: she is not tied to a man through the restrictions of the old virtues and graces. It is telling that Mary's last real encounter with Dick (before she speaks to him on the papal rock above the beach as he leaves for ever) is the "prank" she plays with Lady Caroline Sibley-Biers, a prank that is fittingly a dissolution of sexual identities. Lady Caroline is introduced as the extreme incarnation of the new woman. Her theme song is "There was a young lady from hell! Boom-boom! Toot-toot." She is utterly and totally irresponsible, bringing to a final surge the strength of the evil that is the central characteristic of the brave new world of gilt hot cats. But if Lady Caroline feels the gilt she feels absolutely no guilt. A selfish, thoughtless bitch, she was in the wrong, and she created the trouble. But there is a complete "lack, in Lady Caroline's face, of any sense of evil, except the evil wrought by cowardly Provencal girls and stupid police" who had caught Lady Caroline in her own "prank." Dick is "torn between a tendency to ironic laughter and another tendency to order fifty stripes of the cat and a fortnight of bread and water" (p. 322). Conduct may be founded on the hard rock or the wet marshes, but after a certain point Nick-Dick-Scott doesn't care what it's founded on. And the prank? Consider the boygirls and the girlboys—Mary and Lady Caroline had been "boys," dressed up in French sailor suits, picking up girls to bring to a hotel room. In Lady Caroline there is not even a vestige, as there is still in Mary, of gratitude for the doctor who helps her in her plight. She owes nothing to anyone—the extreme extension of the new Nicole, she disclaims any claims upon her. She will not even repay old Gausse the money he has put up to buy her out of jail. In Dick's world, Rosemary, Mary, and Nicole had been alike in that "they preserved their individuality through men and not by opposition to them. They would all three have made alternatively good courtesans or good wives, not by the accident of birth but through the greater accident of finding their man or not finding him" (p. 112). But these women of the new world! "I have never seen women like this sort of woman," says old Gausse. "I have known many of the great courtesans of the world, and for them I have much respect often, but women like these women I have never seen before" (p. 325). For *that* had Gatsby followed the green light. For *that* had Dr. Richard Diver given his life in the re-education of his Adam's rib, that "broken side." And to that has the heritage of the Abe and Mary of the North descended.

Baby Warren, the man of the family, does not indulge in the

pranks of Lady Caroline. But, the respectable summation of the
world of "this sort of woman," she is the obverse side of the same
coin. In her awareness of her male economic power, she tries to
play the man's old role, insisting on order and proprieties. But it's
a farce, an ignorant imitation, for what is left is empty formalisms,
manners left after the morale and the morals had long since
cracked. She doesn't know what she is imitating, and takes the "refined" English manner as the *ne plus ultra* of the great world to
which she belongs. Neither man nor woman, there is "something
wooden and onanistic about her" (p. 44), and she keeps crossing
and uncrossing her legs in the nervous manner of perpetual, restless virgins (p. 43), whether technically possessing a hymeneal
layer or no. As Dr. Diver finds out and finds out and finds out, the
problem of his world is hardly a physiological question. When the
girl who has inherited daddy's wealth and power goes into action,
she is in the man's role.

Coming to Dick's aid when he is beaten and imprisoned by the
Italian police, she takes control, menacing and browbeating the
carabinieri.

At the Embassy, the disintegration of sexual identities, so closely
woven in this novel with a disintegration of national identities, is
turned to a fine, tight twist.

On an upper landing, just aroused from sleep and wrapped in a white
embroidered Persian robe, stood a singular young man [*the Ambassador of the United States!*]. His face was of a monstrous and unnatural
pink, vivid yet dead, and over his mouth was fastened what appeared
to be a gag. When he saw Baby he moved his head back into a shadow.
"What is it?" he repeated.
Baby told him, in her agitation edging forward to the stairs. In the
course of her story she realized that the gag was in reality a mustache
bandage and that the man's face was covered with pink cold cream
. . . (p. 247).

Fittingly, her unmannerly wrath is repulsed by an English butler, and it is the "English" manners of the Ambassador that resist Baby. "He was of the Eastern seaboard and too hard for her," and as he "maneuvered her to the door for an instant the violet dawn fell shrilly upon his pink mask and upon the linen sack that supported his mustache . . ." (pp. 248, 249). When she arrives at the Consulate, however, Baby is in full possession of her sense of identity: a Warren. She knows how to cut across the manners and proprieties at the same moment she continues her absurd Anglophilism. " 'We're people of considerable standing in America—' Her mouth hardened as she continued. 'If it wasn't for the scandal we can—I shall see that your indifference to this matter is reported in the proper quarter. If my brother-in-law were a British citizen he'd have been free hours ago, but you're more concerned with what the police will think than about what you're here for.' " She sweeps away her own irresponsible self-contradictions together with the Consul's protests.

" 'You put on your hat and come with me right away.'

"The mention of his hat alarmed the Consul, who began to clean his spectacles hurriedly and ruffle his papers. This proved of no avail: the *American Women*, aroused, stood over him; the clean-sweeping irrational temper that had broken the moral back of a race and *made a nursery out of a continent*, was too much for him. He rang for the vice-consul—*Baby* had won" (pp. 250–51, italics mine).

Just as "inevitable became evitable" in *Daddy's Girl*, what Fitzgerald called a "tragic sense of life," indeed life itself, is shut out by Baby's moral and imaginative shallowness and her need for being seen enjoying "the best things in life." On the magnificent funicular ride, she travels "first class . . . the hearse part behind the chauffeur—shut in with curtains for a rainy day, so you can't see anything. But sister's very dignified—" (p. 41). She faces males "with the impetus that sent her out vagrantly toward all new men, as though she were on an inelastic tether and considered

that she might as well get to the end of it as soon as possible."
She "had certain spinster's characteristics—she was alien from
touch, she started if she were touched suddenly, and such lingering touches as kisses and embraces slipped directly through the
flesh into the forefront of her consciousness. She made few gestures
with her trunk, her body proper" and she "relished the foretaste
of death, prefigured by the catastrophes of friends" (p. 188).

Her measurement of people is as insensitive as Barban's, for
she is a moral barbarian in her first-class carriage. She fixes on the
English for all that is "proper," and her conception of that is
the limit of her evaluation of human beings. Dick, who has the
only constantly trustworthy moral view of the creatures who
inhabit the novel, begins to find "something antipathetic in the
English lately. England was like a rich man after a disastrous orgy
who makes up to his household by chatting with them individ-
ually, when it is obvious to them that he is only trying to get back
his self-respect in order to usurp his former power" (p. 211). Baby's
young Englishman at Gstaad is a ruddy ass, braying pretentiously
romantic noises about loving his friend the more he hit him, and
betraying his sophomoric limitations at every bray. Lady Sibley-
Biers is an English representative. Yet, when Baby thinks that for
appearances sake, Nicole is well enough to stop living at a clinic
or "that hermit's life on the Riviera, up on a hill away from anybody," she adds, "I didn't mean to go back to that life. I meant,
for instance, London. The English are the best-balanced race in
the world . . . . They are. I know them, you see. I meant it might
be nice," she advises Dick, "for you to take a house in London for
the spring season—I know a dove of a house in Talbot Square you
could get, furnished. I mean, living with sane, well-balanced English people" (pp. 232–33). Her smug and limited view of people
makes her evaluations irresponsibly and hurtfully arrogant and
simple. When she sizes up Franz, she makes "a quick examination
of him and, failing to find any of the hall-marks she respected, the

subtler virtues or courtesies [*not* Dick's!] by which the privileged
classes recognize one another, treated him thereafter with her
second manner" (p. 189). The fact that Franz helped cure Nicole
is unimportant: that was his service job, for which he was hired.
People who are not "English" are just hired hands, to be used. She
can't be bothered with responsibility. As for Nicole, "What am *I*
supposed to do?" she demands. The answer is simple. With Baby's
connections at the University, with her endowment money, she'll
simply buy some good doctor for Nicole to fall in love with, "buy
her a nice young doctor," and let others take care of the mess (p.
45). With the incredible arrogance of her monied smugness, she
is obtuse enough to advise Dick about the care of Nicole—she who
does not even understand that the mess to be cleaned up was of
Warren making in the first place. She is perfectly capable of telling
Dick that she thinks Nicole should "get out of that atmosphere
of sickness and live in the world [the English world of proper
society, of course] like other people," the "right" people, who are
the only people there are (p. 232). She can forget quite conveniently that when Dick and Franz were talking about buying a clinic
that she thought "that if Nicole lived beside a clinic she [Baby]
would always feel quite safe about her," for "others" could take
care of her (p. 192). "Others," less than people, are all hired mess-
cleaners indeed. When she bailed Dick out of the Italian jail,
"she had the satisfaction of feeling that, whatever Dick's previous
record was, they," the Warrens—the cattle-crook, mess-making,
incestuous Warrens!—"now possessed a moral superiority over
him for as long as he proved of any use" (p. 253). How else can
she think of morality but in terms of acceptable social appearances?
How else think of relations to "others" but in terms of their usefulness? When this "baby" who inherits the nursery-nation speaks
of money and the prerogatives it brings her, she hardens and becomes "suddenly her grandfather, cool and experimental" (p. 191).
As inhuman as it is, it is not astonishing that this granddaughter

of the horse-thief founder of great American wealth should even think of Dick's marriage to Nicole as a matter of convenience and usefulness to her. She is totally unaware of the goodness, sacrifice, true virtues and graces that went into the marriage, and could no more be expected to be aware of them than a she-wolf running down prey.

When Dick muses about the transference necessary for Nicole's recovery, he says,

"It's possible that I was the wrong person for Nicole. . . . Still, she would probably have married someone of my type, someone she thought she could rely on—indefinitely."
"You think she'd be happier with somebody else?" Baby thought aloud suddenly. "Of course it could be arranged."
Only as she saw Dick bend forward with helpless laughter did she realize the preposterousness of her remark.
"Oh, you understand," she assured him. "Don't think for a moment that we're [always that *we* as a phalanx closed to "others"] not grateful for all you've done. And we know you've had a hard time—" (pp. 233–34).

She knows he's "had a hard time" about as much as she could be an earth-mother. Her "gratitude" and "tragic sense of life" become perfectly clear when she is annoyed that Dick doesn't know how to play the "English" game by "decently" clearing out without being seen as he takes leave forever of his wife, his children, his life. When Nicole protests that Dick is not to be simply discarded as an obstacle, a leftover, and that he did devote all his attention during six years of marriage to protecting and curing her, Baby's response is typical. "Baby's lower jaw projected slightly as she said: 'That's what he was educated for' " (p. 331).

Baby had bought "her nice young doctor." Doctor Diver was at liberty. Baby—"the clean-sweeping irrational temper that had broken the moral back of a race and made a nursery out of a continent"—had won. "Before her tiny fist the forces of lust and corruption rolled away; nay, the very march of destiny stopped, inevitable became evitable; syllogism, dialectic, all rationality fell away." Daddy's Baby of the national nursery had won. The war was over. Dick had been able to meet the world only with the weapons of his visions and memory and hopes—his ideals. He had refused to be the one to initiate young Rosemary into the new world of Daddy's Girl translated from movies into "reality." In turning down her plea to be seduced, he had said, "So many people are going to love you and it might be nice to meet your first love all intact, emotionally too. That's an old-fashioned idea, isn't it?" All he could do, though, was to turn the job over to some nameless Barban. As the character whose function, as babe, is to dramatize the growing up of the new generation, with the heartbreaking perversion of all its dewy potential, Rosemary will not long be called—as Dick calls her—"child." She will harden and age. "Do you mind if I pull down the curtain?" "Please do. It's too light in here." "Are you actually a virgin?" "No-o-o."

Dick had lost his war, and the final sign of it was his being rescued by Baby from combat with men. How completely Baby had won. In her triumph, as in the metaphor of *Daddy's Girl*, is Fitzgerald's dramatization of a nation reduced to juveniles and the mindlessness of its adolescent popular values and culture. In his love or his recoil, Americanness is as much the center of Fitzgerald's novels as of his personality.

In examining the meaning of the breakdown of sexual identities, I have tried to suggest the frequency with which the liberation of the new woman from "old-fashioned ideas" is cast in terms of combat and warfare in the novel. Today, much of this may seem silly. What Dick represents, in the light of the sexual revolution of today, can seem too old-fashioned indeed: not merely silly, but repressive. Certainly, it does not seem worth the anguish of Dick's career and the metaphor of war. The same is true in the motif of disintegrating national identities, at a moment when national identity is seen more and more intensely as an ideological

danger that can destroy the planet. It is necessary to remember that
what Fitzgerald is talking about is moral responsibility: not the
mere nature of his materials, but what he does with them. They
are his materials, the *all* he had to work with. He is not interested
in championing repression, prudery, or nationalism. Fitzgerald
is not simplifying morality into mores, but is using mores to represent moral complexities. It is the liberated Nicole with white
crook's eyes who in Barban-like manner oversimplifies the issue:
"So I have white crook's eyes, have I? Very well then, better a
sane crook than a mad puritan" (p. 312). In a moment when social
attitudes and literary fashion have merged in the intentionally
outrageous underground hero, the contemporary audience is apt
to applaud Nicole's statement. Therefore it is especially important to see that the warfare Fitzgerald is writing about is not merely
one of outdated and temporary attitudes, but one in which the
mores that he, in his time, has to work with are signs of a battle
between the dying old world and the flaming new one. Temporal
mores extend beyond themselves in Fitzgerald's fiction as a contrast between *This Side of Paradise* and *The Plastic Age* suggested
even at the very beginning of Fitzgerald's career.

On the level of moralities, there is indeed a basic and overwhelming battle in the novel, just as in *The Great Gatsby*. Sexual
freedom and nationalism are no more the real issues in *Tender
Is the Night* than bootlegging and bucketshopping were in *The
Great Gatsby*.


Fitzgerald dissolves national identities in the same way and
for the same purposes of moral evaluation that he dissolves sexual
identities. The characters' names and origins are confusing. Señor
Luis Campion speaks with a British accent; Mrs. Abrams "was not
a Jewess, despite her name." There is a parallel to Nick's old
timetable, with its hilarious names, in Tommy's copy of the Paris

edition of the New York *Herald:* representative of the "people" who occupy the world of *Tender Is the Night* are the anomalies in the pages of an American Parisian paper. " 'Well, what nationality are these people,' " demands the half-American Tommy, reading "with a slight French intonation. 'Registered at the Hotel Palace at Vevey are Mr. Pandely Vlasco, Mme. Bonneasse'—I don't exaggerate—'Corinna Madonca, Mme. Pasche, Seraphim Tullio, Maria Amalia Roto Mais, Moises Teubel, Mme. Paragoris, Apostle Alexandre, Yolanda Yosfuglu and Geneveva de Momus!' " (pp. 73–74). Nicole adds "Mrs. Evelyn Oyster" and "Mr. S. Flesh" to the group. Mary North changes from Abe's Mary to the Contessa di Minghetti. But even that is too clear an Italian identity, for it turns out that the Conte di Minghetti is "not quite light enough to travel in a pullman south of the Mason-Dixon line," and, a "ruler-owner of manganese deposits in southwestern Asia" is of "the Kabyle-Berber-Sabaean-Hindu strain that belts across north Africa" (p. 277). Furthermore, the name of this Hindu is "a papal title." How's that, Fitzgerald seems to be saying, for confusing identities? Fitzgerald's notes indicate that puns on names are intentionally significant (like Barban for barbarian) and the names indicate identity according to functions that destroy recognizable and dependable identities. So the "man," Campion ("camping" was contemporary slang for homosexual activities), chums around with a royal dumphrey, and Barban, who combines warfare with loss of national identity, insists that Chicago-bred Nicole speak in French. Half American, half French, he "was educated in England and since [he] was eighteen [he wore] the uniforms of eight countries" (p. 87). In the transportation of Hollywood to the Riviera, Rosemary sees in the studio "a decayed street scene in India, a great cardboard whale, a monstrous tree bearing cherries as large as basketballs," all as "autochthonous as the pale amaranth, mimosa, cork oak, or dwarfed pine" (p. 79). On the set she meets Earl Brady, a Cockney director who is filming a scene with a French

actor and an American actress. "Here and there figures spotted
the twilight, turning up ashen faces to her like souls in Purgatory
watching the passage of a mortal through" (p. 79). When Rosemary is last seen, she is considering marriage to Signor Nicotera.
McKisco's name sounds like "a substitute for gasoline or butter."
When Abe North returns to Paris he is thought to be "Mr. Afghan
North," in a queer foreshadowing of Mary's changed identity, and
he is known by "his carte d'identité" (p. 157). The French Negro restaurateur in "Afghan North's" mixup is confused with
an American Negro, who in turn is mistaken for another
American Negro who is introduced as "Mr. Jules Peterson of
Stockholm." Tommy Barban turns up in the Marienplatz in
Munich with a White Guard Russian prince, both of them wearing clothes made in Poland by "Pilsudski's own tailor." The national identities that are at best marginal are representative of the
marginal humanity that exists in the golden new world. Lady
Caroline Sibley-Biers (and her life is the bier of the old virtues and
graces) is introduced on a yacht named the *Margin*, owned by a
money-man named Golding. Utilizing ship names, as he did with
the *Tuolomee* in *The Great Gatsby*, Fitzgerald epitomizes Baby's
world of rapacious and predatory personalities in the name of the
boat that tows Dick on the aquaplane. The boat in attendance on
the public disclosure that he no longer is the "good swimmer" that
he was when he was differentiated from the "light people" at the
beach, is the *Baby Gar*. When Rosemary hears that Dick is in
disgrace, defeated, the news comes fittingly from the mouths of
"some State Department people on the boat—Europeanized Americans who had reached a position where they could scarcely have
been said to belong to any nation at all." It is in this world, where
people "belong" only to "a Balkan-like state composed of similar
citizens," that "the name of the ubiquitously renowned Baby
Warren had occurred" in conversations about the doings of "the
world" (p. 305). In all cases, names and titles refer to no reliable

identities and are all mixed up together. All the old dependabili-
ties are gone.

Fitzgerald weaves the idea of broken identity in the disintegration of sexual and national roles through the metaphor of war
that becomes a summary motif in the novel. The war of sex, love,
money, nations is the explosive destruction of Dick's old world.
When the girl-goddess, Rosemary, is introduced, her hair is called
"an armorial shield" of "lovelocks" and "gold" (p. 59). Tommy,
the most de-nationalized figure in the book, is totally and constantly associated with wars, going to wars, the uniforms of the wars of
various nations. In significant and irresponsible fashion, he doesn't
care which side he fights on. The Negroes involved in "Afghan's"
deadly fiasco are called a tracking war party of "hostile and friendly
Indians" (p. 172). The gay young people of the new golden world
are referred to as "the Sturmtruppen of the rich" (p. 187), as the
new women beyond Gausse's comprehension are called "emergent
Amazons" (p. 193). But the death of self-sacrificial love once made
possible by established and dependable identities is most clearly
anchored in the background of a world war, which broods over
the opening of the novel. It is at the moment of the dying of the
old world and the birth of the new—the convulsive parturition
known as World War I—that Dick Diver is brought to the blurring
identities of the international scene.

Revisiting a battlefield with Abe and Rosemary, Dick mourns a
terrible loss. "All my beautiful, lovely safe world blew itself up
here with a great gust of high explosive love." He recognizes what
it is that died in these trenches.

This western-front business couldn't be done again, not for a long
time. . . . This took religion and years of plenty and tremendous
sureties and the exact relation that existed between the classes. . . .
You had to have a whole-souled sentimental equipment going back
further than you could remember. You had to remember Christmas,
and postcards of the Crown Prince and his fiancée, and little cafés in

Valence and beer gardens in Unter den Linden and weddings at the
Mairie, and going to the Derby, and your grandfather's whiskers. . . .
This kind of battle was invented by Lewis Carroll and Jules Verne
and whoever wrote *Undine,* and country deacons bowling and mar-
raines in Marseilles and girls seduced in the back lanes of Württemberg
and Westphalia. Why, this was a love battle—there was a century of
middle-class love spent here. This was the last love battle (pp. 117–18).

At the moment Dick makes this speech, he admits that he is a
*romantic.* He does not yet know the truth of his own statements.
He still believes, as yet only partly ruined, in the new world to
which his generation has emerged from the war. He still believes
in its freedoms and its millennial possibilities. Even later, when
Rosemary has deepened his growing disquietude, he still tries to
believe in the present. In a restaurant, Dick, Nicole, and Rosemary
observe a table of "gold star muzzers," come to visit their sons'
graves. As Dick looked at them, "in their happy faces the dignity
that surrounded and pervaded the party, he perceived *all the maturity of an older America* [italics mine]. For a while the sobered
women who had come to mourn for their dead, for something they
could not repair, made the room beautiful. Momentarily he sat
again on his father's knees, riding with Mosby while the old loyalties and devotions fought on around him. Almost with an effort
he turned back to his two women at the table and faced the whole
new world in which he believed" (p. 162). It is significant that
Fitzgerald at once associates the gold star mothers, like the trenches, with a deep nostalgia, with memory of lost, irretrievable, and
younger days, with the one fixed point of desirable and stable
identity in the whole, whirling horizon that opened after the War.
And it is beginning to be "an effort" for Dick to still value the
new world above the old departed one, which he buries finally
with "all his fathers." Never missing a touch, Fitzgerald immediately juxtaposes the jazzy easiness of the new world upon the
vision of old memories: "with an effort he turned back to his two

women at the table and faced the whole new world in which he believed.

"—Do you mind if I pull down the curtain?" (p. 162).

Until Dick is ruined—he had always known that he needed a little ruin, and that the price of his intactness was incompleteness —he cannot know in his deathwishing bones the truth of what he was saying in the visit to the trenches. And how he will know it at the graveside of his father! But until he knows the nature of the new world that has replaced the dead old one, his nostalgic sense of the past is marred by a faint sentimentality. The reader is grateful for Abe's puncturing the pose: "Abe yelled from the next traverse:

" 'The war spirit's getting into me again. I have a hundred years of Ohio love behind me and I'm going to bomb out this trench' " (p. 118). The reader is grateful because Dick's truth is as yet merely nostalgic. The meanings of nostalgia have not yet been measured on the scales of his own ruin: "indeed, he had made a quick study" of the whole battlefield, "simplifying it always until it bore a faint resemblance to one of his own parties" (p. 120).

Dick carries on his own war of affection and love and discipline against the forces of disintegration. But he makes a fatally exhausting expenditure of his creative energies in a war not worth waging and impossible to win—the saving of an unredeemable sick world interested only in irresponsibly using its saviors (Christ would be welcomed with excitement for the fun he would furnish and be done to death a second time at parties). As the War is simplified until it bears a faint resemblance to one of Dick's own parties, so Dick's parties bear a faint resemblance to war. As Rosemary observes one of Dick's parties in action, she admires Dick's "technic of moving many varied types, each as immobile, as dependent on supplies of attention as an infantry battalion is dependent on rations . . ." (p. 139). The party reaches its peak of hilarity when the revelers roused a hotel staff for emergency service to "General

Pershing," played by Abe North, while the tired, befuddled waiters "stood up and mumbled remembered fragments of war songs
at him" (p. 139). And when Dick becomes aware of the waste of
his energies in the amusement, care, and feeding of the brave
new world, "the reaction came when he realized the waste and
extravagance involved. He sometimes looked back with awe at
the carnivals of affection he had given, as a general might gaze
upon a massacre he had ordered to satisfy an impersonal blood
lust" (p. 84).

Dick's waste of his potential—exactly as with Gatsby, turning his
dream into the reality of the golden world of hot cats is the destruction of the dream identity—is a constant warfare of attrition. The
morning that Dick awakens to hold the interview about "battle"
with his eczema-patient, he awakens after he has already begun to
realize the attrition of his life: "Dick awoke at five after a long
dream of war." The images of war as a metaphor for the reality of
the battle between sets of values, or values and irresponsible value-
lessness, typified in the identity-destroying battle of the sexes, come
to a climax during the scene in which Abe, "tired of women's
worlds," departs from the Gare Saint-Lazare. A casual acquaint-
ance of Nicole, Maria Wallis, an "emergent Amazon" described
as "a tall girl with straw hair like a helmet," shoots down her man.
As Dick, Mary, Nicole, and Rosemary watch, horrified, the "young
woman with the helmet-like hair . . . made an odd dodging little
run away from the man to whom she had been talking and plunged
a frantic hand into her purse; then the sound of two revolver shots
cracked the narrow air of the platform. . . . But before the crowd
closed in, the others had seen the shots take effect, seen the target
sit down upon the platform" (p. 145). When Dick finds out what
had happened, what he reports is terribly fitting: "they had an
awful time finding out who [he was], because *she shot him through
his identification card*" (p. 146, italics mine). The tiny toy-like
pearl revolver, the petite instrument of the new woman's power,

is as potent in the station of Lazarus (no one rises from the dead of Dick's world, and only the representations of war or of corruption rise, like Devereux Warren, and walk again) as is Baby or Rosemary or Nicole in the sun-bright new world they own. The two porters who hold a post-mortem outside the station sum it up perfectly in their excited conversation.

" 'Tu as vu le revolver? Il était très petit, vraie perle—un jouet.'

" 'Mais assez *puissant!*' said the other porter sagely. 'Tu as vu sa chemise? Assez de sang pour se croire *à la guerre*' " (p. 147, italics mine).

In its summary symbolic energy, the scene, minor as it is, is the turning point of the novel. Up until that moment, Fitzgerald has allowed the reader to know of Dick's increasing disintegration, but only by seeing into Dick's hidden mind. From this scene on, Fitzgerald externalizes Dick's growing defeat and impotence, and allows Dick to be seen for the first time in ineffectual poses and impotent attitudes. For the first time, Nicole takes over and firmly prevents Dick from acting as savior, party-director, doctor. Dick's first impulse is to serve, to be used, to help Maria Wallis. For the first time, someone else can do better than Dick; for the first time Nicole herself says so: "[Maria is] married to a Frenchman, and he can do more than we can" (p. 146). Those sounds of identity-destroying war cracking the narrow air of the station platform sound the crack-up beneath the manner, which is the dramatic function of all the action that makes up the rest of Dick's story. "Then, as if nothing had happened, the lives of the Divers and their friends flowed out into the street.

"However, everything had happened . . . this afternoon had ended the time in Paris [the time when the logistics of Dick's energies could be devoted to fun and games]. Or perhaps the shots, the concussions that had finished God knew what dark matter, had terminated it. The shots had entered into all their lives . . ." (p. 147). And later, during another "war," the "Indian war" in which

Jules Peterson is killed, even Rosemary, "who was accustomed to having shell fragments of such events (as the Maria Wallis affair) shriek past her head," "piled up" a "totality of shock" (p. 147) within her, and cried, "Do all the Americans in Paris just shoot at each other all the time?" (p. 173). Dick, the pacifier, who catches the shock of shell fragments from all sides, ironically classifies his own "long dream of war" as "Non-combatant's shell-shock" (p. 196).

The greatest shock is to discover that the armaments of the old world that blew up with World War I are ineffectual—they merely result in the victory of the same forces that the enemy, the moral irresponsibility of the new world, begets. Mrs. Elsie Speers is a "gold star mother" of that older America. The mother, indeed the Mother, of Mama's girl-Daddy's Girl, she has lost two *soldier* husbands. Rosemary's father had been an army doctor (shades of Dick Diver), and Mrs. Speers's second husband had been a cavalry officer. Both of these warriors, old-school officers, "left something to her that she tried to present intact to Rosemary" (p. 68). That something is what makes Dick and Mrs. Speers understand each other—they both recognize and appreciate in each other the discipline, courage, and responsibility that characterize the old virtues and graces. Indeed, "by not sparing Rosemary [Mrs. Speers] had made her hard—by not sparing her own labor and devotion she had cultivated an idealism in Rosemary," and Rosemary develops "a mature distrust of the trivial, the facile, and the vulgar" (p. 68). When Rosemary falls in love with Dick, she keeps the affair on a nursery footing, annoying to Dick, and does so partly because she is a baby and partly because she sees so much of her mother in Dick. Rosemary Hoyt is prepared, by a mother whose name from her second marriage is itself the name of a weapon, so that "she was protected by a double sheath of her mother's armor and her own" (p. 68). But armed for what? Armed for combat with men—"economically you're a boy, not a girl"—for a place in the sun that turns Barban's skin not to tan but to old leather. That is,

all the idealisms, virtues, and graces that are the heritage of what
Rosemary too could call "all my fathers" end up as—*Daddy's Girl.*
*That's* the "boy" Mama, who has been "father and mother both,"
gives birth to. Mrs. Speers can no more create the world in which
her armed daughter, emergent Amazon, will triumph, than Dick
Diver, who is "father and mother both" to Nicole, can create the
world in which the "daddy's girl" he arms and fortifies will emerge
as a triumphant Amazon. Going lax in Barban's world, as Nicole
discards Dick's armaments of old moralities, she became the "prototype of that obscure yielding up of swords that was going on in
the world about her." Dick's good war against irresponsibility is
defeated by the identity-smashing war of the "liberated" new
world. Both Dick and Mrs. Speers belong to the same world, and
that world is dead. "Mrs. Speers was fresh in appearance but she
was tired; deathbeds make people tired indeed and she had
watched beside a couple" (p. 81). Dick is also tired as father-and-
mother-both. Nicole is "afraid of what the stricken man [Dick] . . .
would feed on while she must still continue her dry suckling at
his lean chest" (p. 297). Mrs. Speers labors to give Rosemary freedom from dependence upon her; Dick labors for the same thing
for Nicole. The irony, of course, is in what the new freedoms mean.
Rosemary is deliberately liberated from being "Mama's girl" only
to become *Daddy's Girl* and then grow up to be hard and self-
protective so that she can be victorious in the bright world of
boygirls after her first flush of youthful innocence has passed.
Nicole is deliberately liberated by Dick from being her "daddy's
girl." She needs the further transference that will allow her final
freedom from any figure who is "father and mother both" so that
she too can play in her bright hard new world. What dismays Dick
and disgusts him is the irresponsible avidity with which Nicole
eagerly shucks him off after she has used him up—finally, in the
last analysis, there is no moral difference between Nicole and
Baby, who wants to buy a doctor in order to conveniently and

selfishly use him for the purposes to which he's been educated.
Rosemary knows that Mama has plans for her. Nicole knows that
Dick has plans for her. Always "she felt that a plan underlay his
... actions and she was afraid of his plans" because she sensed that
they meant she would have to stand, *armed*, on her own feet, free
at last. And, of course, at the same time, she is "like a happy child,
wanting the completion as soon as possible, and knowing vaguely
that Dick had planned for her to have it" (p. 307). But, as the plans
are nothing, Dick and Mrs. Speers cannot plan for themselves or
each other in the war of the worlds and the sexes. Dick saw that
Mrs. Speers made no provision for Nicole and him in permitting
Rosemary her spree. As long as certain proprieties are observed,
Mrs. Speers can watch the love-battle "with as much detachment
and humor as a eunuch" (p. 176). Turned eunuch by the battle,
Mrs. Speers tiredly lasts into the new world only long enough to
protect the product of her former potency. Then she soon fades
and it is time to say goodbye to her as to Gstaad, the "lovely, safe
old world," and all Dick's fathers. The whole novel is one long
taking of farewells. Dick and Mrs. Speers can understand each
other's similar virtues and graces, and with her he can be honest,
in a passage that recalls Lincoln, Grant, and another, older war.
"My politeness is a trick of the heart," says Dick.

"This was partly true. From his father Dick had learned the
somewhat conscious good manners of the young Southerner coming north after the Civil War. Often he used them, and just as
often he despised them because they were not a protest against
how unpleasant selfishness was, but against how unpleasant it
looked" (p. 176). Knowing the real point of all the manners that
the Sibley-Bierses lack, Dick can distinguish between old Mrs.
Speers and young Rosemary. " 'You and Rosemary aren't really
alike,' he said. . . . She doesn't think; her real depths are Irish and
romantic and illogical." In the scene of farewell to Mrs. Speers,

the references to war and combat indicate a woman with a lasting identity very different from that gained in battle by the emergent Amazons of the new world.

"Saying good-bye, Dick was aware of Elsie Speers' full charm. . . . She had an air of seeming to wait, as if for a man to get through with something more important than herself, a battle or an operation, during which he must not be hurried or interfered with. When the man had finished she would be waiting, without fret or impatience. . . ."

" 'Good-bye . . .' " (p. 177). Good-bye to the world Dr. Diver came from and from which his plans and visions grew.

Dick's victory as a doctor is his defeat as a human being. His case is successful, for the patient is cured. But as a man, an identity, he is totally used up, like Abe, like Mrs. Speers, for he cannot cure Nicole into his world of the old virtues and graces. The final moment when the emergent Amazon emerges into her new freedom is a final moment of warfare between two worlds. All Dick has at his command is intelligence, truth, and morality, all worn out and defunct armaments of a dead world. Nicole "began to feel the old hypnotism of his intelligence, sometimes exercised without power but always with substrata of truth under truth which she could not break or even crack. Again she struggled with it, fighting him with her small, fine eyes [her white crook's eyes], with the plush arrogance of a top dog, with her nascent transfer to another man, with the accumulated resentment of years; she fought him with her money and her faith that her sister disliked him [Baby is now the arbiter of what is "good" or "bad"!] and was behind her now; with the thought of the new enemies he was making [epitomized by Lady Caroline Sibley-Biers] with his bitterness, with her quick guile against his wining and dining slowness, her health and beauty against his physical deterioration, her unscrupulousness against his moralities—for this inner battle she used even her

weaknesses, fighting bravely and courageously with the old cans
and crockery and bottles, the empty receptacles of her expiated
sins, outrages, mistakes. And suddenly, in the space of two minutes, she achieved her victory and justified herself to herself without lie or subterfuge, cut the cord forever. Then she walked, weak
in the legs and sobbing coolly, toward the household that was
hers at last.

"Dick waited until she was out of sight. Then he leaned his
head forward on the parapet. The case was finished. Doctor Diver
was at liberty" (pp. 319–20).

Nicole was at liberty. It was no contest. The new world has won,
and Richard Diver was dead. Shot through the identification card.
No Lazarus he.


With the "female" all bound up in his mind with the morality
developed in the images and events of the novel, Fitzgerald felt—
as was the case with Dick, walking the block around Rosemary's
studio—that the "goodness" of the book was a "tribute to things
unforgotten, unshriven, unexpurgated" in his life. He felt that
the enlargement of the "feminine" in the book, compared to *The
Great Gatsby*, not only gave the novel room for more complex
and delicate observation, but also a promise of wider sales. Writing to Perkins about the possible circulation of the book, Fitzgerald asserted, "I don't think there is a comparison between this
book and *The Great Gatsby* as a seller. *The Great Gatsby* had
against it its length and its purely masculine interest. This book,
on the contrary, is a woman's book."[31] What Fitzgerald was recalling was his old fear that there had not been enough of a
woman's point of view in *The Great Gatsby*, that one never really
saw Daisy's reactions from the inside. But in *Tender Is the Night*,

[31] March 4, 1934, *Letters*, p. 247.

not only does one see through Nicole's eyes, but the cast of female characters is enlarged. The world of bootlegging and gangsterism, which Fitzgerald associated with the Tom world and used invisibly and ironically as the source of Gatsby's social identity, disappears in favor of a setting which one would associate with a novel of manners, with the tragi-comedies of an Austen or a James.

All things considered, Fitzgerald was convinced that the "feminine" enlargement of the scope of *Tender Is the Night* was in itself an advance over *The Great Gatsby* precisely because the Jamesian "scene" allowed for "philosophical, now called psychological" delicacies and complexities that were foreshortened in the Buchanan-Barban male world. The enlargement and delicacy of sensibility, personified in Dick, was what Fitzgerald meant when he referred to *Tender Is the Night* as a "philosophical" novel, as he explained to John Peale Bishop:

On receiving your first letter with its handsome tribute and generous praise I realized that I had been hasty in crediting that you would make such a criticism as "this book is no advance on *Gatsby*." You would be the first to feel that the intention in the two books was entirely different [Fitzgerald always associated Bishop with the "feminine," with delicate sensibility, almost with aestheticism], that (to promote myself momentarily) *Gatsby* was shooting at something like *Henry Esmond* [his example of the "dramatic novel"] while this was shooting at something like *Vanity Fair*. The dramatic novel has canons quite different from the philosophical, now called psychological, novel. One is a kind of *tour de force* and the other a confession of faith. It would be like comparing a sonnet sequence with an epic.

The point of my letter which survives is that there were moments all through the book where I could have pointed up dramatic scenes, and I *deliberately* refrained from doing so because the material itself was so harrowing and highly charged that I did not want to subject the reader to a series of nervous shocks in a novel that was inevitably close to whoever read it in my generation.

Contrariwise, in dealing with figures as remote as are a bootlegger

and crook to most of us, I was not afraid of heightening and melo-
dramatizing any scenes; and I was thinking that in your novel I would
like to pass on this theory to you for what it is worth. Such advice
from fellow-craftsmen has been a great help to me in the past, indeed
I believe it was Ernest Hemingway who developed to me, in conversation, that the dying fall was preferable to the dramatic ending under
certain conditions, and I think we both got the germ of the idea from
Conrad.[32]

When one thinks of the scenes from which Fitzgerald refrained,
they are, as he himself pointed out, scenes—with the two excep-
tions of Rosemary's viewing Nicole's hysteria in the bathroom and
of Nicole's breakdown at the fair—of sensation, of mental disorder.
Nicole's incestuous affair is given briefly at second hand, her life
in the sanatorium is only hinted at through letters, and Dick's own
duties as a psychiatrist are presented swiftly in condensed scenes,
none of them garish. Fitzgerald avoids the sensational at all costs
in his mad scenes, which indicates that he was not writing a "psychological" novel in the sense of case history, that he was subordinating the luridness of emotional abnormality to the larger,
parallel purposes of examining social and moral sickness. And it
is significant that he ties the terms "dramatic" and "melodramatic"
not to *Tender Is the Night*, with all its psychiatric materials, but
to *The Great Gatsby*. The scenes, however, in which are hinted
the effects of the social and moral world on Dick are developed
meticulously. In short, what Fitzgerald had learned about plotting
from Hollywood and the slicks he used in setting moral landscapes
in *Tender Is the Night*, not in the lyric "sonnet sequence" language of *The Great Gatsby*. Clearly, the "tour de force" reference
to Gatsby is associated with what Fitzgerald had called "overlapping blankets of prose" and "heightening." Yet, in refraining
from the "lyrical" and the "melodramatic" in *Tender Is the Night*,
Fitzgerald made the novel much more of a "scenario" and less of

[32] April 7, 1934, *ibid.*, p. 363.

a "sonnet" than *The Great Gatsby*. The critical consensus agrees
with Fitzgerald, for most readers judge the dramatic novel, *The
Great Gatsby*, to be the perfect "poem" of a book, while *Tender
Is the Night*, considered more rich, more ambitious, much larger
and more intricate and less perfectly finished, is a complex of nov-
elistic scenes.

Both before and after writing *Tender Is the Night*, Fitzgerald
constantly polarized in his mind the opposing associations that
went into the novel: the weak "female" charm of selfish impulse
versus the charm of discipline and courtesy; American actuality
versus American expectation; wealth and the hard, gross new
world versus the sweet, thin sadness evoked by the death and decay
of an older world irrevocably lost. "Park Avenue girls are hard,
aren't they?" he wrote to Scottie, summing up in "Park Avenue
girls" all the Sibley-Biers qualities on the destructive, "Barbara
Hutton" side of the opposing values. "Usually the daughters of
'up-and-coming' men and, in a way, the inevitable offspring of
that type. It's the 'Yankee push' to its last degree, a sublimation
of the sort of Jay Gould who began by peddling bad buttons to a
county and ended, with the same system of peddler's morals, by
peddling five dollar railroads to a nation."[33] The attitudes Fitzgerald hated were not confined to a class. He despised the gangster-
ish newspaper vendor he created in *Tender Is the Night*, the
American of the lower class, who, with a newspaper cartoon of
wealthy Americans in his pocket, exists only in greedy and pathetic
anticipation of the moment when he too can push into the great
American hog trough of wealth. Fitzgerald had contempt and
loathing for the pretentious hauteur of the ignorant immigrant
whose claim to arrogance was gaudy affluence, and he caricatured
such people in his letters and stories. But the man with the peasant's smoldering hatred of the world he feared and envied always
reserved his deepest, though not his easiest reaction, for the gilded

[33] November 17, 1936, *ibid.*, p. 12.

world he saw to be destructive of any possibility of responsible
goodness:

I shall somehow manage not to appear in a taxi-cab on Thanksgiving
and thus disgrace you before all those "nice" girls [he wrote to Scottie].
Isn't it somewhat old-fashioned to describe girls in expensive backgrounds as "nice?" I will bet two-thirds of the girls at Miss Walker's
school have at least one grandparent that peddled old leather in the
slums of New York, Chicago, or London, and if I thought you were
accepting the standards of the cosmopolitan rich, I would much rather
have you in a southern school, where scholastic standards are not so high
and the word "nice" is not debased to such a ludicrous extent. I have
seen the whole racket, and if there is any more disastrous road than
that from Park Avenue to the Rue de la Paix and back again, I don't
know it.

They are homeless people, ashamed of being American, unable to
master the culture of another country; ashamed, usually, of their husbands, wives, grandparents, and unable to bring up descendents of
whom they could be proud, even if they had the nerve to bear them,
ashamed of each other yet leaning on each other's weakness, a menace
to the social order in which they live—oh, why should I go on? You
know how I feel about such things. If I come up and find you gone
Park Avenue, you will have to explain me away as a Georgia cracker
or a Chicago killer. God help Park Avenue.[34]

The restless and disappointed "Park Avenue" energies of
Baby Warren remained, for Fitzgerald, the sign of the restless
mobility of the new America: "You speak of how good your generation is," he lectured his daughter, "but I think they share with
every generation since the Civil War [which for Fitzgerald was the
real breaking point in American history, culminating in the
emergent "new" America following World War I] in America
the sense of being somehow about to inherit the earth. You've
heard me say before that I think the faces of most American
women over thirty are relief maps of petulant and bewildered

[34] Undated fragment of a letter, *ibid.*, pp. 101–2.

unhappiness." As always, when he speaks of an America that died
with Father Abe and took a dive, a dying fall from a past of young
hope to a world of emergent Amazons, he speaks in the same
breath of the death of a sense of responsibility, of "next things,"
of the old virtues that come from the discipline of hopeful struggle, of "what, for lack of a better phrase, I might call the wise and
tragic sense of life.

"By this I mean the thing that lies behind all great careers,
from Shakespeare's to Abraham Lincoln's, and as far back as there
are books to read—the sense that life is essentially a cheat and its
conditions are those of defeat, and that the redeeming things are
not 'happiness and pleasure' but the deeper satisfactions that come
out of struggle."[35]

There can be no more sense of "the deeper satisfactions that
come out of struggle" for the "Mrs. Oyster" and "S. Flesh" who
inhabit this novel than for the animals and vegetables who inhabit *The Great Gatsby*. In the using and breaking of Dick Diver,
and all he is and stands for, by the world of Warren-Barban-
Buchanan and all they stand for, is Fitzgerald's expression of the
anger, resentment, and smoldering hatred that he poured into
the portrait of Baby and expressed in the letters to Scottie and
Helen Hayes. The attitudes articulated through "the authority
of failure," failure realized in hard fact and emotion beyond all
the premonitory imaginings of Amory Blaine, beyond the failure
of Anthony Patch, beyond the wonderful expectation of "being
somehow about to inherit the earth" that characterized the life
of that poor son of a bitch, Gatsby, are the attitudes turned into
the goodness of art that made *Tender Is the Night* so important
for Fitzgerald. It must have been absolutely inevitable for Fitzgerald to have turned his story into a national and even international biography of Western moralities and wealth and in the

[35] October 5, 1940, *ibid.*, p. 96.

stunningly fitting metaphor of war that permeates the novel to detail the dying fall of Dick Diver's lovely old world as the history of the loss of his own hopeful past.

Even in the flush of triumph that Fitzgerald felt on completing *The Great Gatsby*, even that early he was explicit—if a bit shrill and sweeping—about his repudiation of the hard new generation that inherited the gold-bright world that emerged from the self-sacrificial death of the Dick Diver America. "You are thrilled by New York," he wrote Marya Mannes in October, 1925, "—I doubt you will be after five more years when you are more fully nourished from within. I carry the place around the world in my heart but sometimes I try to shake it off in my dreams. America's greatest promise is that something is going to happen, and after a while you get tired of waiting because nothing happens to people except that they grow old, and nothing happens to American art because America is the story of a moon that never rose," Fitzgerald said, unconsciously, perhaps, plagiarizing from Rosenfeld's review of *The Beautiful and Damned*. He wrote to Scottie about "the majority of pretty girls whose lives in America are lopsided, backward-looking, and wistful."[36] In his letter to Miss Mannes he indicated how much he understood about the empty golden moment that was the subject of his own fiction:

Nor does "the minute itself" ever come to life either, the minute not of unrest and hope but of a glowing peace—such as when the moon rose that night on Gerald and Sara's garden and you said you were happy to be there. No one ever makes things in America with that vast, magnificent, cynical disillusion with which Gerald and Sara make things like their parties. . . .

The young people in America are brilliant with secondhand sophistication inherited from their betters of the war generation who to

36 January 1939, *ibid.*, p. 47.

some extent worked things out for themselves. They are brave, shallow, cynical, impatient, turbulent and empty. I like them not. The "fresh strong river of America!" My God, Marya, where are your eyes . . . ? America is so decadent that its brilliant children are damned almost before they are born . . . . If it is fresh and strong to be unable to endure or tolerate things-as-they-are, to shut your eyes or to distort and lie— then . . . no one has ever misinterpreted the flowers of civilization, the Greek or Gallic ideas, as

Your sincere admirer,
F. Scott Fitzgerald.[37]

The statements in this letter will both date Fitzgerald and introduce him to newer young generations; regardless of the modifications, agreements, or disagreements one would want to make, the important point is that Fitzgerald was no longer echoing a merely fashionable American anti-Americanism. It is always annoying to find (as Fitzgerald found) that the most deeply imagined, bitterly earned criticism of America that permeates so much of the most serious American fiction should be vitiated by the modish posturings of "liberated" people who have only contempt and impatience for the critics of a previous generation. He was still young and glittering when he wrote to Miss Mannes, but he had finished *The Great Gatsby* and was no longer a Younger Generation acolyte of Nathan, Mencken and Co. And by the time he finished *Tender Is the Night*, he was no longer even fighting. In his aging, beaten, tired, dogged courage, he yearned with fatigue for repose in the dead, older America he imagined into a life it never had, and which he saluted as Dick had saluted all his fathers. "Baltimore is warm and pleasant," Fitzgerald wrote his secretary. "I love it more than I thought—it is so rich with memories—it is nice to look up the street and see the statue of my great uncle and to know Poe is buried here and that many ancestors of mine have walked in the old town by the bay. I belong here,

[37] October 1925, *ibid.*, pp. 488–89.

where everything is civilized and gay and rotted and polite. And
I wouldn't mind a bit if in a few years Zelda and I could snuggle
up together under a stone in some old graveyard here. That is
really a happy thought and not melancholy at all."[38] The distance
between the "Lucky Dick" Fitzgerald, who knew that he was to
inherit the earth, and the European, Franz Gregorovius, who
looked out his window at the monuments to the buried past that
defined him in his family ties, was diminished noticeably by the
"tragic sense of life" and the "authority of failure" that had been
such a large part of the "goodness" that went into *Tender Is the
Night*.

All in all, it was the loss of goodness with which Fitzgerald
wished to suffocate his reader. The dying fall with which the book
ends is Fitzgerald's method for summing up the choking nostalgia
for all that's been lost, for spotlighting what the book is all about.
The power of the nostalgia, as ruined Dick leaves his children, his
beach, the world he had made, and disappears into oblivion in
places where nothing ever happens, save for occasional tawdry
and meaningless affairs, is Fitzgerald's way of controlling his reader's reaction to what it is that has fallen, how far it has dived, and
how irrevocably it has died. The nostalgia forces the reader into an
*emotional* judgment that parallels and intensifies the moral judgment. The dying fall, in short, is a technique whereby Fitzgerald
absorbs the reader into an emotional recognition of Dick's life as
the microcosmic center of the world in which that life is exhausted.
Not only is Dick lost, the reader is made to feel, but the possibilities envisioned in the "good gone days" are lost too. The world is
different now, even for you and me. The function of the dying
fall is important, for it is an ultimate hint about choice in the
perennial controversy about whether the first edition or the revised edition is the preferable version of *Tender Is the Night*.

Fitzgerald was conscious of the dying fall as an effect that linger-

[38] To Laura Guthrie, September 23, 1935, *ibid.*, p. 531.

ingly ensnares readers rather than releases them through a burst of
action or emotion or rhetoric. A month after *Tender Is the Night*
was published, Fitzgerald wrote to Hemingway about his sources
for the dying fall.

> To go back to my theme song [Fitzgerald's preference for composite
> borrowings], the second technical point that might be of interest to
> you concerns direct steals from an idea of yours, an idea of Conrad's
> and a few lines out of David-into-Fox-Garnett. The theory back of it
> I got from Conrad's preface to *The Nigger* [*of the Narcissus*], that the
> purpose of a work of fiction is to appeal to the lingering after-effects
> in the reader's mind as differing from, say, the purpose of oratory or
> philosophy which respectively leave people in a fighting or thoughtful
> mood. The second contribution to the burglary was your trying to
> work out some such theory in your troubles with the very end of *A
> Farewell to Arms* [which was very much a dying fall]. I remember that
> your first draft—or at least the first one I saw—gave a sort of old-fash-
> ioned Alger book summary of the future lives of the characters: "The
> priest became a priest under Fascism," etc., and you may remember
> my suggestion to take a burst of eloquence from anywhere in the book
> that you could find it and tag off with that; you were against this idea
> because you felt that the true line of a work of fiction was to take a
> reader up to a high emotional pitch but then let him down or ease him
> off. You gave no aesthetic reason for this—nevertheless you convinced
> me. The third piece of burglary contributing to this symposium was
> my admiration of the dying fall in the aforesaid Garnett's book and I
> imitated it as acurately as it is humanly decent in my own ending of
> *Tender,* telling the reader in the last pages that, after all, this is just
> a casual event, and trying to let *him* come to bat for *me* rather than
> going out to shake his nerves, whoop him up, then leaving him rather
> in a condition of a frustrated woman in bed.[39]

He was firm and clear in his choice of the ending. The month the
book was published he told John Peale Bishop that "There's a
deliberate choice in my avoidance of a dramatic ending—I deliberately did not want it . . . . Without making apologies, I'd

[39] June 1, 1934, *ibid.,* pp. 309–10.

prefer to *fade off* my book, like the last of *The Brothers Karama-zov*, or *Time Regained*, and let the belly carry my story. . . ."[40]

Two years after he published the book, Fitzgerald was still certain about the "belly" rightness of what he had learned from the ending of *A Farewell to Arms* and of the deliberateness with which he applied the lesson to the story of Dick Diver: ". . . when Ernest was writing *Farewell to Arms* he was in doubt about the ending and marketed around to half a dozen people for their advice. I worked like hell on the idea and only succeeded in evolving a philosophy in his mind utterly contrary to everything he thought an ending should be, and [he] later convinced me that he was right and made me end *Tender Is the Night* on a fade-away instead of a staccato."[41] Through all his doubts about the structure of *Tender Is the Night*, Fitzgerald never wavered in his certainty about the rightness of the dying fall as a deliberate intention. In the month he published the book, he was already unhappy about the first part of the novel, already aware that introducing Diver's story through Rosemary's point of view was a false beginning. It is interesting that when he considered the possibility that the beginning was misplaced, he remained sure about the intentions of nostalgia in the dying fall, where all the energies of the action and language are concentrated not on anyone external to Dick, but on Dick himself.

I would like to say in regard to my book [he wrote to Mencken] that there was a deliberate intention in every part of it except the first. The first part, the romantic introduction, was too long and too elaborated largely because of the fact that it had been written over a series of years with varying plans, but everything else in the book conformed to a *definite intention* and if I had to start to write it again tomorrow I would adopt the same plan, irrespective of the fact of whether I had in this case brought it off or not brought it off. That is what most of the critics fail to understand (outside of the fact that they fail to

40 April 2, 1934, *ibid.*, pp. 362–63.
41 To John O'Hara, July 25, 1936, *ibid.*, p. 538.

recognize and identify anything in the book): that the motif of the "dying fall" was absolutely deliberate and did not come from any diminution of vitality but from a definite plan.[42]

That definite plan was to trace the devolution of Dick from his high potential to *homme épuisé,* and to make his vulnerability and decline the center of the novel. It is important to remember that, because Dick's diminishing career, in its relation to the nostalgic function of the dying fall, becomes another hard fact toward decision in the vexed question of choice of editions of the book. In the uncertainty created in Fitzgerald by the arrangement of the first edition of the book, wherein Rosemary's perceptions rather than Dick's are introduced as the center of the novel, Fitzgerald groped toward strengthening Dick. He knew that in all events Dick had to be the center of the novel. A few weeks before publication date of the book (it had already appeared in serial), Fitzgerald told Perkins that

the more I think of it, the more I think that it is absolutely necessary for the unity of the book and the effectiveness of the finale to show Dick in the dignified and responsible aspect toward the world and his neighbors that was implied so strongly in the first half of the book. It is all very well to say that this can be remedied in book publication but it has transpired that at least two dozen important writers and newspaper men are reading the book in the serial and will form their impressions from that. I have made cuts in Section IV [which was merged into Book III of the three part structure the novel was put into in the first edition] —a good bit of the last scene between Dick and Tommy—but . . . if I do not hold these two characters to the end of the book it might as well never have been written. It is legitimate to ruin Dick but it is by no means legitimate to make him an ineffectual. In the proof I am pointing up the fact that his intention dominated all this last part [that Dick deliberately and agonizedly "transferred" Nicole to Tommy in order to effect a final cure] but it is not enough and the foreshortening [cutting from serial to book] without the use of this scene, which was a part of the book structure from the first, does

[42] April 23, 1934, *ibid.,* p. 510.

not contain enough of him for the reader to reconstruct his whole personality as viewed as a unit throughout—and the reason for this is my attempt to tell the last part entirely through Nicole's eyes. I was even going to have her in on the Cannes episode but decided against it because of the necessity of seeing Dick alone.[43]

In a letter to Edmund Wilson, Fitzgerald again paired the dying fall with his preference for the last half of the book, once he had gotten past the problem of switching from Rosemary as the center and of flashing back in time in order to bring the reader up to the moment that Rosemary introduces.

By the way [he wrote], your notion that Dick should have faded out as a shyster alienist was in my original design, but I thought of him, in reconsideration, as an "homme épuisé," not only an "homme manqué."
...I...wish that you, and others, had read the book version rather than the magazine version which in spots was hastily put together. The last half for example has a *much* more polished facade now. Oddly enough several people have felt that the surface of the first chapters was *too* ornate.[44]

The point is that even before Fitzgerald had completed the revisions for publication in book form, the dying fall had focused his attention on the main problems he faced. First, he had to make Dick heroic and noble even though Dick is weak and ruined—the reader must feel lingering in the "belly" the wide significance of the loss that is created in Dick's ruin. Second, Fitzgerald had to do something to the structure of the book that would make Dick not only central but developmentally clear and coherent, standing out alone, so that the reader would be aware of the enormous sacrifice Dick makes in his curing Nicole. There used to be a common opinion among critics that Fitzgerald began to think of changing *Tender Is the Night* only after it was coolly received: he wanted to revise the book in the face of public aloofness in

[43] February 5, 1934, *ibid.*, pp. 240–41.
[44] March 1934, *ibid.*, p. 346.

order to make it a better seller. Of course he did. But the opinion, unmodified, is insupportable as it stands. In actual fact, Fitzgerald worried and fussed about the structure and felt dissatisfied with it long *before* the book was published and reviewed. The revisions of the book and Fitzgerald's letters make it clear that he wished to do something to the structure every time he thought of what he was trying to do with Dick, before there was a critical reaction to set Fitzgerald off. Even four years after book publication, when the novel was being turned into a stage adaptation, Fitzgerald wrote to the playwright, still concerned that Dick be properly understood, still concerned that Dick had not come clear in the book version as it had been published. Writing about the stage characters, Fitzgerald said:

also Tommy seemed to me less integrated [in the play] than he should be. He was Tommy Hitchcock in a way whose whole life is a challenge —who is only interested in realities, his kind—in going into him you've brought him into the boudoir a little—I should be careful of what he says and does unless you can feel the strong fresh-air current in him . . . .

If it has to be cut, the children will probably come out. On the stage they will seem to press, too much for taste, against distasteful events. As if Dick had let them in for it—he is after all a sort of superman, an approximation of the *hero* seen in overcivilized terms—taste is no substitute for vitality but in the book it has to do duty for it. It is one of the points on which he must never show weakness as Siegfried could never show physical fear. I did not manage, I think in retrospect, to give Dick the cohesion I aimed at, but in your dramatic interpretation I beg you to guard me from the exposal of this. I wonder what the hell the first actor who played Hamlet thought of the part? I can hear him say, "The guy's a nut, isn't he?"[45]

Fitzgerald's problem was to show that *as Dick developed* in the Warren's world, he was not a moral representative of it—in fact repudiated it—but paradoxically was weak and vulnerable enough

45 To Mrs. Edwin Jarrett, February 7, 1938, *ibid.*, pp. 566–67.

precisely in his sense of responsibility, his need to serve, to be victimized by it. Fitzgerald wanted to use his own experiences to say what he had said in *Gatsby* about the Buchanan world, and he borrowed, as always, from the world he had shared with Zelda. "Never in her whole life did she have a sense of guilt," Fitzgerald wrote to his daughter, "even when she put other lives in danger—it was always people and circumstances that oppressed her." The trick was to capture nostalgia not for the loss of the irresponsible days of wine and roses, but for the loss of the effectiveness of the romantic expectation, self-sacrificial and heroic in its discipline, in all the old graces and virtues. The belly-felt loss in the dying fall was what Fitzgerald felt in the romantic poets and what he learned from them fully as much as he did from Hemingway or Conrad. As his sense of the dying fall was all tied up with the problem of presenting Dick clearly through a straight-line, cohesive, and coherent picture of Dick's development, so too, therefore, his sense of the dying fall was all tied up with the golden moment—the sad, sad sense in the present of the destruction of the fulfilled future in the loss of the wistful past, where all was hope. A few months after the book was published, Fitzgerald made the associations clear in a letter to Perkins: "What family resemblance there is between we three [himself, Thomas Wolfe, and Ernest Hemingway] is the attempt that crops up in our fiction from time to time to recapture the exact feel of a moment in time and space, exemplified by people rather than things—that is, an attempt at what Wordsworth was trying to do rather than what Keats did with such magnificent ease, an attempt at mature memory of a deep experience."[46] And again, writing to James Boyd he said, ". . . I've had several clippings lately that found qualities in common between your work and mine. I was trying to think what they were, for God knows our subject matter, pasts, etc., have been miles apart, but I think I know—it's a sort of nostalgic sadness

[46] July 30, 1934, *ibid.*, p. 251.

that runs through them. I don't know whether it's because we both read Keats a lot when we were young. . . ."[47] The very title of the book is perfectly clear in the context of what Fitzgerald was trying to do. The man who loved Keats and the "Ode to a Nightingale," which he could "never read through without tears in my eyes,"[48] took a line from the poem which, to him, evoked most richly of all literature the "nostalgic sadness" that comes from a realization of the loss of romantic expectations. *Tender Is the Night* is Fitzgerald's deepest summation of his books, all of which are filled with ghosts of and farewells to a past that has departed and left him forlorn, bereft of the fondest dreams of his fancy. As Keats discovered with his nightingale, Fitzgerald discovered with his dream of the golden moment that the imagination that can create the enormous and deep significance of the desire for the dream in art is overwhelmed by the dissolution of the imaginings in life.

> Forlorn! the very word is like a bell
>     To toll me back from thee to my sole self!
> Adieu! the fancy cannot cheat so well
>     As she is famed to do, deceiving elf.

The irresponsibility that destroys creative imagination and that results in broken decalogues is exactly what Fitzgerald's Keatsian nostalgia—precisely because of what it longs for—repudiates. The novel's themes merge, in this consideration, with Fitzgerald's attempt to retain some "goodness." *Tender Is the Night*, in literary fact, in biographical fact, and in the psychology of Fitzgerald's intentions, is the sign of the morality of art, of Fitzgerald's imagination miraculously preserved within the crack-up of his life. As always, Fitzgerald was feeding his life into a renewal of his literature; but in this book he was also feeding his literature into a renewal of his life. Memory and desire, loss and hope, were the

---

[47] August 1935, *ibid.*, p. 528.
[48] To Scottie, August 3, 1940, *ibid.*, p. 88.

refractors through which Dick's life, as representative of national history, would give Fitzgerald the meaning and uses of his own personal history. The novel as "good" book, and the novel as nostalgic book, in short, are the same. It was the culmination of the long learning process in which Fitzgerald had come to discover that the personalism of art is also social morality.

Even his attitude toward advertising the book is instructive. He had never liked ballyhoo ads, but now he needed money and he was starved for recognition. It is not surprising, when one considers what the book was to him, that he should itch for it to be famous and loved. He had been defending himself for years, even to the sympathetic Maxwell Perkins, against hints that he was washed up, and he knew he was long overdue for a lucky hit that would also be a *succes d'estime*.

I wrote young [he had told Perkins], and I wrote a lot and the pot takes longer to fill up now but the novel, my novel, is a different matter than if I'd hurriedly finished it up a year and a half ago . . . . How much time . . . between *The Genius* and *The* [*sic*] *American Tragedy* . . . ? I think it seems to go by quicker there in America but time put in is eventually time taken out—and whatever this thing of mine is it's certainly not a mediocrity like *The Women of Andros* and *The Forty-Second Parallel*. "He's through" is an easy cry to raise but it's safer for the critics to raise it at the evidence in print than at a long silence.[49]

He was already desperate (Perkins hadn't accused him of anything) when he wrote that letter. And yet, two years later, he still hadn't finished the novel and he was aware that in the public mind he had long since taken a dying fall into failure and oblivion: "At last," he wrote to Perkins, "for the first time in two years and a half I am going to spend five consecutive months on my novel . . . . Am replanning it to include what's good in what I have. . . . Don't

[49] Early May 1930, *ibid.*, pp. 221–22.

tell Ernest or anyone—let them think what they want—you're the only one who's ever consistently felt faith in me anyhow."[50]

Still, it took even *another* two years before *Tender Is the Night* was published. The temptation to do anything, advertise in skywriting, matchbooks, Coke bottlecaps, any way that would recoup his fortune, rebuild his fame, renew his respect, was a great and deep one. Yet, so sure was he of *Tender Is the Night* as a complete testament of "goodness" that he could not bring himself to cheapen it even in advertising. He was still disturbed only by his doubts about the book's structure, not about the book as a redeeming intention in his life. He himself selected nine blurbs for the dust jacket, and all were testimonials to his skill in *The Great Gatsby*, not as the scintillating young personality of a writer, but as the personage of an artist. What he really wanted was endorsement by T. S. Eliot, who had been enthusiastic about *The Great Gatsby* (he had called it the first real advance in American fiction in recent years), by James Joyce, whom Fitzgerald considered the great, classic, living modern master, and by Gertrude Stein, who Fitzgerald thought of as an avant garde beacon in the serious world of modern high art. In every instruction to Scribner's, he made it clear that he was concerned primarily with the honesty and integrity of his book and that it should not be misrepresented, even for increased sales. "I should be careful in saying that it's my first book in seven years, *not to imply that it contains seven years' work*. People would expect too much in bulk and scope.

"This novel, my fourth, completes my story of the boom years. It might be wise to accentuate the fact that it does *not* deal with the depression. [Critics and book buyers were sympathetic to books about "real life" in the hard depression years, not books about the "frivolous" boom years.] *Don't* accentuate that it deals

[50] Mid-January 1932, *ibid.*, p. 226.

with Americans abroad—there's been too much trash under that banner.

"No exclamatory 'At last, the long awaited, etc. . . .' "[51]

Again:

In advertising the book some important points are: Please do not use the phrase "Riviera" or "gay resorts." Not only does it sound like the triviality of which I am so often accused, but also the Riviera has been thoroughly exploited by E. Phillips Oppenheim and a whole generation of writers and its very mention invokes a feeling of un-reality and unsubstantiality. . . . If it could be done, a suggestion that, *after a romantic start, a serious story unfolds* would not be amiss . . . . [Italics mine. Always he was hounded by the continual uneasiness about the book's beginning the way it did.] In general, as you know, I don't approve of great ballyhoo advertisements, even of much quoted praise. The public is very, very, very weary of being sold bogus goods and this inevitably reacts on solider manufactures.[52]

Always the same concern about the clarity of his central intention: "Don't forget my suggestion that the jacket flap should carry an implication that though the book starts in a lyrical way, heavy drama will presently develop."[53]

The implications in Fitzgerald's worries about the nature of the advertising, the function of the book in his own life, and the function of Dick in the novel's life make one thing clear: Fitz-gerald was to be trusted more than his critics in the problem of the clarity of the book's structure. He felt something was wrong while he was writing it, while he was revising it, and after it was published. All the revisions that Matthew Bruccoli details in *The Composition of Tender Is the Night* are lessons in literary evolu-tion. Consciously and unconsciously Fitzgerald was moving stead-ily toward the incremental delineation of Dick as the central

---

[51] To Maxwell Perkins, October 19, 1933, *ibid.*, p. 237.
[52] To Maxwell Perkins, February 5, 1934, *ibid.*, pp. 241–42.
[53] To Maxwell Perkins, January 13, 1934, *ibid.*, p. 239.

character whose meaning he had to clarify in order to make any meaningful moral consolidation out of all the past of his own art and life. What Fitzgerald knew in his bones, and what so many critics have missed in the argument about preferable editions, is that the simple core question is: what arrangement will make Dick consistently central in such a way that the development of his meaning throughout the book will create the deepest belly-sense of loss in the dying fall? There are many kinds of arguments that can be and have been made: arguments about the history of the publication of the novel, about the possibilities of suspense or the loss of suspense, about what Fitzgerald would have had to add or delete if he had lived to complete the revision. But unless conclusions are reached on the basis of the central question of the book's thematic purpose and of Fitzgerald's own relationship to it, all arguments will remain a schoolish skirmish that has little to do with what the book is all about.

Encouraged by his early success, Fitzgerald had had high hopes of moving quickly into the world of the great literary innovators. Fed by the artistic excitements of the twenties, he had thought of the manuscript that was to become *Tender Is the Night* as a charge into greatness at the head of the literary makers and finders. In May of 1925, when he first began to work on the novel, he had written Perkins, "The happiest thought I have is of my new novel—it is really something NEW in form, idea, structure—the model for the age that Joyce and Stein are searching for, that Conrad didn't find."[54] At exactly the same time, he was writing to Mencken that the new novel "will have the most amazing form ever invented."[55] Much later, looking back in what was to be the year of his death, and writing to Perkins about his new book, *The Last Tycoon*, he saw *Tender Is the Night* not as an innovation but

[54] *Letters*, p. 182.
[55] *Ibid.*, p. 481.

as an error in form: ". . . I hope I shan't again make the many
mistakes of *Tender*."[56] For all the central and complex reasons
that he had consistently felt that all "the many mistakes of *Tender*"
grew from the structure, he began to feel his way toward realign-
ing parts of the book in order to sharpen the focus and clarity of
Dick's development. There could be no better arrangement than
beginning at the beginning, at the heights, at the opening of Dick's
life, and carrying that declining life straight through to the dying
fall, so that when Rosemary's point of view took over for a while,
the readers, knowing what Rosemary did not, would intensify in
their bellies the sense of what was happening to Dick, rather than
misplace him. I suspect that Fitzgerald was delayed by *The Great
Gatsby* in finding the simple, chronological structure he was looking for. In that book, he created a belly-sense of the action by
allowing the narrator to discover the meaning of that summer
along with the reader. The reader's knowledge that the narrator
had already lived through the action and had reached moral conclusions about it gave the reader confidence in Carraway, so that
as Carraway's discoveries and the reader's coincided, the mutuality
of experience further identified the reader's moral responses with
those that Carraway had already prepared out of his previous
knowledge. All that Fitzgerald had to do was to have Carraway
disclose affairs in a reproduction of events as he had been involved
in them. I cannot prove that Fitzgerald associated suspenseful disclosure, flashback, intricacies in chronological structure, with
the success of the book as good art, but it is a fact that Fitzgerald
delighted in creating something "radiant," "intricate," and "new"
in *Gatsby* and that he had announced expectations of going further with experiments in form in *Tender Is the Night*. With all the
reasons within him pushing for the creation of something better,
something truly splendid in *Tender*, Fitzgerald must have felt the

---

[56] May 20, 1940, *ibid.*, p. 288.

need for out-Joycing Joyce and out-Steining Stein, but most of all for out-Gatsbying *Gatsby* in his new novel. He had been explicit about feeling that following the line he had begun in *Gatsby* was what he should have done with his life—"without this I am nothing." Perhaps I am on weak ground here, for a critic cannot rest an argument on "feeling" alone; yet I feel certain that in his desire to wow the world, Fitzgerald had serious and perhaps pretentious inclinations to surpass himself (and everybody else) in form when he was writing *Tender*. In any case, the strength of my feeling that memory of *The Great Gatsby* hindered Fitzgerald is hardly my main argument, for whatever delayed Fitzgerald in moving toward the simpler chronology in the revised version of *Tender Is the Night,* the main point is that for years, his doubts and worries and instincts did move him toward the very chronology that he resisted, for whatever reason he did resist.

In later years, as desperately as he wanted *Tender Is the Night* to be reprinted and kept alive, and no matter how afraid he was of jeopardizing his chances by suggesting the additional costs of rearrangement, nevertheless he did so. When he was diffidently negotiating with Bennett Cerf about the possibility of a Modern Library edition of the novel, he could not help but make clear the kind of thing he was after and what it was that had been bothering him about the book all along. "The revision job would take the form, to a large extent, of a certain new alignment of the scenes— without changing their order in any case. Some such line as this:

"That the parts instead of being one, two, and three (they were one, two, three and four in the magazine serial) would include in several cases sudden stops and part headings which would be to some extent explanatory; certain pages would have to be inserted bearing merely headings. Part two, for example, should say in a terse and graceful way that the scene is now back on the Riviera in the fall after these events have taken place, or that this brings us up to where Rosemary first encounters the Divers . . . I have not the plan with me. . . . But I know what printing costs are. It was evolved to have a very minimum of replacement."[57] Fitzgerald's diffidence had not been groundless. Whatever printing costs meant in the midst of the depression, Cerf was not willing to take the chance and nothing ever came of the negotiations.

But Fitzgerald persisted, increasingly sure of his insight into the necessary structural rearrangement of the book. The very logic of his life in his dying fall led him to the true logic of the structure, and, in what was to become an oft-quoted letter, he explicitly identified what had always bothered him as "errors" and "mistakes" in the novel. When, two years after his unsuccessful correspondence with Cerf, he wrote to Perkins, with whom he could be much more frank and open, he was bolder about stating what he really wanted to do. Urging a new edition of the novel, he summed up what all his other comments had been leading to over the years.

But I am especially concerned about *Tender* [he wrote] —that book is not dead. The *depth* of its appeal exists—I meet people constantly who have the same exclusive attachment to it as others had to *Gatsby* and *Paradise*, people who identified themselves with Dick Diver. Its great fault is that the *true* beginning—the young psychiatrist in Switzerland—is tucked away in the middle of the book. If pages 151–212 were taken from their present place and put at the start, the improvement in appeal would be enormous. In fact the mistake was noted and suggested by a dozen reviewers. To shape up the ends of that change would, of course, require changes in half a dozen other pages.[58]

This letter has been a constant embarrassment to critics who argue against the revised version. Antirevisionists explain it away in various ways, but none convincingly.

There are two main headings under which all the antirevisionist arguments can be subsumed. One is the kind most carefully ad-

[57] August 13, 1936, *ibid.*, p. 540.
[58] December 24, 1938, *ibid.*, p. 281.

vanced by Matthew Bruccoli, and it is an argument on the basis of evidence:

The alleged confusion in Fitzgerald's treatment of Dick Diver [says Bruccoli] is frequently connected with the alleged confusion in the structure of *Tender Is the Night* . . . I . . . defend . . . Fitzgerald's original structure. Again the evidence is mainly negative: there is no other discarded structure, and there is no indication that Fitzgerald had any doubts about his narrative plan while he was writing the novel. But there is also the author's summary of Book III in which he flatly states that the withdrawal of Dick Diver from the center of the narrative, which has puzzled some critics, was the intended effect: "All Dick's stories such as are *absolutely necessary* . . . must be told without putting in his reactions or feelings. From now on he is mystery man, at least to Nicole with her guessing at the mystery."[59]

The argument about lack of a discarded, alternative structure is negative evidence indeed. In fact, if there *had* been an alternative structure that had been discarded in favor of the first-edition structure, that *then* would be evidence that despite Fitzgerald's doubts about the book, he had nevertheless insisted on retaining the *un*revised structure. But, if the facts of evidence are at issue, the case is that Fitzgerald always *had* had doubts, and had defined those doubts with increasing explicitness through time, and that he *did* in fact create an alternative structure with which he wished to replace the first edition, but was never given a chance. The explicitness is clear not only in the letter about "the true beginning," but in the ineluctable fact, after all, that up until he died, Fitzgerald was in actuality engaged in revising the book into a new structure. He left full and specific details as far as he went before he died. He left notes about further revisions he intended to make had he lived to complete his way through the entire novel. That is, Mr. Bruccoli's "negative evidence" about a nonexistent alternative structure before the novel was published is not negative evi-

---

59 Bruccoli, *The Composition of Tender Is the Night*, p. 14.

dence but simply no evidence at all. Of anything. If one is really talking about *evidence*, one can only say this: the first-edition structure of the novel was what Fitzgerald wanted when he first published it in book form, but that he *did* have some doubts about it even then. As his doubts grew more precise and strong through time, he *did* create an alternative structure in his own revision of the book, and he left at least that evidence that he did *not* prefer the first-edition structure.

Furthermore, the evidence that does exist suggests that Fitzgerald had real doubts about how the parts of the book fit one another even prior to the publication of the first edition. When he was working with Perkins on the revision of the serial form, he wrote, two months before the book was published, "I find that revising in this case is pulling up the weakest section of the book and then the next weakest, etc. First Section III was the weakest and Section IV the strongest, so I bucked up III; then IV was the weakest and is still, but when I have fixed that Section I will be the weakest. The section that has held up best is Section II."[60] It should be noted that Section I, which displeased Fitzgerald the most, is the key to the difference between the first edition and the revision, for that section, "Rosemary's Angle," is what he wanted to move farther back into the book in order to begin with Dick Diver. As his instructions about advertising make clear (tell prospective buyers that the real drama begins once they are through the romantic, "lyrical" beginning), he remained uneasy about the arrangement of parts as the book was going to press.

The argument about Dick's "disappearance" from the book is a hole-in-the-corner business at best, for the only section in which Dick is not the center is Section I of the first edition, whose placement the antirevisionists *defend*. Neither in Sections II, III, or IV of the serial, nor in Sections II or III of the first edition is there ever a "withdrawal of Dick Diver from the center of the narra-

[60] To Maxwell Perkins, February 5, 1934, *Letters*, p. 242.

tive" as Mr. Bruccoli characterizes it. Fitzgerald does not have Dick tell the reader what he is feeling; Fitzgerald only shows Dick's reactions without ever removing Dick from the center of the reader's vision. Dick is "withdrawn" from the narrative, and for obvious reasons, only during the scene of the liaison between Nicole and Tommy. To say that Fitzgerald does not give the reader statements by Dick of what Dick is thinking and feeling is hardly the same as saying that Dick is withdrawn from the center of the narrative. And Fitzgerald himself never said that it was his purpose to withdraw Dick: he is quite clear that what he wants to do is to make Dick's plans a mystery to Nicole, for her to guess at ("from now on he is mystery man, at least to Nicole with her guessing at the mystery"), and that he wants to portray Dick through his actions rather than through direct statement. When one considers Fitzgerald's determination to create the belly-sense of the dying fall, Fitzgerald's plans are wholly appropriate, nice, deft. By forcing the reader to assume what Dick must be going through *while presenting Dick centrally at every moment except for the Tommy-Nicole episode,* Fitzgerald creates the same kind of sympathetic merger of reader and Dick that he did in the coalescence of Carraway, Gatsby, and the reader. It seems clear beyond argument that the book demands that the reader sympathize strongly with Dick even when—perhaps especially when—as Dick deteriorates, he becomes increasingly unsympathetic and nasty to the people he has spent his life serving. Again, Fitzgerald's own instincts about the relationship between the structure and what the book is all about remain most trustworthy, and he was right in wanting to tear the book apart and reassemble it. It is understandable, and probably just, that critics should be more timid than Fitzgerald since Fitzgerald is not here to complete the surgery himself. But the argument about revision is not a matter of scholarly unimpeachability; it is a matter of the very core and life of the novel. The problem of Dick as "mystery man" is one of showing the extent to which Dick is alone, isolated, no longer "received"—the extent to which Dick is withdrawn not from the center of the novel but from the center of the world he had tried to serve and save. The best evidence for that is not only Dick's relations with Nicole as he effects the final transference to Tommy, but also the powerful and explicit interview with Mary North Minghetti during those stifling and moving moments when Dick bids farewell to Gausse's beach and the world it has become.

Bruccoli is quite right when he says that it "is not easy to comprehend the basis of the complaints about the narrative difficulty of *Tender Is the Night*, which involves one flashback sequence and three obvious shifts in point of view." The first edition is not hard to follow at all. The revision was prompted not by Fitzgerald's sense of obscure narrative thread, but of improperly woven narrative thread. Always one must come back to the book itself, what it is about, what Fitzgerald wanted to do with it. In those terms, the problem, again and again, is one of developing Dick centrally, in a straight-line dive from transcendent potential to dying fall so that the fall itself, in relation to the career that precedes it, creates a heavy, sinking belly-sense of all the possible goodness that has disappeared into nothing and has been lost, lost, lost. Bruccoli himself is quite aware that "Fitzgerald's later decision to revise the structure of the novel was not prompted by the desire to circumvent the possible confusion caused by the flashback. The removal of the flashback was the result of Fitzgerald's desire to emphasize the documentation of Dick's decline. . . ."[61]

The second major line of argument against the revised edition stems from Arthur Mizener's brilliant study, *The Far Side of Paradise*. Like Bruccoli, Mizener recognizes the evidence that supports a revised edition, but then concludes that the first edition is preferable because if the story were unfolded in straight chronological development, suspense would be lost. The question, of

[61] Bruccoli, *The Composition of Tender Is the Night*, pp. 7–8.

course, is the nature and purpose of the suspense. Put most simply, the suspense boils down to, what *did* Violet McKisco see in the bathroom of the Villa Diana? That is unfairly put, but it is accurate, for the nature of the suspense revolves around disclosure of Devereux Warren's incestuous relation with Nicole and around disclosure of the details of emotionally abnormal behavior—which, as I have tried to indicate, are not the real center of Fitzgerald's "philosophical, now called psychological" novel. And when one considers the purpose of suspense, one must consider the purpose of the novel. Is it a suspense novel or is it something else? Again, I have phrased the question with deliberate unfairness—but, I think, still with accuracy, nonetheless—in order to make perfectly clear what the nature of the critical choice is. Suppose one were to say that the nature of the details suspensefully disclosed concerned the substance of Dick's disintegrating world rather than psychiatric details. Then one is confronted with a choice between suspense in that disclosure and "the desire to emphasize the documentation of Dick's decline." For Fitzgerald the choice was clearly the latter. And for the reader that must be the choice, too, if one considers the whole point of the book. If suspense were preferred in this novel, it would have to be preferred for its own sake, and could be preferred only if the book were tedious in the revised edition. No one has argued that, and no one sanely could, for the book moves swiftly in either version. Whatever is lost in "suspense"— and suspense for its own sake is quite beside the point in this novel—in abandoning the first edition is gained in exactly what Fitzgerald wanted to achieve in the revision: the central, step-by-step disintegration of Dick, so that the whole sweep of his life is the documentation of excruciating personal, national, human loss.[62]

---

[62] The task that remains is editorial. Someone—Mr. Bruccoli would be a good choice—should publish a painstakingly careful, complete, and definitive edition of the revised version that was so usefully begun by Malcolm Cowley in the text he published, the text used for this analysis of the novel.

In the revised version, Dick does indeed begin at the top of his
form in Fitzgerald's brilliant weaving of the theme of American
identity. He is contrasted to a Europe "washed . . . by the waves of
thunder around Gorizia and . . . the cataracts along the Somme
and the Aisne," as he studies in a Switzerland filled with either
"sick" or "intriguing strangers." The young American student,
the new man with unlimited possibility ahead of him, he learns all
there is to know about the psychology of the day and, dewy and
strong in his confident youth, writes pamphlets in a Vienna that
"even then . . . was old with death." Wrapped in a floor rug, burning memorized textbooks and notes for warmth, the young newcomer "had no idea that he was charming, that the affection he
gave and inspired was anything unusual among healthy people."
The early beginnings, when all is health (Dick "swam in the winter Danube"), youth (he was twenty-five years old in Vienna),
and promise ("I've only got one [plan] . . . and that's to be a good
psychologist—maybe to be the greatest one that ever lived"), is
the period of illusion, "the illusions of a nation, the lies of
generations of frontier mothers who had to croon falsely that
there were no wolves outside the cabin door" (p. 5). That gold-
en morning moment in the present, when one foresees a fulfilled future as the culmination of the wistful, hopeful past, is
where the envisioned attainment exists and where the creative
energies of expectation are strongest. "Most of us have a favorite,
a heroic period in our lives and that was Dick Diver's" (p. 4).

Beginning with "the illusions of eternal strength and health,"
"the illusions of a nation," American Dick is warned by a Ruman-
ian intellectual that "you're not a romantic philosopher—you're
a scientist. Memory, force, character—especially good sense. That's
going to be your trouble—judgment about yourself" (p. 5). Aware
of his illusions as the source of his hopeful strength, Dick is also

aware of his romantic strength as "American." He hopes for
"faint" destruction, for "a little misfortune," feeling too invulnerable in the Lucky-Dick excitement of total expectation. "He
mocked at his reasoning, calling it specious and 'American'—his
criterion of uncerebral phrase-making was that it was American.
He knew, though, that the price of his intactness was incompleteness" (p. 5). Dick has two strikes against him from the start, and
they are the strikes pitched up by his very advantages: his romantic, excited, American creative hopefulness and his trained,
ordered intelligence. Indeed, he meets Nicole with "fewer Achilles' heels than would be required to equip a centipede, but with
plenty." That is, his romantic Americanness, his sense of indestruc-
tibility (Franz remarks on Dick's "unaging American face") allows
him to consider something as crazy as marrying a patient whose
life might possibly be his one, continuing case. His eager, impulsive responses to challenge, to the possibility of redeeming,
saving, effecting a total cure, serving, are all part of his romantic,
American illusions. What provides his young strength also destroys
him. At the same time, strike two, he has the intelligence to realize
that those illusions require destructive experience for a full selfhood. Nicole, "sweet poison," fits both needs. He falls in love with
the illusions that betray and destroy him. Nicole is the breath of
decay and the promise of destruction, and she is also the essence
of Dick's American illusions. "Now there was this scarcely saved
waif of disaster bringing him the essence of a continent"; she and
Dick played her phonograph and "they were in America now;
even Franz with his conception of Dick as an irresistible Lothario
would never have guessed that they had gone so far away. They
were so sorry, dear; they went down to meet each other in a taxi,
honey; they had preferences in smiles and had met in Hindustan,
and shortly afterward they must have quarrelled, for nobody knew
and nobody seemed to care—yet finally one of them had gone and
left the other crying, only to feel blue, to feel sad" (p. 26). The

American songs recall the emotional associations of transcendent, expectant youth with the rinky-tink Americanness of the home of our youth, and bring to American Dick in Europe the flavor of all his expectations. "The thin tunes, *holding lost times and future hopes in liaison*, twisted upon the Swiss night" (p. 26, italics mine). Later, Dick was to know that his need to serve and be loved, a vain need that came from the dying America he represented, was his own essential Americanness that had found in Nicole exactly the fascination to which, Gatsby-like, he responded. When called to help Mary Minghetti and Lady Caroline Sibley-Biers out of their "prank," he sees the parallel between his aiding them and devoting his life to Nicole: "He would have to fix this thing that he didn't care a damn about, because it had early become a habit to be loved, perhaps from the moment when he had realized that he was the last hope of a decaying clan. On an almost parallel occasion, back in Dohmler's clinic on the Zürichsee, realizing this power, he had made his choice, chosen Ophelia, chosen the sweet poison and drunk it. Wanting above all to be brave and kind, he had wanted, even more than that, to be loved. So it had been. So it would ever be" (p. 321).

In the revised version Fitzgerald begins Dick's "moment," at his topmost heights in his creative-destructive heritage of Americanness. He introduces Dick at his moment of newness, inheriting the world. If there are any similarities between fresh, new America and tired, old Europe, it is where Europe still seems to promise the infinite: "Zurich was not unlike an American city," and when Dick realizes why, he sees it is because Zurich does not have the French topography's sense of the "finite," but rather leads the eye upward so that "life was a perpendicular starting off to a postcard heaven" (p. 7). Yet even Zurich is not a place of romantic sweep and total expectation, but a place of the infinite patience and precision of toymakers—a value that Dick, as scientist, does "not underestimate." Salzburg makes Dick feel "the superimposed quality of a bought and borrowed century of music." Franz, "the third of the Gregoroviuses," is associated with old history: "his grandfather had instructed Kraepelin when psychiatry was just emerging from the darkness of all time," and "the original genius of the family had grown a little tired." If Dick hoped to be the greatest psychologist who ever lived, "Franz would without doubt become a fine clinician" (p. 7). The difference between the vision catapulted into the future by a past of the most transcendent romantic illusions and the vision diffidently groping for the future out of a restrictively overwhelming past—the difference between the Emersonian, "liberated" American and the European aware of history—is made clear in Franz's response to Dick's assertion that he wishes to be the greatest psychologist that ever lived.

Franz laughed pleasantly, but he saw that this time Dick wasn't joking.
"That's very good—and very American," he said. "It's more difficult for us." He got up and went to the French window. "I stand here and I see Zurich—there is the steeple of the Gross-Münster. In its vault my grandfather is buried. Across the bridge from it lies my ancestor Lavater, who would not be buried in any church. Nearby is the statue of another ancestor, Heinrich Pestalozzi, and one of Doctor Alfred Escher. And over everything there is always Zwingli—I am continually confronted with a pantheon of heroes" (p. 22).

Dick's response is sympathetic, but he maintains his American point of view, and in his joking reply continues to associate newness and possibility with the power of America. Emerson, in his acute and essential Americanness, had written, "Our age is retrospective. It builds the sepulchres of the fathers .... The foregoing generations beheld God and nature face to face; we through their eyes. Why should we also not enjoy an original relation to the universe? Why should not we have [our own world] . . . of insight and not of tradition . . . not the history of theirs?. . . why should we grope among the dry bones of the past . . . ? There are new

lands, new men, new thoughts. Let us demand our own works
and laws and worship." So Dick replies, "Everything's just starting
over," and then continues, "I draw military pay all the rest of
the year if I only attend lectures at the university. How's that
for a government on the grand scale that knows its future great
men?" (p. 22).

Franz abandons their old scheme of a clinic for billionaires in
New York as "students' talk," but Dick "felt vaguely oppressed"
by his visit to Franz's world, "not by the atmosphere of modest
retrenchment, nor by Frau Gregorovius, who might have been
prophesied, but by the sudden contracting of horizon, to which
Franz seemed so reconciled. For him the boundaries of asceticism
were differently marked—he [Dick] could see it as a means to an
end, even as a carrying on with a glory it would itself supply, but
it was hard to think of deliberately cutting life down to the scale
of an inherited suit. The domestic gestures of Franz and his wife
as they turned in a cramped space lacked grace and adventure. The
post-war months in France, and the lavish liquidations taking
place under the aegis of American splendor, had affected Dick's
outlook" (pp. 22–23).

But like the American Nicole, the heritage of America has already been corrupted in its very lavishness and splendor. Fitzgerald suggests another aspect of the meaning of America at the
same time he presents, through young Lucky Dick, the creative
vision of its expectant hopefulness. Switzerland, for instance, is
presented as a bourgeois nation of "diamond salesmen and commercial travellers," assuring "the Swiss heart" only through "withered" paper posters of "the Swiss defending their frontiers in
1914" that "it had shared the contagious glory of those days" (p.
3). America is immediately presented as "sister republic" to that
nation, a sister that merely "bungled its way into the war" (p. 3).
If there was any similarity between Europe and the America of
lavish promise, the similarity existed only where Europe offered

occasionally infinite prospects. But the similarity betwen Europe
and the emergent, new America exists where Europe is characterized by Switzerland's commercialism and sentimentalization of
what was once deep feeling. It was Dick's American uniform that
had first attracted Nicole to him (she had never seen one before),
but when that attracted American "essence of a continent" writes
letters, the surface, beneath which the "helpless caesuras" and
"darker rhythms" lurked, are foreshadowings of the destructive
sentimentality of *Daddy's Girl:* "it was easy to recognize the tone—
from *Daddy-Long-Legs* and *Molly Make-Believe,* sprightly and
sentimental epistolary collections enjoying a vogue in the States"
(p. 10). The madness ends resemblance there, but in the context
of what will be introduced with Rosemary and Baby, it is fitting
that the national vogue, in its titles, should have a relation to the
make-believe that is a consequence of the reality of daddy-long-
legs. That is, because the revision allows Fitzgerald to begin at
once with his intricate cross-associations and counter-meanings in
his presentation of America, the implications of the Rosemary section, when it does appear, take on added richness *because* of what
is already known, and if the implications become more visible
at the cost of lost "suspense," they become more meaningful,
complex, and profound. So, if Dick is The American, so too
at one and the same time is Devereux Warren, and the other
America, the hopeful idea of America that Dick represents in his
heritage, is distinguished from the emergent America, the historical actuality increasingly indistinguishable from Europe, that Warren represents in his heritage. Warren, in *his* youth and wealth,
"was a strikingly handsome man looking less than forty. He was
a fine American type in every way, tall, broad, well-made . . ." (p.
15). The "fine American type," beneath its appearances, has a
crook's reality of horse-trading, cattle-stealing, and the stockyards.
The vast size and wealth of America is not immune to corruption
and disease. Dr. Dohmler had once thought of settling in Chicago,

but when "he had thought of what he considered his own thin knowledge spread over that whole area, over all those wheat fields, those endless prairies, he had decided against it. But he had read about Chicago in those days, about the great feudal families of Armour, Palmer, Field, Crane, Warren, Swift, and McCormick and many others, and since that time not a few patients had come to him from that stratum of Chicago and New York." Appropriately, at the moment that Warren discloses that he was able to get a United States cruiser to run the submarine blockade and bring his daughter to Switzerland, this fine American type adds, "that as they say: money is no object" (p. 17). Immediately, American wealth is associated not only with corruption of the beautiful young thing, the Diver-Gatsby "essence of a continent," in the incest visited upon Nicole, but also with its basic power and irresponsibility. Warren prepares his Baby in his every disclaimer of cleaning up messes and buying doctors to do so. He is about to run away from his responsibility to Nicole, back to America. When Dohmler insists that he must come to the clinic, Warren replies, "But look here, Doctor, that's just what you're for." When the swinishness of Warren's impulsive irresponsibilities is exposed, Dohmler makes a gesture that associates this "fine American type" with the cattle and pig warrens of the stockyards.

"As the story concluded Dohmler sat back in the focal armchair of the middle class and said to himself sharply, 'Peasant!' . . . Then he said:

" 'I would like for you to go to a hotel in Zurich and spend the night and come see me in the morning.'

" 'And then what?'

"Doctor Dohmler spread his hands wide enough to carry a young pig.

" 'Chicago,' he suggested" (p. 19).

In a rising obbligato, Fitzgerald associates the new America that emerges from the war with international crass wealth, intense

motion, and swinish usages. The war is scarcely over and Europe
is a "mound of debris," but the greedy little merchants of the
"sister republic" in Berne and Lausanne "eagerly asked if there
would be Americans this year— 'By August, if not in June?' " (p.
39). Even Rosemary and Mrs. Speers are related to imperial wealth
in their Americanness: "After lunch they were both overwhelmed
by the sudden flatness that comes over American travellers in quiet
foreign places. No stimuli worked upon them . . . and missing the
clamor of Empire they felt that life was not continuing here" (p.
69). Fitzgerald uses every possible characterization at his disposal,
even distinguishing between the haughty, impersonal business
rush of American trains and the organic quality of French trains:
"Unlike American trains that were absorbed in an intense destiny
of their own and scornful of people on another world less swift
and breathless, this train was part of the country through which it
passed" (p. 70). When Dick speaks of Mrs. Speers's "other America"
qualities, he insists that "she has a sort of wisdom that's rare in
America" (p. 94). When Barban wants another shot at McKisco,
he insists on a world where the unreal miracles of *Daddy's Girl*
do not prevail: " 'The distance was ridiculous,' he said. 'I'm not
accustomed to such farces—your man must remember he's not now
in America' " (p. 108). Dick bets that "no American men had any
repose" (p. 110), and the nervous, goalless wealth of American
flux and energy bear him out. He wins his bet. A party he or-
ganizes "was overwhelmingly American and sometimes scarcely
American at all," but when its American features are specified,
the details are those of the speed of social motion: "The trio of
women at the table were representative of the enormous flux of
American life. Nicole was the granddaughter of a self-made American capitalist and the granddaughter of a count of the house of
Lippe-Weissenfeld. Mary North was the daughter of a journeyman
paper-hanger and a descendent of President Tyler. Rosemary was
from the middle of the middle class, catapulted by her mother to

the uncharted heights of Hollywood" (p. 111). When Fitzgerald identifies the hostess in "The Frankenstein" of an ultra-modern apartment that Dick and Rosemary visit, he identifies her as "another tall rich American girl, promenading insouciantly upon the national prosperity." The guests are either vicious bitches— American—or distasteful, pathetic girls—American—desperately on the make to bigger and brighter contacts (pp. 134–35). All the other rich Americans promenading insouciantly upon the national prosperity are no better in their irresponsibility.

Nearby some Americans were saying good-bye in voices that mimicked the cadence of water running into a large old bathtub. Standing in the station, with Paris in back of them, it seemed as if they were vicariously leaning a little over the ocean, already undergoing a sea-change, a shifting about of atoms to form the essential molecule of a new people.
So the well-to-do Americans poured through the station onto the platforms with frank new faces, intelligent, considerate, thoughtless, thought-for (p. 145).

All that is potentially good in those faces is cancelled by the mindlessness, unreality, and irresponsibility of a world made by "a new people" that wanted only the cardboard showbiz of *Daddy's Girl*. Actors "were risen to a position of prominence in a nation that for a decade had wanted only to be entertained" (p. 231). The girls that daddies "bring out" in such a world are characterized in Dick's professional visit to "an American girl of fifteen who had been brought up on the basis that childhood was intended to be all fun—his visit was provoked by the fact that she had just hacked off all her hair with nail scissors" (p. 202). The big American wealth-babies had always been prefigured in Fitzgerald's imagination, in his early heuristic depictions of his hot cats and golden girls, as he saw retrospectively in "Early Success":

The uncertainties of 1919 were over—there seemed little doubt about what was going to happen—America was going on the greatest, gaudiest spree in history and there was going to be plenty to tell about it. The whole golden boom was in the air—its splendid generosities, its outrageous corruptions and the tortuous death struggle of the old America in prohibition. All the stories that came into my head had a touch of disaster in them—the lovely young creatures in my novels went to ruin, the diamond mountains of my stories blew up, my millionaires were as beautiful and damned as Thomas Hardy's peasants. In life these things hadn't happened yet, but I was pretty sure living wasn't the reckless, careless business these people thought. . . ."[63]

The outrageous corruptions that the wealth comes from and results in are part of the golden boom the wealth could produce in its splendid generosities—the crass wealth which is all, finally, America comes to mean to the Europeans, and for good reason. When European Franz comes to Dick to propose that they open a clinic together, the great question he leads up to is, will he be able to get in on all that swell American corruption? "Franz threw up his chin, his eyebrows, the transient wrinkles of his forehead, his hands, his elbows, his shoulders; he strained up the muscles of his legs, so that the cloth of his trousers bulged, pushed up his heart into his throat and his voice into the roof of his mouth.

"There we have it! Money!" he bewailed. "I have little money. The price in American money is two hundred thousand dollars. The innovation—ary—" he tasted the coinage doubtfully "—steps that you will agree are necessary will cost twenty thousand dollars American. But the clinic is a gold mine—I tell you, I have seen the books. For an investment of two hundred and twenty thousand dollars we have assured income of—"
Baby's curiosity was such that Dick brought her into the conversation.
"In your experience, Baby," he demanded, "have you found that when a European wants to see an American *very* pressingly it is invariably something concerned with money?"
"What is it?" she asked innocently.

63 *The Crack-Up* (New York, 1956), p. 87.

"This young Privat-dozent thinks that he and I ought to launch into big business and try to attract nervous breakdowns from America" (p. 191).

When Baby, who financially is very, very responsible, advises that Dick go ahead, she does so in the hard-headed moral irresponsibility of the assurance that someone else would clean up the mess of Nicole. "Baby was thinking that if Nicole lived beside a clinic she would always feel quite safe about her." Franz, in his request, simply looks to what America shows. Imagining what the Psychiatric Congress will be like, Dick envisions it all. There will be the American announcing the removal of teeth or tonsils as a panacea for schizophrenia, and the Europeans, out of respect for American wealth and power, will only half deride the quack. There will be dozens of hangdog, greedy, and mendacious American psychiatrists who attend only to strengthen their reputations vicariously in order to be better able to cash in on the lucrative criminal practice. The superior European training, however, would tell; but just as the Europeans would be ready to assert their professional superiority, the Americans would announce their enormous gifts and vast endowments, their huge new facilities and wealthy schools, "and in the presence of the figures the Europeans would blanch and walk timidly" (p. 211).

Baby's experience with the Ambassador and the Consul from America, pink cold cream and all, is one more telling sequence, as is Kaethe's and Franz's argument about Dick, an argument in which Franz shouts, "Hold your tongue—that kind of talk can hurt me professionally, since we owe this clinic to Nicole's money . . . ."

"Kaethe realized that her outburst had been ill-advised, but Franz's last remark reminded her that other Americans had money, and a week later she put her dislike of Nicole into new words" (p. 258). Also damning is the "insistent American, of sinister aspect, vending copies of the *Herald* and of the *Times* fresh from New

York . . . . He brought a gray clipping from his purse—it cartooned millions of Americans pouring from liners with bags of gold. 'You think I'm not going to get part of that? Well I am' " (p. 328).

But perhaps the crescendo of the motif and of Fitzgerald's skill in handling it is reached in the hotel scene when Tommy and Nicole first bed together. The fornication that announces Nicole's "liberation" from Dick and all he stands for is accompanied by increasingly insistent references to America in images and incidents that are associated not with the idea, the metaphor of America that is Dick's world, but with the gross world of force and power that emerges from the death of the young promise. When Tommy and Nicole arrive at the hotel, "at the desk an American was arguing interminably with the clerk about the rate of exchange" (p. 312). Outside the hotel, a counterpointing noise punctuates the noises of Nicole's emergence into the hot new world; the sounds of accompaniment are American.

Tommy peered cautiously from the balcony and reported:
"All I can see is two women on the balcony below this. They're talking about weather and tipping back and forth in American rocking-chairs."
"Making all that noise?"
"The noise is coming from somewhere below them. Listen."
          *"Oh, way down South in the land of cotton*
          *Hotels bum and business rotten*
          *Look away—"*
"It's Americans" (p. 313).

The America insinuated into the scene is both the America of brute Buchanan-Warren power and the pretentious hypocrisy and philistine gentility that tries to mask the basic facts. Tommy, at least, is a man of few but basic facts. At the moment that he tells Nicole that all his old Languedoc peasant remedies will take care of white crook's eyes, she responds, "Kiss me on the lips, Tommy."

" 'That's so American,' he said, kissing her nevertheless. 'When I was in America last there were girls who would tear you apart with their lips, tear themselves too, until their faces were scarlet with the blood around the lips all brought out in a patch—but nothing further' " (p. 314). The girls are like the two English ladies in their American rocking chairs, pretending to ignore the raw fact of the American navy and the brawling sailors and the sailors' whores. "They're here on an economical holiday, and all the American navy and all the whores in Europe couldn't spoil it' " (p. 315). In perfect union with the relationship between the motifs of sexual identity, warfare, and America, the sounds of warfare, of "two American sailors fighting and a lot more cheering them on," become an external rhythm that is an obbligato for the rhythm in the room where the new "doctor," Barban, administers his Languedoc peasant remedies to Nicole. The navy that Warren commissioned ("Hit him where it hurts!") to bring his daughter to Europe ("Yah-h-h!") to bring her out of her illness ("Hey, what I tell you get inside that right!") is in attendance as she finally emerges from it with a new, hard, fighting man ("Come on, Dulschmit, you son!"). The emergent Amazon ("Yaa-Yaa!") takes her place in the regnant world that commands United States cruisers ("*YA-YEH-YAH!*"), and the sounds of her scene of triumph are the sounds of the instruments of warfare: "then a sound split the air outside: Cr-ACK—BOOM-M-m-*m*! It was the battleship sounding a recall" (p. 315). The end of the "orgastic future," the noises of the departing sailors, are a farewell in a new America, not the farewell to all his fathers that Dick had made. The sounds of this world are like the sounds that cracked the narrow air of the station platform when Maria Wallis shot her man through his identification card, the sounds of energy, turmoil, confusion, the gross noises of violent action and of money whose coda is reached in a Nicole-Daisy voice stripped naked to the actuality that underlies the glittering, beautiful appearances of the golden girl, the tones of the whore:

Now, down below their window, it was pandemonium indeed—for the boat was moving to shores as yet unannounced. Waiters called for accounts and demanded settlements in impassioned voices; there were oaths and denials, the tossing of bills too large and change too small; passouts were assisted to the boats, and the voices of the naval police chopped with quick commands through all voices. There were cries, tears, shrieks, promises, as the first launch shoved off and the women crowded forward on the wharf, screaming and waving.

Tommy saw a girl rush out upon the balcony below waving a napkin, and before he could see whether or not the rocking Englishwomen gave in at last and acknowledged her presence, there was a knock at their own door. Outside, excited female voices made them agree to unlock it, disclosing two girls, young, thin, and barbaric, unfound rather than lost, in the hall. One of them wept chokingly.

"Kwee wave off your porch?" implored the other in passionate American. "Kwee please? Wave at the boy friends? Kwee, please. The other rooms is all locked."

"With pleasure," Tommy said.

The girls rushed out on the balcony and presently their voices struck a loud treble over the din.

"By, Charlie! Charlie, look *up!*"

"Send a wire gen'al alivery Nice!"

"Charlie! He don't see me."

And then, at the moment that Fitzgerald has made clear the parallel between Nicole and Tommy inside the room and the sailors and whores outside, has made clear that the difference is not one in moral identity but merely in the kinds of noises that are made, in appearances only, he makes explicit in one pure stroke what the national heritage of the Fathers that are Cody, Carraway's grand-uncle, Buchanan, Demaine, Daddy Warren long-legs has come to be: "One of the girls hoisted her skirt suddenly, pulled and ripped at her pink step-ins, and tore them to a sizable flag; then, screaming 'Ben! Ben! she waved it wildly. As

Tommy and Nicole left the room it still fluttered against the blue sky. Oh, say can you see the tender color of remembered flesh?—while at the stern of the battleship rose in rivalry the Star Spangled Banner" (pp. 315–16).

So much for the promise of Grant in Galena, of Father Abraham, of Emerson and the salvation of the world, of that gorgeous, golden land of the republic rolling on westward there, under the night. Oh land that I love. Except for Twain and Whitman, no American writer has had so sadly, with such fascination, repudiation, and longing, such an intense love affair with his country, and no writer has calibrated the affair as delicately as did Fitzgerald. The love affair is paralleled in his affair with Zelda, which again is paralleled in Dick's affair with Nicole fully as much as in Gatsby's affair with Daisy. Nicole is America to Dick's American as Daisy is to Gatsby's, and the transcendental, expectant devotion ending in whorish betrayal is the same in both stories. At the beginning of the novel, Nicole is associated with two things: a need to be guided and fulfilled, and essential Americanness. The story begins on a metaphoric level in which Dick Diver, the archetypal American, is to cure, express, and fulfill an America that has been hideously raped by the wealth that has sired her. He is to redeem America from her own life, and Nicole looks pathetically for guidance.

"The blind must be led," writes the young Nicole from the clinic. Her home is gone, her place of being lost, and she can find hope neither in the past nor the future. "Here they . . . sing Play in Your Own Backyard as if I had any backyard to play in or any hope which I can find by looking either backward or forward" (p. 13). Yet at the same time, her homeplace, her Americanness, sounds notes to which Diver responds, notes that are part of Diver himself: "I think love is all there is or should be," writes Nicole, and Dick, considering the sick young girl, says, "She seems hopeful and normally hungry for life—even rather romantic" (p. 21).

When she smiles at Dick she smiles "a moving childish smile that was like all the lost youth in the world," and the association with youth and the past is immediately connected to all that was summed up in Daisy Buchanan's whispering voice: "there was that excitement about her that seemed to reflect all the excitement of the world" (p. 25). Like her records, playing in the Swiss night, Nicole brings Dick the essence of the American continent. The two of them, "Dicole," as they will be called, stand out against the tired old Europe. Youth, adolescence, is American; practical maturity, adapting to tiredness and limitation, is European. Fitzgerald uses them both—transcendence and history—as universal realities of men of all nations, but reserves the highest fascination and the deepest corruption for America. The adolescence is the excitement and promise whose reality in time lies in the past, and which in the past took its excitement from its romantic readiness for an unlimited future. But Europe is Vienna "old with death," French finiteness, Zurich toymaking, Swiss small-scale petit bourgeois greed, Franz's inherited suit of a life and the view from his window. Europe is Franz's middle-class humorlessness, his lack of imaginative daring, his extremely non-Emersonian subservience to the past of his fathers, his fear of the wide-ranging idea of Dick's "A Psychology for Psychiatrists." He "considered it a rash business," and said to Dick: "You are an American. You can do this without professional harm. I do not like these generalities. Soon you will be writing little books called 'Deep Thoughts for the Layman,' so simplified that they are positively guaranteed not to cause thinking." Franz asserts that his father, were he alive, would fold up his napkin and grunt with the hopelessness of trying to explain to a foolish American how pretentious Dick's sweeping and revolutionary professional plans are. But Dick, in turn, is annoyed with the prudential smallness that identifies grand vision as foolishness.

  " 'I am alone today,' said Dick testily. 'But I may not be alone tomorrow. After that I'll fold up my napkin like your father and grunt' " (p. 29). Europe is the shabby, grubby materialism in which the Swiss sell the Italians their used cables because a funicular accident would be too much of a threat to the tourist business in Switzerland. Europe is the bourgeois drabness and respectability that envies and dislikes opulent America and is only too glad to have a chance to use that opulence.

But Europe is also the realistic honesty with which Dohmler refuses to take on all that huge midwestern country, in direct contrast to the American "commercial alienists" with their confusion of values, their pretentious sham, their second-rate training. Europe is also Freud, Jung, Forel, Bleuler, at the Psychiatric Congress in contrast to the American quickie-cure-all quacks. In brief, there are two Europes in the novel, just as there are two Americas. As in the novels of James, Europe is grubby, grabby, shabby materialism cloaked in the traditional forms of outworn conventions and respectabilities; it is a repression of the adolescently generous, free, naive, creative, openhearted imagination. But Europe is also maturity in history, the consolidation of a great past, a realistic and productive adulthood that comes from a recognition of mortal limitation and circumstance. America is "a willingness of the heart"—precisely the adolescently generous, free, naive, creative, openhearted imagination that to the European, who misunderstands it, is foolishness. It is bigness, newness, hope, creative energy, and promise for an unlimited future liberated from mortal limitation and circumstance. America is also that heritage of the hopeful, youthful past, changed, in all its unbelievable spiritual splendor, into irresponsible and irresistible materialistic power. It is as if the worst of the two Europes were suddenly to be made childishly mindless and multiplied in its wealth a thousand times. What Fitzgerald does in the breakdown of sexual and national identities in this novel is to indicate that the best of Europe and the best of America are disappearing in a century whose humanity is increasingly lost in irresponsible wealth and power, and that the worst of America and the worst of Europe are merging in an international glittering world of precisely that irresponsible wealth and power that is destroying the best that humanity offers. In the worst ways Europe and America, Europeans and Americans, become indistinguishable from each other. And that's the story of the novel's international setting and characters. So too is it the story of Dick's Nicole.

At the beginning the young, raped Nicole is all the lost youth and excitement of the world, is the essence of a continent; she suppresses the impulse to be a Warren in order to get what she wants and forces herself to responsibility rather than allowing herself to confuse values. Wanting Dick desperately, "for a moment she entertained a desperate idea of telling him how rich she was, what big houses she lived in, that really she was a valuable property—for a moment she made herself into her grandfather, Sid Warren, the horse-trader. But she survived the temptation to confuse all values . . ." (p. 35).

But as she grows stronger on her use of the Americanness that she represents to Dick and he to her, she, like Europe, becomes destructive of the "willingness of the heart" that had given her sustenance and support, and she ends up with Sid Warren's eyes. She is gorgeous in the process, as she is in her shopping spree. Without question, the new America of hot cats emerging from the death of another America appears to be the golden moment to the world. Nicole has everything: youth, vigor, beauty, wealth, power. When Dick meets her on the funicular, the world of that summer morning is one of brilliant, sparkling blue and green and white, of lake and sky and tennis courts and clouds, "the heartless beauty" of "the true center of the Western World" (p. 40). The fluffy golden clouds, the trailing roses, are icing on the gorgeous cake of a blue-and-white world. Nicole bursts into the scene with her light golden "fine-spun hair . . . fluffed into curls," and in her "sweater

of powder blue and a white tennis skirt she was the first morning
in May" (p. 41). Her hair is "new," she "floats" as she sways in the
funicular "between the blues of two heavens," and rises to the
fresher air of a higher world as the car that takes on the burden of
liquid descends to pull her up her rose-bestrewn way. She emerges
into a newer heaven as Dick, taking on her burden, is to "dive"
in a long dying fall in a relationship that makes the funicular
ride a symbol of the central plot. As she emerges toward her new
heaven of the golden world she had been locked out of, she begins
almost at once, within her diffidence and fearful newness, to assert
her Sid Warren eyes, with tennis skirt to match. She accuses Dick
of not giving her a chance to make him fall in love with her, to
which Dick replies, " '*What!*'

"The impertinence, the right to invade implied, astounded
him. Short of anarchy [which Nicole would eventually welcome
in the love of Tommy Barban] he could not think of any chance
that Nicole Warren deserved" (p. 47). She wants Dick and wants
to use him to go into final liberation into the golden world of new
Amerope-Eurica. She heals under Dick's protection, "under a
roof of umbrellas" on the sun-scarred beach; "her beauty, tentatively nesting and posing, flowed into his love, ever braced to
protect it" (p. 192).

But in Dick's world she does not have the Warren world she
wants. Inevitably she must become restive as she becomes stronger,
for she has nothing but the self Dick gives her so that when Dick
is gone she is nothing, has nothing. "She led a lonely life owning
Dick, who did not want to be owned.

"Many times he had tried unsuccessfully to let go his hold on
her. They had many fine times together, fine talks between the
loves of the white nights, but when he turned away from her into
himself he left her holding Nothing in her hands and staring at
it, calling it many names, but knowing it was only the hope that
he would come back soon" (pp. 196–97). The identities of the

old virtues and graces don't work anymore in the new world of broken decalogues. Ironically, the only real identity available to the Warren girl is the Warren identity that had raped her; her hardening into health is her hardening into perfect, joyful adaptation to the diseased, irresponsible, glittering world from which Dick had saved her by giving her himself—a self that in all its implications was rapidly becoming literally and metaphorically exhausted into nonexistence.

In marrying Dick, Nicole had made the first necessary transference—had married a "father" she could trust. He knows that she would "have married someone of my type, someone she thought she could rely on—indefinitely." But like the child who wants both protection and freedom, Nicole loves and hugs Dick at the same time that she wishes for his destruction so that she can be free of the restrictive decencies he imposes on her, the Nothing left over from another world. In the mad scene at the fair, Nicole, having wrecked the car, laughs "hilariously, unashamed, unafraid, unconcerned . . . .

" 'You were scared, weren't you?' she accused him. 'You wanted to live!' " (p. 208). Because the Nicole Dick creates out of moral and psychological ruin is only as "good," as "real" as Dick is, and the measure of his being is in her identity, she is and has Nothing without him. As she takes on her old Warren identity anew in the strength that ironically flowed into her from Dick, "Dicole" dissolves into Nicole and a used-up Dick. The ruin of Dick is the ruin of *his* Nicole in the new re-creation of the real Nicole. Having used him to death with the burden of herself, in one soft moment of remorse, regret, grief, love, and pity, Nicole is ready to join Dick in death as, saying "You ruined me, did you? . . . Then we're both ruined" (p. 292), he seems ready to dive to suicide off Golding's yacht. But the main direction of Fitzgerald's development of her is one of awakening and then triumphant Warrenism. Her first reaction to the full thought of independence is fear and

disbelief. Tommy tells her she shouldn't let Dick drink. " 'I!' she
exclaimed in amazement. '*I* tell Dick what he should do or
shouldn't do!' " (p. 293). But it isn't long before the seed planted
by Tommy sprouts. " 'She was somewhat shocked at the idea of
being interested in another man—but other women have lovers—
why not me? . . . Why shouldn't I?' " (p. 295). In the world of deteriorating identities, Dick makes Nicole able to be a woman (she
thinks of an affair against a conversation of two gardeners—"I laid
her down there"—in which the sexual conflict is reawakened as
she overhears "the male world" with all the inhibitions it gives
her in memories of the brutalized use of it made by her father),
to really be a woman again. He does restore her strength and
Tommy consummates it. The incident of the jar of camphor-
rub intensifies Nicole's direction into her Warrenish path as she
goes more surely and swiftly from the "female" moonworld of
Dick to the hardmale sunworld of glittering heat. Trusting Dick
completely in her use of him, she has no doubts about what will
happen when Dick is finished with her, which is when she will be
finished with Dick. She yearned for the life afterwards, without
Dick; all she feared was the moment of the break itself, when she
would first stand free of him. "For what might occur thereafter
she had no anxiety—she suspected that that would be the lifting
of a burden, an unblinding of eyes. Nicole had been designed for
change, for flight, with money as fins and wings. The new state of
things would be no more than if a racing chassis, concealed for
years under the body of a family limousine, should be stripped to
its original self. Nicole could feel the fresh breeze already—it was
the wrench she feared, and the dark manner of its coming" (p.
298). But after that, o new, new world! Breezy inconstancy, jetset
change, frolic, sunlit gratification, o white-eyed Warren world!
When it is Dick that's down, sunk beneath the burden of her and
unable to get up and aquaplane, there will not be a reversal of
roles. "Her panic changed suddenly to contempt . . . Nicole was

annoyed—everything he did annoyed her now" (p. 303). The sustaining, self-preserving, and selfish impatience of the child who is grown enough to be unable to wait to be through with daddy is what is necessary for the break into one's own life. And like the child, Nicole cannot stop to consider which daddy really gave her life.

Daddy Dick, in his self-annihilating and total devotion of love and service, planned to give Nicole life even at the expense of his own. A good psychiatrist, he knew the role he played in Nicole's life, and in Tommy Barban prepared the male that the golden girl would leap to when she "divorced" her daddy. "Tommy is one of those men that Dick's passed along to Nicole" (p. 101). In the passage she will go from the controlled sunlight of Dick's umbrella-managed beach to the glare of Tommy's beach, the garish thing that had been made out of Dick's beach. "Since the evening on Golding's yacht," she had known "a renewal of her apprehension that Dick was contriving at some desperate solution" (p. 298). She "had a sense of being cured in a new way. Her ego began blooming like a great rich rose [of the funicular: *"Défense de cueillir les fleurs"*] as she scrambled back along the labyrinths in which she had wandered for years. She hated the beach, resented the places where she had played planet to Dick's sun" (p. 307). And though she "was afraid of what was in Dick's mind; again she felt that a plan underlay his current actions and she was afraid of his plans," she knew that *this* good and all-wise daddy, this planet-controlling, non-scorching sun, would somehow manage to plan for her what she wanted. Indeed, in total self-sacrifice to her, he does just that: " 'Why, I'm almost complete,' she thought. 'I'm practically standing alone, without him.' And like *a happy child*, wanting the completion as soon as possible, and knowing vaguely that Dick had planned for her to have it, she lay on her bed as soon as she got home and wrote Tommy Barban in Nice a short provocative letter" (p. 307, italics mine).

All Baby will say is, "That's what you were educated for, Doc."
Nicole, in modification of the statement, at least says, "Thanks."
But when she's "all new *like a baby*," she's new "with white eyes"
(p. 313, italics mine). So, "with the opportunistic memory of
women she scarcely recalled how she had felt when she and Dick
had possessed each other in secret places around the corners of
the world, during the month before they were married. Just so
had she lied to Tommy last night, swearing to him that never
before had she so entirely, so completely, so utterly . . ." (p. 318).
And so, entirely, completely, and utterly does Fitzgerald carry
through the part of his "General Plan" for the novel, a part that
reads, "The Divers, *as a marriage*, are at the end of their resources.
Medically Nicole is nearly cured but Dick has given out and is
sinking toward alcoholism. . . . His hold is broken, the transference
[to him] is broken. He goes away. He has been used by the rich
family and cast aside."

When Dick's bitterness shows, as he comes to the end of his
case and the end of his "moment," his "intricate destiny," Nicole
throws all the blame on him. Feeling "sorry for Dick as she had
sometimes felt for Abe North and his ignoble destiny" and suspecting that Dick had consciously brought about his loss of control
over her, Nicole takes the bait, engages Dick in a furious argument, and calls him coward. Repudiating him with all the power
of her money, ownership, selfishness, and position, Nicole justifies
herself to herself and closes the case. "Doctor Diver was at liberty"
(pp. 319–20).

At the moment she beats Dick, there is little difference between
American Nicole's victory and that of the Australian parents of
Dick's patient, Von Cohn Morris: "the gross parents, the bland,
degenerate offspring: it was easy to prophecy the family's swing
around Europe, bullying their betters with hard ignorance and
hard money" (p. 271).

Nicole, of course, is substantially different from the Morrises in that for much of the book she is a sympathetic character and expresses a sense, derived from most intimate experience, of how good Dick really is. But in the Warrenizing of her Americanness is her essential community with the world of Barban and Baby, Rosemary and Sibley-Biers, Minghetti and Von Cohn Morris. Not alone, she has good company in Franz among those who have used Dick, gained life and strength from him, and then repudiated him and cast him off when he no longer fits one's needs—"he's not received anywhere anymore." Rosemary's "democratic manners of America" are "superimposed" (p. 63), and when Baby searched for help "her heart lifted at the word 'American' on the sign" of the American Express Company in the Piazza di Spagna (p. 249). But it is not the superimposed Americanness or the commercial company in the Spanish Plaza in Italy or the Warren triumph of the new Nicole world that Dick represents. He stands out against all that, disappearing at the end of the book as his heritage did, a heritage that dies and is linked indissolubly with the long, old past before the Civil War, the long, old dream of the West and Indian names, the hard pioneer days when the land was to have blossomed into millennium:

Only as the local train shambled into the low-forested clayland of Westmoreland County did he feel once more identified with his surroundings; at the station he saw a star he knew, and a cold moon bright over Chesapeake Bay; he heard the rasping wheels of buckboards turning, the lovely fatuous voices, the sound of sluggish primeval rivers flowing softly under soft Indian names.

Next day at the churchyard his father was laid among a hundred Divers, Dorseys, and Hunters. It was very friendly leaving him there with all his relations around him. Flowers were scattered on the brown unsettled earth. Dick had no more ties here now and did not believe he would come back. He knelt on the hard soil. These dead, he knew them all, their weather-beaten faces with blue flashing eyes, the spare violent bodies, the souls made of new earth in the forest-heavy darkness of the seventeenth century.

"Good-bye, my father—good-bye, all my fathers" (p. 222).

The motif of the fathers is one of the major unifying devices
Fitzgerald uses to develop the thematic significances of the
"Dicole" plot. There seem to be the European fathers and the
American fathers, but the distinctions merge, like all identities,
into an international amalgam of opposites, the old world and the
new, the past and the present. The older Europe—Franz's fore-
bears, the view from his window, "the Swiss piety of a huge claret-
colored photo of [his father] on the wall" (p. 9) are an oppressive
past, but a past of patience, discovery, and honorable achievement
at the "heart of the great Swiss watch." But like Dick's father,
that past is faded, like Amiens, so sadly ruined by the all-significant
War. "In the day-time one is deflated by such towns, with their
little trolley cars of twenty years ago crossing the great gray cobble-
stoned squares in front of the cathedral, and the very weather
seems to have a quality of the past, faded weather like that of old
photographs" (p. 120). "The original genius of the [European]
family had grown a little tired" and it is the new American who
opens the windows in the smoky air of Franz's study and lets fresh
air and a "cone of sunshine" into the room (p. 9). The heritage of
the fathers has deteriorated in Franz to merely careful, prudent
clinical work that in its scientific timorousness is handmaiden to
the prudential respectability and materialistic selfishness manifested in Franz's use of Dick. Like all the rest of the world, like
the essence of America, Europe is caught in the flux of change as
the brassy, jazzy, gilt new world emerges from the death of the old
one. The change is epitomized by the departure of the Russians,
whose princesses write memoirs of "the dim conventions of the
nineties" (p. 70), and who left their "scent ·. . along the coast—
their closed book shops and grocery stores. Eleven years before,
when the season ended in April, the doors of the Orthodox Church
had been locked, and the sweet champagnes they favored had

been put away until their return. 'We'll be back next season,'
they said, but this was premature, for they were never coming
back any more" (p. 71). It is not that Fitzgerald associates Czarism
with the departed graces and virtues; through Dick he makes clear
his attitude toward Tommy's killing of three young Red soldiers
to rescue the papier maché relic of a Russian prince. Rather, what
he does is to continually suggest in various ways what he had introduced with the war motif and the American theme: the past is
gone and its values, for good and bad, can no longer be active in
the new world to which it has given birth—everywhere the novel
is a long series of good-byes. As a modern, as a progressive, as a
visionary, Dick had believed in and aligned himself with the new
world until he discovered that its corruptions were even more
immoral, more dehumanizing in its broken decalogues, than the
old one had been, that older world of certainties and identities
Dick described on the visit to the trenches of World War I. So
Barban, the man who "rescues" relics of the past into the new
world, the deliverer from the new world to whom the new world
golden girls are delivered, has a simple sense of his history, his
allegiances—his "fathers." His resistance to change is not part of
the old world graces and virtues, but the simplest reaction of the
selfishness that is jet-set cousin to the heavy, genteel, pedantic,
bourgeois, selfish carefulness of Franz. " 'Well, I'm a soldier,' "
said "Barban pleasantly. 'My business is to kill people. I fought
against the Riff because I am a European, and I have fought the
Communists because they want to take my property from me" (p.
92). The quarrel about socialism between McKisco and Barban is
indicative of Fitzgerald's own ambivalences and opposition of attitudes within himself that went into everything he wrote. On
the one hand, Barban is not a sympathetic character, and his resistance to the "great new experiment" would have overtones of
meaning for Fitzgerald's readers of the 1930's that would not obtain today. On the other hand, Fitzgerald cannot adopt a doc-

trinaire approval of the changed new world in the making, no
matter how much he sympathizes with his own times. In his own
"other Americanness" of the old virtues and graces he gives the
defense of the new times to the confused and inept McKisco. But
change is inevitable in the history this novel presents, and in their
new world money, the Divers too (like Nicole on her shopping
spree) represent the change even in the manners of the very class
that survives change because of its money. "At the moment the
Divers represented externally the exact furthermost evolution of
a class, so that most people seemed awkward beside them—in reality a qualitative change had already set in that was not at all
apparent to Rosemary" (p. 77), but that becomes more and more
apparent to Dick as he sees every aspect of the world he would
save metamorphosed into the glittering features of the emergent
new world that repels him.

Rosemary, before she changes into her hard maturity, thinks
that the laws of the world of her "fathers" (Mrs. Speers and her
two husbands and their values of next things and responsibility)
are still operative, but she finds them operative only in her own
mother and in Dick. "Now—she was thinking—I've earned a time
alone with him. He must know that because his laws are like the
laws Mother taught me" (p. 94). But as she grows up to become
adept in the Barban male world, the world of Earl Bradys and
Signor Nicoteras, her heritage from her fathers devolves into the
same heritage that Nicole has from hers. In a quick and subtle
thrust, Fitzgerald even has Rosemary and Nicole discover that
parts of their youths touched in the past, and that "gray echoes of
girlhood" emanate from two buildings, directly across from each
other, where they each lived in—of all places—"the Rue des Saints-
Pères" (p. 129).

Regardless of whether the heritage is from the good American
fathers or the bad, the result, claimed by the new world, is the
same just as it is in the European heritage of the fathers. The good

American fathers, Dick's, are also "of tired stock," like Franz, but they raised themselves to the moral effort of inculcating the old virtues and graces.

Dick loved his father—again and again he referred judgments to what his father would probably have thought or done. Dick was born several months after the death of two young sisters; and his father, guessing what would be the effect on Dick's mother, had saved him from a spoiling by becoming his moral guide. He was of tired stock yet he raised himself to that effort . . . . "Once in a strange town when I was first ordained, I went into a crowded room [Dick's father told him] and was confused as to who was my hostess. Several people I knew came toward me, but I disregarded them because I had seen a gray-haired woman sitting by a window far across the room. I went over to her and introduced myself. After that I made many friends in that town."

His father had done that from a good heart—his father *had been sure of what he was* [italics mine], with a deep pride of the two proud widows who had raised him to believe that nothing could be superior to "good instincts," honor, courtesy, and courage (p. 221).

The death and description of Dick's father, which comes directly from Fitzgerald's own life, left Dick, in his memories, like Fitzgerald in his, "remembering so many things . . . and wishing he had always been as good as he had intended to be" (p. 221).

But the heritage of the good American fathers is buried under the land of old Indian names. What survives is something quite else. It is the Mrs. Abramses of the world who are "preserved by an imperviousness to experience and a good digestion into another generation" (p. 62). And Daddy-Long-Legs Warren doesn't die and get buried—he continues on, at home in the new world. He just gets up off his deathbed and walks. "He was supposed to be *dying of general collapse* . . . he got up and walked away, *back to Chicago*, I guess . . ." (p. 268, italics mine). The corruptions of the old world, unlike the virtues and graces, do not collapse and die under their own old weight, but always continue to come home in

the new world. Daddy's girl and her doctor husband, in the marriage that becomes a microcosm of the breakdown of the old world,
sit alone when they have learned that Devereux still walks, and
the music they hear on a phonograph now is not the music that
twisted on the Swiss night air so long ago. It is now the music that
follows the triumph of Devereux, of Baby, of *Daddy's Girl*. It is
"The Wedding of the Painted Doll" (p. 269).

The good past is too far buried to be retrievable. Abe ruminates
about his own new-world, self-indulgent failure and says, "it was
such a long way to go back in order to get anywhere" (p. 143). He
drinks to regain that long way back, "happy to live in the past. The
drink made past happy things contemporary with the present, as if
they were still going on, contemporary even with the future, as
if they were about to happen again" (p. 165). Dick, increasingly
drunk and self-indulgent in his own ruin, continues to struggle.
"He had been swallowed up like a gigolo and had somehow permitted his arsenal to be locked up in the Warren safety-deposit
vaults.

" 'There should have been a settlement in the Continental
style; but it isn't over yet. I've wasted nine years trying to teach
the rich the ABC's of human decency, but I'm not done. I've got
too many unplayed trumps in my hand' " (p. 219). But he is done.
Tommy was right. Nicole has too much money. As he sinks more
deeply into a parallel with Abe's premonitory career, his sadness
over an irrecoverably lost past a long way back, and talents and
futures and hopes broken along with decalogues, is played within
him against a significant exterior rhythm (one of Fitzgerald's
favorite tricks) that is a tired reminder of the war.

He slept deep and awoke to a slow mournful march passing his window. It was a long column of men in uniform, wearing the familiar
helmet of 1914, thick men in frock coats and silk hats, burghers, aristocrats, plain men. It was a society of veterans going to lay wreaths on
the tombs of the dead. The column marched slowly with a sort of swag-

ger for a lost magnificence, a past effort, a forgotten sorrow. The faces were only formally sad, but Dick's lungs burst for a moment with regret for Abe's death, and his own youth of ten years ago (p. 217).

Sadly and ironically the wreaths can only commemorate what has been war-lost, not what has been preserved. The deaths, the past, the sacrifices have been mislaid. When the American girl comes to place a wreath on her brother's grave, she cannot find the marker, for the War Department has given her the wrong number.

Always the past is misused by the present. Even Tommy's tradition of the duel degenerates into a Gallic squabble about who will pay for the services of the seconds and the doctors. As talent has been bought, so too honor becomes money. All the old virtues and graces are broken by "hard ignorance and hard money." It's too easy, with money, to remake the past any way you want it. The snow of winter isn't real snow—you just pay a little money and it goes away. The affluent present makes the past anything it wants it to be. When the fully "emerged" Rosemary meets Dick after so many years, she says, "we're making *The Grandeur that Was Rome*—at least we think we are; we may quit any day" (p. 224). They make their movie-version of the past in a "huge set of the forum, larger than the forum itself" (p. 230). All that's left of the grandeur that was Rome is in the air of the Italian night in which Dick has his debauched fight with the cabbies and cops: "a sweat of exhausted cultures tainted the morning air" (p. 242). No one is exempt and no culture, no empire. If the heritage of the fathers in Rome has become the cabbies and cops and Signor Nicotera in a movie set, the British Empire has become Lady Caroline Sibley-Biers. "She was fragile, tubercular—it was incredible that such narrow shoulders, such puny arms could bear aloft the pennant of decadence, last ensign of the fading empire" (p. 289).

Dick was doomed from the start. The new world was too powerful for him. He could not shape it according to the ABC's of human decency he had learned from his father, and his own attempt to transmit the good heritage of the fathers becomes as corrupted as any aspect of the heritage of goodness. His beach, for instance, is "perverted now to the tastes of the tasteless; he could search it for a day and find no stone of the old Chinese wall he had once erected around it, no footprint of an old friend" (p. 299). The past cannot exist even in enclaves in this nostalgic novel. The world of the new people who come to Dick's beach, which significantly was handmade with care and order for the preservation of creative routine on a shore that had been untamed and inhospitable to swimmers, is a world in which relationships and identities among the sexes are ironically destructive of the carefully ordered identities that Dick had created the beach to help preserve. The new people are not swimmers, as are the old people—Dick is a very good high diver and aquaplaner, and Abe North is first distinguished as "a good swimmer." The new people are pale and hung over, as the old people have grown tan and healthy on Dick's beach. Fitzgerald uses water and swimming briefly as a motif that separates and defines groups of people. In contrast to the crushing sun, the "water . . . pulled . . . [Rosemary] tenderly down out of the heat," but, neophyte that she is, she could swim only "a choppy little four beat crawl" (p. 60). Campion, on the other hand, warns people out of the water and complains of sharks. The tan folk are graceful aquapeople and the light ones are not. McKisco flails away at the Mediterranean, exhausts his breath, and stands up amazed to find himself still in the shallows, just a few feet from where he started. He never understood, he admits to Rosemary, how swimmers breathe.

Violet McKisco is clumsy getting up onto the raft, and has to be helped by one of the tan people, Abe. In contrast to the McKiscos and Rosemary, who is "suddenly conscious of the raw whiteness of her own body," Abe "shoved off into the water and his long body lay motionless toward shore.

"Rosemary and Mrs. McKisco watched him. When he had exhausted his momentum he abruptly bent double, his thin thighs rose above the surface, and he disappeared totally, leaving scarcely a fleck of foam behind.

" 'He's a good swimmer,' Rosemary said" (pp. 64–65).

On the raft, McKisco wishes for a cigarette, but the Diver group when swimming is entirely engrossed in "the utter absorption of the swim" (p. 77). When Abe tries to help McKisco out of his nervous funk before the duel, he says, "Do you want to take a quick dip and freshen up?" "No-no, I couldn't swim," McKisco replies (p. 104).

Though not much of a swimmer, Rosemary is willing to try. She got pneumonia making a picture, swimming and diving again and again, all morning, though she had the grippe and didn't know it. She is at least ashamed of her whiteness and admires good swimming. When she looks at the white, bad swimmers, "she did not like these people, especially in her immediate comparison of them with those who had interested her at the other end of the beach" (p. 63). Rosemary, in transition between the two worlds of dewy youth and the past and of golden fame and the future, ironically will triumph in the only world that emerges, the new world of the new, white people, where sexual and national identities break down. Ironically too, the new world is a triumph not of the cool tender water and umbrella-controlled tan, but of glaring sunheat—in a motif reminiscent of *The Great Gatsby*—where people either remain a decadent slug-white or where they become burnt-out black like Tommy Barban. Diver's world, superior and admirable, is doomed before the invasion of the new people. The arrangements of parasols, mats, and umbrellas make a clear distinction between the new and old worlds. Rosemary could see that "Farther up, where the beach was strewn with pebbles and dead sea-weed [where Dick had not yet done his cleansing and restorative and civilizing work], sat a group with flesh as white as her

own. They lay under small hand-parasols instead of beach umbrellas and were obviously less indigenous to the place. Between
the dark people and the light, Rosemary [symbolically] found
room . . ." (p. 60). Soon the white people would take over, and
appropriate completely the world Dick had prepared for them,
and like Tommy Barban in his many wars, turn dark. And Rosemary, too, would join the world of the "light people" turned fashionably dark after she had used Dick for her first "experience."
Soon Rosemary, too, would try to imitate Nicole's shopping. Dick,
indeed, worries about Rosemary's skin—tries to control her emergence into the strong light. He arranges "an umbrella to clip a
square of sunlight off Rosemary's shoulder." Tommy's skin, on the
other hand, becomes "so dark as to have lost the pleasantness of
deep tan, without attaining the blue beauty of Negroes—it was
just worn leather" (p. 288). The "light people" say, "We wanted
to warn you about getting burned the first day . . . because *your*
skin is important, but there seems to be so darn much formality
on this beach that we didn't know whether you'd mind," but
they are useless in preventing Rosemary from burning her legs
crimson. It is the "formality," the virtues and graces, with which
Dick, with strenuous and unremitting effort, manages the fine line
between emerging to strong new light and abandoned immersion
in it, between freedom and chaotic anarchy. He creates neither
the black leather of Tommy's brutal experience and hard, rapacious sun-strong maleness nor the sickly whiteness of the new
people just emerging into the sun-world. He creates the fine tan
that is the careful, balanced order in which potentially destructive
experience is turned into humanly usable and creative intensity.
He promises to buy Rosemary a sun-hat to save her "sanity." It is
not just Nicole that he guards, but the values of a world.

The protective "Chinese wall" of rational order, umbrellas,
careful exposure to sunheat, a careful mingling of black and white
into regulated tans, all the careful, cleansing work Dick had done

on the beach, was now the home of "new paraphernalia, the trapezes over the water, the swinging rings, the portable bathhouses, the floating towers, the searchlights from last night's fêtes, the modernistic buffet, white with a hackneyed motif of endless handlebars." And as for the water for "good swimmers," well, "few people swam anymore in that blue paradise . . . most of Gausse's guests stripped the concealing pajamas from their flabbiness only for a short hangover dip at one o'clock" (p. 299).

In a world that misuses the goodness in its past, Nicole becomes adapted to the world of *her* father. Dick is careful when he and Nicole sing

> "Thank y' father-r
> Thank y' mother-r
> Thanks for meeting up with one another—"

" 'I don't like that one,' Dick said, starting to turn the page.

" 'Oh, play it!' she exclaimed. 'Am I going through the rest of life flinching at the word "father"?' " (p. 308). And when, built for change, with money for wings and fins, Nicole adapts to the world of her father, Dick goes off by himself for a few days, now out of her world. Her new caller is Tommy, and Nicole "felt her lips' warmth in the receiver as she welcomed his coming" (p. 308), which was so conveniently and deliberately prepared for by Dick.

As in *The Great Gatsby*, time, manifested in history, is the great antagonist of the romantic readiness, the transcendental dream. Dick knows that he can only pretend "that the world was all put together again by the grey haired men of the golden nineties who shouted old glees at the piano" (p. 190), for the actuality beneath the pretense is one of irresistible change. "He had lost himself . . . . Between the time he found Nicole flowering under a stone on the Zürichsee and the moment of his meeting with Rosemary the spear had been blunted" (p. 218). On his mountain-climbing trip, he never does get to the top of his mountain, for "at mid-day the weather changed to black sleet and hail and mountain thunder" (p. 219). Change and time defeat Dick's transmission of the virtues and graces of the good fathers at every point in the triumph of the bad ones. When he is completely locked up in Nicole's world, he had to adapt every bit of his control and order and talent to her needs, and when he "could no longer play what he wanted to play on the piano, it was an indication that life was being refined down to a point. He stayed in the big room a long time, listening to the buzz of the electric clock, listening to time" (p. 183). Dick's battle against time is for wider social purposes than Gatsby's personal one, but as with Gatsby, "his girl" is at the golden center of his losing battle, and no more than Gatsby can he turn the clock back, old sport.

The very magazines the age reads are periodicals of flight, movies, of an impermanence as socially wide as in *The Great Gatsby*. The magazines "available on the station quays" are "the *Century*, the *Motion Picture*, *L'Illustration*, and *Fliegende Blätter*" (p. 211). The "Frankenstein" of an apartment that Dick detests, telling Rosemary that "You're not going to like these people," is on the surface a house from the old European heritage. It was "hewn from the frame of Cardinal de Retz's palace in the Rue Monsieur, but once inside the door there was nothing of the past, nor of any present" even. "The outer shell, the masonry, seemed rather to enclose the future," o brave new world, "so that it was an electric-like shock, a definite nervous experience, perverted as a breakfast of oatmeal and hashish, to cross that threshold, if it could be so called, into the long hall of blue steel, silver-gilt, and the myriad facets of many oddly bevelled mirrors" (p. 133). Dick, in his heritage, thinks he has trumps yet left to play, but "the Frankenstein took down Dick and Rosemary at a gulp" (p. 134). The "future" is filled with insincerity, "living all in the upper registers," with a "wild beating of wings," with irresponsible innuendo, rumor, vicious gossip, selfish and desperate egoes of people who are all unsure of who they are. Fitzgerald makes Dick's farewell to his fathers an international lament in a world whose new sex-battles are worse than the old love-battles, whose new dehumanizations are so much more nervous and perverted than the old ones. As Fitzgerald had written to Zelda, if their own lives had been a destruction of goodness and identity, "the world has certainly caught up" with them.

In the movietime rush of history, as pervasive in this novel as in *The Great Gatsby*, Nicole is best able to keep up with time. For Dick "time stood still and then every few years accelerated in a rush, like the quick rewind of a film, but for Nicole the years slipped away by clock and calendar and birthday, with the added poignance of her perishable beauty" (p. 196). She's satisfied with perishable time and change. As she looks at her naked body, which she prepares for Tommy, she gives herself " 'about six years, but now I'll do—in fact I'll do as well as anyone I know. . . .' Whereas a girl of nineteen draws her confidence from a surfeit of attention, a woman of twenty-nine is nourished on subtler stuff . . . . Happily she does not seem, in either case, to anticipate the subsequent years when her insight will often be blurred by panic, by the fear of stopping or the fear of going on. But on the landings of nineteen or twenty-nine she is pretty sure that there are no bears in the hall" (pp. 309–310). She does not try to make time stand still, much less turn the clock back, as the ABC's of human decency are transmitted in the face of that terrible "rush, like the quick rewind of a film," but what she foresees is a continuum of change, "peopled with the faces of many men, none of whom she need obey or even love" (p. 312).

Even the many transatlantic crossings the Fitzgeralds made are used in the novel as metaphors for time, change, nationality, and identity. "One hurries through, even though there's time; the past, the continent, is behind; the future is the glowing mouth in the side of the ship; the dim, turbulent alley is too confusedly the present.

"Up the gangplank and the vision of the world adjusts itself, narrows. One is a citizen of a commonwealth smaller than Andorra, no longer sure of anything" (pp. 222–23). The buzz of time, the death of certainties, and the Frankenstein swallows us up at a gulp.

The swiftness and unreality of modern life, as it is refracted through Fitzgerald's belly-sense of broken decalogues, is given a metaphor, as in *The Great Gatsby*, in showpiece surfaces and movies. Fitzgerald used every weapon from his arsenal of experience in this war novel, and no one can guess how great his Hollywood novel, *The Last Tycoon*, would have been had he lived to finish it. That unfinished work is full of promises of the familiar motifs being used for the same purpose in one last and perhaps highest key. In *Tender Is the Night*, at any rate, the uses of the movietime metaphor are clear.

The movies become the American statement of surface appearances in which youth, luck, and wealth make the evitable inevitable and the inevitable evitable, "a confusion of all values." The appearances, like Buchanan's house and the sugar-lump city of New York, merely mask an ugly reality of identitylessness and corruption. The clinics, like Devereux Warren's appearances, hide a story of swinishness or madness or both. No matter how silly the sickness with which the clients come, one doesn't use the word "nonsense" in "a rich person's clinic," as Franz warns (p. 8). Wealth is catered to, ugly truths hidden, so that as in *The Great Gatsby* money serves as a means to irresponsibility where surfaces protect the rich in the realities of their lives. "No layman would recognize [Dohmler's rich person's clinic] as a refuge for the broken, the incomplete, the menacing of this world." Warren dumps his problems in the laps of the doctors, and in his anxiety about appearances after his first collapse, he seemed chiefly concerned as to whether the story would ever leak back to America" (p. 20). And Dick doctors the rich, makes a carefully regulated movie-world in which they can ease their broken psyches. In his own clinic for broken rich babies, "the bright colors of the stuffs they worked with gave strangers a momentary illusion that all was well, as in a kindergarten" (p. 198). Nicole's set-designs for the clinic were so good that no "visitor would have dreamed that the light, graceful filigree work at a window was a strong, unyielding end of a tether" (p. 199). In his personal life, exquisitely conscious of others and exemplifying the ABC's of human decency, Dick creates illusions and surfaces for friends and guests. "Then, without caution, lest the first bloom of the relation wither, he opened the gate to his amusing world. So long as they subscribed to it completely, their happiness was his preoccupation, but at the first flicker of doubt as to its all-inclusiveness he evaporated before their eyes, leaving little communicable memory of what he had said or done" (p. 84). The Villa Diana, with its "intensely calculated perfection," is like the movie-illusion clinics. Built of Warren money, it is a disguise shielding and hiding madness and corruption. The garden, Nicole's masterpiece, is exquisite, and the dinner that evening in the garden is Fitzgerald's presentation of the movietime loveliness that can be created for surfaces that become a life style (the table seems to rise "a little toward the sky like a mechanical dancing platform" [p. 91]). When Dick awakens to the unreality, to the realization that his dedication to others is, in the Warren world, merely a pimpish service and not moral redemption, the movie is over. All the gardens, clinics, villas, manners, and surfaces simply become one more service for the predatory irresponsibility and putrescence of the rich, gilt world. Devereux Warren's hotel suite is a summation. "The suite in

which Devereux Warren was gracefully weakening and sinking
was of the same size as that of the Señor Pardo y Ciudad Real—
throughout this hotel there were many chambers where rich
ruins, fugitives from justice, claimants to the thrones of media-
tized principalities, lived on the derivatives of opium or barbitol
listening eternally, as to an inescapable radio, to the coarse melo-
dies of old sins" (p. 266). It's a swell hotel, like Jordan Baker's
Plaza.

But whatever dark flowers the rich pluck at their whim and
leisure, those on their way up, "out of their depth," as Baby has it,
must not pick flowers. One is aware, as Rosemary is, that "up north
the *true* world thundered by," and feels the place where one is
is empty by comparison (p. 70). Rosemary admires what she sees
on the Divers' beach, which is "the first burst of luxury manu-
facturing after the war." On another buying spree with Nicole,
once again Rosemary admires the lavishness of Nicole's spending,
and "once again they spent their money in different ways, and
again Rosemary admired Nicole's method of spending. Nicole was
sure that the money she spent was hers—Rosemary still thought
her money was miraculously lent her and she must consequently
be very careful of it" (p. 158). But she'll learn. Fast and well. She'll
belong, and having made her way up will pick all the flowers she
wants. Her movie appearance will become her movietime reality.

The golden appearances of wealth are enviable indeed, and
when the Diver household debarks from a train—trunks, satchels,
suitcases, servants, sporting goods, grips, packages, and pets, "the
village people watched the debarkation with an awe akin to that
which followed the Italian pilgrimages of Lord Byron a century
before" (p. 276). The Minghetti entourage is there to meet them,
and "when these princely households, one of the East, one of the
West, faced each other on the station platform, the splendor of
the Divers seemed pioneer simplicity by comparison" (p. 277).
Just like in the movies. But the Minghetti gorgeousness simply

masks the silliness and vanity and hauteur that Mary has become in her new appearances. Her identity *is* a movie identity, which is one of the constant points Fitzgerald makes about wealthy hot cats. They're as unreal people as the names in Nick's old train schedule or the names in Tommy's newspaper, and like Baby and Mary and, eventually, Rosemary and Nicole, become the irresponsible and self-gratifying images of their own status. Nicole can say of Abe what, in effect she will even say of Dick. She "shook her head right and left, disclaiming responsibility. . . . 'So many smart men go to pieces nowadays' " (p. 160). But her responsibility for Dick, disclaimed though eventually it may be, is total. The recipient of the services of this curative master illusionist, she wants to absorb him in ownership, the relationship her wealth has taught her to assume to the world. The bars of gilt metal that Dick uses as paperweights, weighing down his uncompleted manuscripts, are fitting appurtenances indeed. "Naturally Nicole, wanting to own [Dick], wanting him to stand still forever, encouraged any slackness on his part, and in multiplying ways he was constantly inundated by a trickling of goods and money. The inception of the idea of the cliff villa, which they had elaborated *as a fantasy* one day, was a typical example of the forces divorcing them from the first simple arrangements in Zurich.

" 'Wouldn't it be fun if—' it had been; and then, 'Won't it be fun when—'

"It was not so much fun. His work became confused with Nicole's problems; in addition, her income had increased so fast of late that it seemed to belittle his work" (p. 183). The movie appearances of wealth are not so much fun in the realities of identity and morality when the man who cries "Use me!" offers his services to personalities who thoughtlessly see all creation and its people as their servants to be bought, to be used, and then to be thrown away when, used up, they become inconveniences. They are jokes, like the nose of the silver-polishing butler in *The Great*

*Gatsby.* The mindless unreality of the movies is not so much human fun, after all.

Not literally in the movies, Dick is of them all the time. The movie world itself, with its shallow, hard, brash, showbiz egos, its struggle for notoriety and youth and status, the mindless entertainments of its productions, is summed up in the "ickle durl" cardboard emptiness of *Daddy's Girl* and the bluff hardness of Earl Brady. Brady's "heartiness became, moment by moment [at the Divers' party], a social thing instead of a crude assertion and reassertion [which ordinarily it was] of his own mental health, and his preservation of it by a detachment from the frailties of others" (p. 91). In this, he is the total opposite of Dick, who seeks completion through "a little misfortune" and who sacrificially uses his own mental health to take on the burdens of others. Dick sees in the movies all the brainless, philistine harlotry and confusion of values with which the new world breaks decalogues and destroys virtues and graces. He refuses Rosemary's offer of a screen test. "The pictures make a fine career for a woman—but my God . . . I'm an old scientist all wrapped up in my work" (p. 131). Appropriately, Nicole and Mary are "faintly annoyed" that they weren't asked. But for Dick, the movies represent everything he tries to combat and cure and repudiate, and they sum up the nursery condition of the Baby-world that is his opponent. Dick "closed the subject [of the screen test] with a somewhat tart discussion of actors: 'The strongest guard is placed at the gateway to nothing,' he said. 'Maybe because the condition of emptiness is too shameful to be divulged' " (p. 131).

But Dick's own immersion in the moral, human unreality of the world he creates makes him very much "of" the movies himself and occasionally makes Dick's pronouncements seem pathetically and faintly priggish. In his exquisite social tact he is, as a friend and host, a movie director; in his professional role he is involved in the rich man's world of corruption and emptiness. His

undoing is his discovery that in his professional life spent trying
to teach the rich the ABC's of human decency he was in the
movies all along. His directorial equipment becomes increasingly
useless as his central "patient" learns from him how to do without
him—whatever his failings, Dick is the perfect doctor. So, the
megaphone he uses with which to talk to Nicole across the garden
is belittled by the ease with which her unaided voice reaches him,
but he "raised it stubbornly," insisting on its use as his efforts
become less and less necessary (p. 84). Dick's perfect scenario, the
dinner party in the garden, feeds innocence and mindlessness as
much as *Daddy's Girl* ever did. It provides illusions by which egos
maintain themselves, false dreams and empty hopes, for a gorgeous,
enchanted moment. So Rosemary, the naif, rich with the wealth of
the America she so essentially characterizes and which characterizes her, for a moment can believe that she truly belongs to the
grand world that, with Baby-like anti-Americanism, she associates
with the heritage of the "European" fathers. "Rosemary, as dewy
with belief as a child from one of Mrs. Burnett's vicious tracts, had
a conviction of homecoming, of a return from the derisive and
salacious improvisations of the frontier" (p. 91). What seizes on
Dick's talent is the snobbish "otherness" with which those who can
afford it separate themselves from "American" commonness, from
consequences, from limitation, and it was to this, *this,* that Dick's
American, romantic, visionary idealism, in its self-deluded hopefulness and expectation, cried "Use me!" So Fitzgerald does not
neglect to observe that when McKisco makes it big and Violet
enters her longed-for great role—she "was very grand now, decked
out by the grand couturiers"—she comes to it with a "soul born
dismally in the small movie houses of Idaho" (pp. 223–24). She
and Mary Minghetti, like everyone else in the novel, once differentiated by their placement inside or outside Dick's beach-world,
now occupy the same glittering and sham Riviera-world.

When Rosemary first declares her love for Dick, what Dick is

aware of in "the too obvious appeal" is "the struggle with an un-
rehearsed scene and unfamiliar words" (p. 95). Dick, as director
of the lovely world he would create for people, is naturally a force
to which the baby, Rosemary (who keeps insisting, "I'm not a
baby," but who infuses her romance with a "flavor of the nursery")
is attracted. "Like most women she liked to be told how she should
feel, and she liked Dick's telling her which things were ludicrous
and which things were sad" (p. 119). Obsessed by his infatuation
with Rosemary, Dick observes the bank tellers, deciding which one
would least notice his depression. He "decided to go to Pierce,
who was young and for whom he would have to put on only a
small show. It was often easier to give a show than to watch one"
(p. 151). Rosemary's first sight of Dick is one in which he "was giving a quiet little performance for [his] group" (p. 61). When Rosemary weeps, "I've loved you so-o-o," Dick replies, "Not only are
you beautiful but you are somehow on the grand scale. Everything
you do, like pretending to be in love or pretending to be shy, gets
across" (p. 125). And Rosemary, astonished at the words of passion
coming out of her, "was calling on things she had read, seen,
dreamed through a decade of convent hours. Suddenly she knew
too that it was one of her greatest roles and she flung herself into
it more passionately" (p. 126). Later, when she reiterated her love
for Dick, "It was time for Rosemary to cry, so she cried a little in
her handkerchief" (p. 136). When she and Dick are in the Frankenstein apartment, which is pressure-packed with modish people
and their hot egos, thousands of pounds to the square inch, "Rosemary had the detached false-and-exalted feeling of being on a set
and she guessed that everyone else present had that feeling too"
(p. 133). The "most sincere thing" that Rosemary ever says to Dick
is "Oh, we're such *actors*—you and I" (p. 167).

When Rosemary thinks of loving Dick "she exhausted the future
quickly, with all the eventualities that might lead up to a kiss,
but with the kiss itself as blurred as a kiss in pictures" (p. 97). The

movies are not concerned with being, but with the excitement of the golden moment of becoming, with gratification of impulse, not with next things. As in his very first book, *This Side of Paradise,* Fitzgerald associates the golden moment with a carelessness about next things and a carelessness about next things with ego-ridden, impulsive gratification. There was always, in Fitzgerald's erotic imagination, an association between promiscuity—translated either into the popularity of the golden deb or marital infidelity— and a repudiation of next things. With Zelda's infidelity, the association took on more specific dimensions, and infidelity became one of the features of the bad side of what was "female" in his world. The carelessness about the real world of next things in the mindless golden moment on the silver screen became part of Fitzgerald's view of his nation's sex-worship and youth-worship which, always implicit in the mythic dream of America, were midwifed into full birth by the movies. It is fitting that Rosemary's naive vision of life with Dick is as tenuous as the dissolving image of the final clinch in the happy ending before the lights come on in "the erotic darkness" where Rosemary watches her imaginings. It is fitting that the sexuality that Campion represents should be associated with the movies. He weeps and one thinks of the weeping woman who almost stole the show from Rosemary in *Daddy's Girl.* "He was weeping hard and quietly and shaking in the same parts as a weeping woman. A scene in a role she had played last year swept over her irresistibly and advancing she touched him on the shoulder" (p. 98). Like the pointless and corrupt drift of the rich world of hot cats, in the deepest human, moral terms, nothing is real in the movies as Fitzgerald uses them, and in their unreality they in turn become an agent of dissolution of deepest human and moral reality. So, when Rosemary overhears the real passion in Nicole's "Oh, do I!"—the response to Dick's question, "So you love me?"— Rosemary enters into the passion with which Dick and Nicole make an assignation at the hotel, and "however far she was from it her stomach told her it was all right—she had none of the aversion she had felt in the playing of certain love scenes in pictures" (p. 113). Humanity lives in a saintly, angelic trick of the heart, but Franco-American Films lives "at 341 Rue des Saintes Anges—ask for Mr. Crowder" (p. 112).

When Dick tries to explain to Rosemary the difference between human and theatrical reactions to life, the essence of his explanation is artificiality and ego. The actress burlesques "the correct emotional responses—fear and love and sympathy" in order "to get the audience's attention back on herself" (p. 306). Nicole, annoyed with everything Dick does lately, listens to the dissertation with mounting impatience. To her the talk is simply a dull exposure of the false world in which Dick moves, forgetful, as ever, that *his* direction, *his* artificial world, was not that of the movies but of sanative perservation of the order, control, virtues, and graces that allow one to come back, finally, to come to grips with reality. It had done just the opposite of what the movies do in the novel. But Nicole, anxious to shed Dick, can see no distinctions through her newly regained Warren eyes. When Rosemary turns to Topsy and says, " 'Would you like to be an actress when you grow up? I think you'd make a fine actress,' Nicole stared at her deliberately and in her grandfather's voice said, slow and distinct:

" 'It's absolutely *out* to put such ideas in the heads of other people's children' " (p. 307).

But who is saying what to whom? With the whole world in the fast-movietime of the new beach, with the repudiation of Dick as director, the whole world is at the movies, in the movies, and not the movies of Dick's master illusions. Nicole herself "was enough ridden by the current youth worship, the moving pictures with their myriad faces of girl-children, blandly represented as carrying on the work and wisdom of the world, to feel a jealousy of youth" (p. 309). The new love is movie love in which one watches

"Nicotera, one of the many hopeful Valentinos, strut and pose before a dozen female 'captives,' their eyes melancholy and startling with mascara" (p. 230). The completeness with which the parallel between the movies and the social scene is drawn is part of the belly-felt intention of the dying fall that Fitzgerald so wonderfully manages. As the whole world comes to the post-Dick beach and is part of it, the whole world comes to the world of movie images and values and no one is exempt. When Dick sees a pretty young girl in a cabaret, he says, "She looks like somebody in the movies." The response of Collis Clay is hilarious—Collis Clay, that stuffy, harmless, pretentious, obtuse, perpetual fraternity boy whose last name specifies his soul and body and mind: " 'I'd like to get in the movies," said Collis thoughtfully" (p. 241). Even more improbable people than Collis are ludicrously corrupted into the new, emergent world.

"I think," says Kaethe Gregorovius, "Nicole is less sick than anyone thinks—she only cherishes her illness as an instrument of power. She ought to be in the cinema, like your Norma Talmadge—that's where all American women would be happy."

"Are you jealous of Norma Talmadge, on a film?" asks Franz.

"I don't like Americans. They're selfish, *sel*fish!"

"You like Dick?"

"I like him," she admitted. "He's different, he thinks of others."

—And so does Norma Talmadge, Franz said to himself. Norma Talmadge must be a fine, noble woman beyond her loveliness. They must compel her to play foolish roles; Norma Talmadge must be a woman whom it would be a great privilege to know.

For Kaethe, Norma Talmadge was merely "a vivid shadow that she had fretted bitterly upon one night as they were driving home from the movies in Zurich" (pp. 257–58). Everyone is at the movies. Hossain Minghetti is most curious to know, above all, "about stocks and about Hollywood" (p. 278). Everyone. Nicole tells Tommy that he looks "just like all the adventurers in the movies. . . ." Tommy replies, "I only know what I see in the cinema . . . ."

" 'Is it all like the movies?'

" 'The movies aren't so bad. Now this Ronald Colman—have you seen his pictures about the Bataillon d'Afrique? They're not bad at all.'

" 'Very well, whenever I go to the movies I'll know you're going through just that sort of thing at the moment' " (p. 288). When an older, more expert Rosemary returned to Gausse's new beach, she "was acting amusement, joy, and expectation—more confident than she had been five years ago" (p. 300). Mary Minghetti makes the situation clear. "We're all there is!" she cried to Dick, having told him that he's no longer the continuing source of entertainment, ready to be exploited, that he used to be. " 'If you don't like nice people, try the ones who aren't nice, and see how you like that. All people want is to have a good time and if you make them unhappy you cut yourself off from nourishment.'

" 'Have I been nourished?' he asked," as "down the steps tripped Lady Caroline Sibley-Biers with blithe theatricality" (p. 332).

Everyone. That's all the anyone there is. All everyone wants is "the lush midsummer moment outside of time," the fast-movietime of no care and no reality. But as Dick's career closes down, so too, the book implies, has time also caught up with the rotten crowd on the corrupted beach. For a long time there had been "a hint in the air that the earth was hurrying on toward other weather," and that the lush midsummer moment "was already over" (p. 175). The hint is not in any action, but in the completeness with which the world is given over to mindlessness and corruption, in the completeness with which Diver's fate had been the test of his society. Unwritten at the end of the book are invisible words that are the summation of Fitzgerald's evaluation: *mene mene tekel upharsin.*

In catering to the world of wealth, even those whose fathers represent a heritage of next things point in subtle ways toward the heartless use of people that irresponsibility and selfishness create. Franz was willing to use Dick as Nicole's initial transference; Dohmler was almost willing to let Dick commit himself to Nicole (pp. 30–32). And Dick, the source of all hope and comfort, will be used to be loved. He is a source of knowledge—"a man knows things and when he stops knowing things he's like anybody else" (pp. 56–57). Always the "excitement . . . generating under the umbrella . . . came from the man in the jockey cap" (p. 66), and "his voice promised that he would take care of [one], and that a little later he would open up whole new worlds . . . unroll an endless succession of magnificent possibilities" (p. 72). In the things Dick does and the way he lives, one can feel "a purpose, a working over something, a direction, an act of creation different from any . . . [one has] known" (p. 74). In his delicate and sensitive considerateness, Dick always has "his arms full of the slack he had taken up from others" (p. 90), so that those he cares for always seem to be "still under the beach umbrella" (p. 111), even at rambling parties in Paris. In Dick, Fitzgerald makes the case more complex than in any of his other composite, autobiografictional selves, for Dick is self-conscious enough to see what makes him tick. Although deep within one part of himself he knows that "you can't do anything about people" (p. 140), "on the other hand, there was a pleasingness about him that simply had to be used— those who possessed that pleasingness had to keep their hands in, and go along attaching people that they had no use to make of" (p. 149). He is at once the Gatsby-dreamer, filled with adolescent, Lucky-Dick visions of a possible self, and the self-conscious Carraway rolled into one. "A part of Dick's mind was made up of the

tawdry souvenirs of his boyhood. Yet in that somewhat littered
Five-and-Ten, he had managed to keep alive the low painful fire
of intelligence" (p. 212). As much romantic as doctor, as much
doctor as romantic, even in his deterioration, when the cloud
would lift from the heartsickness that was Dick's cold self-awareness and clear view of what his life had been devoted to, he would
bring "out all his old expertness with people, a tarnished object
of art" (p. 300). In his own depression and decline, he can never
resist the creative-destructive self-sacrificing selfishness of his vision
of self. Finding a "lost and miserable family of two girls and their
mother" touring Europe, "an overwhelming desire to help, or to
be admired, came over him: he showed them fragments of gaiety;
tentatively he bought them wine, with pleasure saw them begin
to regain their proper egotism" (p. 224). Even when called on for
help by the Mary Minghetti and Caroline Sibley-Biers who had
most insulted and snubbed him, "his self-knowledge assured him
that he would undertake to deal with it—the old fatal pleasingness,
the old forceful charm, swept back with its cry of 'Use me!' " (p.
321). One can call Dick "organizer of private gaiety, curator of a
richly incrusted happiness" (p. 137). One can call him pimp. One
can call him fool. There is some justice in all the appellations.
But one misses the point, and remains confused about Dick, unless
one measures him always and only within the context for moral
evaluations provided by the world Fitzgerald creates in the novel.
Everyone in this world is morally doomed as the old world dies
with a whimper and the new one triumphs with bingo! bango!
But everyone else uses people for selfish vanities and gratifications.
It is essential to notice that Dick uses *himself*, is used by others,
for the vanities and private gratifications that drive him. His
Americanness is like that of Wilsonian Democracy—in its foolish
and naive sense of transcendental possibilities it does stupid, even
arrogant and hurtful things. But mixed in with all the shoddy
motives is what is used and abused by the shoddy motives—the

millennial sense, the willingness of the heart to change the world, the sense of being big, good, brave, wise, grand enough so that the vain and generous self-sacrifice will be redemption. If everyone is driven by secret vanities to be gratified, Dick's at least remain the only helpful, hopeful dreams of salvation in a nursery of murderously thoughtless babies. He is a fool, but he is a human and wise one. He is an impulsive romantic, but he is also a mature one. He is sucked into the glittering world of hot cats, but he is also a man of next things. Disintegrating though he is under the onslaught of the irresponsibility with which the world responds to his cry of "Use me!" still, he is the only constant moral point in a Frankenstein world of mindless flux and selfish change.

It is, I think, quite appropriate to say that Dick indeed *is* Fitzgerald's most complex, composite self in all of what I have called Fitzgerald's autobiografiction. He brings to an apogee the American need for esteem that permeated his other novels, and having explained that need in *This Side of Paradise* and, especially, *The Great Gatsby*, went on in *Tender Is the Night* to show the relationship of that need, intelligently understood within and by the American imagination, to the rest of the world. One might say that in his vision of the death of the idea of the America he so loved, Fitzgerald was writing his deepest statement of defense and affection for America in the very novel in which Devereux Warren is the "fine American type in every way." In every way but the one that is most essentially the idea of America—the visionary vanity, the millennial expectation of a Dick Diver who can also outshine his European colleagues in the brilliance of the very technology they introduced to the world. Fitzgerald might have been writing of himself when he wrote about the creative need for love that drove Dick to adopt other personalities and incorporate parts of them forever until his own self became one complex composite integration of conflicting fragments. Dick tried to dissect the "very charm" that "for Dick . . . always had an independent existence," tried to dissect "courageous grace," and trying to "dissect [charm, virtues, and graces] into pieces small enough to store away," realized

that the totality of a life may be different in quality from its segments, and also that life during one's late thirties seemed capable of being observed only in segments. His love for Nicole and Rosemary, his friendship with Abe North, with Tommy Barban in the broken universe of the war's ending—in such contacts the personalities had seemed to press up so close to him that he became the personality itself; there seemed some necessity for taking all or nothing; it was as if the remainder of his life he was condemned to carry with him the egos of certain people, early met and early loved, and to be only as complete as they were complete themselves. There was some element of loneliness involved—so easy to be loved—so hard to love (p. 263).

The "lesions of vitality" that Fitzgerald described as "bankruptcy" in "The Crack-Up" articles are exact parallels to the waste of resources and extravagant expenditure of self that characterize Dick. One of "his most characteristic moods" was

the excitement that swept everyone up into it and was inevitably followed by his own form of melancholy. . . . This excitement about things reached an intensity out of proportion to their importance, generating a really extraordinary virtuosity with people. Save among a few of the tough-minded and perennially suspicious, he had the power of arousing a fascinating and uncritical love. The reaction came when he realized the waste and extravagance involved. He sometimes looked back with awe at the carnivals of affection he had given, as a general might gaze upon a massacre he had ordered to satisfy an impersonal blood lust (p. 84).

The shots from Maria Wallis's gun signal the externalization of the change and degeneration that had already begun in Dick's life under the seminal impact of his own self-awareness and his knowledge of what he was devoting his Warren-bought life to. From that moment on the novel is a dramatization of the increasing visibility of the morale that had cracked even though the manner lasted for a while. The events are those that indicate a growing rift between Dick and Nicole, and Dick's hardening himself to life without her. His pilgrimagelike walk around the block where Rosemary's studio is located—Rosemary, who is his last blooming, fresh reminder of the potential his own youth had been—is a payment of "tribute to things unforgotten, unshriven, unexpurgated" (p. 153). Going nowhere and running hard to keep up with Nicole's growing wealth and Warren-strength, Dick, who was going to write a great, ordered new psychology, make sanity out of madness, and be the greatest psychologist who ever lived, never even finishes his series of small pamphlets. Becoming increasingly tired and exhausted, he parallels all the careers of destruction that impinge upon his. Like Abe and his ugly drunken escapade with some Negroes in Paris, Dick in his drunkenness has an ugly moment with a Negro orchestra leader in a cabaret (p. 240). Previously the darling of the Europeans, whether his peers or his servants, Dick is now to Kaethe Gregorovius "no longer a serious man" (p. 259); to Augustine, his drunken cook, he becomes just one more "disgusting American" (p. 284), and even this harridan can frustrate Dick and make him look clumsy. But the nadir of the debasement of the man who has become "the Black Death" and doesn't "bring people happiness anymore" (p. 237) comes after the traumatic and dramatic fight with the cops and cabbies. Not only does Dick—*Dick*!—come to feel a "vast criminal *irresponsibility*" (p. 251, italics mine), but to the onlooker he is no longer distinguishable from what the reader knows the reality of the incestuous pederast, Devereux Warren, to be: as he went through the courtyard to the courtroom, "a groaning, hissing, booing sound went up from the loiterers in the courtyard, voices full of fury and scorn . . . . A native of Frascati had raped and slain a five-year-old child and . . . the crowd had assumed it was Dick" (p. 252). Daddy Dick, the child-raper. Richard Diver, M.D.

In self-loathing, disgust, and fury with the world he has come too late to see clearly, he wishes to smash as earlier he had wished to create. His hatred of the emergent world is equal to his contempt for himself, and as his self-destructiveness is dramatized in his drinking, his hatred of the world that used him is dramatized in the things he says—fittingly—to Lady Caroline, to Mary Minghetti, but most of all, to Nicole. The sameness of Dick and Abe is not Lincolnesque, not that of the promise of Grant any longer, but has become the bitter use of words like "spic" and "smoke" and "nigger." Dick, who had been father confessor and moral guide to a world (Rosemary felt "the smooth cloth of his dark coat like a chasuble. She seemed about to fall on her knees" [p. 95]; thinking of the Divers, Rosemary imagines them singing "a hymn, very remote in time and far away" [p. 98]), is reduced to the spoiled priest indeed by the end of the book. His last gesture is the drunken benediction of his hand raised in a papal cross above his ruined beach, fit symbol of his "broken universe of the war's ending" and all the broken decalogues. Returning to an America that is the isolation and provincialism of upper New York state, and not the lavish promise associated with America at the beginning of the book, Dick, "Grant," the man who had been central in the vision and imagination of all who came into the action of this novel, disappears "in that section of the country, in one town or another" (p. 334).

The tremendous sense of enormous loss and waste, a belly-sense evocation of great nostalgia, is generated incrementally in the reader by the direct line of descent, or dive, or dying fall, from the early beginning of Dick's career to the end in the revised edition. But Dick himself is not as aware as the reader of when the change was consolidated. The shock of the murder committed by Maria Wallis tells the reader what Dick only suspects. "Dick had no suspicion of the sharpness of the change; he was profoundly unhappy and the subsequent increase of egotism tended to blind him to what was going on round about him, and deprive him of the long ground-swell of imagination that he counted on for his judgments" (p. 148). But the reader is aware, in this very statement, that what Dick had sensed for a long time was now visible and in the dramatic foreground of the book's actions. The shots "had entered into all their lives" and "terminated" "the time in Paris." In fact, the lush midsummer moment outside of time is quite translated into something else. When they leave the station, "in the square, as they came out, a suspended mass of gasoline exhaust cooked slowly in the July sun" (p. 148).

The relationship between heat, sun, and infidelity that went into *The Great Gatsby* was inevitably recalled, consciously or unconsciously, by the relationship between infidelity and the Warren world to which Nicole belongs. There is absolutely no need to try to extricate and identify the complex lines of composite character—Zelda in Nicole, Scott in Dick, Josanne in Barban—because what's there is there so obviously and what's merged and confused exists not in Fitzgerald's art but in the life and memory from which the art came. It is sufficient here simply to point out the parallels to what Fitzgerald had done with the composite memories in *The Great Gatsby*, to suggest the significance of gasoline exhaust cooking slowly in the July sun. Warren's eyes are veined not only by whiskey, but, like Jordan Baker's, by sun (p. 15). The "nothingness of the heartless beauty" of the "true center of the western world" that the Warrens epitomize (p. 40) is the setting of the meeting between the released Nicole and the Dick she claims, as by *droit de seigneur*, at the meeting. "It was a bright day, with sun glittering on the grass beach below and the white courts of the Kursaal" (p. 40). Nicole's blue-and-white clothes, her gold hair, are restatements of the *mise en scène* and indications of her oneness with a golden setting in which "the thousand windows of a hotel burned in the late sun" (p. 42). The entire funicular scene is a climbing toward the sun, counterpointed against the promise of a long descent and the rise of one car at the expense of a burdened other.

The world that Diver regulates with umbrellas is too strong to take without protection. "Out there the hot light clipped close . . . [Rosemary's] shadow and she retreated—it was too bright to see. Fifty yards away the Mediterranean yielded up its pigments, moment by moment, to the brutal sunshine; below the balustrade a faded Buick cooked on the hotel drive" (p. 59). The colors of the sea, like those of Nicole's garden, are constantly associated with the lovely world one sees when one looks at the surfaces of the Divers' life—"a sea as mysteriously colored as the agates and cornelians of childhood, green as green milk, blue as laundry water, wine dark" (p. 71), and in its loveliness is associated with evening or early, cool morning throughout the book. But the sunheat of a world in which total exposure turns Barban's skin to old leather fades the pigments. As the new world of success does to the young Rosemary, "all dewy with belief," with "the dew . . . still on her," the sun of the Barban-Warren world dries out freshness as it climbs the sky. All is cool and lovely in the fresh early morning, but after the sun is well advanced, "bus boys shouted in the hotel court; the dew dried upon the pines. In another hour the horns of motors began to blow down from the winding road . . ." (p. 58). When "noon dominated sea and sky . . . even the white line of Cannes, five miles off . . . faded to a mirage of what was fresh and cool," and in the deliberate symbolism with which Fitzgerald invests Dick's beach, "it seemed there was no life anywhere in all this expanse of coast except under the filtered sunlight of those umbrellas, where something went on amid the color and the murmur" (p. 66). Dick's concern about sunburn and umbrellas, about sunhats to save "sanity," his difference from the white people and the black Barban, who all turn out to be the same anyway, is his preservation of "color," like Christmas-tree

Gatsby. The Diver's garden is always damp and cool. It exists in a "fuzzy green light" and is a "scherzo of color" (p. 83), and the party in the garden is set in the cool twilight and warm evening. At Tarmes there is "the fresher air" (p. 85). As the faces of the Diver children are aglow in the slant of "the late sunshine," Fitzgerald again introduces the name of the Divers' home at Tarmes. The Villa Diana is the home where the moon is the deity, where the children sing "Au claire de la lune" (p. 86). When Dick says farewell to Gstaad, where he feels he is saying farewell to the identity of his youth, the imagery is energetic: "They passed the crisp green rinks where Wiener waltzes blared and the colors of many mountain schools flashed against the pale-blue skies . . . .

"Good-bye, Gstaad! Good-bye, fresh faces, cold sweet flowers, flakes in the darkness. Good-bye, Gstaad, good-bye!" (p. 195).

The dying fall is one long series of farewells to fathers, pasts, youth, hope, to "those illusions that give such *color* to the world." Always the pigment-destroying sun-world destroys the illusions. When Nicole, in her sun-colored dress, breaks down into mad hostility at the fairgrounds, "a high sun with a face traced on it beat fierce on the straw hats of the children" (p. 204). Tommy, the sun-child, is scared only when he is cold, but Dick Diver's fathers and the land of his fathers is associated with a "star . . . and a cold moon bright over Chesapeake Bay" (p. 222), like Gatsby's memories. When Rosemary's face is transfigured by Dick's "looking up at it, there was the eternal moonlight in it" (p. 229). Nicole hears that Tommy is in Nice "in the first hot blast of June," and the day Dick leaves Gausse's beach is one of totally white sun-glare. "A white sun, chivied of outline by a white sky, boomed over a windless day" (p. 330). Not characterized by the tan in Dick's colored world but by the stark white of sun-heat and the black of Tommy's skin, Nicole and Tommy, now on *their* beach, are "black and white and metallic against the sky" so white and hot (p. 332). Dick's mixture of black and white, his tan, the colors of his sensibility, the colors of his gardens, umbrellas, and parties, disappear into the black-and-white gold-world of the rich new people. Even as a host he disappears and becomes merely the bad guest, while the new host, in white suit, is a man of brute power who, with his enormous paws, waves couples into dance aboard his yacht, and whose name is Golding. The day of the showdown between Tommy, Dick, and Nicole, like the crucial day for Gatsby at the Plaza, is one of heat, with the "perfumed breeze of the fans" in the hairdressing parlors and the coiffeuse "faintly sweating" in her "white uniform" (p. 326). Dick, "nourished" as he is in the world of Minghettis, can no longer get his mixture of black and white, though Tommy and Nicole get what they want. All Dick can get is an invitation to take a walk for himself. Tommy gets the demi he orders, Nicole gets her golden sun drink, "a citron pressé," and Dick orders the "Blackenwite with siphon." But,

" 'Il n'y a plus de Blackenwite. Nous n'avons que le Johnny Walkair' " (p. 327). And Dick takes his walk and—a perfect image of the course of his life—his figure diminishes in the dying-fall distance "until it became a dot and mingled with the other dots in the summer crowd" (p. 329). At the crucial point, Fitzgerald reinforces the important fact of self-sacrifice: even in his deterioration Dick could perform his deliberate transference of Nicole to Tommy for the final cure. "Nicole felt outguessed, realizing that from the episode of the camphor-rub, Dick had anticipated everything" (p. 329). At his lowest, Dick is worth so much more than what Carraway had called "the whole rotten crowd."


Though working *generally* as they did in *The Great Gatsby*, colors—black, white, silver, gold—are less prominent in *Tender Is the Night*. But the essentials are the same, the farewells are the same, the moral identification of the cast of characters the same. Most important, the talent is still strong and high, the art is the same—even richer—in this superb book, and that is miraculous. It is even more astonishing that Fitzgerald should have made such a brilliant beginning on *The Last Tycoon*, which, unfinished as it is, cannot receive treatment here. For everything was deserting him; he had said all his farewells to his talent and identity and youth and past, his Gstaad and his fathers. But Fitzgerald was not Diver. How did he do it?

He was often in the valley of depression, often in the valley of the shadow. As he wrote Scottie, a year and a half before he died:

One of the reasons I find myself so consistently in valleys of depression is that every few years I seem to be climbing uphill to recover from some bankruptcy. Do you know what bankruptcy exactly means? It means drawing on resources which one does not possess. I thought I was so strong that I never would be ill and suddenly I was ill for three years, and faced with a long, slow, uphill climb. Wiser people seem to manage to pile up a reserve. . . . But I think that like me, you will be something of a fool in that regard all your life, so I am wasting my words.[64]

Just before publication of *Tender Is the Night*, Fitzgerald wrote Perkins a letter in which a few sentences indicate how clearly he had taken stock of himself. He knew that after having depleted his resources as badly as he had, he would probably always be poor, but he was determined never again to be bankrupt. At least in whatever frugality his life dictated, he would conserve the treasure of his talent, and that required conservation. It was not the facile, quick talent that has so often been attributed to him, unless one is talking about his easy flair for cheap magazine fiction. But even then, one must be very careful, for on closer examination many of the magazine stories (but by no means all) turn out to be anything but cheap fiction, and often he had to sweat and groan over the hack stuff he turned out for bread. At any rate, in the necessary new economy of his life, he would paste together some of the

[64] April 5, 1939, *Letters*, p. 55.

broken decalogues in order to preserve the "line" he should have followed after *The Great Gatsby*. The economy would never be parsimony—Fitzgerald wasn't built that way, and there would always remain in him an impulsive, large, wasteful, romantic streak. But he knew himself now, knew what he must control, knew all about the golden moment and how much he had to work in a relentless labor of next things.

After all, Max, I am a plodder. One time I had a talk with Ernest Hemingway, and I told him, against all the logic that was then current, that I was the tortoise and he was the hare, and that's the truth of the matter, that everything that I have ever attained has been through long and persistent struggle while it is Ernest who has a touch of genius which enables him to bring off extraordinary things with facility. I have no facility. I have a facility for being cheap, if I wanted to indulge that. I can do cheap things. I changed Clark Gable's act at the moving picture theatre here the other day. I can do that kind of thing as quickly as anybody but when I decided to be a serious man, I tried to struggle over every point until I have made myself into a slow-moving behemoth (if that is the correct spelling), and so there I am for the rest of my life.[65]

What he wrote was not entirely true, for he always retained a facility for language that allowed him a gift with descriptive phrases as Hemingway's allowed him a gift with structure and conversation. But in essence, he was a man of revisions and persistence and perseverence and courage. He was a writer who put into *Tender Is the Night* the kind of complexity that gave him the right to complain "that a whole lot of people just skimmed through the book for the story and it simply cannot be read that way."[66] It is marvelous that so much richness came out of so much bankruptcy. The wonder is not that he died so young. The wonder is that, depleted as he was, he kept going as long, as persistently, and as brilliantly as he did.

[65] March 4, 1934, *ibid.*, p. 247.
[66] To Gilbert Seldes, May 31, 1934, *ibid.*, p. 513.

It is very moving that within the forces of the ambitions and vanities and generosities and ego and discipline that drove him and of the dissipation and bankruptcy that impeded him, he saved his goodness, and that he finally was a writer who was "good, good, good." What seems incredible to me—and I am grateful for the mystery—is what no one ever fully understands about an artist who is truly good. What I don't understand, all his ruin and ruinousness considered, is how he ever got that way.

Wright Morris once wrote, "In plumbing [nostalgia] . . . to its depths, rather than merely using or abusing it [as Thomas Wolfe did], Fitzgerald dropped to the deep, dead-end center of the American mind. He let his line out deeper than Hemingway and Twain, deeper than the Mississippi and the Big Two-Hearted River, down to that sunken island that once mythically flowered for Dutch sailors' eyes." Fitzgerald, like the Americans he wrote about at the end of *The Great Gatsby*, was "borne back ceaselessly into the past" in an interweaving process in which he created his fiction out of himself by creating and expressing a composite self through his fiction. Because that self was a process of history— a tension between past, present, and future, between lost hopes of the "Irish," "romantic," "female" self and the very world of wealth and power that the lost self had dreamed for its future, a tension between the future-facing "progressive" and "liberal" in Fitzgerald and the past-gazing "conservative" in him—that self became a sign of the tensions of the America from whose history the materials of the self's stories were taken. In many ways Fitzgerald illustrates the dilemma of the liberal in America, and in this provides another reason why his culture finds him so perennially fascinating and significant: American liberalism and progressivism, as Russell Nye has pointed out, is fully and deeply as native as any of our know-nothingisms, xenophobias, and reactionary impulses. Since the 1930's, despite its periodic and dramatic reversals, liberalism is probably the reflection of the majority in

American life, and readers sense constantly in Fitzgerald's fiction
not only a mythic but also a political area of applicability to their
own Americanness.

In the past that Fitzgerald evokes, the liberal, up through the
time of Emerson, was associated with a repudiation of the past.
Jefferson and his agrarianism in an earlier day, Thoreau and his
pastoralism in a later one, are transmuted into industrial and
urban liberal and radical ideologies in the America that emerged
from the Civil War and World War I. The stance of the good man,
the new man—the true American—in the continuum of progres-
sivistic thought was one in which the future was American, to be
made new and whole out of populistic and democratic and transcendent possibilities, free of the stink and corruption of the past,
of Europe, of commercialism, of history. Yet ideologies being what
they are, the future-facing sense of newness was also a mindless
and popular insistence on a new model each year, a new label
on the soap-wrapper, a new address to signify a new man, as Fenimore Cooper early saw and as West Egg made clear—it was as much
a brutalized debasement as it was a sense of a meaningful tradition
in social and political thought. The liberal's expectations for
change in man and society and the mindless mobility and materialism that the liberal deplores have their American roots in the very
same native assumptions about what is good. This is not to say
that they are the same, but that they are closely related enough to
explain why American liberalism is at once better able than conservatism to articulate the vague hopes of the American mass and
yet is perpetually unable to effect any radical change in the basic
psychology of that mass. Fitzgerald found himself at once identified with Dick and Gatsby and the liberals of his day in opposition
to the Grundyism and the robber-baron capitalism that encouraged a debased defense of a status quo which expressed both conservative and reactionary ideologies; and yet he found himself

unable to bear much of the "progressive" new nation that was emerging from the lost past. He faced both past and future at once, facing the future with all his American sense of the way a good man should face, and yet facing the past with all his sense of the need for conserving something good that was being destroyed. He expressed better than any of his contemporaries, perhaps better than any American writer except, possibly, Whitman, the rich ambiguities and ambivalences and complexities of the future-facing man turning to the past for good values because it was in the past that the sense of the future was best and purest. When he sank his imagination into the vastness and pastness of the republic that rolls on and on, he found that because America had always been a process of futurizing, both in the best and in the most care-less, selfish, and brutalizing aspects of the sense of transcendent possibility, there was no stable point in history on which to rest and say, "There, *that's* what we lost." Rather, as his novels show, our culture is filled with people who are driven by unspecified longings and unarticulated wistfulness into an identity-yearning mobility. Fitzgerald found that America's history of futurizing (a history which leads me to claim for liberalism the majority voice of America) was a process in which the best was constantly being turned into the careless, selfish, and brutal. Nostalgia becomes a yearning not for an actual time in the past, but for a state of hope which has been lost through initiation into America's wasteful and careless historical process, and as I have tried to demonstrate in this book, that's what the autobiografiction of Fitzgerald's composite characters is all about.

Yet, Fitzgerald could never abandon his liberalism even though the time-direction that his nostalgia made him face associated him with the alignments of conservatism. For one thing, too many of the ideologies had switched sides. The laissez-faire that had once been a radical and future-facing doctrine, optimistically based on and associated with Jeffersonianism, had become an argument used by conservatives who had enormous economic interest in the maintenance of the status quo. The pastoralism that had been associated with the radicalism of Jefferson, Emerson, and Thoreau had been subverted in the reactionary ruralism of political factions in an industrial and urban age. But one thing remained constant. The conservative, from Hamilton and John Adams on, in a distrust of the human animal, had argued for order. Like liberalism, American conservatism embodies both the best and the most debased aspects of American life. At its best it is an insistence on the inescapability of history, on the equality and primacy of law to establish harmony. At its worst it is an ideological and hypocritical mask for privilege often further debased into the heedless maintenance of the status quo at whatever expense of authoritarian brutality under the banner of law and order. Whether noble or debased, liberalism is associated with innovation, social experiment—futurizing. Whether noble or debased, conservatism is associated with stability, law, precedent—past-gazing. Of course the categories are not unmixed. Of course there are significant crossovers and meeting points and historical contradictions. What I am talking about is not the important modifications made by the facts of history, but the large, often unarticulated generalizations by which people identify themselves and others and which produce the facts of history. I hope that I have shown that if Fitzgerald was anything he was American to the marrow. His politics were increasingly progressivist and left-wing, though he never was the Marxist he thought himself to be (he found many of the Marxists he knew as repellant as he found Party dogma). His politics were intermeshed with that part of his Americanness that reflected liberalism—the Gatsby-Diver dream of change and possibility. Though he could portray a Marxist labor organizer with sympathy and understanding in *The Last Tycoon*, he was aware if anyone ever was that American expectation was a huge, amorphous, nationality-identifying stance, or dream, rather than any one set of political dicta.

Paradoxically (one of the essential paradoxes of American politics), it is the nature of that American stance, or dream, that drew Fitzgerald inexorably into the past, into that aspect of his Americanness that was conservative. As I have suggested, the essence of the dream is not really a dream of community, despite the many American utopian experiments and communities, but a dream of self. Where does the essential American imagination go when it has to try to find its manifestations in community, in rules and laws and politics rather than in the "Great New West?" It is driven into the future, into its transcendent sense of change, its "liberalism," in the face of the inevitable limitations of actual history, and into its hungry sense of the past, its desire to identify the roots of its history, its "conservatism," in the face of the constant dissolution of its futurizing hopes. Fitzgerald knew what Hawthorne, Emerson, and Thoreau had known in the depth of their involvement with communitarian contemporaries, that the necessities and the dogmas of the community were ever at odds with the transcendent dream of the self, the true dream of the Great New Golden Virgin Land. In this tension, the enormous complexities and crossovers of the ideologies of liberalism and conservatism cannot possibly begin to be discussed here. It is enough to point out here that part of the difficulty encountered by nineteenth- and twentieth-century revolutionary immigrants—and I am not talking about the forces of establishmentarian authority aligned against them but about the mass American psychology in which those forces found such fertile ground to work—came from the antagonism between the essence of the American myth about the possibilities of and for the self and the statist theories of the new arrivals. Again, at its best the conflict was an expression of the

arguments about the priorities to be assigned to the individual or
the community, which is one of the continuing arguments in
American Constitutional interpretation. At its worst, the conflict
finds national expression in xenophobia and know-nothingism:
the individual is aware in varying ways and degrees that his goal
is his new self and that the unrestricted new self is to be found
only here in this perpetually new Eden. The psychology is one in
which the vaguely yearning, wistfully hopeful American says,
"Hands off—this is *me* we're talking about now. *This* is America,
ain't it? Who do those Jew-bastards think they are to come *here*
and tell us what to do? If they don't like it here. . . ." Whether in
intelligent Constitutional debate or in chauvinism, in Transcen-
dentalism or capitalist ideologies, the expression is one of the
essential, individualist Americanness of what Fitzgerald saw the
dream to be—which explains, I think, why anti-revolutionary
pressures find such willing acquiescence in an American population which thinks of itself as a revolutionary leadership in world
history and why "American heartland" states like Wisconsin and
Minnesota astonish the world by representing at one and the same
time both progressivist politics and 200 per cent super-American
reaction. Native progressivism, in the self-center of its dream, in
the American heartland psyche that the Minnesotan, Fitzgerald,
came from, is as closely related to reaction in the general populace
as conservatism is. Fitzgerald both deplores reactionary xenophobia and takes "whacks at Jews" and Negroes. He is at once the
populist and the smouldering peasant and yet is drawn magnet-
ically to the society that most seems to symbolize the successful
world of the American dream-self. He is both democrat and snob.
He is opposed to reaction and has his progressivist roots in its most
American sources. It is both idiosyncratic and American of
Fitzgerald that the typical attitude toward time in the psycho-
geographical landscape of his fiction is that of the midwestern
youth, all ambition, vanity, and hopeful dreams mixed with snob-

bish visions of social glory, gazing future-eastward toward the expected American fulfillment of the self dreamed out of his past. What is most germane to my evocation of Scott Fitzgerald, whether as progressive or provincial, easterner or midwesterner, modern liberal or conservative, is the inevitability in the American imagination of the congruence of finding self and finding values in a civilization whose history provides no fixed point of actualization of the dream of identity. Fitzgerald had to go back, back, back into himself in order to define his values and his Americanness. He had to find, evaluate—perhaps to invent—his fathers, all his fathers, in whom to base an imaginative understanding of his history, in which he could find himself. His father always remained a crucial point of reference in his mind, and he referred to his memories of his father and his father's values in his own search for identity and values even though—perhaps because—he knew at the same time that his father was the tired ending of a history and not its triumphant culmination. I will go so far as to say that when one considers Fitzgerald's artistic purposes, Hemingway was dead wrong in his argument against Fitzgerald's evocative creation of composite characters, who always turned out to be himself. What Fitzgerald was looking for, after all, was the face and spirit of a nation, and in this he displays his firm and important place in a long and rich continuum of American literary impulses that, as Emerson made clear, are based in a national ethic which, when understood, will reveal the universal meaning of America in the continuing history of all mankind and the significance of all human aspiration. Fitzgerald was looking for the soul of America, and, like Whitman before him, found his fantastic, lovely, beloved republic turning more and more into gross body. What he confronted in embodying the liberal's dilemma was the basis of the fiction that arose from and was to rise past all his vanities and ambitions of self.

Without doubt and almost without peer he has become one of

the most "American" writers this nation has produced. I don't mean that just because he is American he is therefore good. I do mean that like all good writers who capture greatly the peculiarities of their national experience, he touches upon one depth or another of the composite, personal experience of all men everywhere. He brought from America and gave to the world "the long ground-swell of imagination" that so richly nourishes the responding imaginations of all readers and that periodically makes Americans want to begin his books all over again. And that is just exactly as it should be, for they find in Fitzgerald's novel what he himself never found—what no man could find—in life: the golden moment organized into all its meanings. In wry and limping doggerel he asked the question made inevitable by the pandering whisper of the golden girl, the Helen whose promising gorgeousness launched all those ships. Was there a promised land? Did the golden moment become millennium in a new, enchanted place where we would live immortally? Tell me, baby, in jazz as we launch the

> Thousand-and-First Ship
>
> In the fall of sixteen
>     In the cool of the afternoon
> I saw Helena
>     Under a white moon —
> I heard Helena
>     In a haunted doze
> Say: "I know a gay place
>     Nobody knows."
>
> Her voice promised
>     She'd live with me there,
> She'd bring everything —
>     I needn't care:
> Patches to mend my clothes
>     When they were torn,
> Sunshine from Maryland.
>     Where I was born.

My kind of weather,
   As wild as wild,
And a funny book
   I wanted as a child;
Sugar and, you know,
   Reason and Rhyme,
And water like water
   I had one time.

There'd be an orchestra
   Bingo! Bango!
Playing for us
   To dance the tango
And people would clap
   When we arose,
At her sweet face
   And my new clothes.

But more than all this
   Was the promise she made
That nothing, nothing,
   Ever would fade
Nothing would fade
   Winter or fall,
Nothing would fade,
   Practically nothing at all.

Helena went off
   And married another,
She may be dead
   Or some man's mother.
I have no grief left
   But I'd like to know
If she took him
   Where she promised we'd go.

Never.

No man ever gets there. He tried to find the way alone and he tried to find the way with Zelda and he never got there either. But he learned that all things fade and that the golden moment glistens lastingly only in memory. The golden girl never guided him to the enchanted land he imagined. But in his dark, destructive reconnaissance, as he journeyed alone within his talent, he found the only permanent radiance he was to know—the true and lasting gold of his own bright art.

A Note on the Author

Milton R. Stern is professor of English at the University of Connecticut. He received his B.A. at Northeastern University, his M.A. at the University of Connecticut, and his Ph.D. at Michigan State University (1955). He has been awarded an American Council of Learned Societies Research Grant (1960), a Fulbright Professorship at the University of Warsaw, Poland (1964–65), and the Distinguished Teaching Award of the University of Connecticut (1969). His other books are *The Fine Hammered Steel of Herman Melville* (1957), *Herman Melville's Typee and Billy Budd* (editor, 1960), *Discussions of Moby Dick* (editor, 1960), and *The Viking Portable Survey of American Literature* (editor with S. L. Gross, 4 volumes, 1962; revised and expanded with S. L. Gross, 1968).

UNIVERSITY OF ILLINOIS PRESS